9

Part One – R1

CERTIFICATE OF PROFESSIONAL COMPETENCE

ROAD HAULAGE

2022 EDITION

A COMPLETE CPC OPERATORS COURSE

R1 AND R2

Foreword

There have been changes to the syllabus for the Operator Certificate of Professional Competence (CPC). These commenced following the changes made to the old syllabus on 4 December 2011. They now incorporate both National and International qualifications as one.

The CPC is the Certificate of Professional Competence in Road Haulage and Passenger Transport. These qualifications are for individuals who want to enter the profession of Transport Manager or demonstrate their professional competence to meet Operator Licensing requirements - holding a CPC is one of the elements an applicant must satisfy for the Transport Commissioner to grant an O license. After 4th December 2011, the examinations changed to the new requirements for 2012.

The new exam consists of a single multiple-choice assessment and a single case study assessment. Both elements will test national and international knowledge/application. So, to achieve a new International CPC, candidates will only need to take two units.

The multiple-choice assessment R1 is available as a paper-based test from March 2012. From June, it is also available on screen and on demand, allowing candidates to sit or re-sit an assessment at a time convenient for them and to enable them to receive their results quickly.

We have covered the R1 syllabus in this first manual.
(Please note that some subject areas in the sections of the syllabus appear to duplicate with each other. Therefore, this relevant information has been repeated accordingly. This will help reinforce the knowledge required.)

The second manual, R2, covers the second part of the exam, the case study. A scenario will be issued with the papers at the start of the two-hour fifteen-minute assessment. This shorter case study will contain no distractions and will only contain information that will enable the candidate to demonstrate application of the knowledge they have acquired. It now only assesses the core areas. Candidates will need to achieve 50% over the whole paper to pass. The case study will focus on the application of knowledge. Candidates will be able to take any notes or books of their choice into the case study assessment and questions will test application of knowledge only. For example, candidates will no longer be asked to identify and explain but just to explain, allowing them to demonstrate they can apply their knowledge and use relevant sources of information.

The multiple-choice element will be assessed by one OCR set and marked timetabled assessment consisting of 60 multiple-choice questions (and thus 60 marks). In order to pass this unit, candidates must achieve a score of at least 70% across the paper. This paper will test knowledge of both national and international elements of the syllabus. The minimum and maximum number of questions will be asked from each broad area (A, B, C, etc.) of the syllabus.

CASE STUDY ASSESSMENT (R2)

This paper will be assessed by means of a marked timetabled assessment of a case study with extended answer questions. This paper tests applications of knowledge of both national and international elements of the syllabus. There will be between five and eight questions. Each question is worth between seven and twelve marks; there are 60 marks available in the case study paper. There will be no part A and part B. In order to pass this unit, candidates must achieve a score of at least 50% of the marks available across the paper. All questions will be based upon a single scenario that will be given to candidates as a separate booklet made available at the start of the assessment. The assessment will be two hours fifteen minutes in length. This paper will be open book. Candidates will be allowed to take any notes or texts of their choice into the assessment.

The following syllabus areas will be tested in every case study paper:

C4 Drivers' hours, working time and records.
E7 Operational costings
F1, F2, F3 Operating licensing
At least one of F1, F2 or F3 will be tested in each paper.

The following syllabus areas may be tested in a case study paper:

A5 Compensation claims (see syllabus)
E6 Budgets
E8 Organisational charts
G2 Vehicle selection
G5 Vehicle maintenance and roadworthiness
G6 Safe loading of vehicles (see syllabus)
G8 Dangerous goods and waste
H1 Driver licensing
H3 Vehicle checks

Contents

Section A1 A2 A3 A4 - Contracts of Carriage, Compensation and CMR

Civil Law

Understanding Contracts

Haulers and their customers conduct business based on contracts. These agreements are not always formally presented in writing but may be the consequence of a telephone conversation requesting a pickup and delivery of a load of goods. Such a casual conversation does, however, constitute a binding contract.

For a legally binding contract to exist it must include:

- An offer.
- An acceptance.
- Consideration (payment).
- An intent by both parties to be legally bound by the contract.

Essentially then, a contract is said to exist when an offer has been made and accepted. There is no requirement for the arrangement to be set in writing.

The individuals concluding the arrangement must have the capacity to contract. In general terms, this means the agreement must be concluded between two individuals age 18 or older, who are in a sound mental state and not intoxicated. Corporate bodies have the capacity to contract, so long as the authority is specifically stipulated in the Memorandum of Association.

A contract is discharged when the parties are free of their obligation either by entire, substantial, or partial performance, by frustration or by breach.

- Entire Performance – Both parties have fulfilled their obligations.
- Substantial Performance – A legal term used in completion disputes in which the court finds that one party is not required to fulfil each term of the contract to be liable.
- Partial Performance – One party will accept and pay for lesser performance than that stipulated in the contract.
- Frustration – A contract proves impossible to fulfil, and is therefore void.
- Breach – An unlawful failure by one or more parties to meet the terms of a contract.

In instances of breach, damages may be claimed by the plaintiff (the party suffering the loss). Compensation in the form of damages may take the form of either:

- Ordinary Damage – Arise naturally from the breach of contract for losses that cannot be proven positively. The amount is at the discretion of the court, as it perceives the plaintiff's degree of injury.

- Special Damages – Losses that do not arise naturally from the breach of contract and are rewarded for losses that can be proven positively.
- Exemplary and Aggravated Damages – Additional damage awarded for actual loss and as a punishment and deterrent to the defendant and to others for future conduct in a similar vein. (Often called punitive damages.)

Each time a carrier accepts goods from a customer to be carried to a specific destination, that carrier has entered into a contract.

In most cases, the goods are accepted in the role of a private carrier so that the carrier's liability is limited to the terms specified in the conditions of carriage. These conditions are the method whereby the carrier protects himself by stipulating terms that define the extent of his liability to his own negligence and that of his employees.

(Common carriers have no conditions of carriage and hold themselves out to carry for all without reserving the right to refuse goods tendered. As such, the liability for loss or damage to the goods (irrespective of the degree of negligence) is unlimited.)

The consignor accepts the conditions of carriage whether they have been directly or indirectly drawn to his attention. Generally, the conditions of carriage are printed either on the back of a carrier's business paper, on his quotation sheets, or they are posted in his office.

The conditions of carriage limit the haulier's responsibility for loss or damage up to a maximum limit of £800/£1,300 or more per tonne. He is not liable for loss or damage in excess of this value unless he has been informed of the value of the goods and undertakes to carry and to insure them in excess of the amount over the standard. (For goods in excess of this value extra cover should be arrange with the Goods in Transit insurers.)

The conditions of carriage cannot, however, include a clause exempting the carrier from liability for a fundamental breach of contract. This means simply that the carrier cannot fail to do what he has contracted to do and not be held liable.

Carriers have a right to lien or to take possession of goods until the carriage charges are paid. Particular lien means that a specific consignment may be held, general lien that any goods may be held. Particular lien is a standing right of law, but general lien must be stated in the conditions of carriage. The right to lien is nothing more than the right to hold goods. The carrier cannot charge for their storage, nor can he sell the goods to recover his loss unless such actions are stipulated in the conditions of carriage.

Further, a haulier may detain goods that cannot be delivered, known as bailment, which carries the responsibility to guard the goods from loss and damage through negligence. The goods may be held until the carriage charges are paid and if the conditions of carriage include the necessary provision, demurrage or charges for delay may be raised.

Legal Obligations - Understanding Torts and Liabilities

As it applies to transit scenarios, negligence is defined as a failure to exercise proper care in dealing with goods or property, or care in maintaining the vehicles on which goods are carried or the premises on which goods are held or stored. Negligence can be committed by the road transport operator or by his employees. When the operator enters into a contract with a third party, he becomes responsible for incidents of negligence, which in legal terms is referred to as "liability for torts" (breach of duty that may be redressed by a claim for damages by the aggrieved party).

The operator's liability for torts is important. Examples of the operator's duties include:

- exercising the proper care in carrying and storing goods
- ensuring that the goods are not lost or damaged due to negligence from:
- failure to adequately secure a load
- failure to shield the load from weather
- failure to maintain a vehicle
- avoiding unreasonable delay with resulting damage

Other aspects of liability a private carrier might face include loss or damage due to unreasonable delay in transit where such loss could be foreseen (for instance fruit that goes bad). There is no liability, however, if the consignor stops delivery. Liability applies if the goods are subject to wrongful delivery due to wilful misconduct but not mere negligence. No liability is attached to dangerous goods in situations where the carrier is ignorant of the danger.

- ensuring the use of proper lifting equipment
- ensuring the goods are not left outside and subject to the elements

If damage does occur, the customer or plaintiff can seek an award of damages for negligence in a legal proceeding.

Operators must also consider their liability for instances of public nuisance, the commission of which is a crime. A public nuisance is defined as loss to a "class" of people beyond the discomfort or inconvenience suffered by the public at large. An example might be obstruction of a public right of way or highway, excessive noise at unsociable hours, or creating an exceptional odour. The event or circumstance must affect a number of people, for instance all the residents of a row of houses.

A private nuisance may affect one person if the unlawful act concerns land. The offender may, for example, interfere with an individual's ability to enjoy land occupied by him by obstructing his access to the land, by blocking light, or by allowing the land to be otherwise effected by noise, smells, water, germs, or rubbish. It is also an offence to obstruct the police in the execution of their duties. Such an offence would be committed by an individual who failed or refused to provide information about alleged offences and crimes or who refused to follow a directive given by an officer. In relation to transport, such an incident might involve refusing to move a vehicle, to produce a driving license or other documents, or to answer a police officer's questions forthrightly when apprehended.

Liability for Employee Actions

When wrongful or negligent acts are committed by an employee engaged in activities that fall within the scope of their employment, the employer is liable for the consequences of the acts. If, however, the act could be classed as "deviation or departure" (engaging in a "frolic of his own") from the employee's stated duties, the liability falls on the employee.

A television salesman would engage in a "frolic of his own" if in visiting a customer, he attempted to repair the individual's existing set. The employer could argue that the employee was hired to be a salesman, not a repairman, and had thus deviated from his stated duties.

The employer cannot escape liability by simply prohibiting an employee from taking certain actions or for performing tasks for a specific third party, if, for example, an employer forbade his repairman to work on a television owned by Mr. X, but the repairman disregarded the prohibition and did the repair anyway, the employer is liable for any negative consequences.

The employer is also held liable in cases where the employee fails to meet specific legal requirements relative to the execution of his job. The employer can also be prosecuted for offences relating to his employee's failure to comply with statutory requirements.

Liability by Virtue of Occupancy

In occupying premises, two types of individuals are encountered by the occupier. Visitors and employees have explicit or implied permission to be there, and trespassers who have no such authority.

Under the terms of the Occupiers' Liability Acts of 1957 and 1984, the occupier owes a common duty of care toward visitors and employees. This means the occupier must ensure said individuals are reasonably safe by giving adequate warning of any dangers present with particular care given to the presence of children. The occupier must be prepared for the fact that children will exercise less care than adults and are likely to be attracted to dangerous objects or areas. (The occupier may only need to give sufficient warnings to the adult or competent person supervising the child to circumvent this liability.)

Under the provisions of the Guard Dogs Act of 1975, guard dogs are not allowed to roam loose or to be present on the premises unless clear notice is posted warning of their presence and of the danger attached.

Trespass is defined as the forcible and direct interference with the possession of another person's land without lawful justification. This includes walking on to the land or remaining on the land after permission to be present has been revoked. (This definition applies to English law with different circumstances applying to trespass in Scotland.)

As a duty of common humanity, the transport operator has an obligation to warn trespassers of dangers present or to warn them to take reasonable steps to avoid said dangers. If activities on the land are liable to cause danger, even to unauthorised trespassers, the land should be fenced. If a trespasser suffers injuries, liability to the landowner can still apply.

Principals and Subcontractors

There is a special legal relationship between principals and agents.

An agent has authorisation to act on behalf of a principal and to represent the business interests of that person. In legal terms, the agent is a firm or person who has agreed to conclude a contract between the principal and a third party. The agent may or may not be the principal's employee. There are two types of agents, special and general. A special agent has authority to act on behalf of the principal for a specific purpose. A general agent possesses general authority to act for the principal across a range of business activities. An agency agreement may be created orally, stipulated in writing, or implied by the relative actions of the principal and the agent. Once the principal gives authority to the agent, the principal becomes responsible for the agent's actions or omissions.

The extent of the authority held by the agent depends on the authority expressly conferred by his principal or implied by the principal in words and actions. In general, agents may not delegate their powers or duties to another person without permission of the principal who is entitled to expect the agent to personally discharge his duties.

Any contract executed by the agent is a contract between the principal and a third party. The agent is not a party to the contract. The principal is bound to the terms of the contract only so long as the agent acted within the definition of his assigned authority. By the same token, the principal can only enforce contracts made by the agent if the agent acted within his granted authority.

A principal may not terminate his responsibility for his agent's actions simply by telling the agent not to act. If the agent continues to act for the principal in an unauthorised capacity, the people contracting with the agent have the right to assume the agent is still authorised to act until they are informed otherwise.

If a principal wishes to terminate an agent's authority, steps should be taken to inform potential customers of the fact. This can be a lengthy and expensive process involving advertisements in newspapers and trade papers, direct mail to customers, and such other methods of communication as prove necessary.

An agent has a responsibility to:

- use ordinary care and skill in executing his duties
- use judgment and discretion honestly
- maintain information in confidence
- avoid conflicts of interest
- keep accurate financial accounts
- refuse bribes, secret commissions, or similar benefits

The agent may expect to be remunerated for his services, reimbursed for legitimate expenses and outlays, and indemnified against liabilities incurred from performing his authorised duties. Agents have a right of lien over their principal's property in respect of all legal claims against the principal. An agent is personally liable, however, if he does not disclose the name of his principal when carrying out acts on his behalf. The agent may not be liable, however, if he discloses the existence of an unnamed principal. It is illegal for an agent to make secret profits in his deals, and if such profits are made and are discovered, they must be returned or the principal may sue the agent. The profits do not have to be returned to the customer.

Contractors and Subcontractors

An operator who accepts instructions to deliver goods that a principal contractor has initially agreed to deliver, the subcontractor is not an employee of the contractor and is usually hired when the principal contractor's own fleet is fully utilised, when the delivery is outside the normal working territory, or when the price is poor but the contractor feels obliged to accept instructions for delivery.

Principal Contractor's Responsibilities

The customer expects the principal contractor to:
- carry the goods on a suitable vehicle
- in the hands of a reliable driver
- with proper protection against loss or damage
- with adequate insurance
- to the correct location
- by the specified time

In selecting a subcontractor, the principal contractor should make sure that each of these expectations can be met. The contractor is fully liable to the customer for loss or damage to the goods even when they are in the possession of a subcontractor and the subcontractor is at fault.

Subcontractor's Responsibilities

The contractor expects the subcontractor to:

- follow the instructions given for collection and delivery
- carry the load without risk of loss or damage
- have adequate insurance coverage
- provide proof of delivery in the form of a signed receipt note

If the customer, the original consignor of the goods, has to make a claim for loss or damage, the claim is made to the principal contractor who then seeks redress from the subcontractor. The principal contractor cannot legally escape responsibility for the safekeeping and proper delivery of the goods.

CMR Liability

Operators who carry goods internationally must comply with the stipulations of the Contract for the International Carriage of Goods by Road 1956 (CMR - Convention Merchandises Routiers) in regard to liability and documents. (The UK adopted the Convention as the Carriage of Goods by Road Act 1965.)

The countries that are party to the CMR Convention are:

- Austria
- Belarus
- Belgium
- Bosnia-Herzegovina
- Bulgaria
- Croatia
- Czech Republic
- Denmark
- Estonia
- Finland
- France
- Germany
- Gibraltar
- Greece
- Hungary
- Italy
- Kazakhstan
- Latvia
- Lithuania
- Macedonia
- Moldova
- Morocco
- Netherlands
- Norway
- Poland
- Portugal
- Romania
- Russian Federation
- Serbia and Montenegro
- Slovak Republic
- Slovenia
- Spain
- Sweden
- Switzerland
- Tajikistan
- Tunisia
- Turkey
- Turkmenistan
- Uzbekistan

The terms of the Convention apply to all contracts for the carriage of goods by road for hire or reward between one country and another. For the terms to apply, at least one of the countries involved must be a party to the Convention.
Exemptions include:

- own-account operations
- carriage under an International Postal Convention
- furniture removals
- funeral consignments

The CMR does not apply to international haulage between the UK (and Northern Ireland) and the Republic of Ireland or between the UK mainland and the Channel Islands. The Convention's principal conditions are:

1. The terms apply to the complete carriage whether it is wholly by road or only partially.
2. The carrier is responsible for the actions and omissions of his agents and those of any other individuals whose services are used as an aspect of the carriage.
3. The contract of carriage is confirmed with a CMR consignment note with three original copies signed by the carrier and the sender. Each retains one copy with the third accompanying the goods.
4. If the goods travel on different vehicles or if they are divided owing to a difference in nature, separate consignments notes must be made out for each vehicle or load.
5. There is a required form for the consignment note but it may also contain additional information for use by the parties to the contract.
6. The sender is responsible for all expenses, losses, and damages sustained by the carrier that are a result of inaccurate or incomplete information supplied by the sender on the consignment note.
7. The carrier must check the accuracy of the consignment note and the condition of both the goods and their packaging upon receipt of the goods.
8. The sender is liable for damages and expenses caused by defective packing unless the defect was revealed to the carrier when taking over the goods.
9. The sender must supply the necessary documents for customs purposes with the consignment note.
10. The sender has the right of disposal, to stop transit, or to change the delivery address up to the time of delivery to the consignee unless the consignment note confers these rights on the consignee. Once the goods are delivered to the address on the consignment note the consignee has the right of disposal.
11. If the carrier fails to follow the instructions on the consignment note or follows them without requesting the first copy of the note to be produced, the carrier is liable for loss or damage caused by the failure.
12. The carrier must provide a second copy of the consignment note to the consignee at the time of delivery.
13. If the carrier cannot follow the instructions on the consignment note he must ask either the sender or the consignee (whichever has the right of disposal) for additional instructions.
14. Between the time the carrier accepts and delivers the goods he is liable for

total or partial losses and damage unless the loss, damage, or delay was caused by the claimant's neglect or wrong doing. (The burden of proof rests with the carrier.)

15. If the carrier fails to deliver the goods within 30 days of the specified time limit, or within 60 days from the time the carrier took over the goods with no time limit applied, the goods are considered to be lost.

16. The carrier must be apprised of the nature of dangerous goods and of the appropriate precautions.

17. If goods are lost or damage, the calculation of compensation is based on the value of the goods at the time and place of their acceptance for carriage. (Compensation will not exceed a set value.)

18. In the event of total loss (and proportionally in the event of partial loss) carriage charges, customs duties, and other charges are to be refunded.

19. Where the value or a special interest in delivery has been declared or where a surcharge has been paid in respect of a declared value exceeding the limited (mentioned in 17), higher levels of compensation may be claimed.

20. If goods are damaged the carrier is liable for the amount the goods have been diminished.

21. The claimant in a dispute may demand interest at 5 percent per annum from the date on which the claim was sent to the carrier.

22. If goods are damaged due to wilful misconduct or default constitution wilful misconduct, the carrier cannot avail himself of exclusions or limiting clauses.

23. If the consignee does not indicate reservations about the goods at the time of receipt or within seven days of receipt (excluding public holidays and Sundays) it is assumed that the goods were in satisfactory condition.

24. In legal proceedings the plaintiff may bring the action in any court or tribunal of a contracting country, of a country in which the defendant is a resident, of the country where the defendant has his principal place of business, the country where the goods were delivered, or that in which they were designated for delivery but not in any other court or tribunal.

25. A period of limitation for an action is one year, three in cases of wilful misconduct.

26. Where successive road carriers are involved in a contract each is responsible for the whole operation as a party to the contract. Each successive carrier must present the previous carrier with a dated receipt and must enter his name and address on the second copy of the consignment notice.

27. A carrier who has paid compensation arising from a claim may recover the compensation with interest, costs, and expenses attached from other carriers who were parties to the contract subject to: (a) the carrier responsible for the loss or damage paying the compensation (b) each carrier responsible for loss or damage jointly caused shall be liable to pay proportionate compensation or compensation proportionate to their share of the carriage charges if responsibility can be apportioned.

28. If a carrier due to pay compensation is insolvent, the other carrier's party to the contract must pay his share.

CMR Liability Insurance

In Britain, transport operators carry goods under their own conditions of carriage or those of the Road Haulage Association and their liability is covered by Goods in Transit insurance. The insurance varies from the minimum £800 per tonne to £1,300 (the current RHA standard.)

Updated for 2020, the RHA Conditions are recognised as the industry standard. Only fully paid up members of the Road Haulage Association can legally use RHA Conditions of Carriage.

If you do not use conditions of carriage correctly; under Common Law you can be held responsible for the full value of a load, irrespective of the value placed on the load by the customer. You can also be held responsible for consequential losses arising from non-delivery or damaged delivery.

Older conditions remain valid until you advise your customers that you intend to trade subject to the new conditions. We recommend that you start trading as soon as possible under the new conditions to benefit from the changes that have been made.

You must also inform your insurer or broker and secure any necessary adjustments to existing insurance covers.

RHA members should contact The Road Haulage Association with their membership number to access a copy of the updated 2020 RHA Conditions of Carriage.

In international road haulage operations (but not own-account operations), the terms of the International Convention on the Carriage of Goods 1956 (CMR) automatically apply. The carrier's liability is determined by a measure known as "special drawing rights" (SDR). SDRs are defined by the International Monetary Fund and converted to the national currency of the country in which a claim is dealt with in court. The value used for calculation is that of the date of judgment or a date agreed upon by the parties. According to the SDR measure compensation cannot exceed 8.33 units of account per kilogram of gross weight short (GWS.)

There is a financial limit to the haulier's liability which is expressed in terms of "special drawing rights" (S.D.R.s). The liability is 8.33 S.D.R.s per kilogram of weight and the value of and S.D.R. changes on a daily basis.

In recent times the limit has varied between £6,000 and £8,000 per tonne. This marks a substantial increase from domestic conditions of carriage – compare R.H.A liability at £1,300 per tonne.

In addition a haulier is liable for delay but this is limited to the carriage charges. There is further liability for refund of the carriage charges, customs duties and other charges incurred.

Since international road haulage is subject to CMR, any liability is at the CMR levels. Operators need to make sure they have appropriate cover for those levels.

In some instances, a domestic haulier may unwittingly participate in international movement without adequate cover to reach CMR liability levels. If a haulier is asked to carry a loaded trailer from one place to another in the UK, but the trailer entered the UK from abroad and has not been unloaded, the internal movement is still part of the international transit and subject to CMR. A similar situation would be a case in which a haulier was asked to take a loaded trailer to port for outward shipment or to an inland clearance depot. If the trailer goes forward loaded, the haulier needs to be covered for CMR level liability.

CMR Consignment Notes

CMR consignment notes must include the following details:

1. The date and the place where the consignment note is made out.
2. The sender's name and address.
3. The name and address of the carrier and those of any subsequent carriers.
4. The place and date of taking over the goods and the designated delivery destination.
5. The consignee's name and address.
6. A description in common use of the nature of the goods and how they are packed. (With dangerous goods, their generally recognised description.)
7. The number of packages, their special marks, and numbers.
8. The gross weight or quantity otherwise expressed.
9. Carriage charges, supplementary charges, customs duties, and other charges likely to be incurred between the making of the contract and the delivery.
10. Instructions for customs and other formalities.
11. A statement that the carriage, notwithstanding any clause to the contrary, is subject to the CMR.

Where applicable the following should also be included:

1. A statement forbidding transhipment.
2. The charges the sender undertakes to pay.
3. The amount of COD charges.
4. A declaration of the value of the goods and of the amount of special interest in delivery.
5. The sender's instruction to the carrier regarding insurance.
6. The agreed time limit for the carriage to occur.
7. A list of documents given to the carrier.

The consignment note should include any other information the parties to the contract feel would be useful. The document must be carried by the driver on all hire and reward journeys abroad.

Blank CMR consignment notes are available from the Road Haulage Association and the Freight Transport Association.

Section B1 B2 Business Contracts and Company Law

Commercial Law

Trading Law

Businesses are formed in a variety of organisational structures with the most basic being the sole trader or proprietor who works on his own account. Larger operations are formed as partnerships or limited liability companies, while national and international firms are normally public limited companies. Each organisational structure carries different legal obligations and each has relative advantages and disadvantages attached.

Sole-Traders

Any person can start a business with negligible start up costs and minimal legal requirements. The owner's primary responsibilities are to himself and to his customers. The main advantage of sole proprietorship is that there is no need to comply with Companies Act legislation involving legal registration and a range of complex financial and structural formalities.

The primary disadvantage is the lack of protection for the proprietor from personal liability to meet creditors' payment demands. The owner's belongings and home may even be sold to pay such obligations. The typical scenario that results in this kind of action is when the business requires capital for expansion. The bank takes a second charge on the proprietor's home and if repayments are not made, the house is seized to recover the debt. An added financial disadvantage is the fact that all business profits become the proprietor's income and must be declared for taxation.

Partnerships

In a partnership arrangement, two or more individuals share equally (or in agreed upon proportions) in the ownership, work, and profits associated with a business. The partners are personally liable for debts incurred by the partnership. Each partner serves as an agent for the partnership, which is usually referred to as a "firm". As agents, a single partner can bind the other partners in a contract with or without specific authorisation to do so.

A partnership can be sued in its business name or by separate writ to each of the individual partners. A partner who is sued individually may be entitled to receive contribution towards damages against him from the other partners, even if they were not named individually in the suit.

A partnership cannot buy and have land conveyed to it, only to one or more of the partners as individuals who can declare a trust for sale for all the partners who own equity in the business.

Most partnerships are "general partnerships" with all partners being equally liable. The Partnership Act 1907, however, allows for the formation of a limited partnership in which individual partners' liabilities may not exceed the amount they have invested in the business. In such a case, however, there must be one designated general partner with unlimited liability.

Typically, a partnership agreement outlines the responsibilities and liabilities of each partner in proportion to their share of ownership and provides for the proportionate distribution of excess profits. In the absence of such an agreement, the Partnership Act 1890 applies wherein each partner is assumed to be equal. The partners are then "jointly and severally" liable for the business' debts. This means that if the other partners have no personal assets, a single partner with assets could be left to meet the tax liabilities and other debts of the partnership in the event of a business failure.

The advantage of a partnership lies in the ability to share the burdens of work, decision making, providing security, and worrying. The disadvantage, however, is that people do not always agree and contentious episodes of anger and distrust can sink a business. Arguments can arise over management issues, as well as the apportionment of work and profits.

Upon the dissolution of a partnership, the business assets are sold and the funds are applied to outstanding debts, loans, and other liabilities such as the tax and National Insurance contributions of the partners and employees. If there is a shortfall, the partners must personally meet the outstanding amounts. If there is a surplus, the amount is distributed equally or proportionately as per the terms of the partnership agreement.

If a partner dies, the surviving partners must account to the personal representative of the deceased for the amount of his interest in the firm. All tax due prior to the death normally becomes due immediately, unless special arrangements are made with the HM Revenue & Customs (HMRC) about continuation of the partnership with the remaining members. Most partnerships take precautions against such an event with appropriate insurance cover to provide adequate funds to meet payments due both to the HMRC and to the estate of the deceased.

Limited Liability Companies

A limited liability company (under the provisions of the Companies Act 2006) provides a means for a person or persons to remove the risk of the loss of personal property and possessions in a business failure. Such a company is a legally corporate body on record with the Registrar of Companies. The owners of the business are the shareholders and may hold their shares in equal or unequal proportions. The company's name must be approved by the Registrar of Companies and may not be confused with that of another registered company. The name may not be sensitive, meaning that it cannot imply royal connections or be suggestive of national authority nor may it be offensive. The word "limited" must be added as the last word of the name.

UK private limited companies must have at least one director at all time during its existence. There is currently no upper limit. Since 6th April 2008, there is no longer a requirement to have a minimum of one company secretary. Prior to 1 October 2009, where the company opted to have a secretary and there was a single director, the secretary would have to have been another person. The position is slightly different following the Companies Act 2006 changes introduced on 1 October 2009 which now permits a sole director to also act as a company secretary. Thus a single person can now occupy the three essential positions when incorporating a company; those of director, secretary and subscriber.

Essentially, this means that only one person is required to register a limited company and a single individual can occupy all three positions; that is, those of director, secretary and subscriber.

In forming a private limited company, friends or relatives may be asked to buy shares for the purpose of raising capital but shares may not be advertised for sale to the general public. Some or all of the shareholders may be elected as company directors. They choose a chairman from their ranks to conduct meetings and to cast the deciding vote in situations of stalemate.

When the company is formed, the founders determine the amount of shares that will form the legally constituted "share capital". For instance, if there are 100 shares at £1 each, the entity is a £100 share-capital company. The shares are divided among the subscribers according to their contribution and according to the decision regarding who will have controlling interest.

When the share capital and the individual holdings of each subscriber are determined, this becomes the maximum personal liability of each individual in the event of liquidation. If their shares are fully paid up, shareholders need not make further contributions toward company debts. If the shares are not paid up, the subscribers become liable to pay the balance of their allocation. So, if a £100 company has issued two £1 shares, in liquidation each would be responsible for an additional £49 (assuming each had equal shares).

Company directors carry considerable legal responsibilities and can be held liable for approximately 200 company law-related offences. Directors have a fiduciary duty to the company (a duty of trust to safeguard its property and assets). They must act in good faith and must not allow personal interests to conflict with those of the company. Under the Companies Act 2006, directors are responsible for the preparation of financial statements that give a true and fair view of the company's state and the degree of surplus or deficit present annually. In preparing such financial statements, directors must:

- select and consistently apply suitable accounting policies
- make reasonable and prudent judgments
- state whether applicable accounting standards have been followed, subject to any material departures disclosed and explained in the financial statements
- prepare the financial statements on a going concern basis, unless it is inappropriate to assume the company will stay in business

The directors are responsible for ensuring the company keeps reasonably accurate accounting records which disclose the financial state of the company and which enable the directors to make sure the financial statements comply with the Companies Act 2006. By the same token, the directors are responsible (in so far as they are able) to protect the company's assets and to attempt to prevent and to detect fraud and other irregularities.

If directors fail in their duties, they are held personally liable for any loss that can be tied to their negligence or for any act taken outside their authority or in breach of duty or trust.

Public Limited Companies

When a large company's capital requirements require investment, rather than loans, that company takes steps to become quoted on the stock market and to sell its shares to all interested buyers, thus becoming "public". Such companies are required to use the letters "plc" for "public limited company" after their company name.

The money shareholders pay for their shares generates capital for the business. The shares may be a new issue representing an increase in the company's share capital or they may be original shares released by the founders. (In the latter case, however, the money raised goes to the founders not into the company.)

A limited company must have an authorised share capital of £50,000 or more to go public. There must be at least two shareholders and a satisfactory performance history with good future prospects and evidence of sound management. Once a company has gone public, its shares are quoted on the Stock Exchange with daily value fluctuations reported in the financial columns of the daily media.

Other Organisational Forms

A non-profit organisation may form a special type of limited liability company that is guaranteed by its members who pledge to pay a small amount in the event of collapse or liquidation.

A cooperative is a business organisation formed and operated by a group of people who have a financial interest in its success. Profits after expenses are shared among members and management is carried out by elected member committees. This is a common arrangement in agriculture where individual farmers cannot afford to buy machinery or pay for other aspects of large-scale production.

Company Law

There are two avenues of creation for limited companies. They may be specially formed to suit the requirements of a particular business or they may be "off the shelf" or "readymade", a service offered by specialised firms situated near Companies House. While the procedure is identical in both avenues, the readymade companies are less expensive to organise and are afforded faster protection from liability. Such companies have their share capital established, name registered, Articles of

Association and Memorandum printed, and legal formalities completed for immediate operation. (While the advantages of speed and economy apply to the readymade solution, bear in mind that the company name may not be suitable and the Articles may not be sufficiently comprehensive).

In creating a new company, an accountant or solicitor is employed and often his office is quoted as the registered office of the company. In forming a company, the following must be established:

- a name followed by the word "Limited"
- share capital
- names of the original two (or more) subscribers
- names of the first directors and company secretary
- registered office for the company
- Articles of Association and Memorandum

The Articles of Association and Memorandum may be likened to the company rulebook. The documents specifically define the company, its name, and the objects for which it was formed. The Memorandum must contain:

- a name followed by the word "Limited"
- location of the registered office
- objects for which the company was formed
- statement of limited shareholder / member liability
- share capital amount divided into a number of shares with a value attached
- names of the original subscribers and their share holdings

The Articles of Association must contain:

- a statement that the provisions of the Companies Act 1985 (as amended in 2006) apply
- details of the capital structure, types of shares, and how they may be transferred
- voting rights of shareholders
- details of appointment and duties of directors
- company's borrowing powers
- appointment of a company secretary
- requirements for notification of company meetings
- names of the first directors (not less than one and no more than seven)
- names and addresses of original subscribers

Companies registered with the Registrar of Companies are given a number and are required to have an official seal for use on legal documents and share certificates. A Certificate of Incorporation is provided that includes the company name, registration number, and date of first registration. The certificate is to be displayed in the company's registered office.

A printed set of the Articles and Memorandum will be placed on file with the Registrar of Companies, along with copies of the formation documents. It is fairly routine for the company's bank to require copies of the Articles and Memorandum in order to understand the company's borrowing powers and any legal restrictions on its operation.

Legal Operation of Companies

Under the requirements of the Companies Act, a limited liability company must meet the following:

- The Certificate of Incorporation must be displayed at the registered office.
- The company name must be shown on the exterior of the business and on all documents including cheques.
- All business paper must include:
  - The address of the registered office, if different from the trading address.
  - The registration number.
  - Whether registered in England and Wales, Scotland, or Northern Ireland.
  - Name of directors may be shown if all directors are included with their first names or initials.
  - The VAT number if VAT registered.
- The company's accounts must be audited annually by a professional auditor who is not an employee of the company. This individual must also prepare a trading account and balance sheet.
- An annual meeting must be held at which the directors and shareholders approve the annual accounts.
- An annual return of directors, a copy of the minutes of the annual meetings, and the accounts must be placed on file with the Registrar of Companies. (Small companies with a turnover less than £632,000 may produce a simplified "the Companies Act ").
- The Registrar of Companies must be notified of any changes of secretary, shareholders, directors, or of the registered address.
- Details of any charge or mortgage against the company or against its property must also be recorded at Companies House.

Any interested person may pay a small fee and examine the records relating to limited companies. As an alternate service, researchers at Companies House will gather the information and provide copies of the data for a fee.

Accounts filing options for small companies.

Micro-entities

Micro-entities are very small companies. Your company will be a micro-entity if it has any 2 of the following:

- a turnover of £632,000 or less
- £316,000 or less on its balance sheet
- 10 employees or less

If your company is a micro-entity, you can:

- prepare simpler accounts that meet statutory minimum requirements
- send only your balance sheet with less information to Companies House
- benefit from the same exemptions available to small companies

Abridged accounts

You must meet at least 2 of the following:

- turnover is no more than £10.2 million
- balance sheet total is no more than £5.1 million
- average number of employees is no more than 50

Full accounts with HMRC

These joint accounts are suitable for small companies who are audit exempt and need to file full accounts to us and HMRC. You can also file your tax return with HMRC at the same time.

Dormant company accounts

These accounts are suitable for companies limited by shares or by guarantee that have never traded and can be filed using our WebFiling Service.

Further details: https://www.gov.uk/file-your-company-accounts-and-tax-return

Duties and Liabilities of Company Directors

Directors of a public limited company owe it to every other director to act in accordance with legal requirements especially in regard to the interests of shareholders, employees, and those with whom the company comes into contact. The directors are trustees of the company assets and must guard against personal interest interfering with the execution of their duties. They must act honestly and in good faith and not engage in or allow the company to engage in wrongful or fraudulent trading, for which they could be held personally liable in the event of insolvency. Further, directors must not be party to secret profits and are personally liable to compensate for same if they are discovered to exist.

The statutory duties of directors include:

- the keeping of proper accounts and the preparation of annual accounts
- the filing of legal documents with Companies House
- the maintenance of the company's statutory books
- the disclosure of company contracts in which they have a personal interest

- the refusal to accept or make substantial personal property investments in connection with the company (in excess of £100,000 or 10 percent of the company's value)
- the exercise of care and skill in operation and management
- honest dealings with shareholders regarding company activities, profits, and share value
- the avoidance of negligent statements or misrepresentations about the company in promotional literature

Liquidation of a Business

The Insolvency Act 1986 (updated 16 September 2020.) makes it illegal for a company to continue operations when its financial difficulties no longer allow it to meet creditor demands. At this point, various courses of action are available to the owners.

The first step may be an attempt to arrange an agreement with creditors to accept debt reduction or deferred payments. The second may be gaining an administration order preserving the firm intact and preventing creditors from forcing it into bankruptcy. This move buys time for an appointed administrator to attempt to save the business or to sell it as a going concern.

If neither of these methods is relevant, a receiver can be voluntarily appointed to take charge of the company's affairs and to pay off the creditors so far as the 1assets allows preparatory to shutting down the business. Alternately one or more of the creditors or all the creditors as a group may appoint a receiver.

Charges may be brought against the proprietor, partners, or directors for such actions as misappropriation of funds or they could be judged personally bankrupt.

Once a receiver is appointed he becomes legally responsible for collecting debts due to the business, for selling off its assets, for paying off creditors, and for meeting employee wages. Some preferential creditors such as banks or Inland Revenue will be given first share of any such monies paid out. (The receiver is allowed to charge his fees first.)

When all of the assets have been realised and distributed and the shareholders of a limited company have met outstanding commitment on shares, they are finished with the proceeding. In non-limited funds, the receiver is responsible for securing the personal assets of the proprietor or partners even to the extent of forcing the sale of their homes and possessions. A similar misfortune may befall a director of a limited liability company who has given personal guarantees or secured his personal assets against business loans.

Section C1 C2 C3 Social Law and Industrial Relations

Transport managers routinely come into contact with a broad and complex body of social legislation that has evolved over many years. Much of this legislation pertains to all aspects of employee interaction, compensation, and conflict resolution.

Tribunals and Trade Unions

There are a number of bodies concerned with arbitration and the resolution of employment issues, as well as those that provide a means of appeal to a higher authority.

ACAS - The Advisory, Conciliation and Arbitration Service

ACAS deals with employment disputes and is an official body, staffed by civil servants with a council comprised of a chairman and nine members. The members are appointed in groups of three after consultations with employers' organisations, trade unions, and independent members (usually academic). When a worker makes a complaint to an employment tribunal, ACAS has a statutory duty to secure settlement if possible by conciliation between the parties, so as to avoid a tribunal hearing.

The role of the ACAS is to:

- Offer advice to employers, employers' associations, individual employees, and trade unions on industrial relations and employment policies.
- Provide a conciliation service to help settle employment disputes.
- Provide conciliation officers when necessary to try to settle complaints before and after matters are taken to employment tribunals.
- Refer disputed matters to arbitration or to the Central Arbitration Committee (CA).
- Look into employment relations generally or to examine particular industries or employment sectors.
- Publish codes of practice and advisory literature for employers, trade unions, and others.

Employment Tribunals

Tribunals function as a type of court convened specifically to deal with employment disputes. Matters before the tribunal are considered by a chairman with legal training and two "lay" members. The intent is to provide a less formal way to address disputes and to provide employees with redress for breach of statutory duties on the part of their employers.

Tribunals deal with:

- discrimination (gender, race, disability)
- equal pay

- employment protection, employee rights
- transfer of undertakings
- payment of the national minimum wage
- violations of working-time regulations
- wrongful (unfair) dismissal
- health and safety in the workplace

Central Arbitration Committee (CAC)

The CAC arbitrates wage/pay disputes and assists recognised trade unions with the exercise of their statutory rights to obtain information for purposes of collective bargaining with firms employing their members.

Certification Officer

As an independent statutory authority, the Certification Officer is responsible for ensuring:

- the independence of trade unions
- that trade unions and employers' associations keep accounting records, undergo proper audits, and submit annual returns
- periodic actuarial examination and separating funding of members' superannuation schemes
- observance of statutory procedures for transfers of engagements, amalgamations and change of name
- supervision of the statutory requirements for the establishment and operation of political funds, dealing with members complaints about breaches of the rules governing such funds, and trade union elections
- the refund of certain costs incurred by independent trade unions in the holding of secret ballots for specified purposes
- the availability of documents, including annual returns and rule books of trade unions and employers' association for public inspection

Commissioner for the Rights of Trade Union Members

The Commissioner assists trade union members who intend to take or who are already taking, legal action against unions. (Examples might be issues over balloting, elections, and political expenditures.)

Trade Union Membership

A recognised trade union is one that is acknowledged by an employer or group of employers for purposes of collective bargaining on wages and other employment terms and conditions. Such a trade union is also recognised by the parties to a union agreement within the firm, or one the ACAS recommends as worthy of recognition.

Employees have the right not to be victimised or discriminated against as individuals (short of dismissal) for the purpose of:

- preventing or deterring them from becoming members of a trade union
- preventing or deterring them from taking part in trade union activities at any appropriate time (outside working hours or at a time when the employer has given permission for such activities)
- compelling them to be or to become a member of a trade union

If any such actions are taken against an employee, he may complain to an employment tribunal within three months of the action. The tribunal can award just and equitable compensation in relation to any loss the employee suffered as a consequence.

Trade Disputes and Picketing

A trade dispute occurs between an employer and his employees in relation to:

- The terms and conditions of employment or the physical conditions of the employment.
- The engagement or non-engagement of one or more workers; the termination or suspension of their employment or the duties of their employment.
- The allocation of work or duties of employment between employees or groups of employees.
- Matters of discipline among employees.
- Membership or non-membership of a trade union.
- The provision of facilities for trade union officials.
- The machinery for negotiation or consultation and other procedures relating to any of the above matters, including recognition by employers or employers' associations of the right of a trade union to represent workers in any such negotiation or consultation or in carrying out such procedures.

Trade disputes involving industrial action may take place between employers and employees or employee groups. These actions are only subject to legal action if they have not been instigated by a properly conducted ballot. Without such a ballot, the trade union and its officers have no legal immunity. Secondary industrial action, where a person is induced to take industrial action against an employer who is not party to a trade dispute, in most cases can result in legal action for damage. Picketing to further a trade dispute is legal if it is intended to peacefully communicate information, to persuade a person to refrain from or to engage in work, and is carried out near the place of work. It is not illegal to picket elsewhere, but can result in claims for damages by those who suffer a loss as a result.

Employment and Health and Safety

Terms and Conditions of Employment

As soon as a job offer has been tendered and accepted, a contract of employment exists. By reporting on time to start the job, the employee signifies acceptance of the terms described at the interview or contained in their letter of confirmation. The contract does not have to be in writing; however, within two months of starting work the employee must be given a written statement detailing:

- the parties of the contracted
- the date employment began and, in the instance of a fixed term, when it will end
- the date when continuous employment began
- rates of pay
- when payment will be made
- normal and irregular hours of work
- holiday entitlements and pay
- sick pay and provisions
- pensions and pension schemes
- notice of termination requirements
- job title
- the duration of a temporary contract
- the date of termination of a fixed-term contract
- where the job is outside the UK for more than one month the details of the length of the posting and the terms and conditions of return to the UK in addition to the payment currency and details of any additional benefits that will accrue
- disciplinary rules (unless fewer than 20 people were employed when continuous payment began)
- the name of the person to whom appeals on disciplinary matters can be referred
- the name of the person to whom an employee can apply to seek redress of grievances
- how such applications are to be made

If the terms of employment set out in the written statement change, the employer must give the employee the new details within one month.

Part-Time Workers

The Part-time Workers Prevention of Less Favourable Treatment Regulations 2000 introduced new rights to protect part-time workers. Such employees are entitled to the same:

- hourly rate of pay
- access to pension schemes
- entitlements to annual and maternity/paternity leave on a pro rata basis
- contractual sick pay
- access to training

Itemised Pay Statements

Employees are entitled to an itemised pay statement on or before the pay day including:
- gross amount of pay

- amount and reason for deductions (except if fixed deductions are regularly made)
- net amount payable
- where the net amount is paid by different means, the method of that payment (part cheque / part cash)

Guarantee Payments

If the employer cannot find work on a given day for an employee who has worked continuously for at least a month, the employee is entitled to be paid a guaranteed payment for that workless day. (This does not apply if the workless day occurs as a result of a trade dispute.) Payment need not be made if the employee was offered alternative work and refused, or if the employee does not comply with reasonable requirements to make sure his services are available. Guarantee pay is limited to five days in any three-month period for a five-day-week worker. Payment of guarantee pay does not affect the right of the employee to receive any other pay under his contract. If the employer fails to pay all or part of the guarantee pay due, the employee can complain to an employment tribunal.

Suspension on Medical Grounds

Under the Health and Safety at Work Codes of Practice an employee suspended from work by his employer on medical grounds must be paid for up to 26 weeks. The employee is not entitled to such payment for any time when he is unable to work if:

- he had not been continuously employed for at least one month prior to the suspension
- the employment is under a fixed-term contract not exceeding three months
- he is suffering disease or mental or physical disablement
- the employer has offered suitable alternative work
- he does not comply with reasonable requirements to make his services available

The amount of remuneration is one week's pay for every week's suspension starting on the day before the suspension begins, and proportionate payment for part-weeks. The employee has recourse to an employment tribunal if the payments are not made.

Time Off

An employee must be given time off with or without pay for the following circumstances.

Trade Union Duties

If an employee is an official of a recognised trade union he must be given paid time off to carry out duties concerned with industrial relations between the employer and employees and to undergo training in industrial relations relevant to his duties and approved by the union or the Trade Union Congress (TUC).

The amount of time allowed is described as "reasonable in all the circumstances." The pay given the employee must match his normal pay or in the instance of variable pay, an average for the time.

Trade Union Activities

Employees who are not union officials must be given unpaid time off to take part in the activities of a recognised union of which the employee is a member excluding those actions in relation to industrial action or the furtherance of a trade union dispute. The amount of time allowed is described as "reasonable in all the circumstances". If the employer fails to grant the time, the employee may complain to an employment tribunal which will award equitable compensation if the decision is in the employee's favour.

Public Duties

Employees who fulfil certain public duties must be given a reasonable amount of unpaid time off to attend to said duties. These circumstances pertain if an employee is a:

- Justice of the Peace
- member of a local authority, but not elected councillors
- member of a statutory tribunal
- member of a regional or area health authority or of a family practitioner committee
- member of the managing or governing body of an educational establishment maintained by a local education authority
- member of the National Rivers Authority

Qualifying duties would include attending meetings and discharging other functions. The amount of time allowed is described as "reasonable in all the circumstances".

This is judged by the amount of time required to fulfil the duties, how much time has already been taken in that respect, and the effect of the employee's absence on the business. If the employer fails to grant the time, a complaint can be lodged with an employment tribunal within three months of the incident. (Employees listed for jury service must also be allowed non-paid time off.)

Looking for Work or Arranging for Training

An employee who has been given notice of dismissal by reason of redundancy must be given reasonable paid time off to look for new employment or to make arrangements for training for future employment. If the employer refuses the time off, the employee is entitled to an amount equal to the pay he would have been entitled to had he taken time off.

A complaint may be made to an employment tribunal within three months of such an incident and if compensation is awarded, it may be equal to up to two-fifths of a week's pay.

Maternity Rights

Although more detailed information is available from the Department of Trade and Industry, the key aspects of the rights due an employee absent from work wholly or partly as a result of pregnancy or confinement include:

- 26 weeks continuous leave before and/or after childbirth
- paid time off for antenatal examinations
- no risk of dismissal during the pregnancy and maternity leave other than in exceptional circumstances unrelated to the pregnancy
- preservation of contractual rights while on maternity leave
- pay at the sick-pay rate during the period of maternity

Maternity Leave

Regardless of the length of an employee's tenure on the job, 26 weeks ordinary maternity leave apply. Pregnant employees who have completed 26 weeks' continuous service by the beginning of the 14th week before the expected week of childbirth (EWC) can take additional leave starting immediately after the ordinary maternity leave and continuing for an additional 26 weeks making for a total of 52 weeks.

A pregnant employee must notify her employer of her intention to take maternity leave by the end of the 15th week before her EWC unless it is not reasonably practicable to do so. She must tell her employer she is pregnant, supply the date of the week in which the child is expected to be born, and the date she wants the maternity leave to begin. (The employee can change her mind on the start date if she gives her employer 28 days advance notice unless it is not reasonably practicable to do so.)

A woman intending to return to work at the end of her maternity leave is not required to give further notification to her employer, however, if she wants to return to work before the end of her leave she must give the employer 28 days notice.

Maternity Pay

Statutory Maternity Pay (SMP) is paid for up to 39 weeks. You get:

- 90% of your average weekly earnings (before tax) for the first 6 weeks
- £151.20 or 90% of your average weekly earnings (whichever is lower) for the next 33 weeks

SMP is paid in the same way as your wages (eg monthly or weekly). Tax and National Insurance will be deducted.

Women are entitled to statutory maternity pay (SMP) if they were:

- employed by their present employer in the 15th week before the birth of their child

- employed by that employer for at least 26 weeks into the 15th week before the birth
- earn adequate wages on average to be relevant for National Insurance purposes

Pregnant women who have been recently employed but who do not qualify for SMP or those who are self-employed can apply for 26 weeks of maternity allowance (MA) at a Job Centre Plus.

Employee's Right to Return to Work

Employees have the right to return to their job if they take only:

- Ordinary Maternity or Ordinary Adoption Leave
- Ordinary Paternity Leave
- Additional Paternity Leave
- 4 weeks or less of parental leave

The rules are different if the employee takes:

- Additional Maternity or Additional Adoption Leave
- more than 4 weeks of parental leave

In this situation, employees have the right to their job or a similar job (if it's not possible to give them their old job). Similar means the job has the same or better terms and conditions. If the employee unreasonably refuses to take the similar job the employer can take this as their resignation.

An employee's right to return to work after pregnancy or confinement is subject to:

- employment with the original employer or his successor
- the job previously held
- the original contract of employment
- terms and conditions no less favourable than those applicable had she not been absent

If changed circumstances do not allow the employee to return to the original job, a suitable alternative vacancy must be offered under a new contract of employment that is not substantially less favourable than the original.

An employee exercising her right of return must give 28 day written notification. An employer may write to the employee up to 49 days after the notified date of confinement asking for written confirmation of her intent to return to work. If a reply is not tendered in 14 days, the right to return to work is lost. The employer may postpone the date of return for no more than four weeks, provided the employee is notified of the postponement.
The employee may postpone the date of return for no more than four weeks and must produce a medical certificate showing the reason she cannot return.

Parental Leave

A mother must take a minimum of 2 weeks' maternity leave following the birth (4 if she works in a factory). The adoptive parent getting Statutory Adoption Pay must take at least 2 weeks' adoption leave following the placement.

Parental leave may be taken by employees who have or who expect to have parental responsibility for a child. Parents have the right to take time off to look after a child, to make arrangements for the child's welfare, and to spend more time with their children to strike a better balance between their work and family lives.

To qualify, employees must have a year's continuous service with the current employer after which they may take 13 weeks leave in total for each child (twins are also counted individually). The parents of disabled children (those for whom an award of Disability Living Allowance has been made) receive 18 weeks total.

Parental leave may be taken in short or long blocks, depending upon agreement with the employer and contingent upon correct notice.

Termination of Employment

Specified minimum periods of notice apply to notices of termination whether given by the employer or by the employee.

Termination by the Employer:
If a person has been employed continuously for four weeks or more, the following periods of notice of termination apply:

- Less than 2 years, 1 week
- More than 2 but less than 12 years, 1 week for each continuous year
- More than 12 years, at least 12 weeks

Termination by the Employee:
After being employed for four or more weeks, an employee must give one week's termination notice. If a contract of employment stipulates a shorter period, the one week still applies but either party may waive the right to notice or accept payment in lieu of notice.

Dismissal

Certain conditions must be observed when an employer dismisses an employee depending on the circumstances of the case. Dismissal includes:

- termination of employment with or without notice
- the term of a contract expiring without renewal
- termination by the employee with or without notice due to the employer's conduct
- failure by an employer to let an employee return to work after pregnancy or confinement

Statement of Reasons for Dismissal

An employee is entitled to request a written statement detailing the justification for dismissal within 14 days if:

- he is given notice of termination for employment of more than 26 weeks
- he is dismissed without notice
- a fixed-term contract expires without being renewed

If the employer fails to produce a written statement or if the reason given is inadequate or known to be erroneous, the employee can complain to an industrial tribunal within 3 months of the dismissal. If the tribunal finds in the employee's favour an award may be made equal to two weeks' pay.

Fair and Unfair Dismissal

For an employee to be fairly dismissed, the employer must show the reason for dismissal in one of the following areas:

- the capability or qualification of the employee for the work involved including his fitness to perform the work
- the conduct of the employee
- redundancy of the employee
- contravention of legal restrictions by the employee in connection with his work

In stipulating one of the above reasons, the employer must show that he acted reasonably in treating the cause as sufficient for dismissal.

Dismissal Relating to Trade Union Membership

Dismissal for trade union membership, refusal of membership, or participation in union activities is unfair.

Dismissal on Redundancy

Dismissal for redundancy if the employee was selected for dismissal for an inadmissible reason or was selected in contravention of customary arrangements or agreed procedures is unfair.

Dismissal on Pregnancy

Dismissal for pregnancy or for any reason connected with pregnancy, except if the employee is incapable of doing her job because of the pregnancy or cannot do her job due to her pregnancy without contravention of legal restrictions is unfair.

Dismissal on Replacement

If an employee is hired to work as a replacement for an employee on pregnancy leave, it is not unfair to dismiss the employee when the pregnant employee returns to work if the replacement employee was warned dismissal would occur.

Dismissal on Industrial Action

Dismissal for an employee conducting or institution a lock-out or who was taking part in a strike or other industrial action is unfair.

Qualifying Period and Age Limit for Dismissal

A claim of unfair dismissal can be lodged with an employment tribunal within three months. Such a claim cannot be made if the following circumstances apply:

the employment was in a firm with more than 20 employees and -
   • the employee was employed for less than 2 years; 1 year if the employment began before 1 June 1985 (if he worked for 16 or more hours per week)
   or
   • the employee was employed for less than five years (if he worked 8-16 hours per week)

In the case of a firm with less than 20 employees, unfair dismissal cannot be claimed if the employment was for less than two years.

Remedy for Unfair Dismissal

In cases of unfair dismissal, an employee may lodge a complaint with an employment tribunal within three months of the dismissal. In well-founded cases reinstatement or compensation may be awarded.

Redundancy

The need to make an employee redundant may arise when a job ceases to exist, when the demand for a product or service ceases to exist, or when a business closes down. Employees are not redundant if they are replaced by new or other employees. Under employment legislation, for an employee to claim a redundancy payment he must have been continuously employed by that employer for at least two years since reaching age 18 years and must not have unreasonably refused an offer of suitable alternative employment.

The redundancy payment depends on age, length of service, and weekly rate of pay. The redundancy pay rates are as follows:

   • Half a week's pay for each year continuously employed if you were under 22.
   • One week's pay for each year continuously employed from ages 22 to 40.
   • One and a half week's pay for continuously employed for ages 41 or older.

Length of service is capped at 20 years.

Your weekly pay is the average you earned per week over the 12 weeks before the day you got your redundancy notice.

If you were paid less than usual because you were 'on furlough' because of coronavirus, your redundancy pay is based on what you would have earned normally.

If you were made redundant on or after 6 April 2020, your weekly pay is capped at £538 and the maximum statutory redundancy pay you can get is £16,140. If you were made redundant before 6 April 2020, these amounts will be lower.

The employer pays the redundancy amount, unless he is insolvent at which time the payment comes from the Secretary of State for Education and Employment. Redundancy payments made by employers are not recoverable from the Government. The payments and payments in lieu of notice are not normally subject to income tax deductions.

Redundancy pay (including any severance pay) under £30,000 is not taxable. Your employer will deduct tax and National Insurance contributions from any wages or holiday pay they owe you.

The following are not entitled to redundancy payments:

- self-employed people
- individuals employed continuously for less than two years since age 18
- people employed less than 16 hours per week
- the husband or wife of an employer
- people engaged on a fixed-term contract for two years or more or those who have agreed to forfeit any right to redundancy
- people outside Britain at the time of being made redundant, unless they normally work in Britain
- share fishermen
- merchant seamen (a master or seaman on a British seagoing vessel with a gross registered tonnage of 80 tons or more)
- registered dock workers

Consultation/disclosure

An employer wishing to make an employee redundant must consult the person's trade union representative. The requirement is to consult, not to inform. The consultation should begin 30 days before dismissal when 10 or more employees are to be made redundant in a period of 30 days, and 90 days when 100 or more are to be made redundant in 90 days.

An employer must disclose the following to the trade union representative:

- the reason for the redundancy
- the number and description of employees proposed for redundancy

- the total number of comparable employees
- the proposed selection method for employees to be dismissed
- the proposed methods of dismissal and the period in which they will take effect

If requested to do so by the trade union representative, the employer should provide this information in writing. The employer must consider and reply to any representations made by the trade union representative during consultation and to supply reasons for their rejection.

Failure to comply with these regulations allows the trade union to complain to an employment tribunal. An employer also must notify the Secretary of State for Education and Employment of proposed redundancies. The notification must occur 30 days in advance when proposing to dismiss 10 or more employees and 90 in advance of dismissing 100 or more.

Statutory Sick Pay

Under the Social Security Contributions and Benefits Act 1992, employers are required to make sickness payments to employees who satisfy rules regarding periods of incapacity, entitlement periods, and qualifying days. Certain small employers may reclaim the full payments made to employees (including National Insurance contributions) by deductions from his payments of National Insurance contributions to HMRC - Small Employers' Relief (SER). State sickness benefit still apply for special cases, such as an individual who must regularly miss work for long-term medical treatment or for those who do not qualify for or who have exhausted their SSP entitlements.

Employees qualify for SSP after four days of a period of incapacity for work (PIW) due to physical or mental illness or disablement. A number of periods can be linked if each is of a minimum of four days. The first three days of a PIW are waiting days. Sickness payment is only made in respect of qualifying days, which count from the fourth day onwards. The maximum entitlement to SSP in any period of incapacity from work is 28 weeks after which a new PIW begins.

The notification of sickness can be made by using the DSS self-certification form, by submitting a doctor's medical certificate, or by any scheme of self-certification instituted by the employer.

The SSP amount is based on the employee's average gross weekly pay according to a specified limit set by the Government.

National Minimum Wage

On 1 April 1999 the National Minimum Wage Act 1998 came into effect in the UK with subsequent amendments reflecting hourly minimum rate increases. The minimum wage applies to most employees included agency workers, part timers, casual workers, and those paid on commission. (Current rates available at www.direct.gov.uk)

Assessing Minimum Pay

In assessing minimum pay, bonuses, incentives, and performance related awards count, but other allowances not consolidated into the employee's pay do not. Overtime payments and shift payments do not count. Benefits in kind including overnight subsistence, meals, and allowances for work wear and uniforms are also excluded.

To determine if the hourly rate matches the national minimum, subtract deductions and reductions from the gross pay and divide the resulting amount by the number of hours worked.

Types of Work

The work hours for which an employer must pay are calculated by the type of work.

- Time work is where an employee is compensated for a set number of hours or a set time period.
- Salaried work is where an employee has a contract for a number of basic hours in return for an annual salary distributed in equal instalments.
- Unmeasured work is where employees are paid to do specific tasks but is not set to specific hours. (The employer must agree in writing with the employee on a realistic daily average to carry out the assigned tasks.)

Enforcement of Penalties

HMRC and employees themselves enforce the minimum wage provisions. Employers have a responsibility to keep accurate records for three years of hours worked and wages paid in case the information is called into question. An employee may make a written request to access their own records and the employer must comply within 14 days, unless extended by agreement. In disputes the burden of proof falls to the employer. Refusal to pay the minimum wage is a crime carrying a maximum fine of £5,000. Dismissal of an employee who becomes eligible for minimum wage or a higher rate of pay constitutes unfair dismissal.

Discrimination

There is a range of applicable legislation protecting workers from discrimination based on gender, colour, race or creed in recruitment, training, promotion, pay, terms of employment, and working conditions.

Equal Pay Act 1970

This legislation, as amended by the Equal Pay Regulations 1983, affects any employer who hires women and was introduced to prevent gender-based discrimination in terms and conditions of employment which must be equal for men and women employed in "like work".

The problem for the employer lies in determining what constitutes "like work" or "work rated as equivalent". The Act defines "like work" as that which is the same or of a broadly similar nature. In comparing a woman's work to that of a man, regard must be given to the frequency with which any differences occur in practice as well as to the nature and extent of the differences. "Work rated as equivalent" means the woman's job must be given equal value as the man's in terms of effort, skill, and decision. In negotiating pay deals, the employer must consider the requirements of the act.

Any aggrieved person under the terms of this Act may make a claim with an employment tribunal within six months of employment termination or at any time while still employed. Any awards give can equal up to two years' arrears of pay.

Sex Discrimination Acts 1975 and 1986

In firms with more than five employees, discrimination on the grounds of gender or marital status in relation to employment, training, promotion, employment benefits, and dismissal is illegal. The genders must be afforded equal opportunities with the most significant factor for many employers arising from advertised vacancies. Such an ad may not be worded so as to imply that applicants of only one gender need apply. There are obvious exemptions, such as the recruitment of females for the women's branches of the armed services or attendants in toilets. The transport operator, however, must exercise care and not indicate a "tea lady" is required or ask for an "attractive young lady" to serve as a receptionist.

Even when seeking staff for driving, maintenance, warehouse, or traffic office positions the wording of an advertisement must not suggest that only males will be employed. It is permissible to describe the duties of a position as physically arduous, with the implication that men might be more suited to the task, but strong women must not be excluded.

In general, the media will not accept advertising worded in such a way as to infringe the provisions of the act, but the employer should also be aware of materials posted on internal notice boards or in publications such as a company newsletter.

Disabled Persons

Under the terms of the Disabled Persons (Employment) Acts of 1944 and 1958 and the Disability Discrimination Act 1995 (DDA), disabled individuals are protected from discrimination in seeking employment or in working on their own account. For these purposes, a disabled person is either an individual registered under the Disabled Persons (Employment) Act 1944 or a person with a disability as defined in the DDA as "a physical or mental impairment which has a substantial and long-term adverse effect on their ability to carry out normal day-to-day activities".

Physical and Mental Impairment

Physical impairments include those affecting hearing and sight, while mental impairment results from or consists of a clinical illness recognised by bodies such as the World Health Organisation or by qualified medical practitioners. Examples might include manic depression, schizophrenia, or depressive psychoses. Impairments that do not qualify include alcoholism, nicotine and substance addictions, arson, thieving, exhibitionism, voyeurism, and physical or sexual abuse of other persons.

Discrimination against the Disabled

Discrimination against the disabled can occur in one of two ways. If the employer treats the person less favourably than able-bodied employees and cannot justify the treatment, the employer is guilty of discrimination. By the same token, if the employer fails to make reasonable adjustments in relation to the disabled person and cannot justify the failure, the failure is discriminatory.

The 1995 Act contains complex definitions of each discriminatory circumstance. Examples of reasonable adjustments might include:

- making adjustments to premises
- allocating some of the disabled person's duties to another employee
- transferring him or her to fill an existing vacancy
- altering his or her working hours
- assigning him or her to a different work place
- allowing for absences during work hours for rehabilitation, assessment or treatment
- giving or arranging for training
- acquiring or modifying equipment
- modifying instructions or reference manuals
- modifying testing assessment procedures
- providing a reader or interpreter
- providing supervision

Remedies for Discrimination against Disabled Persons

Within three months of an act of discrimination a disabled person may lodge a complaint with an employment tribunal. The period may be longer for just and equitable circumstances. In cases where other employees commit the discrimination, the employer is liable unless he can show that reasonable steps were taken to stop the incidents. If the claim of a disabled person is successful, the discriminator will be required to take action to end the discrimination and compensation may be awarded with no ceiling on the amount.

Race Relations Act 1976

This act, as most recently amended in 2003, prohibits racially based acts of discrimination and makes it illegal to treat another person less favourably or to apply requirements on a person or group of people which cannot be justified irrespective of colour, race, nationality, ethnic, or national origins. Discrimination is not allowed in regard to offering employment, to the terms on which the employment is offered, or on refusal of employment. It is also illegal to offer or refuse to offer promotion opportunities, training, benefits, or services on racial grounds and to dismiss a person or subject him to other detriments on the same grounds.

Fair Employment (Northern Ireland) Act 1989

This act applies solely to the province of Northern Ireland and came into effect on 1 January 1990. It ensures that Catholic and Protestant workers in Northern Ireland have equal job opportunities. The act established a Fair Employment Commission and a Fair Employment Tribunal and requires compulsory registration of employers with the Commission. Employers must review their recruitment, training, and promotion procedures and monitor their workforces and job applicants to ensure the provisions of the act are upheld. Failure to do so can result in criminal penalties and economic sanctions. Victims of religious discrimination can be awarded compensation by the Tribunal up to £30,000.

Public Disclosure

An employee can officially "shop" an employer who contravenes the law under the "whistleblowers" Public Interest Disclosure Act which took effect on 1 January 1999. When employees disclose such information, they are legally protected from detrimental treatment, especially when the disclosure is in the best interest of the public. A road transport worker might disclose information in instances of:

- the use of ill-maintained or unsafe vehicles
- the use of unlicensed, untaxed, or uninsured vehicles
- encouragement by an employer for drivers to exceed the speed limit or to overload their vehicles
- the setting of unreasonable work and delivery schedules
- the use of illegal "red" diesel
- encouraging or coercing drivers to exceed their hours limitations
- falsified or fraudulent tachographs
- contravention of transport or employment legislation

Any worker, including agency workers, may make such disclosures even where no conclusive proof is available. The person making the disclosure need only have a reasonable belief that:

- A criminal offence has been, is being, or is likely to be committed.
- A person has failed, is failing, or is likely to fail to comply with a legal obligation.
- A miscarriage of justice has occurred, is occurring, or is likely to occur.

- An individual's health and safety has been, is being, or is likely to be endangered.
- The environment has been, is being, or is likely to be damaged.
- Information regarding any of the above has been, is being, or is likely to be deliberately concealed.

A "protected disclosure" is one that is made:

- in good faith to an employer
- to another person where the malpractice related to the other person's conduct
- to another person with legal responsibility for the subject of the disclosures
- where the worker uses an employer's authorised procedure
- where the worker seeks legal advice
- where the worker, in good faith, makes a disclosure to regulatory authorities
- to anybody if:
- The disclosure is made in good faith.
- The disclosure is made with no intent to seek personal gain.
- The disclosure contains true information.
- Disclosure to the employer might result in suffering detrimental treatment.
- The complainant believes that disclosure to the employer would result in the concealment or destruction of evidence.
- The complainant has previously reported the matter to the employer with no response.

Employers may not prevent or persuade employees not to make disclosures, nor may they negotiate contracts prohibiting disclosure. Instead, employers must establish procedures to address complaints of malpractice that include provisions for proper investigation and action. The dismissal of an employee for making a public disclosure is unfair and would lead to a compensatory award by an industrial tribunal for an unlimited amount.

Working Time

A number of new working time provisions were introduced by Council Directive 93/104/EC of November 1993 (known as the Working Time Directive). It included the maximum 48-hour work week and shift working restrictions limiting night workers to no more than an average 8 hours per 24. The Directive specifically excluded the transport sector, by implication meaning that while drivers may be excluded other workers employed in associated transport operations like vehicle maintenance, warehousing, and administrative functions are not.

When adopted in November 1993, the Working Time Directive (93/104/EC) excluded the air, rail, road, sea, inland waterway and lake transport, sea fishing, offshore work and the activities of doctors in training as it was decided that these sectors required individual specific legislation to accommodate working time measures. A further Directive covering these sectors, known as the Horizontal Amending Directive (HAD) (2000/34/EC), was adopted on 1 August 2000.

Three further sectors specific Directives have also been adopted:

The Road Transport Directive (RTD) which was formally adopted on 23 March 2002 makes provision in respect of breaks, rest periods and working time for those subject to Council Regulation No. 3820/85 on the harmonisation of certain social legislation relating to road transport, otherwise known as "the European drivers' hours regulations". The RTD was implemented in April 2005.

The Aviation Directive, concluded by the Social Partners in the civil aviation sector, limits annual working time of mobile personnel (as defined inn the Directive) to 2000 hours, covers some elements of standby time and restricts flying time to 900 hours. The Directive also requires "appropriate" health and safety protection for all mobile personnel and contains provisions for a monthly and yearly number of rest days. Member States have until 1 December 2003 to implement the Directive. The Department for Transport will be consulting on its proposals to do this shortly.

The Seafarers' Directive on the organisation of working time, concluded by the social partners, is based on the International Labour Organisation (ILO) Convention No. 180. The Directive provides for a maximum working week of 72 hours and 14 hours' rest in any 24 OR a minimum weekly rest requirement of 77 hours and 10 hours in any 24-hour period. It also provides for 4 weeks' paid annual leave and health assessments. The Department for Transport implemented this Directive through the Merchant Shipping (Hours of Work) Regulations 2002 (SI 2002/2125) which came into effect on 7 September 2002.

The regulations impose a range of legal obligations on employers that may be enforced by the Health and Safety Executive (HSE) and by local authorities for premises for which they are responsible. Failure to comply by an employer is an offence under the Health and Safety at Work Act and may result in a fine up to £5,000 and, on indictment by the Crown Court in serious cases, imprisonment.

Duty of Employers

Employers are specifically required by the regulations to do the following:

- Limit average weekly work to 48 hours, including overtime calculated over successive periods of 17 weeks for the period of employment if less than 17 weeks. (Workers may agree individually or as an aspect of a collective or workforce agreement to waive the maximum but detailed records must be kept.)
- Limit night worker to a maximum of 8 hours in 25 taken on a 17-week average. (For night workers or those who work at least 3 hours at night and who face special hazards or heavy physical or mental strain, the limit is a straight 8 hours in 24 with no averaging.)
- Provide night workers with free health assessments and the opportunity to transfer to days in cases in which night work affects their health.
- Allow workers a daily rest period of a minimum 11 hours in 24 and an

uninterrupted 20-minute break when their daily work exceeds 6 hours.

- Allow workers a rest period of not less than 24 hours per seven days.
- Allow workers employed continuously for 13 weeks a minimum of four weeks annual paid leave that may not be exchanged for payment, except where it occurs on termination of employment.
- Keep adequate records of workers' hours to show compliance with legal requirements and to retain said records for two years from the date on which they were made.

Young workers are protected by more restrictive standards and certain special classes of workers such as Crown servants, the police, trainees, and agricultural workers are exempt. The Horizontal Amending Directive (HAD) (Directive 2000/34/EC) amended the Working Time Directive and set rules for those sectors expressly excluded from the Working Time Directive such as non-mobile transport workers and mobile workers not covered by EU drivers' hours rules.

The Road Transport Directive (RTD) (Directive 2002/15/EC) from 23 March 2005 deals specifically with working time for persons performing mobile transport activities under the EU drivers' hours rules. This is the main area of concern for hauliers and own account transport operators. RTD supplements the current EU drivers' hours regulations 3829/85/EEC and the AETR Agreement, so drivers who fall within the scope of these regulations when driving a goods vehicle must also take note of and comply with the provisions of the RTD.

Unfair Dismissal

New amendments to the Employment Rights Act 1996 make it unfair to dismiss an employee for refusing to comply with a requirement contrary to these regulations, or to forgo their rights.

Section C4 Drivers' Hours and Tachographs

The limits on drivers' hours are as follows:

Breaks from Driving

A break of no less than 45 minutes must be taken after no more than 4.5 hours of driving. The break can be divided into two periods - the first at least 15 minutes long and the second at least 30 minutes - taken over the 4.5 hours.

Daily Driving

Maximum of 9 hours, extendable to 10 hours no more than twice a week.

Weekly Driving

Maximum of 56 hours.

Two-weekly Driving

Maximum of 90 hours in any two-week period.

Daily Rest

Minimum of 11 hours, which can be reduced to a minimum of 9 hours no more than three times between weekly rests. May be taken in two periods, the first at least 3 hours long and the second at least 9 hours long. The rest must be completed within 24 hours of the end of the last daily or weekly rest period.

Multi-manning Daily Rest

A 9-hour daily rest must be taken within a period of 30 hours that starts from the end of the last daily or weekly rest period. For the first hour of multi-manning, the presence of another driver is optional, but for the remaining time it is compulsory.

Ferry/train Daily Rest

A regular daily rest period (of at least 11 hours) may be interrupted no more than twice by other activities of not more than 1 hour's duration in total, provided that the driver is accompanying a vehicle that is travelling by ferry or train and has access to a bunk or couchette.

Weekly Rest

A regular weekly rest of at least 45 hours, or a reduced weekly rest of at least 24 hours, must be started no later than the end of six consecutive 24-hour periods from the end of the last weekly rest. In any two consecutive weeks a driver must have at least two weekly rests - one of which must be at least 45 hours long. A weekly rest that falls across two weeks may be counted in either week but not in both. Any reductions must be compensated in one block by an equivalent rest added to another rest period of at least 9 hours before the end of the third week following the week in question.

AETR Rules

Journeys to or through the countries that are signatories to the AETR Agreement are subject to AETR rules. AETR rules apply to the whole journey, including any EU countries passed through.

Working Time Regulations

Drivers who are subject to the EU rules on drivers' hours and tachographs normally have also to comply with the rules on working time as laid out in the Road Transport (Working Time) Regulations, which were brought into force on 4 April 2005.

GB Domestic Rules

The GB domestic rules, as contained in the Transport Act 1968, apply to most goods vehicles that are exempt from the EU rules. Separate rules apply to Northern Ireland.

Domestic Rules Exemptions

The following groups are exempt from the domestic drivers' hours rules:

- Drivers of vehicles used by the Armed Forces, the police and fire brigade.
- Drivers who always drive off the public road system.
- Private driving, i.e. not in connection with a job or in any way to earn a living.

Domestic Driving Limits

Driving is defined as being at the controls of a vehicle for the purposes of controlling its movement, whether it is moving or stationary with the engine running, even for a short period of time.

Daily Driving

In any working day, the maximum amount of driving permitted is 10 hours. The daily driving limit applies to driving on and off the public road. Off-road driving for the purposes of agriculture, quarrying, forestry, building work or civil engineering counts as duty rather than driving time.

Day: The day is the 24-hour period beginning with the start of duty time.

Daily Duty

In any working day the maximum amount of duty permitted is 11 hours. A driver is exempt from the daily duty limit (11 hours) on any working day when he does not drive.

A driver who does not drive for more than 4 hours on each day of the week is exempt from the daily duty limit.

Duty: In the case of an employee driver, this means being on duty (whether driving or otherwise) for anyone who employs him as a driver. This includes all periods of work and driving, but does not include rest or breaks.

Employers should also remember that they have additional obligations to ensure that drivers receive adequate rest under health and safety legislation.

For owner-drivers, this means driving a vehicle connected with their business, or doing any other work connected with the vehicle and its load.

Drivers of certain vehicles are exempt from the duty but not the driving limit, namely - goods vehicles, including dual-purpose vehicles, not exceeding a maximum permitted gross weight of 3.5 tonnes, when used:

- By doctors, dentists, nurses, midwives or vets.
- For any service of inspection, cleaning, maintenance, repair, installation or fitting.
- By commercial travellers.
- By the AA, RAC or RSAC.
- For cinematography or radio and television broadcasting.

Record Keeping

You must keep written records of your hours of work on a weekly record sheet. Operators are expected to check and sign each weekly record sheet.

Record books containing weekly record sheets are not available from The Stationery Office.

Alternatively, an EU-approved and sealed tachograph may be used to record a driver's activities while he is subject to domestic drivers' hours rules. When recording in this manner, and where domestic records are legally required (see flowchart below), all rules on the fitment and use of the tachograph must be complied with.

Where a tachograph is fitted to a vehicle subject to the domestic rules, but is not used to produce a legally required record, the operator and driver should nevertheless ensure that the tachograph is properly calibrated and sealed.

The tachograph does not have to be recalibrated provided the seals remain intact and the vehicle remains out of scope of the EU rules.

Emergencies

The GB domestic rules are relaxed in cases where immediate action is needed to avoid:

- Danger to the life or health of people or animals.
- Serious interruption of essential public services (gas, water, electricity or drainage), of telecommunication or postal services, or in the use of roads, railways, ports or airports.
- Serious damage to property.

In these cases the driving and duty limits are suspended for the duration of the emergency.

Records for Vehicles carrying Postal Articles

Tachographs must be fitted and used on all vehicles with a permissible maximum weight in excess of 3.5 tonnes that carry parcels and letters on postal services. Drivers of such vehicles may be exempt from the EU rules on drivers' hours (see EU rules exemptions) but, if so, must still comply with the UK domestic rules.

Travelling Abroad

The GB domestic rules apply only in GB, but you must observe the national rules of the countries in which you travel. The embassies of these countries will be able to assist in establishing the rules that might apply.

For example, German national rules require drivers of goods vehicles between 2.8 and 3.5 tonnes to record details of their journeys in an AETR-style log book. This means that UK drivers have to use the logbook when they set out and while driving through the countries on journeys to or through Germany.

Mixed Vehicle Types

If it occurs that a driver divides his time driving goods vehicles and passenger vehicles under GB domestic rules, then in any working day or week, if he spends most of his time driving passenger vehicles then the appropriate GB rules for passenger vehicles apply for that day or week.

Working Time Regulations

Drivers who are subject to the UK domestic rules on drivers' hours are affected by four provisions under the UK's Working Time Regulations 1998 (as amended).

Mixed EU/AETR and GB Domestic Driving

Many drivers spend some of their time driving under one set of rules and some under another set, perhaps even on the same day. If you work partly under EU/AETR rules and partly under GB domestic rules during a day or a week, the following points must be considered (the EU rules take precedence over the GB domestic rules):

- The time you spend driving under EU rules cannot count as an off-duty period under GB domestic rules.
- Driving and other duty under GB domestic rules (including non-driving work in another employment) counts as attendance at work but not as a break or rest period under EU rules.
- Driving under EU rules count towards the driving and duty limits under GB domestic rules.
- Any driving under EU rules in a week means that you must take a daily rest period on those days when you actually drive under EU rules, as well as a weekly rest period.

Driving Limits

GB domestic limit (a maximum of 10 hours of driving a day) must always be obeyed. But at any time when you are actually driving under the EU rules you must obey all the rules on EU driving limits.

Other Duty Limits

GB domestic limit (i.e. no more than 11 hours on duty) must always be obeyed. But when working under EU rules you must also obey all the rules on breaks, daily rest (only on those days when actually driving) and weekly rest.

Rest Periods and Breaks

Again, you must always obey the EU rules on rest periods and breaks on days and weeks in which driving in scope of EU rules is carried out.

A weekly rest period is not required in a fixed week where a driver does not drive under EU rules. Where a driver works under EU rules in one week and under GB domestic rules in the following week, the driver may take either a regular or a reduced weekly rest in the first week. If the driver takes a reduced weekly rest, compensation will be required by the end of the third week following the week in question. If this working pattern continues, the driver may take either a regular or reduced weekly rest period every other week.

Where a driver works under GB domestic rules in week one and the EU rules in the second week, the weekly rest required in week two must start no later than 144 hours following the commencement of duty on or after 00.00 hours on Monday.

Driver's Hours Update – 2020

Changes to the driver hour's laws are now in operation and will continue to apply in the UK after Brexit.

The legislation caps the amount of time that driver can work away from home.

Among the changes, drivers are now required to return home every four weeks, the law also clarifies that normal length weekend rests cannot be taken in the vehicle cab.

Driver's week ended outside their home state can take two consecutive weekly rest period of 24 hours, but in any four week period four weekly rests must be taken, at least two of which must be regular weekly rest periods.

When two consecutive reduced weekly rests have been taken, the next weekly rest must be preceded by a rest period to compensate for the two reduced weekly rests.

In a forthcoming reform, drivers will be required to retain tachograph records for 56 days, rather than the current 28 days.

This change will not come into force until 31st December 2024.

The requirement to have tachograph fitted is to be extended to include goods vehicles of 2.5 – 3.5 gvw on international hire & reward from July 2026.

The updated UK government guidance for good vehicles driver's hours is available from:
https://www.gov.uk/guidance/drivers-hours-goods-vehicles

Records

During a week in which the in-scope driving has taken place, any previous work (including out-of-scope driving since the last weekly rest period), would have to be recorded as "other work" on a tachograph chart, printout or a manual entry using the manual input facility of a digital tachograph, or a legally required GB domestic record on a log book.
When driving a vehicle subject to EU or AETR rules, a driver is required to produce on request tachograph records (including other work records described above) for the current day and the previous 28 calendar days.

An approved tachograph is the required instrument by which the activities of drivers subject to the EU or AETR drivers' hours rules, and the vehicle's speed, distance and time are recorded. There are two main types of tachograph - analogue and digital. The only exception is when driving a vehicle engaged in the collecting of sea coal. In this one case you are subject to the EU rules on drivers' hours but do not need a tachograph.

The resulting record is to be used to monitor compliance with rules on drivers' hours. The rules on using the tachograph are contained in Regulation (EC) 3821/85 (as amended), and these depend on whether the vehicle is fitted with an analogue or digital tachograph. These rules must be observed by both drivers and operators of vehicles that fall within the scope of Regulation (EC) 561/2006 or the AETR rules.

The driver of a vehicle that is exempt from or out of scope of the EU rules is not required to use the recording equipment, even if it is fitted, unless the vehicle is operated by a universal service provider (USP).

From 2 March 2015 the distance threshold were raised from a 50 kilometres (kms) radius from base to 100 kms radius from base for the following derogations which apply only to journeys wholly within the United Kingdom.

The following derogation became an exemption (under Article 3 of EC 561/2006) and will also have a threshold of 100 km radius from base instead of a 50 km threshold:

Vehicles or combinations of vehicles with a maximum permissible mass not exceeding 7,5 tonnes used for carrying materials, equipment or machinery for the driver use in the course of his work on condition that that driving the vehicles does not constitute the driver's main activity

Analogue or digital: Vehicles first registered on or after 1 May 2006 must be fitted with a digital tachograph. Those vehicles registered before that date can be fitted with either analogue or digital equipment.

Analogue Tachographs

Analogue tachograph recordings are made by a stylus cutting traces into a wax-coated chart.
Three separate styluses mark recordings of speed, distance travelled and the driver's activity (known as the 'mode'). The inner part is used by the driver to write details of his name, location of start of journey, end location, date and odometer readings.

The reverse of a tachograph chart normally contains an area for recording manual entries and details of other vehicles driven during the period covered.

The Tachograph Chart

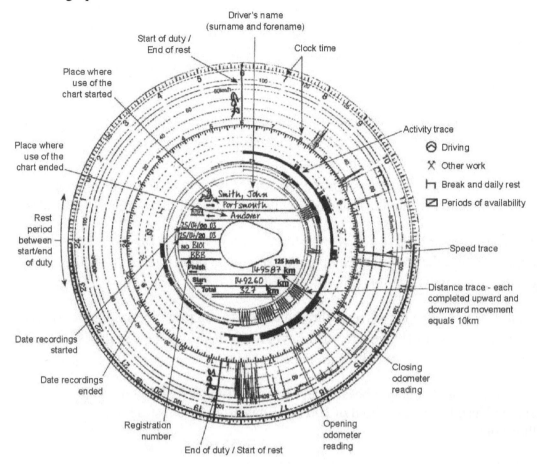

Driver's name
(surname and forename)

Start of duty /
End of rest

Clock time

Place where
use of the
chart started

Place where
use of the
chart ended

Rest
period
between
start/end
of duty

Date recordings
started

Date recordings
ended

Registration
number

End of duty / Start of rest

Opening
odometer
reading

Closing
odometer
reading

Distance trace - each
completed upward and
downward movement
equals 10km

Speed trace

Activity trace

⊘ Driving

✕ Other work

⊢ Break and daily rest

▨ Periods of availability

Smith, John
Portsmouth
Andover
25/04/20 03
25/04/20 03
NO B101
BBB
Finish
Start   149260
Total   327
149587 km
km
125 km/h

Charts and Records

Drivers are responsible for operating the tachograph correctly in order to record their activities accurately and fully. Specifically, drivers must:

- Verify, before using an instrument, that it is correctly calibrated via the attached plaques and ensure that the time displayed is set to the official time of the country in which the vehicle is registered.
- Carry enough charts for the whole journey, including spare charts in case any become damaged or dirty.
- Use a second chart if a chart is damaged while in use and attach this one to the first chart on completion. There are other occasions when use of a second chart in a 24-hour period is unavoidable, namely when a driver changes to a vehicle with an incompatible tachograph to the chart in use or he changes vehicle so many times that all the details cannot be accommodated on one chart.
- Ensure that the correct type of chart is being used for the specific model of tachograph in use and that enough spare charts are carried.
- Not use a chart to cover a period longer than 24 hours.
- Enter centrefield details at the first use of the chart, when changing vehicles and when completing the use of the chart.
- Correctly operate the mode switch in order to record their activities accurately.
- Make manual entries on the chart in respect of their activities away from the vehicle where the rules have been exceeded in an emergency, or to correct a recording.
- Make manual entries when the equipment malfunctions and report any such malfunctions to the operator or employer.
- Return used charts to the operator within the 42 days. This requirement must be complied with even when a driver changes employer.
- Permit an Authorised Examiner or police officer to examine the tachograph instrument;
- Not remove the chart from the instrument before the end of their duty period unless authorised to do so. The rules do not specify who can authorise removal of the chart, but cases where charts can be removed include, a change of vehicle.
- To make manual entries in the event of an emergency, equipment malfunction etc. and be able to produce at the roadside, charts and any legally required manual records for the current day and the previous 28 calendar days; and the driver's digital smart card if they hold one.

Time tips: Make sure the time is correct for am or pm - both times are displayed identically on an analogue tachographs 12-hour clock face. Analogue tachographs must continue to display the correct time - which for the UK includes adjustments for British Summer Time.

Activity record: Most analogue tachograph instruments in use are 'automatic'. This means that the instrument will automatically record activity as driving when the vehicle is moving and defaults to the mode switch setting when the vehicle stops.

Driver cards: Drivers who have been issued with a driver card are committing an offence if they are unable to produce this during a roadside inspection, even if they only drive analogue tachograph- equipped vehicles.

Centrefield Entries

A driver is required to enter the following information on the centrefield of a tachograph chart that he is using to record his activities:

- Surname and first name (the law does not stipulate which order the names are put in - but your employer may have a policy on this).
- The date and place where the use of the record sheet begins and ends. The year may be written in full or abbreviated - so both '2007' and '07' are acceptable. If the start and finish places are the same, both must be written on the chart - ditto marks are not acceptable.
- The registration number(s) of vehicle(s) driven (which should be entered before departing on a new vehicle).
- The time at which any change of vehicle takes place; and the odometer readings:
- At the start of the first journey.
- At the end of the last journey.
- At the time of any change of vehicle, recording the readings from both vehicles. Note that the 'total km' field does not have to be completed.

It is not acceptable for written entries to extend outside the centrefield area if they might interfere with chart recordings. If, for example, the driver's name or a place name is so long it must be abbreviated in order to avoid any possible interference with the recordings, the full name should be noted on the reverse of the chart.

Tachograph charts are required to provide space on their reverse side to record the additional information required in connection with changes of vehicles.

Manual Entries

Drivers must produce a record of their whole daily working period. So when drivers are unable to operate the instrument, have not been allocated a vehicle, or are working away from the vehicle and have had to remove their tachograph chart, they must manually record their activities on the chart. Manual entries may also be needed at other times - for example, if the tachograph develops a fault, or in the event of an emergency. Employers may also ask drivers to indicate on a chart where their duty (or rest) begins and ends, so that they can ensure that a full record has been submitted. Most analogue charts have a specified place to make manual entries (usually on the reverse). However, manual entries can be made anywhere on the chart, provided that they are clear and do not obliterate other recordings.

Digital tachographs work by storing digital data on the driver and vehicle in their own memory and separately on a driver's smart card. Transport undertakings must periodically download this data from the digital tachograph (known as the Vehicle

Unit or VU) every 90 days and from driver cards every 28 days and analyse the information to ensure that the rules have been complied with.

Driver Cards and Records

It is a legal requirement for a digital tachograph-equipped vehicle driven in scope of EU rules that the driver must use a driver card.

If the vehicle is used without a card being inserted, the system will not prevent the vehicle from being driven, but the VU will record the fact that the vehicle has been used without a card. Drivers may only be in possession of one driver's smart card, and must never use anyone else's card or allow another driver to use their card.

When driving a vehicle that is equipped with a digital tachograph, drivers should:

- Ensure that the instrument is calibrated by inspecting the calibration plaque or interrogating the instrument.
- Ensure that their driver card is inserted into the correct slot (driver in slot 1, second driver in slot 2) from the moment they take over the vehicle, and that it is ready for use, before the vehicle is moved.
- Record the country in which they begin and end their daily work period. This must always be carried out at the time of the start or end of the period, even if the card is not to be withdrawn or inserted (for example if the card is left in overnight).
- Carry sufficient supplies of type-approved print roll on board the vehicle so that a printout can be produced at an enforcement officer's request.
- Ensure that all duties conducted since the driver card was last removed from a tachograph are manually entered onto the card record, using the manual entry facility on the tachograph.
- Ensure that the tachograph is working properly.
- Ensure that through the daily working period the mode button is used correctly to record other work, periods of availability, and rest and breaks.
- Take reasonable steps to protect their card from dirt and damage.
- Use only their own personalised driver card to record driving and other activities they undertake.
- Ensure that the card is not removed from the tachograph during the working day unless otherwise authorised. The rules are not specific on who can authorise removal of the card, but cases where cards can be removed include a change of vehicle, or where another driver will be using the vehicle during a break or rest period.
- On multi-manning operations ensure that their driver card is placed in the correct slot (slot 1 when they are acting as driver and slot 2 when co-driver on a double-manned journey) when they take over driving.
- Make their cards available for downloading by their employer.
- Be able to produce at the roadside:
- Charts and any legally required manual records for the current day and the previous 28 calendar days; and the driver's digital smart card if they hold one.

Mode switch default: Note that digital tachographs will default to recording 'other work' for driver 1 and 'availability' for driver 2 when the vehicle stops, and drivers must use the mode switch correctly to ensure that rest and break periods are recorded correctly.

How to Apply for Driver Cards

You can get application forms and assistance from the Driver and Vehicle Licensing Agency.
Forms are available to order online at www.dvla.gov.uk. Alternatively, forms should be available from local DVLA offices and testing stations. DVLA will accept payment for up to 25 driver card applications on one company cheque. In Northern Ireland, application forms are available from Driver and Vehicle Licensing Northern Ireland (DVLNI) (call 028 7034 1589) and test centres of the Driver and Vehicle Agency (DVA).

Lost, Stolen or Malfunctioning Driver Cards

Digital tachograph cards have passed all relevant International Organisations for Standardization (ISO) qualified tests and security certification requirements. They are designed to work reliably and securely for their period of validity, but like all smart cards, can be damaged by abuse. Take care of your driver card - treat it as if it were a credit card and do not subject it to excessive force, bending or extremes of temperature.

Where it is impossible to use a driver card (e.g. where it has been lost, stolen or damaged or is malfunctioning) a driver may drive without the card for a maximum of 15 calendar days (or longer if this is necessary for the vehicle to be returned to its premises) provided that he produces two printouts - one at the start of the journey and another at the end.
Both printouts must be marked with:

- The driver's name or driver card or licence number, so the driver can be identified.
- Any manual entries needed to show periods of other work, availability, and rest or break.
- The driver's signature.

The driver must report the problem to DVLA and apply for a new card within seven calendar days.

UTC - the time set on a digital tachograph

The internal clock of a digital tachograph is set to Universal Time Co-ordinated (UTC). The time displayed on the clock face can be set by the driver either to local time or to UTC. However, all data will be recorded by the VU on the time set by the integral clock, which operates on UTC - this is the same as Greenwich Mean Time

(GMT). You will need to remember that UTC is one hour behind British Summer Time (BST). So, between 01.00 on the last Sunday in March and 01.00 on the last Sunday in October, drivers must account for the difference when manually inputting activity details in the digital tachograph.

For example, if drivers carried out other work for two hours between 06.00 and 08.00 in June before taking over the vehicle, they must enter this as between 05.00 and 07.00 in UTC time. As mentioned above, it is possible for drivers to set the display time on the VU to local BST, but this will not prevent the VU recording in UTC. Therefore, it is recommended that drivers leave the display time in UTC as a reminder of the difference.

Manual Records

A digital tachograph offers the ability for a driver to enter activities carried out by him away from his vehicle. This is by means of the manual input facility offered by the instrument.

COMMON RULES

Operation of the mode switch or button

Drivers must ensure that the mode switch on an analogue tachograph or the mode button on a digital tachograph is correctly set to record their activities.

Break or Rest

Covers breaks in work and daily or weekly rest periods. Drivers may not carry out any driving or any other work. Break periods are to be used exclusively for recuperation. During a rest period a driver must be able to dispose freely of his time. If for any reason the tachograph does not make an accurate record of activities (e.g. if the driver inadvertently makes an incorrect manual entry in a digital tachograph, or fails to correctly operate the mode button or switch), it is strongly recommended that the driver makes a manual tachograph record to this effect. For digital equipment, the driver should make and sign a printout for the relevant period with a note giving details of the error and reason at the time the error is made. For analogue equipment, the record should be made at the back of the chart.

Multi-manning - Second Driver Record

Some analogue equipment and all digital tachographs will automatically record all time spent as a second driver when the vehicle is in motion as a period of availability and do not allow the mode to be changed to either 'break' or 'other work'. Provided the second driver is not required to carry out any work during this time, enforcement authorities will accept the first 45 minutes of this time as a break from driving. Any periods of other work, however, must be manually recorded on a printout or chart by the driver.

Travelling Time

In cases where a vehicle that comes within the scope of EU rules is at a separate location that is neither the driver's home nor the employer's operational centre where the driver is normally based, the time the driver spends travelling to or from that location may not be counted as a rest or break, unless the driver is in a ferry or train and has access to a bunk or couchette.

Mixed Records - analogue and digital equipment

It is possible that a driver may during the course of a day drive two or more vehicles where both types of recording equipment are used. Drivers in such a situation must use a driver card to record while driving a vehicle with a digital tachograph and tachograph charts when driving a vehicle equipped with an analogue device. Time away from the vehicle may be recorded on either recording equipment, but there is no need to record it on both.

Note: A driver who is not in possession of a driver card cannot drive a vehicle equipped with a digital tachograph.

Recording Other Work

Drivers must record all other work and periods of availability - including work for other employers - on all driving and non-driving days within a week where they have undertaken driving that comes within the scope of the EU rules on drivers' hours since their last weekly rest.

For example, a driver who works in a warehouse on Monday, Tuesday and Wednesday and wishes to drive a vehicle within the scope of the EU rules on Thursday of the same week must complete records for Monday, Tuesday and Wednesday.

The record must be either:

- Be written manually on a chart.
- Be written manually on a printout from a digital tachograph.
- Made by using the manual input facility of a digital tachograph.

For days where a driver has been subject to the domestic drivers' hours rules and a record is legally required recorded in a domestic logbook.

For the non-driving days, the record may simply show the driver's name, the date, and the start and finish of the shift. These records must be carried on the vehicle by the driver to be produced to enforcement officers for the relevant period (see individual sections on how to make manual entries).

<u>Information to Operators</u>

A driver who is at the disposal of more than one transport undertaking must provide each undertaking with sufficient information to allow them to make sure the rules are being met.

<u>Rest and Other Days Off</u>

The period of time unaccounted for between successive charts produced by a driver should normally be regarded as (unless there is evidence to the contrary) a rest period when drivers are able to dispose freely of their time. In the UK, drivers are not expected to account for this period, unless enforcement authorities have reason to believe that they were working. Nevertheless, on international journeys it is recommended that letters of attestation from the employer are provided for drivers travelling through other countries to cover any sick leave, annual leave and time spent driving a vehicle which is out of scope of EU/AETR rules during the preceding 28 days.

<u>Responsibilities of Operators</u>

Operators of transport undertakings have legal responsibilities and liabilities for their own compliance with the regulations and that of the drivers under their control. Transport undertakings must:

- Ensure that tachographs have been calibrated, inspected and re-calibrated in line with the rules.
- Supply sufficient quantity of type-approved charts and print roll to drivers.
- Properly instruct drivers on the rules.
- Ensure the return of used tachograph charts from drivers. Note that this responsibility continue after a driver has left employment until all charts are returned.
- Properly schedule work so the rules are met.
- Not make payments to drivers related to distances travelled and/or the amount of goods carried if that would encourage breaches of the rules.

Download data from the Vehicle Unit:
- At least every 90 calendar days.
- Immediately before transferring control of the use of the vehicle to another person (for example, when the vehicle is sold or de-hired).
- Without delay upon permanently removing the unit from service in the vehicle.
- Without delay upon becoming aware that the unit is malfunctioning, if it is possible to download data.
- Without delay in any circumstances where it is reasonably foreseeable that data will be erased imminently.
- In any case as often as necessary to ensure that no data is lost (the Vehicle Unit holds 365 days' worth of average data, after which the memory is full and the oldest data is overwritten and lost).

Download data from Driver Cards:
- At least every 28 calendar days.
- Immediately before the driver ceases to be employed by the undertaking (remember that this also applies to agency drivers).
- Without delay upon being aware that the card has been damaged or is malfunctioning, if it is possible to download data.
- Without delay in any circumstances where it is reasonably foreseeable that data will be erased imminently.
- Where it is only possible to download the card via a Vehicle Unit (for example, if the card is stuck), immediately before ceasing control of the use of the vehicle; and any case as often as necessary to ensure that no data is lost (the driver card holds 28 days of average data, after which the memory is full and the oldest data is overwritten and lost. An average day is deemed to be 93 activity changes. In certain operations where more than 93 activity changes are recorded in a day, a driver card may hold less than 28 days of data).
- Make regular checks of charts and digital data to ensure compliance.
- Be able to produce records to enforcement officers for 12 months.
- Take all reasonable steps to prevent breaches of the rules.

Tachograph Calibration and Inspection

All tachographs used for recording drivers' hours, whether analogue or digital, must be properly installed, calibrated and sealed. This task must be performed either by a vehicle manufacturer or an approved tachograph calibration centre. An installation plaque must be fixed to or near the tachograph. Tachograph calibration centres will issue a certificate showing details of any inspection conducted.

Analogue tachographs must be inspected every two years and recalibrated every six years.

Digital tachographs must be recalibrated:
- Every two years.
- After any repair.
- If the vehicle registration number changes.
- If UTC is out by more than 20 minutes.
- After an alteration to the circumference of the tyres or characteristic coefficient.

Inspection and recalibration dates are shown on the plaque and updated by calibration centres.

Operators must ensure that these tachograph requirements are complied with before a new or used vehicle goes into service.

Breakdown of Equipment

EU legislation requires that in the event of a breakdown or faulty operation of the equipment, it must be repaired as soon as possible. If the vehicle is unable to return to its base within a week, the repair must be carried out en route.

UK legislation also provides that a driver or operator will not be liable to be convicted if they can prove to a court that the vehicle was on its way to a place where the recording equipment could be repaired, or that it was not immediately practicable for the equipment to be repaired and the driver was keeping a manual record.

Additionally, they will not be liable where a seal is broken and the breaking of the seal was unavoidable and it could not be immediately repaired, providing that all other aspects of the EU rules were being complied with.

For faults and breakdowns involving digital tachographs, operators should ask the repair centre to download any data held on the unit. If this is not possible, the centre should issue the operator with a 'certificate of undownloadability', which must be kept for at least 12 months.

International journeys: Although this is the position under EU rules, it is not advisable to start or continue an international journey with a defective tachograph, even if manual records are kept. This is because many countries will not permit entry by such vehicles, since their own domestic laws require a fully functioning system.

Digital Tachographs - company cards

Company cards are issued by DVLA in the company name. Company cards do not primarily hold data but act as an electronic key to protect and access data from the digital tachograph. A company can hold up to 2,232 cards, which will have identical card numbers but different issue numbers at the end of the card number that enable operators to tell them apart.

Company cards are needed to download data from the VU - they can be placed in either driver card slot. Company cards are not needed in order to access information from a driver card where it is being downloaded separately from the VU.

Operators may also use the company card to lock in (in other words, protect) their drivers' details. Once an operator has locked in, all subsequent data is protected and the full details may only be downloaded by inserting the same numbered company card. Locking in is especially recommended, since failure to do so could lead to an operator being unable to download its data if this has been protected by a previous user's card.

The cards can be used to lock out when they have finished with a vehicle - for example, if it has been sold or if operators have used a hired vehicle. This will signify the end of their interest in the vehicle and its operations, although failing to do this will not prevent another company protecting its own data by locking in, as locking in will automatically lock out the previous protection.

Operators who use hired vehicles may need to train their drivers, and equip them with the means, to download VU data from vehicles at the point of de-hire where this occurs away from base.

Company Cards

Operators can apply for company cards by calling the DVLA at 0300 790 6109 to obtain an application form (form ST2A). In Northern Ireland, application forms are available from DVA by calling the Driver and Vehicle Licensing Enquiry Section on 0845 402 4000, emailing dva@doeni.gov.uk or visiting https://www.nidirect.gov.uk/articles/digital-tachograph-company-cards

Enforcement and Penalties

Fixed Penalties and Deposits

Following the Road Safety Act 2006, fixed penalties and deposits were introduced during 2009. Infringing drivers with verifiable UK addresses are, in the most routine cases, dealt with by means of a fixed penalty, which can be considered by the driver for up to 28 days. Drivers without a verifiable address are asked to pay a deposit equal to the fixed penalty and further driving is prohibited pending receipt of that payment. DVLA can still take cases to court if it is deemed necessary.

Enforcement Powers and Sanctions

Powers

Legislation has provided authorised DVLA examiners with powers that include:

- The power to inspect vehicles.
- The power to prohibit and direct vehicles.
- Powers relating to the investigation of possible breaches of regulations.
- The power to instigate, conduct and appear in proceedings at a magistrates' court.

Sanctions

Action taken against drivers' hours and tachograph rules infringements is largely determined by legislation, and includes the following:

Verbal Warnings - Minor infringements that appear to enforcement staff to have been committed either accidentally or due to the inexperience of the driver/operator and are isolated instances may be dealt with by means of a verbal warning.
This will include a clarification of the infringement and an explanation of the consequences of continued infringement.

Offence Rectification Notice - These may be issued to operators for a number of infringements not related to safety, and give them 21 days to carry out a rectification of the shortcoming, otherwise prosecution will be considered.

<u>Prohibition - Many</u> drivers' hours and tachograph rules infringements attract a prohibition. A prohibition is not strictly a 'sanction', rather an enforcement tool to remove an immediate threat to road safety. When issued, driving of the vehicle is prohibited for either a specified or an unspecified period until the conditions stated on the prohibition note are satisfied. Where the prohibition is issued for an unspecified period, a note indicating the removal of the prohibition must be issued before use of the vehicle is permitted. In addition to attracting a prohibition, the matter will be considered for prosecution.

<u>Prosecution -</u> If it is considered to be in the public interest, more serious infringements are considered for prosecution, either against the driver, the operator or other undertakings, or against all of them.

<u>Referral to the Traffic Commissioner -</u> Where the driver is the holder of a vocational licence and/or the operator is the holder of an operator's licence, enforcement staff may report infringements by either the driver or the operator to the Traffic Commissioner instead of, or as well as, prosecution. This may occur when enforcement staff believes that the matter under consideration brings into doubt the repute of the driver/operator and subsequently call on the Traffic Commissioner to decide whether any administrative action should be taken against their licences.

Infringements of Domestic Drivers' Hours Rules

Where an infringement of the domestic drivers' hours rules occurs, the law protects from conviction in court those drivers who can prove that, because of unforeseen difficulties, they were unavoidably delayed in finishing a journey and breached the rules. It also protects employers if any driver was involved in other driving jobs that the employer could not have known about.

Infringements of the EU Drivers' Hours Rules

The law protects from conviction in court those drivers who can prove that, because of unforeseen difficulties, they were unavoidably delayed in finishing a journey and breached the rules. The EU rules make transport undertakings liable for any infringements committed by their drivers. However, transport undertakings will not be held responsible for these offences if they can show that at the time of the infringement the driver's work was being organised in full consideration of the rules, and in particular that:

- No payments were made that encouraged breaches.
- Work was properly organised.
- The driver was properly instructed.
- Regular checks were made.

Transport undertakings must also show that they have taken all reasonable steps to avoid the contravention. Employers also have a defence if they can prove that the driver was involved in other driving jobs that the employer could not reasonably have known about. Where it is found that an undertaking has failed in its obligations, prosecution may be considered against the undertaking for a driver's offence.

In the case of infringements concerning records, the law protects an employer from conviction if they can prove that they took all reasonable steps to make sure that the driver kept proper records. Under the EU rules, enforcement action can be taken against operators and drivers for offences detected in Great Britain but committed in another country, provided that the offender has not already been penalised.

To prevent further penalties being imposed for the same offence, enforcement agencies must provide the driver with evidence of the proceedings or penalties in writing. The driver is required to carry the documentation until such time as the infringement cannot lead to further action.

EU Rules: Co-liability

The EU rules also make undertakings such as consignors, freight forwarders, tour operators, principal contractors, sub-contractors and driver employment agencies responsible for ensuring that contractually agreed transport time schedules respect the rules on drivers' hours.

The undertaking must take all reasonable steps to comply with this requirement. If a contract with the customer includes a provision for transport time schedules to respect the EU rules, then the requirement would normally be satisfied. However, a driver employment agency is unlikely to absolve itself from the liability if it is found to have been offering back-to-back jobs to drivers where it will be impossible for the driver in question to take a daily or weekly rest in-between those jobs. We consider the term 'driver employment agency' to include employment businesses as defined in the Employment Agencies Act 1973, Section 13(3).

Penalties for Infringements of the Drivers' Hours Rules in Great Britain

Maximum Fines

As contained within Part VI of the Transport Act 1968 (as amended), the maximum fines that can be imposed by a court of law on conviction are as follows:

- Failure to observe driving time, break or rest period rules: fine of up to £2,500 (Level 4).
- Failure to make or keep records under the GB domestic rules: fine of up to £2,500 (Level 4).
- Failure to install a tachograph: fine of up to £5,000 (Level 5).
- Failure to use a tachograph: fine of up to £5,000 (Level 5).
- Failure to hand over records relating to recording equipment as requested by an enforcement officer: fine of up to £5,000.
- False entry or alteration of a record with the intent to deceive: on summary conviction fine of £5,000, on indictment two years' imprisonment.

- Altering or forging the seal on a tachograph with the intent to deceive: on summary conviction fine of £5,000, on indictment two years' imprisonment; and failure to take all reasonable steps to ensure contractually agreed transport time schedules respect the EU rules: fine of up to £2,500 (Level 4).

Legislation

For reference to the text of the relevant legislation the following links are useful.

United Kingdom
The National Archives, www.legislation.gov.uk The Stationery Office, www.tsoshop.co.uk

European Union
Eur-Lex - the portal for European Union law: http://eur-lex.europa.eu/en/index.htm

Relevant Legislation

EU Rules

EC Regulation 561/2006 on drivers' hours and tachographs
EC Regulation 3820/85 on drivers' hours
EC Regulation 3821/85 on tachographs
EC Regulation 3314/90 on tachographs
EC Regulation 3688/92 on tachographs
EC Regulation 2479/95 on tachographs
EC Regulation 2135/98 and EC Regulation 1360/2002 (as amended)
The Community Drivers' Hours and Recording Equipment Regulations 1986 (SI 1986/1457)
*The Drivers' Hours (Harmonisation with Community Rules) Regulations 1986 (SI 1986/1458)
The Passenger and Goods Vehicles (Recording Equipment) Regulations 1989 (SI 1989/2121)
The Passenger and Goods Vehicles (Recording Equipment) Regulations 1996 (SI 1996/941)
The Passenger and Goods Vehicles (Recording Equipment) Regulations 2005 (SI 2005/1904)
The Passenger and Goods Vehicles (Recording Equipment) (Tachograph Card) Regulations 2006 (SI
2006/1937)
The Passenger and Goods Vehicles (Recording Equipment) (Fitting Date) Regulations 2006 (SI 2006/1117)
The Passenger and Goods Vehicles (Recording Equipment) (Downloading and Retention of Data) Regulations
2008 (SI 2008/198)
The Passenger and Goods Vehicles (Community Recording Equipment Regulations) 2010 (SI 2010/892)

The Community Drivers' Hours and Recording Equipment Regulations 2007 (SI 2007/1819)

<u>AETR Rules</u>

European Agreement Concerning the Work of Crews on Vehicles Engaged in International Road Transport
(AETR) (Cm 7401) (as amended by Cmnd 9037)

<u>Domestic Rules</u>

Transport Act 1968 (Part VI as amended)
The Drivers' Hours (Goods Vehicles) (Modifications) Order 1970 (SI 1970/257)
The Drivers' Hours (Passenger and Goods Vehicles) (Modifications) Order 1971 (SI 1971/818)
The Drivers' Hours (Goods Vehicles) (Modifications) Order 1986 (SI 1986/1459)
The Drivers' Hours (Goods Vehicles) (Exemptions) Regulations 1986 (SI 1986/1492)
The Drivers' Hours (Goods Vehicles) (Keeping of Records) Regulations 1987 (SI 1987/1421)

The Passenger and Goods Vehicles (Recording Equipment) (Tachograph Card Fees) Regulations 2005 (SI 2005/1140)

Working Time Rules

The working time rules that apply to you depend on whether you drive a vehicle in scope of the EU or GB domestic drivers' hours rules.

<u>If you are driving under the EU drivers' hours rules</u>
If you operate a vehicle in scope of the EU drivers' hours rules, then you are subject to the Road Transport (Working Time) Regulations 2005 (as amended - 'the 2005 Regulations'), unless you are an occasional mobile worker.

The main provisions of the 2005 Regulations are as follows:

- Weekly working time must not exceed an average of 48 hours per week over the reference period. A maximum working time of 60 hours can be performed in any single week providing the average 48-hour limit is not exceeded.
- Night work: if night work is performed, working time must not exceed 10 hours in any 24-hour period. Night time is the period between 00.00 and 04.00 for goods vehicles and between 01.00 and 05.00 for passenger vehicles. The 10-hour limit may be exceeded if this is permitted under a collective or workforce agreement.

Breaks
- Mobile workers must not work more than 6 consecutive hours without taking a break.
- If your working hours total between 6 and 9 hours, working time should be interrupted by a break or breaks totalling at least 30 minutes.
- If your working hours total more than 9 hours, working time should be interrupted by a break or breaks totalling at least 45 minutes.
- Breaks should be of at least 15 minutes' duration.

Rest
- The regulations are the same as the EU or AETR drivers' hours rules.

Record Keeping
- Records need to be kept for two years after the period in question.

The reference period for calculating the 48-hour week is normally 17 weeks, but it can be extended to 26 weeks if this is permitted under a collective or workforce agreement. There is no 'opt-out' for individuals wishing to work longer than an average 48-hour week, but breaks and 'periods of availability' do not count as working time.

Generally speaking, a period of availability (POA) is waiting time, the duration of which is known about in advance. Examples of what might count as a POA are accompanying a vehicle on a ferry crossing or waiting while other workers load/unload your vehicle. For mobile workers driving in a team, a POA would also include time spent sitting next to the driver while the vehicle is in motion (unless the mobile worker is taking a break or performing other work i.e. navigation).

In addition, you are affected by two provisions under the Working Time Regulations 1998 (as amended - 'the 1998 Regulations').
These are: An entitlement to 4.8 weeks' paid annual leave (increased to 5.6 weeks from 1 April 2009); and health checks for night workers.

If you only occasionally drive vehicles subject to the EU drivers' hours rules, you may be able to take advantage of the exemption from the 2005 Regulations for occasional mobile workers.

Self-employed drivers are now in scope of the EU Working Time Directive 2002/15/EC which the Road Transport (Working Time) Regulations 2005 implement.

DVLA enforces the provisions of the 2005 Regulations and the requirement for health checks for night workers (under the 1998 Regulations). For further information about matters relating to annual leave, call the Advisory, Conciliation and Arbitration Service (ACAS) national helpline on 08457 47 47 47.

If you are driving under the GB domestic drivers' hours rules (or are an occasional mobile worker). If you drive a vehicle subject to the GB domestic drivers' hours rules or are an occasional mobile worker you are affected by four provisions under the 1998 Regulations. These are:

- Weekly working time, which must not exceed an average of 48 hours per week over the reference period (although individuals can 'opt out' of this requirement if they want to).
- An entitlement to 4.8 weeks' paid annual leave (increased to 5.6 weeks from 1 April 2009).
- Health checks for night workers.
- An entitlement to adequate rest.

Adequate rest means that workers should have regular rest periods. These rest periods should be sufficiently long and continuous to ensure that workers do not harm themselves, fellow workers or others and that they do not damage their health in the short or long term.

The reference period for calculating the 48-hour average week is normally a rolling 17-week period. However, this reference period can be extended up to 52 weeks, if this is permitted under a collective or workforce agreement.

The 1998 Regulations do not apply to self-employed drivers. Please note that this definition is different to the one used under the 2005 Regulations. DVLA enforces the working time limits and the requirement for health checks for night workers under the 1998 Regulations for drivers operating under the GB domestic drivers' hours rules (and occasional mobile workers). If you have any questions about matters relating to rest or annual leave, call the ACAS national helpline on 08457 47 47 47.

For further details on the 1998 Regulations, contact the Department for Business, Innovation and Skills on 020 7215 5000 or access their website at www.bis.gov.uk Further details on the 2005 Regulations can be found on the Department for Transport website at www.dft.gov.uk/pgr/freight/road/workingtime/

Definition of a Self-employed Driver under the 2005 Regulations

'Self-employed driver' means anyone whose main occupation is to transport passengers or goods by road for hire or reward within the meaning of Community legislation under cover of a Community licence or any other professional authorisation to carry out such transport, who is entitled to work for himself and who is not tied to an employer by an employment contract or by any other type of working hierarchical relationship, who is free to organise the relevant working activities, whose income depends directly on the profits made and who has the freedom, individually or through a co-operation between self-employed drivers, to have commercial relations with several customers (Regulation 2 of SI 2005/639).

<u>Definition of an Occasional Mobile Worker under the 2005 Regulations</u>

A mobile worker would be exempt from the 2005 Regulations if:

- He works 10 days or less within scope of the European drivers' hours rules in a reference period that is shorter than 26 weeks

  Or

- He works 15 days or less within scope of the European drivers' hours rules in a reference period that is 26 weeks or longer.

<u>Definition of Self-employed under the 1998 Regulations</u>

You are self-employed if you are running your own business and are free to work for different clients and customers.

Section C5 Driver Licensing

A license showing a full or provisional driving entitlement must be held by any person wishing to drive a motor vehicle on public roads in the UK or within Europe. Drivers of good vehicles require a current license showing an LGV (large goods vehicle) vocational driving entitlement (either full or provisional). Any person found to be driving without a license or without one covering the correct category of vehicle faces heavy penalties. The employer of any person required to drive for business purposes must ensure that his employees, irrespective of their function, status or seniority, are correctly licensed. The fact that a driver may be disqualified or has allowed his license to v lapse is no defence for the employer against prosecution for allowing an unlicensed person to drive.

Driver CPC – Continuous Training

New drivers who obtained an LGV vocational entitlement (C1, C1+E,C or C+E licence) after the 10th September 2009 will have to obtain the Driver CPC Initial Qualification in addition to their licence to drive professionally.

New drivers who undertake a National Vocational Training programme are still able to obtain a vocational licence but can defer the Initial Qualification by up to a maximum of one year whilst, still being able to drive professionally. An example of a National Vocational Training programme would be an Apprenticeship in Driving Goods Vehicles. Drivers intending to use this concession will have to register with the Driving Standards Agency. Existing LGV drivers who held a vocational licence prior to the 10th September 2009 are exempt from the Initial Qualification. This is known as "acquired rights". However, all professional drivers (new and existing drivers) must complete a total of 35 hours Periodic Training every 5 years following their "acquired rights" or Initial Qualification to keep their Driver CPC valid. Existing drivers must complete their Periodic Training by September 2013 (PCV) and September 2014 (LGV).

Note: Offences
Driving or causing or permitting another person to drive a vehicle without a current and valid driving license is an offence. For LGVs the license must also give entitlement to drive category C or C+E vehicles.

Checking Licenses

Haulage employers should check the licenses held by their drivers upon hiring the individual and at regular intervals of three to six months. Only an original license should be accepted for examination and all information should be checked against company records.

Invalidation of Insurance

Driving without a current and valid driving license covering the category of vehicle driven can invalidate insurance cover (which is itself an offence and is usually added to the charges) and could result in rejection of any accident or damage claim by the insurance company.

Legislative Changes Since 1990

Since 1 April 1991 the pink and green European "unified" driving license (Euro-license), which shows all entitlements to drive, has been issued from the DVLA, Swansea. Traffic Commissioners (TCs) no longer issue large goods and passenger vehicle licenses. The Euro-license carries the words "European Communities Model" and has "driving license" printed in the language of the country of issue, that of all EU nations, Greek and Gaelic on the front. British-issued Euro-licenses also show, where appropriate, provisional driving entitlements and any endorsements of penalty points or license disqualification made by the courts. This part of the document is called the "counterpart" and is green.

Existing UK License Holders

For a large proportion of British ordinary driving license holders who currently hold "licenses-for-life," the changes mentioned above will not be noticed unless or until they apply to change the details on their license. At that time they will be issued the Euro-license.

The licensing provisions described in this section are principally contained in the:

- Road Traffic Act 1988.
- Road Traffic (Driver Licensing and Information Systems) Act 1989.
- Road Traffic (New Drivers) Act 1995.
- Motor Vehicles (Driving licenses) Regulations 1996 as amended.
- Motor Vehicles (Driving licenses) (Large Goods and Passenger Carrying Vehicles) Regulations 1990 (which deal with entitlements to drive large goods vehicles over 7.5 tons gross weight and passenger carrying vehicles used for hire and reward operations) plus a number of subsequent amendments.

Changes to the license system made by this legislation involved significant alteration in vocational (HGV/PSV) licensing. The terminology changed so that heavy goods vehicles (HGV) and public service vehicles (PSV) are now called large goods vehicles (LGV) and passenger carrying vehicles (PCV). Additionally, goods vehicles are no longer classified by the number of axles.

Definitions

For driver licensing purposes:

- A "large goods vehicle" is "a motor vehicle (not being a medium-sized goods vehicle) which is constructed or adapted to carry or haul goods and the permissible maximum weight of which exceeds 7.5 tons".

- A medium-sized goods vehicle is defined as one having a permissible maximum weight exceeding 3.5 tons but not exceeding 7.5 tons.
- A large passenger-carrying vehicle has been constructed or adapted to carry more than 16 passengers.
- A small passenger-carrying vehicle carries passengers for hire or reward and has been constructed or adapted to carry more than 8 but not more than 16 passengers.

Unified Licenses

Previously large vehicle drivers required a separate license. Now their qualification to drive such vehicles is referred to as an "entitlement" within the unified license scheme and is shown in the single combined (unified) license document along with the ordinary driving entitlements.

The previous British system of vehicle groups has been changed to the EU system of vehicle "categories". Applicants for new or renewed HGV/PSV licenses are issued a "unified" license showing their goods (LGV) and/or passenger vehicle (PCV) driving entitlements under these new categories.

Photographs on Licenses

To help eliminate misuse and fraud, the new British-issued driving licenses carry the holder's photograph. (Licenses in Northern Ireland already carry a photograph.) Plastic photocard driving licenses for British holders were launched on 23 July 1998. These have now replaced the old paper licenses.

Standard license information includes the individual's name, address and date of birth, the vehicles they are entitled to drive, and the date of issue and expiration. All this is against a pink background in one of the EU's official languages (plus one other language if required). The nationality symbol for the country of issue is shown ("UK" will be used rather than "GB" as shown on vehicle nationality plates) on a blue background and surrounded by the EU's 12 gold stars, together with the holder's photograph.

The new-type license will be issued to new license applicants and to existing license holders who apply for replacements or who wish to change the details on their license – existing licenses will not be recalled for change.

The Issuing Authority

The Driver and Vehicle Licensing Agency (the DETR's Executive Agency – DVLA), Swansea issues vocational driving entitlements. The TCs still retain a disciplinary role in regard to such entitlements.

Age Limits for Drivers

Certain minimum ages are specified by law for drivers of various categories of motor vehicle:

- Invalid carriage or moped* 16 years
- Motor cycle other than a 17 years
  moped* (over 50cc engine
  capacity)
- Small passenger vehicle or 17 years
  small goods vehicle (not
  exceeding 3.5 tons gross
  weight and not adapted to
  carry more than nine people
  including the driver)
- Agricultural tractor 17 years
- Medium-size goods vehicle 18 years
  (exceeding 3.5 tons but not
  exceeding 7.5 tons gross
  weight)
- Other goods vehicles (over 21 years
  7.5 tons gross weight) and
  passenger vehicles with
  more than nine passenger
  seats

*The definition of moped is:
in the case of a vehicle first registered before 1 August 1977, a motorcycle with an engine cylinder capacity not exceeding 50cc equipped with pedals by means of which it can be propelled. In the case of a vehicle first registered on or after 1 August 1977, a motorcycle which does not exceed the following limits: kerbside weight 250kg; cylinder capacity (if applicable) 50cc.

If a goods vehicle and trailer combination exceeds 3.5 tons permissible maximum weight the driver must be 18 years of age; if such a combination exceeds 7.5 tons the driver must be 21 years of age (and will also need to hold an LGV driving entitlement).

Members of the armed forces are exempt from the 21 years age limit for driving heavy goods vehicles when such driving is in aid of the civil community. The limit is then reduced to 17 years. Similarly, exemption from the 21-year minimum age limit applies to learner LGV drivers of vehicles over 7.5 tons gross weight if they are undergoing registered training by their employer or by a registered training establishment. In this case the minimum age is 18 years.

Vehicle Categories/Groups for Driver Licensing

For driver licensing purposes, vehicles are defined according to specified categories shown on licenses by capital letters.

Motorcycles

A
    Motorcycles (with or without sidecar) and scooters but excluding vehicles in category K.
Additional categories covered: B1, K, P

A1
    Light motorcycles not over 125cc and 11kW (14.6bhp).
Additional category covered: P

Cars and Light Vans

B
    Motor vehicles up to 3.5 tons mass and with not more than eight seats (excluding the driver's seat) including drawing a trailer of up to 750kg mass. Including combinations of category B vehicles and a trailer where the combined weight does not exceed 3.5 tons and the weight of the trailer does not exceed the unladen weight of the towing vehicle.
Additional categories covered: F, K, P

B1
    Motor tricycles and three/four-wheeled cars and vans up to 550kg unladen with a design speed not exceeding 50kph and, if fitted with an internal combustion engine, a cubic capacity not exceeding 50cc.
Additional categories covered: K, P

B+E
    Motor vehicles in category B drawing a trailer over 750kg where the combination does not come within category B.

Medium Goods Vehicles

C1
    Medium goods vehicles between 3.5 tons and 7.5 tons (including drawing trailer of up to 750kg – maximum weight of the combination must not exceed 8.25 tons).

C 1 +E
    Medium goods vehicles between 3.5 tons and 7.5 tons and drawing a trailer over 750kg but which does not exceed the unladen weight of the towing vehicle – maximum weight of the combination must not exceed 12 tons.
Additional category covered: B+E

Large Goods Vehicles

C
    Large goods vehicles over 3.5 tons (but excluding vehicles in categories D, F, G and H) including those drawing a trailer of up to 750kg.

C+E
    Large goods vehicles in category C drawing a trailer exceeding 750kg. Some C+E licenses, where the holder was previously qualified to drive vehicles in old HGV class 2 or 3, show a restriction limiting driving to drawbar combinations only.
Additional category covered: B + E

Minibuses

D1   Passenger vehicles with between 9 and 16 seats including drawing trailer up to 750kg.

D1+E   Motor vehicles in category D1 drawing a trailer over 750kg – the weight of the trailer must not exceed the unladen weight of the towing vehicle and the maximum weight of the combination must not exceed 12 tons. Additional category covered: B+E

Passenger Vehicles

D   Passenger vehicles with more than eight seats including drawing a trailer up to 750kg.

D+E   Passenger vehicles in category D drawing a trailer over 750kg. Additional category covered: B+E

Other Vehicles

F   Agricultural or forestry tractors but excluding any vehicle in category H.

G   Road rollers.

H   Track-laying vehicles steered by their tracks.

K   Mowing machine or pedestrian-controlled vehicle (with up to three wheels and not over 410kg).

L   Electrically propelled vehicles.

P   Mopeds.

Vehicle/trailer weights, unless otherwise specified, are to be taken as the maximum authorised mass (mam) which is the permissible maximum weight (pmw) for the vehicle/trailer — commonly referred to as the "gross weight".
https://www.gov.uk/driving-licence-categories

Restricted Categories for Post-1997 Drivers

Since 1 January 1997, drivers who pass the car and light vehicle test (vehicles up to 3.5 tons pmw) may not drive heavier vehicles without securing additional driving categories on their license. This restriction applies only to those who pass the test after the specified date and does not apply retrospectively.

Drivers who pass their car test (category B) may not drive minibuses (D1), medium-sized goods vehicles (C1), or tow large (over 750kg) trailers (B+E, C +E and D1+E). Without testing for those categories.

Any driver wishing to drive a vehicle towing a heavy trailer (gross weight over 750kg) must first pass a test in the associated rigid vehicle. Learner drivers in categories B, C1, C, D1 and D cannot drive a vehicle towing a trailer of any size.

Towed and Pushed vehicles

A person who steers a vehicle being towed (whether it has broken down or even has vital parts missing) is "driving" for licensing purposes and therefore needs to hold current and valid driving entitlement covering that category of vehicle. Conversely, a person pushing a vehicle from the outside (with both feet on the ground) is not "driving" or "using" the vehicle.

Learner Drivers

Learner drivers must hold a provisional driving entitlement shown on the green "counterpart" of the license.

Full category C LGV entitlement holders can use this entitlement in place of a provisional entitlement for learning to drive vehicles in category C+E (drawbar combinations and articulated vehicles). Full entitlements in categories B and C1 cannot be used as a provisional entitlement for learning to drive vehicles in categories C or C +E. A proper provisional entitlement for these classes is required.

When driving on public roads, learner drivers must be accompanied by the holder of a full entitlement covering the category of vehicle driven and must not drive a vehicle drawing a trailer, except in the case of articulated vehicles or agricultural trailers.

An approved "L" plate must be displayed on the front and rear of a vehicle driven by a learner driver. Learners driving in Wales may alternatively display a "D" plate.

Learner drivers (of category B and C1 vehicles) are not allowed to drive on motorways. However, learner LGV drivers seeking a license for category C and C+E vehicles and who hold full entitlements in license categories B and C1, may drive such vehicles on motorways while under instruction.

Compulsory Re-tests for Offending New Drivers

Newly qualified drivers with six or more penalty points within two years of passing the test revert to learner status (with the display of "L" plates and the need to be accompanied by a qualified driver) and have to re-pass both the theory and the practical driving test.

Supervision of "L" Drivers

Qualified drivers supervising learner drivers in cars, and in light, medium and large goods vehicles, must be at least 21 years old with full driving entitlement for a continuous period of at least three years (excluding any periods of disqualification). Those accompanying learner LGV drivers must have held a relevant entitlement continuously since 6 April 1998.

Exemptions from Vocational Licensing

Exemptions from the LGV driving entitlement (categories C or C+E) apply when driving certain vehicles as follows (in most cases such vehicles may be driven by the holder of a category B license):

- Steam-propelled vehicles.
- Road construction vehicles used or kept on the road solely for the conveyance of built-in construction machinery.
- Engineering plant, but not mobile cranes.
- Works trucks.
- Industrial tractors.
- Agricultural motor vehicles which are not agricultural or forestry tractors.
- Digging machines.
- Vehicles used on public roads only when passing between land occupied by the vehicles' registered keeper and which do not exceed an aggregate of 9.7 kilometres in a calendar week.
- Vehicles, other than agricultural vehicles, used only for the purposes of agriculture, horticulture or forestry, between areas of land occupied by the same person and which do not travel more than 1.5 kilometres on public roads.
- Vehicles used for no purpose other than the haulage of lifeboats and the conveyance of the necessary gear of the lifeboats.
- Vehicles manufactured before 1 January 1960 used unladen and not drawing a laden trailer.
- Articulated goods vehicles with an unladen weight not exceeding 3.05 tons.
- Vehicles in the service of a visiting military force or headquarters as defined in the Visiting Forces and International Headquarters (Application of Law) Order 1965.
- Any vehicle driven by a police constable for the purpose of removing it to avoid obstruction or danger to other road users or members of the public, for the purpose of safeguarding life or property, including the vehicle and its load, or for other similar purposes.
- Breakdown vehicles which weigh less than 3.05 tons unladen, provided they are fitted with apparatus for raising a disabled vehicle partly from the ground and for drawing a vehicle when so raised, are used solely for the purpose of dealing with disabled vehicles, and carry no load other than a disabled vehicle and articles used in connection with dealing with disabled vehicles.
- A passenger-carrying vehicle recovery vehicle other than an articulated vehicle with an unladen weight of not more than 10.2 tons which belongs to the holder of a PSV "0" license when such a vehicle is going to or returning

84

from a place where it is to give assistance to a damaged or disabled passenger-carrying vehicle or giving assistance to or moving a disabled passenger-carrying vehicle or moving a damaged vehicle.

- A mobile project vehicle, defined as a vehicle exceeding 3.5 tons pmw constructed or adapted to carry not more than eight persons in addition to the driver and which carries mainly goods or burden comprising play or educational equipment for children or articles used for display or exhibition purposes.

Application for Licenses and Vocational Entitlements

Applications for all driving licenses have to be made to Swansea on Form D1 (obtainable from main post offices, direct from Swansea or from Local Vehicle Registration Offices).

Questions concern personal details of the applicant, the type of license required, any previous license held and whether the applicant is currently disqualified. LGV/PCV entitlement applicants are asked about any convictions recorded against them.

Health Declaration

Applicants are asked to declare information whether they have:

- had an epileptic event
- sudden attacks of disabling giddiness, fainting or blackouts
- severe mental handicap
- had a pacemaker, defibrillator or anti-ventricular tachycardia device fitted
- diabetes controlled by insulin
- angina (heart pain) while driving
- a major or minor stroke
- Parkinson's disease
- any other chronic neurological condition
- a serious problem with memory
- serious episodes of confusion
- any type of brain surgery, brain tumour or severe head injury involving hospital in-patient treatment
- any severe psychiatric illness or mental disorder
- continuing or permanent difficulty in the use of arms or legs which affects the ability to control a vehicle safely
- been dependent on or misused alcohol, illicit drugs or chemical substances in the previous three years (excluding drink/driving offences)
- any visual disability which affects both eyes (short/long sight and colour blindness do not have to be declared)
- sight in only one eye
- any visual problems affecting either eye
- angina
- any heart condition or had a heart operation

Where a license applicant has previously declared a medical condition they are required to state what the condition is, whether it has worsened, and whether any special controls have been fitted to the applicant's vehicle since the last license was issued.

Considerations for Vocational Entitlements

Applicants for vocational driving entitlements must meet specified conditions:

- They must be fit and proper persons.
- They must meet laid-down eyesight requirements.
- They must satisfy a medical examination and specifically must not have had an epileptic attack in the previous 10 years or suffer from insulin-dependent diabetes.

The decision to grant or deny an LGV driving entitlement rests entirely with the DVLA. Factors considered include any driving convictions in the previous four years for motoring offences, drivers' hours and record offences, and offences relating to the roadworthiness or loading of vehicles, and any offence connected with driving under the influence of drink or drugs 11 years prior. The applicant has to declare such convictions on the application form (D1) but the DVLA has means of checking to ensure applicants have been forthcoming.

Section D1 VAT, Business Taxation and Cabotage

The VAT, a tax on consumer spending, is collected on business transactions and imports by VAT registered persons. In the UK, the tax is paid to HM Revenue and Customs (HMRC).
Most such transactions involve supplies of goods or services.

VAT is payable if they are:
- supplies made in the UK, the Isle of Man or the EU
- by a taxable person
- in the course or furtherance of business
- and are not specifically exempted or zero-rated

Taxable Persons

By definition, a taxable person is an individual, firm or company that is or is required to be registered for VAT. Currently, a person who made taxable supplies of more than the current threshold of annual taxable turnover in the previous 12 months must be registered.

Out-of-Scope Supplies

Supplies outside the scope of VAT include:
- those not made by a taxable person
- those made outside the UK and the Isle of Man (unless they are of certain international services)
- those not made in the furtherance of business

Current VAT Rates

There are currently three VAT rates in the UK:
- a standard rate, currently 20%
- a reduced rate of 5% on domestic fuel and power
- a zero rate on which no VAT is payable although items to which they apply are treated as taxable supplies in all other respects

VAT Exempt Supplies

Some supplies are exempt from VAT:
- building and civil engineering services
- exports
- land and buildings
- education and training
- financial services

- certain insurance services

No tax is payable on these supplies, and the person making the supply cannot normally recover VAT paid on their own purchases.

Zero-Rated Supplies

Certain supplies are zero rated for VAT purposes. Examples include:
- food and drink for human consumption
- some health care services such as drugs and medicines
- some insurance services
- certain transport and cargo-handling services
- sewerage and water supply
- building construction
- imports and exports
- children's clothing and footwear
- gold and bank notes
- charitable and cultural services

VAT Categories

VAT is divided into output and input tax.

Output tax is due on taxable supplies made by a registered person at the value of the sales/supply invoice multiplied by the tax rate (currently 20% in the UK, except as stated above).

Input tax is charged on business purchases and expenses with certain exceptions including car purchases, business entertainment and certain building articles.
Input tax is due on the following:
- goods and services supplied in the UK
- goods imported from outside the EC
- goods acquired from another taxable person within the EU
- goods removed from a warehouse
- certain services received from abroad including banking, financial, consultancy, legal, data and information, engineering, advertising

A VAT-registered person may reclaim input tax by deduction from the amount of payable output tax assuming the output tax is greater than the input tax.

VAT on Cabotage Operations

Internal transport operations under cabotage authorisation require operators to comply with national VAT regulations. For this purpose, operators may need to register in the member states in which they are operating or appoint a suitable VAT agent or fiscal representative to handle these matters on their behalf.

International Freight, calculation for VAT purposes

The nature of your supply can be:

- domestic freight transport – the transport of goods that takes place wholly within one country, the UK
- intra-EU freight transport – the movement of goods from one member state to another
- intra-EU freight transport to the Azores and Madeira
- international freight transport – the transport of goods between the EU and non-EU countries, or wholly outside the EU
- ancillary transport services – includes certain services, handling and storage services in connection with ship and aircraft cargo
- transport and related services connected to imports
- transport and related services connected to exports
- intermediary services – making arrangement for the supply of freight transport or related ancillary services
- freight forwarding services

Freight transport services which occur wholly outside the UK?

Other member states – you may have to register for VAT in those member states and account for VAT at the relevant rate accordingly.

Intra State Transport

If you transport goods...	the place of supply is...	and...
from France to the UK, for a customer who is not registered for VAT	France – the place of Departure	you as the supplier are Responsible for accounting for VAT in that member State.
From the UK to France for a customer who is registered for VAT in the UK	the UK - the place of departure of the goods.	your supply is standard-rated and you, as the supplier, account for the tax.
From the UK to France for a customer who is registered for VAT in	France because your customer is registered for VAT, in a different member	your customer must account for VAT in France under the "reverse charge"

Vehicle Excise Duty

The tax disc, first introduced in 1921, has ceased to exist in paper form since October 2016, with a new electronic system put in its place. This means motorists are no longer required to display a tax disc on their windscreen.

The Driver and Vehicle Licensing Agency (DVLA) and the police now rely on DVLA's electronic vehicle register and tools like Automatic Number Plate Recognition (ANPR) cameras to support VED compliance.

Using or parking an unlicensed vehicle or trade licensed only vehicle on a road for even a short period is an offence.

Exceptions

Certain official vehicles such as those belonging to fire brigades and ambulance services, those operated by the Crown, snow clearance and other public utility vehicles have exemption. Those vehicles used solely for forestry, agriculture or horticultural purposes travelling on public roads for no more than 1.5 kilometres between the land occupied by the same firm or the person who is the registered owner of the vehicle are also exempt.

Concessionary Tax Classes

Vehicles of more than 3.5 tons including mobile cranes, digging machines, works trucks, road rollers and showmen's goods and haulage vehicles belong to a "special concessionary" class that also includes agricultural machines, mowing machines, gritters and snowploughs, electric vehicles and steam-driven vehicles. As such, special and concessionary VED rates apply.

Documents for Licensing

The following documents are required to license a vehicle:

- The form V5 registration document or the logbook in Northern Ireland.
- A current certificate of insurance or a temporary cover note, but not the policy.
- Where applicable, a current MOT or goods vehicle test certificate.
- A completed application form, VE55 for a first registration or form V10 for renewal.
- The type approval certificate for a first registration only.
- A reduced pollution certificate where relevant.
- The appropriate amount of duty.

A registration number will be given upon a vehicle's initial registration which must be made into plates displayed on the front and rear of the vehicle. The vehicle must be taxed at the appropriate VED rate, it is an offence to operate an untaxed vehicle.

Rates of Excise Duty

The Department for Transport consulted on the introduction of the levy for HGVs of 12 tonnes and over, and the principle of an accompanying reduction in VED rates and cessation of RPC VED discounts in October 2012.
The measure was announced at Budget 2013. The HGV Road User Levy Act 2013 implements the Levy from 1 April 2014, introducing a fairer arrangement for UK hauliers by ensuring that foreign hauliers pay to use roads in the UK.

Heavy good vehicle levy and vehicle excise duty rates introduced from April 2014 can be found from the following link: http://tinyurl.com/zgucnmm

The reductions in HGV VED rates will apply to vehicle licences taken out on and after 1 April 2014.
RPC VED discounts conforming with the Euro I, II and III pollutant emissions standards will cease with effect from 1 April 2016, except for HGVs in the Levy whose discounts will cease with effect from 1 April 2014.
RPC VED discounts conforming with the Euro IV, V and VI standards will cease with effect from 1 January 2017, except for HGVs in the Levy whose discounts will cease with effect from 1 April 2014 – grants will apply to these vehicles until 31 December 2016.

Parts III, VI and VIII of Schedule 1 to the Vehicle Excise and Registration Act 1994 (VERA) set rates of VED for HGVs, and discounted rates of VED for reduced pollutant emissions for buses and HGVs.

Legislation was introduced in Finance Bill 2014 amending Schedule 1 to VERA to reduce VED rates for HGVs.

Dual-Purpose Vehicles

A dual-purpose vehicle is one meant for or converted for the purpose of carrying both passengers and goods and has an unladen weight of no more than 2,049kg. If such a vehicle is used to carry goods connected with trade or business and is more than 3,500kg gross weight, the goods vehicle duty must be paid. Other characteristics of such vehicles include:

- four-wheel drive
- a permanently fitted roof
- a permanently fitted single row of transverse seats behind the driver cushioned or sprung with upholstered backrests
- A window on either side to the rear of the driver and one at the rear

The majority of vehicles generally described as estate cars, shooting brakes, station wagons, hardtop Land Rovers and "hatchback" saloons with fold-down seats are classed as dual-purpose vehicles. If they are used in connection with a trade or business, and are more than 3,500kg gross weight, the appropriate goods vehicle rate of duty must be paid.

Reduced Pollution Vehicles

Certain buses, haulage vehicles and heavy goods vehicles built or adapted to produce fewer pollution exhaust emissions under the provisions of the Vehicle Excise Duty (Reduced Pollution) Regulations 1998 can qualify for reduced vehicle excise duty of as much as £1,000 per year for the heaviest vehicles.
The reduced pollution requirement may be satisfied by:

- a new vehicle meeting the required standard
- the fitting of a new engine to a vehicle
- the fitting of a type-approved device (catalyser) for which the manufacturer issues a Certificate of Conformity

The reduced pollution requirements are satisfied if the rate and content of a vehicle's particulate emissions do not exceed the number of grams per kilowatt-hour specified below:

Instrument setting standard to which vehicle was first used	Rate and content of particulate emissions after adaptation (grams per kilowatt-hour)
Directive 88/77/EEC	0.16
Directive 91/542/EEC (limits A)	0.16
Directive 91/542/EEC (limits B)	0.08
European Commission Proposal (Com [97] 627) for a European and Council Directive amending Council Directive 88/77/EEC	0.04

Refunds of Duty

When a license is surrendered, paid duty may be reclaimed for each complete month remaining. Applications for refunds must be made by the last day of the preceding month and the license disc must be surrendered.

Alteration of Vehicles

The Driver and Vehicle Licensing Agency (DVLA) at Swansea must be notified of vehicle modifications.

Fuel Duty

While diesel fuel for road-going vehicles is subject to excise duty, diesel used on farms and sites is not. Duty-free diesel is dyed red and for legal purposes is referred to as "rebated heavy oil". In popular use it is called "red diesel" or "gas oil". (A green version is also available.) The illegal use of red diesel in road-going vehicles is easy to detect and the HMRC conducts roadside checks to make sure the correct duty-paid fuel is used.

UK Trade Tariff: excise duties as of November 2020 - http://alturl.com/hbbk4

Trade Licenses

Trade licenses or trade plates may be obtained and used by manufacturers, repairers or dealers in motor vehicles including motor vehicle delivery firms and vehicle testers. The plates may be used on vehicles that are temporarily in their possession as motor traders, and on vehicles submitted for testing. Trade plates must not be used on recovery vehicles.

Applications for Trade Licenses

Application for a trade license on Form VTL301 must be made to local Vehicle Registration Offices (VROs). The license is valid for one year (or for a lesser period, i.e. 6 to 11 months). If application for a trade license is refused, an appeal can be made to the Secretary of State for Transport.

Trade Plates

Two plates are issued with red letters on a white background; one with the triangular license affixed. This plate must be attached to the front of the vehicle, and the other to the rear.

Use of Trade Plates

Trade plates may only be used by bona fide motor traders and testers in the following instances:

- for test or trial during construction or repair of a vehicle or its accessories or equipment and after completing construction or repair
- when travelling to or from a weighbridge to check the unladen weight or when travelling to a place for registration or inspection by the council
- for demonstration to a prospective customer and when travelling to or from a place of demonstration
- for test or trial of the vehicle for the benefit of a person interested in promoting publicity for the vehicle
- for delivering the vehicle to a purchaser
- for demonstrating the accessories or equipment to a prospective purchaser

- for delivering a vehicle to, or collecting it from, other premises belonging to the trade license holder or another trader's premises
- for going to or coming from a workshop for the fitting of a body, equipment or accessories
- for delivering the vehicle from the premises of a manufacturer or repairer to a place where it is to be transported by train, ship or aircraft or for returning it from a place to which it has been transported by these means
- when travelling to or returning garage, auction where vehicles are stored/sold
- when travelling to a place to be dismantled or broken up

Goods may only be carried on a vehicle operating under a trade license when a:
- load is necessary to demonstrate or test the vehicle, its accessories or its equipment – the load must be returned to the place of loading after the demonstration or test
- load consists of parts or equipment to be fitted to the vehicle being taken to the place where they are to be fitted
- load is built in or permanently attached to the vehicle
- trailer is being carried for delivery or being taken to a place for work to be carried out on it

The only passengers permitted to travel on a trade-licensed vehicle include:

- The driver of the vehicle, who may be the trade license holder or an employee. Other persons may drive the vehicle with the permission of the license holder but they must be accompanied by the license holder or his employee. This latter proviso does not apply if the vehicle is constructed to carry only one person.
- Persons required to be on the vehicle by law, such as a statutory attendant.
- Any person carried for the purpose of inspecting the vehicle or trailer.
- Any person in a disabled vehicle being towed.
- A prospective purchaser or his servant or agent.
- A person interested in promoting publicity for the vehicle.

Trade-licensed vehicles must not be left parked on public roads.

Recovery Vehicles

A separate VED class applies to recovery vehicles which may not be used for recovery operations on trade plates. Any vehicle used for recovery work that does not conform to the definition given below must be licensed at the normal goods vehicle rate according to its class and gross weight. Goods must not be carried on a recovery vehicle when in use, except essential tools or spares.

Definition of a Recovery Vehicle

In regard to this taxation class, a recovery vehicle is one "constructed or permanently adapted primarily for the purpose of lifting, towing and transporting a disabled vehicle or for any one or more of those purposes". A vehicle will no longer qualify under this definition as per the Vehicle Excise and Registration Act 1994 Schedule 1 Part V if at any time it is used for a purpose other than:

- The recovery of a disabled vehicle.
- The removal of a disabled vehicle from the place where it became disabled to a repair premises or scrap facility.
- The removal of a disabled vehicle from one repair or scrap facility to another.
- Carrying any load other than fuel and any liquids required for its propulsion, tools and other articles required for operation or those used in connection with apparatus designed to lift, tow or transport a disabled vehicle.

Plating and Testing of Recovery Vehicles

Recovery vehicles licensed under the recovery vehicle taxation class are not exempt from goods vehicle plating and testing unless they satisfy the definition of a "breakdown vehicle". This is "a vehicle on which is mounted permanently fitted apparatus for raising a disabled vehicle from the ground and for drawing that vehicle when so raised, and which is not equipped to carry any load other than articles required for that operation, the apparatus for repairing disabled vehicles".

Operation of Recovery Vehicles

Recovery vehicle drivers must hold category C driving entitlements and must comply with British domestic driving hours rules. Their vehicles are exempt from "0" licensing, the EU drivers' hours rules and the tachograph requirements.

Road and Bridge Tolls

In both the UK and Europe certain roads, bridges and tunnels are only accessible via a toll levied according to user type including pedestrians, cyclists and motorcyclists, motor cars and light goods vehicles, heavy goods vehicles and passenger vehicles. For the most part tolls defray construction and maintenance costs, although there is a trend towards private or combined construction and maintenance financing so that the toll provides investment returns.

Currently there is a single major road, the M6 Toll and a small number of bridges and tunnels where tolls are collected. In addition, there are also two UK road pricing schemes, the London congestion charge and the Durham congestion charge
The tolled bridges and tunnels are as follows:

- Dartford crossing- Dart Charge or Pre-Pay (i.e. Dartford Tunnel northbound and the Queen Elizabeth II Bridge southbound over the River Thames on the M25 motorway).
- Erskine Bridge over the River Clyde west of Glasgow on the A82.
- Forth Road Bridge over the Firth of Forth on the A90 between Fife and Lothian in Scotland to the west of Edinburgh (connecting with the M8, M9 and M90 motorways).
- Humber Bridge over the River Humber on the A15.
- Mersey Tunnel between Liverpool and Birkenhead.

- Severn Bridge – two crossings of the River Severn on the M4 and M48 motorways between England (Avon) and Wales (Gwent).
- Skye Bridge over the Kyle of Lochalsh on the A87 between the Scottish mainland and the Isle of Skye.
- Tamar Bridge over the River Tamar on the A38 between Plymouth and Saltash (toll payable eastbound only – i.e. into Cornwall).
- Tyne Tunnel under the River Tyne on the A1 to the east of Newcastle upon Tyne.

Kent Access Permit (KAP)

From 1 January 2021, HGV drivers must have a KAP to travel through Kent to the Port of Dover or the Eurotunnel and on to the EU. The permit helps manage traffic by confirming drivers have the right documents for EU import controls.

You must have tested negative for coronavirus (COVID-19) up to 72 hours before you cross the border into France. Check the latest advice for HGV drivers using the Port of Dover or Eurotunnel at: http://alturl.com/n9yja

You do not need a Kent Access Permit (KAP) if the HGV is under 7.5 tonnes or leaving from a different port. Further details here: http://alturl.com/wyx6a

Who needs a Permit

You need a KAP if your HGV is both:

- leaving Great Britain from the Port of Dover or the Eurotunnel
- over 7.5 tonnes

You will need a permit even if the HGV is not carrying goods or if it is only carrying post.
Each permit is valid for 24 hours. You need a new permit each time the HGV leaves Great Britain.
The driver could be stopped and fined up to £300 for entering Kent without having a Kent Access Permit, or for making false declarations when travelling to the Port of Dover or Eurotunnel

Who Does Not Need a Permit

You do not need a KAP if:

- the HGV weighs 7.5 tonnes or less
- you are not leaving Great Britain from the Port of Dover or the Eurotunnel
- you are not travelling internationally, for example you're just driving an HGV through or in Kent

- you are dropping off a trailer that will be taken across the border

You should still check that your vehicle is ready to cross the border even if you do not need a KAP.

What This Service Does Not Do

This service does not provide any customs or goods-specific paperwork apart from a KAP. Before crossing the border, you may also need to:

- make an entry summary declaration (or safety and security declaration) into the Import Control System (ICS) of the EU country you are crossing into
- get a local reference number from the shipper (or 'consignor') supplying the goods, if you're travelling to a customs office of departure before taking the goods to the EU

What You'll Need

You will need:

- the expected date and time of arrival of the HGV in Kent
- the registration number (front number plate) of the HGV

To get a KAP, you will have to confirm which documents you have already. Before you start, check whether you have:

- an EU import document with a barcode (for example from an import declaration or Transit Accompanying Document)
- Admission Temporaire/Temporary Admission (ATA) or Transport Internationaux Routiers (TIR) carnets

Use the service even if you do not need these documents, or you're planning to collect them while travelling to the border. The service will tell you if you do not have a document you need.

If you're carrying specialty, restricted, or controlled goods

You'll need to confirm you have additional documents if you're transporting:

- live animals
- animal products
- fish products
- plants
- other specialty, restricted, or controlled goods

Find out more about the paperwork needed for specialty, restricted or controlled goods. At: https://www.gov.uk/export-goods

Apply for a Kent Access Permit online

To get your permit, you will have to:

- confirm you have the correct customs and export documents before the HGV travels
- complete a self-assessment to confirm you meet EU import requirements

International Vehicle Taxes and Tolls

Goods Vehicle Taxation

Normally, the vehicle taxation system of the country through which goods vehicles pass apply to those vehicles. Britain has, however, accepted the terms of the International Convention on the Taxation of Road Vehicles and as a result of bilateral agreements, goods vehicles are exempt from paying further taxation provided they are correctly taxed in the country of registration. All vehicles must be correctly taxed to meet this requirement.

Countries where further lorry tax (i.e. excise duty) has to be paid are:

- Austria (tax payable on transit of goods vehicles of more than 12 tons)
- Hungary (where single-axle weight exceeds 10 tons or 16 tons on two axles)
- Switzerland (road tax payable based on gross weights and time in country)
- Turkey (transit tax payable)
- Former Yugoslavia (road tax payable for vehicles in transit)

Fuel Duties

Generally, road fuel taxes or duties are paid upon purchase in the country or origin. No additional tax or duty is attached to fuel carried into other county in a vehicle's fuel tank. The general allowance within the EU is 200 litres. Some countries do, however, charge a tax or duty above certain limits for long-range international vehicles with high-capacity fuel tanks.

Motorway Taxes (Vignettes)

Goods vehicles of more than 12 tons gross weight are subject to a motorway tax when travelling to or through Germany, the Benelux countries (Belgium, Luxembourg and Holland), and Denmark. A vehicle certificate (vignette) is issued upon payment of the sliding-scale tax depending on the number of axles and the period of time for which the certificate is required.

A road user charge is imposed in Poland. Motorway vignettes must be purchased in Slovakia for the use of motorways. Similarly, Slovenia charges for the use of certain routes.

Britain's first toll motorway – the 27-mile long, three-lane M6 Toll Road – formerly known as the Birmingham Northern Relief Road (BNRR), opened in December 2003. It was designed to ease traffic and congestion through the West Midlands.

Brexit - New Rules

Brexit: check how the new rules affect you - https://www.gov.uk/transition

COVID-19 test requirements in different countries update, 18 January 2021

Several countries have introduced COVID-19 testing requirements for hauliers. The rules are different in each country. Check the rules before you travel and take the necessary action.   http://alturl.com/n9yja

https://www.gov.uk/export-goods

Corporate and Income Tax

This section is concerned with income tax paid by individuals who may be employees or self-employed persons and corporate taxation levied on the profits of limited liability companies.

Income Tax

Employed individuals and self-employed sole traders and partners in a partnership business are liable to pay income tax based on their earnings, but subject to certain minimum earnings concessions and various personal allowances.
Tax Schedules

Income is assessed according to source "schedule" allocated by HMRC. Broadly, there are four schedules:

- Schedule A, which applies to income from land and property (applicable to individuals and companies).
- Schedule D, which applies to income/profits from trade or a profession, interest on savings/investments, rents and commissions (applies to both individuals and companies).
- Schedule E, which applies to wages and salaries from employment.
- Schedule F, which applies to dividends and the like paid to shareholders by a UK company.

Payment of Income Tax

Payment methods vary by the manner in which the tax was deducted, namely Pay As You Earn (PAYE), and payment of tax by self-employed persons on a twice-yearly basis calculated on their annual income.

PAYE

A relevant amount of income tax determined by the tax code and the National Insurance contribution is deducted from the gross earnings of employees working for a wage or salary. The employer pays these monies to HMRC monthly. Personal allowances to offset the tax due include personal allowance for all individuals, which may vary according to circumstances (for example single-child-one-parent families, blind person allowance, widow's bereavement allowance, medical insurance relief, life assurance relief).

Tax for the Self-Employed

Self-employed people are taxed under a "self-assessment" system on an earnings basis. They must maintain income and expenditure records and make an annual HMRC return reflecting this information. Tax due is payable in January and July.

After the first year in business two payments on account towards the annual tax bill are due on 31 January and 31 July each year with a final payment of any balance due payable the following 31 January. In effect then, in the second year of business the self-employed individual pays one and half years' worth of tax.

Trading Accounts for the Self-Employed

The self-employed are required to compile a complete and accurate account of income received in a tax year and are responsible for the accuracy of the information, even if it is assembled by an accountant.
The report must include two parts: a profit and loss or trading account showing income and expenditure, and a balance sheet showing the assets and liabilities of the business.

For very small businesses, those below £15,000 annual income before deduction of expenses, a simple three-line return will suffice (i.e. turnover, less expenses, equals net profit).

Expenses and Allowances for the Self-Employed

The only business expenses that may be used to offset income to determine gross profit are those related to business activities. Expenses not allowed include:

- personal and domestic

- entertaining and hospitality
- gifts and donations, fines and penalties
- debts other than bad debts
- life insurance and pension premiums on the business proprietor

Employee Benefits

Most benefits in kind provided to an employee in consequence of his employment are taxable. The general rule (subject to many exceptions) is that for employees who are company directors or whose annual income and benefits are more than £8,500, the benefit is assessable for an amount equal to the cost to the employer. For other employees, fringe benefits are not usually assessed.
Taxable benefits include:

- provision of accommodation
- gifts of assets and gift vouchers
- loans
- provision of staff
- childcare facilities
- company car/van and fuel
- luncheon vouchers
- club memberships
- use of mobile phones
- share options
- travel

Certain benefits can be provided free of tax including:

- Canteen facilities, provided the same facilities are available to all employees.
- Car parking at or near the place of work.
- Chauffeur, provided he is only used on company business.
- Childcare facilities provided by the employer and which comply with local authority regulations.
- Clothes such as uniforms, safety clothing or bearing the company logo.
- Company car, covering use of a pool car only for company business.
- Education, full-time, but only where it meets certain criteria.
- Entertainment incidental to the employment.
- Gift, but only if unrelated to employment or not from the employer and not worth more than £150 a year.
- Housing – necessary to perform duty properly, customary for that employment, necessary for security, or free board for agricultural workers.
- Hotel bills, but only necessary food and accommodation (£5 a day personal expenses in the UK and £10 overseas).
- Laundry where the clothing qualifies for tax relief.
- Liability cover or payment, but not for a criminal offence.
- Long service awards for at least 20 years and not more than £50 per year of service.

- Luncheon vouchers, but not if worth more than 15p per working day.
- Medical treatment incurred overseas or for a routine check-up.
- Mobile telephone, but not for personal calls.
- Outplacement counselling for an employee made redundant.
- Parties and functions provided cost does not exceed £150 per person.
- Pension contributions to an approved scheme.
- Relocation up to £8,000.
- Scholarships first awarded before 1983.
- Security measures necessary to protect an employee or his family (but not a vehicle or accommodation).
- Sports facilities provided by an employer.
- Training costs related to an employee's work.
- Training expenses for courses in the UK related to work and lasting four weeks or more.
- Travel and subsistence made in the course of work.

Tax Records

Tax records including all relevant receipts must be maintain for five years from 31 January in the year following that to which the return relates. (Practically, that means six years' of data.)

Corporation Tax

UK-based companies pay corporation or corporate tax based on their annual trading profits and capital gains determined from the company's annual accounts showing sales and purchases. By deducting one from the other the gross profit is calculated. Income may include overseas trading, investment income and dividends received. Purchases/expenditure may include normal business expenses, capital allowances, charitable covenants and patent royalties.

Small Company Corporation Tax

Marginal relief eases the transition from the starting rate to the small companies' rate for companies with profits between £10,000 and £50,000. The percentage used in the calculation of this marginal relief will be 19%. Marginal relief also applies to companies with profits between £300,000 and £1,500,000, The percentage being 30%. The fraction used in the calculation of this marginal relief will be 11/400.

Double Taxation

When the same income and gains are taxable in more than one country double taxation occurs. Double taxation relief is given by:

- means of a double tax treaty with the country concerned, whereby income is exempt from tax in one country and a credit granted for foreign taxes paid on other income;
- allowing the foreign tax paid as a credit against the total UK tax liability
- the foreign tax being considered as a deductible expense in calculating the business profits chargeable to tax (for example the foreign tax being treated like an ordinary business expense).

Double tax treaties take precedence over UK domestic legislation where relief is due. In most cases, the full amount of income, including income from the overseas territory, is calculated for income tax liability for the tax year. The overseas tax paid on the relevant income is then offset as a credit against the total liability to income tax. The credit is limited to the income tax liability on the income that has been subject to overseas tax. There is no relief available for any excess foreign tax paid. Any unrelieved foreign tax cannot be carried forward or back. Generally, only direct foreign taxes are taken into account for the purposes of double tax relief.

National Insurance

Most people who work pay National Insurance contributions in one of five classes: employee, self-employed person, non-employed person or employer. Depending on his status, a person may have to pay more than one class of contribution at the same time. Some contributions count towards benefits such as incapacity benefit and retirement pension.

Self-employed people are liable to pay two classes of contributions: Class 2 and Class 4, which are paid on profits and gains at, or above, a set level.

Class 2 Contributions

Class 2 contributions are a flat rate payment collected by the Contributions Agency from self-employed persons of more than16 years but who are under pension age.

Payment is made in arrears either by quarterly bill every 13 weeks or by direct debit every month.

These contributions do not count for Jobseeker's Allowance but they do count for incapacity benefit, retirement pension, widow's benefit and maternity allowance.

Class 4 Contributions

Class 4 contributions are payable when an individual's profits exceed a certain amount. These contributions may have to be paid in addition to Class 2 contributions. They are based on a percentage of annual profits between a lower and upper profit level. The levels are set each year by the Chancellor in the Budget.

Class 4 contributions are normally assessed and collected by the Inland Revenue together with Schedule D tax, based on the individual's profit assessment. As with tax, if payment becomes overdue, interest may have to be paid. These contributions do not entitle the payee to any benefit, but they do help to share the cost of funding the benefits paid to all self-employed people.

Section D2 Vehicle Taxation

Goods Vehicle Taxation

Normally the vehicle taxation system of the country through which goods vehicles pass apply to those vehicles. Britain has, however, accepted the terms of the International Convention on the Taxation of Road Vehicles and as a result of bilateral agreements, goods vehicles are exempt from paying further taxation provided they are correctly taxed in the country of registration. To ensure that vehicles are correctly taxed to meet this requirement,

Countries where further lorry tax (i.e. excise duty) has to be paid are:

- Austria (tax payable on transit of goods vehicles of more than 12 tons)
- Hungary (where single-axle weight exceeds 10 tons or 16 tons on two axles)
- Switzerland (road tax payable based on gross weights and time in country)
- Turkey (transit tax payable)
- Former Yugoslavia (road tax payable for vehicles in transit)

Amount of Vehicle Taxation – UK

The following tables give the rates of vehicle tax from 1 April 2020. Please refer to your Registration Certificate (V5C) or new keeper details section (V5C/2) for the technical details of your vehicle. You can pay by Direct Debit for certain vehicles, either annually, six monthly or monthly. Where Direct Debit is available the rates are shown.

Standard Rates – The following table contains the rates of vehicle tax for already registered cars

Cars registered between 1 March 2001 and 31 March 2017 based on CO₂ emissions and fuel type		Petrol Car (Tax Class 48) and Diesel Car (Tax Class 49)					Alternative fuel car (Tax Class 59)				
		Non Direct Debit		Direct Debit			Non Direct Debit		Direct Debit		
Bands	CO₂ emission figure (g/km)	12 months	Six months	Single 12 month payment	Total payable by 12 monthly instalments	Single six month payment	12 months	Six months	Single 12 month payment	Total payable by 12 monthly instalments	Single six month payment
Band A	Up to 100	£0	-	-	-	-	£0	-	-	-	-
Band B	101 to 110	£20	-	£20	£21	-	£10	-	£10	£10.50	-
Band C	111 to 120	£30	-	£30	£31.50	-	£20	-	£20	£21.00	-
Band D	121 to 130	£125	£68.75	£125	£131.25	£65.63	£115	£63.25	£115	£120.75	£60.38
Band E	131 to 140	£150	£82.50	£150	£157.50	£78.75	£140	£77	£140	£147.00	£73.50
Band F	141 to 150	£165	£90.75	£165	£173.25	£86.63	£155	£85.25	£155	£162.75	£81.38
Band G	151 to 165	£205	£112.75	£205	£215.25	£107.63	£195	£107.25	£195	£204.75	£102.38
Band H	166 to 175	£240	£132.00	£240	£252.00	£126.00	£230	£126.50	£230	£241.50	£120.75
Band I	176 to 185	£265	£145.75	£265	£278.25	£139.13	£255	£140.25	£255	£267.75	£133.88
Band J	186 to 200	£305	£167.75	£305	£320.25	£160.13	£295	£162.25	£295	£309.75	£154.88
Band K*	201 to 225	£330	£181.50	£330	£346.50	£173.25	£320	£176.00	£320	£336.00	£168.00
Band L	226 to 255	£565	£310.75	£565	£593.25	£296.63	£555	£305.25	£555	£582.75	£291.38
Band M	Over 255	£580	£319.00	£580	£609.00	£304.50	£570	£313.50	£570	£598.50	£299.25

Band K includes cars that have a CO2 emission figure over 225g/km but were registered before 23 March 2006.

First Licence Rates – From 1 April 2020, anyone buying a new car will pay a different rate of vehicle tax. From the second licence onwards, the standard rate of vehicle tax will apply.

First Licence Rates for cars registered on or after 1 April 2020 based on CO_2 emissions & fuel type		Petrol car (Tax Class 48) and Diesel car (Tax Class 49)		Alternative fuel car (Tax Class 59)	
Bands	CO_2 emission figure (g/km)	Petrol Car	Diesel Car	12 months	Six months
Band A	000 to 000	£0	-	£0	-
Band B	001 to 050	£10	£25.00	£0	-
Band C	051 to 075	£25	£110.00	£15	-
Band D	076 to 090	£110	£135.00	£100	-
Band E	091 to 100	£135	£155.00	£125	£65.63
Band F	101 to 110	£155	£175.00	£145	£76.13
Band G	111 to 130	£175	£215.00	£165	£86.63
Band H	131 to 150	£215	£540.00	£205	-
Band I	151 to 170	£540	£870.00	£530	-
Band J	171 to 190	£870	£1,305	£860	-
Band K	191 to 225	£1305	£1,850	£1,295	-
Band L	226 to 255	£1850	£2,175	£1,840	-
Band	Over 255	£2,175	£2,175	£2,165	-

Private or light goods vehicles (PLG) Tax Class 11 (goods vehicles weighing no more than 3500kg)	Non Direct Debit		Direct Debit		
	12 months	Six months	Single 12 month payment	Total payable by 12 monthly instalments	Single six month payment
Not over 1549cc	£165	£90.75	£165	£173.25	£86.63
Over 1549cc	£270	£148.50	£270	£283.50	£141.75

Light goods vehicles Tax Class 39 (weighing no more than 3500kg)	Non Direct		Direct Debit		
	12 months	Six months	Single 12 month payment	Total payable by 12 monthly instalments	Single six month payment
Vehicles registered on or after 1 March 2001	£265	£145.75	£265	£278.25	£139.13

Euro 4 light goods vehicles Tax Class 36 (weighing no more than 3500kg)	Non Direct Debit		Direct Debit		
	12 months	Six months	Single 12 month payment	Total payable by 12 monthly instalments	Single six month payment
Vehicles registered between 1 March 2003 and 31 December 2006 and which are Euro 4 compliant	£140	£77	£140	£147	£73.50

Euro 5 light goods vehicles Tax Class 36 (weighing no more than 3500kg)	Non Direct Debit		Direct Debit		
	12 months	Six months	Single 12 month payment	Total payable by 12 monthly instalments	Single six month payment
Vehicles registered between 1 January 2009 and 31 December 2010 and which are Euro 5 compliant	£140	£77	£140	£147	£73.50

Motorcycles (weighing no more than 450kg unladen) Tax Class 17 Motorcycles (with or without sidecar)	Non Direct Debit		Direct Debit		
	12 months	Six months	Single 12 month payment	Total payable by 12 monthly instalments	Single six month payment
Not over 150cc	£20	-	£20	£21.00	-
151 to 400cc	£44	-	£44	£46.20	-
401 to 600cc	£67	£36.85	£67	£70.35	£35.18
Over 600cc	£93	£51.15	£93	£97.65	£48.83
Tax Class 50 Tricycles (weighing no more than 450kg without a sidecar) (Tricycles weighing over 450kg must be taxed in the PLG class.) Not over 150cc	£20	-	£20	£21.00	-
All other tricycles	£93	£51.15	£93	£97.65	£48.83

Trade licences	12 months	Six months
Trade licences available for all vehicles Trade licences available only for: • bicycles (weighing no more than 450kg without a sidecar) • tricycles (weighing no more than 450kg without a sidecar)	£165 £93 £93	£90.75 £51.15 £51.15

Use the tables below to determine the VED payable for your vehicle based on the revenue weight, axle configuration e.g. a two axle rigid weighing 14,500kgs pays B2 i.e. an annual rate of £105. Note – Where a vehicle exceeds 44,000kgs the VED paid is equal to that for special types vehicles (£1,585 annual/£792.50 six months). The following rates are applicable from 1 August 2020.

VED band	Without RPC					With RPC					RPC discount	
	Non Direct Debit		Direct Debit			Non Direct Debit		Direct Debit				
	12 months	Six months	Single 12month payment	Total payable by12monthly instalments	Single six month payment	12 months	Six months	Single 12month payment	Total payable by12monthly instalments	Single six month payment	12 months	Six months
A0	£165	£90.75	£165	£173.25	£86.63	£160	£88	£160	£1	£84	£5	£2.75
B0	£200	£110	£200	£210	£105	£160	£88	£160	£1	£84	£40	£22

VED band and rate	Total VED & levy without RPC		Total VED, levy and RPC discount/grant		VED rates		Levy band	Levy rates		RPC discount/grant	
	12 months	Six months	12 months	Six months	12 months	Six months		12 months	Six months	12months	Six months
A1	£165	£9	£160	£88.50	£8	£4					
A2	£169	£9	£164	£90.50	£8	£4					
A3	£185	£101	£180	£98.50	£100	£5	A	£85	£51	£5	£2.50
A4	£231	£124	£226	£121.50	£146	£7					
A5	£236	£126.50	£231	£124	£151	£75.50					
B1	£200	£110.50	£160	£90.50	£9	£47.50					
B2	£210	£115.50	£170	£95.50	£105	£52.50	B	£105	£63	£40	£20
B3	£230	£125.50	£190	£105.50	£125	£62.50					
C1	£450	£249	£210	£129	£210	£105					
C2	£505	£276.50	£265	£156.50	£265	£132.50	C	£240	£144	£240	£120
C3	£529	£288.50	£289	£168.50	£289	£144.50					
D1	£650	£360	£280	£175	£300	£150	D	£350	£210	£370	£185
E1	£1,200	£664	£700	£414	£560	£280	E	£640	£384	£500	£250
E2	£1,249	£688.50	£749	£438.50	£609	£304.50					
F	£1,500	£831	£1,000	£581	£690	£345	F	£810	£486	£500	£250
G	£1,850	£1,025	£1,350	£775	£850	£425	G	£1,000	£600	£500	£250

Use the tables below to determine the total VED and levy payable for your vehicle based on the revenue weight & axle configuration e.g. A two axle rigid weighing 14,500kgs pays B2 i.e. an annual rate of £210
Note–Where a vehicle exceeds 44,000kgs the VED paid is equal to that for special types vehicles (£1,585 annual /£792.50 six months), levy band G applies (£1000/£600) and where applicable the maximum RPC grant is allocated (£500/£250).

Rigid goods vehicle					Tractive unit with two axles					Tractive unit with three or more				
Revenue weight of vehicle kg		2 axles	3 axles	4 or more axles	Revenue weight of vehicle kg		One or more semi-trailer axles	Two or more semi-trailer axles	Three or more semi-trailer axles	Revenue weight of vehicle kg		One or more semi-trailer axles	Two or more semi-trailer axles	Three or more semi-trailer axles
Over	Not over				Over	Not over				Over	Not over			
3,500	7,500	A0	A0	A0	3,500	11,999	A0	A0	A0	3,500	11,999	A0	A0	A0
7,500	11,999	B0	B0	B0	11,999	22,000	A1	A1	A1	11,999	25,000	A1	A1	A1
11,999	14,000	B1	B1	B1	22,000	23,000	A2	A1	A1	25,000	26,000	A3	A1	A1
14,000	15,000	B2	B1	B1	23,000	25,000	A5	A1	A1	26,000	28,000	A4	A1	A1
15,000	19,000	D1	B1	B1	25,000	26,000	C2	A3	A1	28,000	29,000	C1	A1	A1
19,000	21,000	D1	B3	B1	26,000	28,000	C2	A4	A1	29,000	31,000	C3	A1	A1
21,000	23,000	D1	C1	B1	28,000	31,000	D1	D1	A1	31,000	33,000	E1	C1	A1
23,000	25,000	D1	D1	C1	31,000	33,000	E1	E1	C1	33,000	34,000	E2	D1	A1
25,000	27,000	D1	D1	D1	33,000	34,000	E1	E2	C1	34,000	36,000	E2	D1	C1
27,000	44,000	D1	D1	E1	34,000	38,000	F	F	E1	36,000	38,000	F	E1	D1
					38,000	44,000	G	G	G	38,000	44,000	G	G	E1

Rigid vehicles pulling trailers of over 4,000kg–Tax Class 02 (trailer) And 46 (RPC)

A rigid HGV of 12,000 kg and over pulling a trailer over 4,000kg must pay a higher rate of tax and levy.

To calculate the amount, first look up the levy band for the vehicle in table T1. Then, look up the VED band and amount payable in table T3. To do so, you need to know whether the vehicle has road friendly suspension, the number of axles on the HGV (not on the trailer), the levy band, the trailer weight category, and the total weight of the HGV and the trailer. (Please note: If pulling a trailer of 4,000 kg and under please use the tables above).

Note–Where a table does not specify a VED rate for a particular vehicle combination, the maximum VED rate applies (£609 annual/£304.50 six months). The levy band and (where applicable) the RPC grant are as set out in tablesT1 and T2.

Note–Where the total weight of the vehicle plus the trailer exceeds the maximum weights shown below, then VED, levy and RPC grant are all calculated based on the highest weight shown. This will be 40,000 kg for a vehicle without road friendly suspension, or when the HGV has two axles, and 44,000kg for other vehicle combinations. For these vehicles (ie rigid vehicles pulling trailers where the total weight exceeds maximum weights in the table), unlike for other HGVs, keepers must contact DVLA directly to tax the vehicle, otherwise incorrect VED/levy may be applied.

Table T1 - levy bands for rigid vehicles with trailers

Weight of rigid		Two-axled rigid	Three- axled rigid	Four- axledrigid
Over	Not over			
11,999kg	15,000kg	B(T)	B(T)	B(T)
15,000kg	21,000kg	D(T)	B(T)	B(T)
1,000kg	23,000kg	E(T)	C(T)	B(T)
23,000kg	25,000kg	E(T)	D(T)	C(T)
25,000kg	27,000kg	E(T)	D(T)	D(T)
27,000kg	44,000kg	E(T)	E(T)	E(T)

Table T2 – levy rates & RPC grant values for rigid vehicles with trailers

Levyband	Levy rates		RPC grant	
	12 months	Six months	12 months	Six months
B(T)	£135	£81	£40	£20
C(T)	£310	£186	£240	£120
D(T)	£450	£270	£370	£185
E(T)	£830	£498	£500	£250

Table T3–VED bands, rates & amounts payable for rigid vehicles with trailers & road friendly suspension

HGV axles(the rigid, not the trailer)	Levy band	Trailer weight category	Total weight of HGV and trailer,not over	VED band (letter) and rate (number)	Total VED and levy without RPC		Total VED, levy and RPC grant		VED rates		Levy rates	
					12 months	Six months	12 months	Six months	12 months	Six months	12 months	Six months
Two	B(T)	4,001-12,000kg	27,000kg	B(T)1	£365	£196	£325	£176	£230	£115	£135	£81
		Over12,000kg	33,000kg	B(T)3	£430	£228.50	£390	£208.50	£295	£147.50	£135	£81
			36,000kg	B(T)6	£536	£281.50	£496	£261.50	£401	£200.50	£135	£81
			38,000kg	B(T)4	£454	£240.50	£414	£220.50	£319	£159.50	£135	£81
			40,000kg	B(T)7	£579	£303	£539	£283	£444	£222	£135	£81
	D(T)	4,001-12,000kg	30,000kg	D(T)1	£815	£452.50	£445	£267.50	£365	£182.50	£450	£270
		Over12,000kg	38,000kg	D(T)4	£880	£485	£510	£300	£430	£215	£450	£270
			40,000kg	D(T)5	£894	£492	£524	£307	£444	£222	£450	£270
Three	B(T)	4,001-12,000kg	33,000kg	B(T)1	£365	£196	£325	£176	£230	£115	£135	£81
		Over12,000kg	38,000kg	B(T)3	£430	£228.50	£390	£208.50	£295	£147.50	£135	£81
			40,000kg	B(T)5	£527	£277	£487	£257	£392	£196	£135	£81
			44,000kg	B(T)3	£430	£228.50	£390	£208.50	£295	£147.50	£135	£81
	C(T)	4,001-12,000kg	35,000kg	C(T)1	£615	£338.50	£375	£218.50	£305	£152.50	£310	£186
		Over12,000kg	38,000kg	C(T)2	£680	£371	£440	£251	£370	£185	£310	£186
			40,000kg	C(T)3	£702	£382	£462	£262	£392	£196	£310	£186
			44,000kg	C(T)2	£680	£371	£440	£251	£370	£185	£310	£186
	D(T)	4,001-10,000kg	33,000kg	D(T)1	£815	£452.50	£445	£267.50	£365	£182.50	£450	£270
			36,000kg	D(T)3	£851	£470.50	£481	£285.50	£401	£200.50	£450	£270
		10,001-12,000kg	38,000kg	D(T)1	£815	£452.50	£445	£267.50	£365	£182.50	£450	£270
		Over12,000kg	44,000kg	D(T)4	£880	£485	£510	£300	£430	£215	£450	£270
Four	B(T)	4,001-12,000kg	35,000kg	B(T)1	£365	£196	£325	£176	£230	£115	£135	£81
		Over12,000kg	44,000kg	B(T)3	£430	£228.50	£390	£208.50	£295	£147.50	£135	£81
	C(T)	4,001-12,000kg	37,000kg	C(T)1	£615	£338.50	£375	£218.50	£305	£152.50	£310	£186
		Over12,000kg	44,000kg	C(T)2	£680	£371	£440	£251	£370	£185	£310	£186
	D(T)	4,001-12,000kg	39,000kg	D(T)1	£815	£452.50	£445	£267.50	£365	£182.50	£450	£270
		Over12,000kg	44,000kg	D(T)4	£880	£485	£510	£300	£430	£215	£450	£270
	E(T)	4,001-12,000kg	44,000kg	E(T)1	£1365	£765.50	£865	£515.50	£535	£267.50	£830	£498
		Over12,000kg	44,000kg	E(T)2	£1430	£798	£930	£548	£600	£300	£830	£498

113

Table T3–VED bands, rates & amounts payable for rigid vehicles with trailers, no road friendly suspension

Axles	Band	Weight range	Weight	Band								
Two	B(T)	4,001-12,000kg	27,000kg	B(T)1	£365	£196	£325	£176	£230	£115	£135	£81
		Over 12,000kg	31,000kg	B(T)3	£430	£228.50	£390	£208.50	£295	£147.50	£135	£81
			33,000kg	B(T)6	£536	£281.50	£496	£261.50	£401	£200.50	£135	£81
			36,000kg	B(T)10	£744	£385.50	£704	£365.50	£609	£304.50	£135	£81
			38,000kg	B(T)7	£579	£303	£539	£283	£444	£222	£135	£81
			40,000kg	B(T)9	£739	£383	£699	£363	£604	£302	£135	£81
	D(T)	4,001-12,000kg	30,000kg	D(T)1	£815	£452.50	£445	£267.50	£365	£182.50	£450	£270
		Over 12,000kg	33,000kg	D(T)4	£880	£485	£510	£300	£430	£215	£450	£270
			36,000kg	D(T)8	£1059	£574.50	£689	£389.50	£609	£304.50	£450	£270
			38,000kg	D(T)5	£894	£492	£524	£307	£444	£222	£450	£270
			40,000kg	D(T)7	£1054	£572	£684	£387	£604	£302	£450	£270
Three	B(T)	4,001-10,000kg	29,000kg	B(T)1	£365	£196	£325	£176	£230	£115	£135	£81
			31,000kg	B(T)2	£424	£225.50	£384	£205.50	£289	£144.50	£135	£81
		10,001-12,000kg	33,000kg	B(T)1	£365	£196	£325	£176	£230	£115	£135	£81
		Over 12,000kg	36,000kg	B(T)3	£430	£228.50	£390	£208.50	£295	£147.50	£135	£81
			38,000kg	B(T)5	£527	£277	£487	£257	£392	£196	£135	£81
			40,000kg	B(T)8	£677	£352	£637	£332	£542	£271	£135	£81
	C(T)	4,001-10,000kg	31,000kg	C(T)1	£615	£338.50	£375	£218.50	£305	£152.50	£310	£186
			33,000kg	C(T)4	£711	£386.50	£471	£266.50	£401	£200.50	£310	£186
		10,001-12,000kg	35,000kg	C(T)1	£615	£338.50	£375	£218.50	£305	£152.50	£310	£186

HGV axles (the rigid, not the trailer)	Levy band	Trailer weight category	Total weight of HGV and trailer, not over	VED band (letter) and rate (number)	Total VED and levy without RPC		Total VED, levy and RPC grant		VED rates		Levy rates	
					12 months	Six months	12 months	Six months	12 months	Six months	12 months	Six months
Three	C(T)	Over12,000kg	36,000kg	C(T)2	£680	£371	£440	£251	£370	£185	£310	£186
			38,000kg	C(T)3	£702	£382	£462	£262	£392	£196	£310	£186
			40,000kg	C(T)5	£852	£457	£612	£337	£542	£271	£310	£186
	D(T)	4,001-10,000kg	31,000kg	D(T)1	£815	£452.50	£445	£267.50	£365	£182.50	£450	£270
			33,000kg	D(T)3	£851	£470.50	£481	£285.50	£401	£200.50	£450	£270
			35,000kg	D(T)8	£1059	£574.50	£689	£389.50	£609	£304.50	£450	£270
		10,001-12,000kg	36,000kg	D(T)1	£815	£452.50	£445	£267.50	£365	£182.50	£450	£270
			37,000kg	D(T)2	£842	£466	£472	£281	£392	£196	£450	£270
			38,000kg	D(T)4	£880	£485	£510	£300	£430	£215	£450	£270
		Over12,000kg	40,000kg	D(T)6	£992	£541	£622	£356	£542	£271	£450	£270
Four	B(T)	4,001-12,000kg	35,000kg	B(T)1	£365	£196	£325	£176	£230	£115	£135	£81
		Over12,000kg	40,000kg	B(T)3	£430	£228.50	£390	£208.50	£295	£147.50	£135	£81
	C(T)	4,001-12,000kg	37,000kg	C(T)1	£615	£338.50	£375	£218.50	£305	£152.50	£310	£186
		Over12,000kg	40,000kg	C(T)2	£680	£371	£440	£251	£370	£185	£310	£186
	D(T)	4,001-10,000kg	36,000kg	D(T)1	£815	£452.50	£445	£267.50	£365	£182.50	£450	£270
			37,000kg	D(T)5	£894	£492	£524	£307	£444	£222	£450	£270
		10,001-12,000kg	39,000kg	D(T)1	£815	£452.50	£445	£267.50	£365	£182.50	£450	£270
		Over12,000kg	40,000kg	D(T)4	£880	£485	£510	£300	£430	£215	£450	£270
	E(T)	4,001-10,000kg	38,000kg	E(T)1	£1365	£765.50	£865	£515.50	£535	£267.50	£830	£498
			40,000kg	E(T)3	£1434	£800	£934	£550	£604	£302	£830	£498
		10,001-12,000kg	40,000kg	E(T)1	£1365	£765.50	£865	£515.50	£535	£267.50	£830	£498

VED and levy bands and rates for combined transport tax class 23 (standard) and 53 (RPC)

Tractive Unit with 3 or more axles used with a semi-trailer with Three or more axles Over 41,000 kgs Not over 44,000 kgs	Total VED and levy without RPC		Total VED, levy and RPC, grant		VED rates		Levy rates		RPC grant	
	12 months	Six months	12 months	Six months	12 months	Six months	12 months	Six months	12 months	Six months
	£650	£389	£280	£204	£10	£5	£640	£384	£370	£185

VED and levy bands and rates for special types vehicles tax class 57 (standard) and 58 (RPC)

Those used to carry very large loads that cannot be separated –in conjunction with a Special Types General Order	Total VED and levy without RPC		Total VED, levy and RPC grant		VED rates		Levy rates		RPC grant	
	12 months	Six months	12 months	Six months	12 months	Six months	12 months	Six months	12 months	Six months
	£2,585	£1,392.50	£2,085	£1,142.50	£1,585	£792.50	£1,000	£600	£500	£250

Special vehicles Tax Class 14 (weighing over 3,500kg)	Non Direct Debit		Direct Debit		
	12 months	Six months	Single 12 month payment	Total payable by 12 monthly instalments	Single six month payment
Showman's goods, showman's haulage, works trucks, digging machines, road rollers ,mobile cranes and pumps	£165	£90.75	£165	£173.25	£86.63
Private HGV Tax Class 10 (weighing more than 3500kg)	£165	£90.75	£165	£173.25	£86.63
Small island vehicles Tax Class 16	£165	£90.75	£165	£173.25	£86.63

Buses Tax Class 34						Reduced pollution buses **Tax Class 38**					
Number of seats (including the driving seat)	Non Direct Debit		Direct Debit			Non Direct Debit		Direct Debit			
	12 months	Six months	Single 12month payment	Total payable by12monthly instalments	Single six month payment	12 months	Six months	Single 12month payment	Total payable by12monthly instalments	Single six month payment
10 to17	£165	£90.75	£165	£173.25	£86.63	£165	£90.75	£165	£173.25	£86.63
18 to36	£220	£121	£220	£115.50	£165	£90.75	£165	£173.25	£86.63	
37to61	£330	£181.50	£330	£231 £173.25	£262.50	£165	£90.75	£165	£173.25	£86.63
62andover	£500	£275	£500	£346.50	£165	£90.75	£165	£173.25	£86.63	

General haulage vehicles Tax Class 55					Reduced pollution general haulage vehicles Tax Class 56				
Non Direct Debit		Direct Debit			Non Direct Debit		Direct Debit		
12 months	Six months	Single 12month payment	Total payable by12monthly instalments	Single six month payment	12 months	Six months	Single 12month payment	Total payable by12monthly instalments	Single six month payment
£350	£192.50	£350	£367.50	£183.75	£165	£90.75	£165	£173.25	£86.63

Recovery vehicles Tax Class 47			Non Direct Debit		Direct Debit		
	Over	Not over	12 months	Six months	Single 12month payment	Total payable by 12 monthly instalments	Single six month payment
	3,500kg	25,000kg	£165	£90.75	£165	£173.25	£86.63
	25,000kg	-	£410	£225.50	£410	£430.50	£215.25

To calculate your tax please visit www.gov.uk/calculate-vehicle-tax-rates
You can get more information on taxing your vehicle on the website at www.gov.uk/vehicletax
Find out about DVLA's online services. Go to www.gov.uk/browse/driving -
http://alturl.com/auw4o

<u>Refunds of Vehicle Excise Duty</u>

You can apply for a refund of vehicle tax if you are the current registered keeper or were the last registered keeper of your vehicle. You'll also need to tell the Driver and Vehicle Licensing Agency (DVLA) why the vehicle no longer needs to be taxed.

DVLA no longer accepts applications for a vehicle tax refund from customers using a V14 form. They will be rejected and returned to the customer.

Since 1 October 2014, you no longer need to make a separate application on a V14 for a refund of vehicle tax. DVLA automatically issues a vehicle tax refund when a notification is received from the registered keeper that the:

- vehicle has been sold or transferred
- vehicle has been scrapped at an Authorised Treatment Facility
- vehicle has been exported
- vehicle has been removed from the road and the person on the vehicle register has made a Statutory Off Road Notification (SORN)
- registered keeper has changed the tax class on the vehicle to an exempt duty tax class

Customers should ensure that the dates of acquisition and/or disposal provided on the notification via the vehicle registration certificate (V5C or logbook), V5C/2 and V5C/3 are current and accurate.

You can tax your vehicle or claim a refund on the 'phone on 0300 123 4321 fully automated 24/7 service. Takes less than 4 minutes and charged at local rate.

<u>You Made a SORN</u>

If you've decided not to use your vehicle on public roads and you already made a SORN, you will be automatically sent a DVLA tax refund for the remaining months that your tax payment wouldn't be used. If you haven't made a SORN yet, you could apply for this online at https://www.sorn.service.gov.uk/. You may also call 0300 123 4321 or send your filled up V890 form to DVLA, Swansea, SA99 1AR.

<u>You Transferred or Sold Your Vehicle</u>

You must let DVLA know if you sold or transferred your vehicle. Do this before you even send the V5C by post. You would need the reference number on the V5C for this process. In case you're acting on behalf of the seller, you would also need their permission. Go to https://www.gov.uk/sold-bought-vehicle in order to start the online process. You could do this from 8:00am to 6:00pm, Monday to Friday. The tax refund would be sent to the person who is the registered keeper on the latest V5C.

It Was Scrapped

Vehicles that can no longer be used must be scrapped at an ATF or Authorised Treatment Facility. If you wish to remove and keep some parts before sending the vehicle to an ATF, you must make a SORN first. In case you also wish to keep the registration number,
you may request this here. https://www.gov.uk/keep-registration-number

You'll need to pay £80 for this. This service is available from 8:00am to 6:00pm, Monday to Friday. Once done with removing the parts you need, you may take the vehicle to an ATF. Go to https://www.gov.uk/find-vehicle-scrapyard to find the nearest ATF in your area. Enter your postcode on the appropriate field and click "Find". Let DVLA know that you had your vehicle scrapped at an ATF.

Your application will be rejected if you don't give these details and a rejection letter sent to you. The name on the refund application should also match exactly what is on your vehicle registration certificate (V5C).

Do not apply for a refund if your vehicle is in the process of having its registration number transferred or retained. The tax will be dealt with at the time of the transfer or retention application.

If your vehicle is being transferred from Great Britain (GB) to Northern Ireland (NI) or NI to GB, you do not need to apply for a refund.

Your vehicle has been stolen

If your vehicle was stolen, you should let the local police know right away. You would be asked for the vehicle's registration number, colour, model and make; then you would be given a crime reference number. You'll need this reference number when claiming for your auto insurance and applying for a DVLA tax refund.

Apply for a tax refund only if your vehicle is not found in one week after it was stolen. Call DVLA at 0300 790 6802 and ask for a V33 form that you need to fill up and send it to the following address:

Refund Section DVLA Swansea SA99 1AL

As many vehicles are recovered within a few days of theft, you should wait at least seven days before applying for a refund. Applying earlier than the seven days may cause your application to be returned to you.

If the vehicle has been recovered, and you still want to apply for a refund, you must tell DVLA what has happened to the vehicle since its recovery.

Trade Licenses

These are issued by the DVLA. Licences last for six or 12 months, and expire on 30 June or 31 December, although there are seven to 11 month licences available for first-time applicants.

To apply for a trade licence, download and complete form VTL301 in accordance with the guidance notes VTL301/1 and take or send it to the DVLA local office nearest to the business premises the trade plates will be kept.

You can also get form VTL301/1 from a DVLA office.

There are two general categories of business that are eligible for a trade licence. These are:

- Motor traders - dealers, manufacturers and repairers of motor vehicles, including those engaged wholly or mainly in collection and delivery, or manufacturers of trailers in conjunction with a business of motor trader or valeters and accessory fitters.
- Vehicle testers - those other than motor traders who regularly in the course of their business carry out testing on public roads of motor vehicles belonging to others.

Recovery Vehicles

Any vehicle used strictly for recovery work is given some exemptions within the law.

- Any recovery vehicle is exempt from operator's licence.
- Any recovery vehicle is exempt from the use of a tachograph.
- Recovery vehicle excise duty (road tax) applies at reduced rate.

Recovery is defined as the movement of any 'mechanically disabled vehicle', i.e. broken down or accident damaged but only to a place of safety.

Section D3 Road Haulage Taxation

<u>Fuel Duties</u>

Generally, road fuel taxes or duties are paid upon purchase in the country or origin. No additional tax or duty is attached to fuel carried into other county in a vehicle's fuel tank. The general allowance within the EU is 200 litres. Some countries do, however, charge a tax or duty above certain limits for long-range international vehicles with high-capacity fuel tanks.

<u>Motorway Taxes (Vignettes)</u>

Goods vehicles of more than 12 tons gross weight are subject to a motorway tax when travelling to or through Germany, the Benelux countries (Belgium, Luxembourg and Holland), and Denmark. A vehicle certificate (vignette) is issued upon payment of the sliding-scale tax depending on the number of axles and the period of time for which the certificate is required.

A road user charge is imposed in Poland. Motorway vignettes must be purchased in Slovakia for the use of motorways. Similarly, Slovenia charges for the use of certain routes.

Vignettes are used in Austria, Bulgaria, the Czech Republic, Hungary, Moldova, Romania, Slovakia, Slovenia and Switzerland. In most of these countries a small, coloured sticker is affixed to a vehicle windscreen, but in Bulgaria, Hungary, Romania, Slovakia and since 2021 in Czech Republic, these have been superseded by electronic vignettes.

Britain's first toll motorway – the 27-mile long, three-lane M6 Toll Road – formerly known as the Birmingham Northern Relief Road (BNRR), opened in December 2003. It was designed to ease traffic and congestion through the West Midlands.

Taxes and Tolls

In both the UK and Europe certain roads, bridges and tunnels are only accessible via a toll levied according to user type including pedestrians, cyclists and motorcyclists, motor cars and light goods vehicles, heavy goods vehicles and passenger vehicles. For the most part tolls defray construction and maintenance costs, although there is a trend towards private or combined construction and maintenance financing so that the toll provides investment returns.
Currently there is a single major road, the M6 Toll and a small number of bridges and tunnels where tolls are collected. In addition, there are also two UK road pricing schemes, the London congestion charge and the Durham congestion charge
The tolled bridges and tunnels are as follows:

- Dartford crossing- Dart Charge or Pre-Pay (i.e. Dartford Tunnel northbound and the Queen Elizabeth II Bridge southbound over the River Thames on the M25 motorway).

- Erskine Bridge over the River Clyde west of Glasgow on the A82.
- Forth Road Bridge over the Firth of Forth on the A90 between Fife and Lothian in Scotland to the west of Edinburgh (connecting with the M8, M9 and M90 motorways).
- Humber Bridge over the River Humber on the A15.
- Mersey Tunnel between Liverpool and Birkenhead
- Severn Bridge – two crossings of the River Severn on the M4 and M48 motorways between England (Avon) and Wales (Gwent)
- Skye Bridge over the Kyle of Lochalsh on the A87 between the Scottish mainland and the Isle of Skye
- Tamar Bridge over the River Tamar on the A38 between Plymouth and Saltash (toll payable eastbound only – i.e. into Cornwall)
- Tyne Tunnel under the River Tyne on the Al to the east of Newcastle upon Tyne

International Vehicle Taxes and Tolls

Goods Vehicle Taxation

Normally the vehicle taxation system of the countries through which goods vehicles pass applies to vehicles. Britain has, however, accepted the terms of the International Convention on the Taxation of Road Vehicles and as a result of bilateral agreements, goods vehicles are exempt from paying further taxation provided they are correctly taxed in the country of registration. You must ensure that vehicles are correctly taxed to meet this requirement.

Austria

In Austria motorway and expressway tolls for vehicles whose maximum admissible weight exceeds 3.5 tonnes are collected electronically, there being no need for the driver to stop or change lanes for the toll to be collected properly. Each vehicle has to be equipped with a cigarette box-sized device called Go Box. It can be bought for 5 Euros (20% VAT included) at one of the 220 selling points in Austria and neighbouring countries. A visual and acoustic signal from the Go Box indicates that the toll has been collected properly each time the vehicle passes under a toll gantry.

Payment:
There are two modes of payment. In the pre-pay system, the driver loads a toll credit on his Go Box. This can be done at any of the Go Box selling points. The first time, a minimum of 45 euro has to be loaded. Each next time, the driver can load from 50 to 500 Euros at a time. The loaded credit remains valid for two years. If the driver loses his Go Box, the unused credit cannot be recovered.

In the post-pay mode, no credit has to be loaded on the Go Box. The vehicle owner periodically receives an invoice for the kilometres covered.

Both in the pre-pay and post-pay modes, payment can be done via Maestro, credit card or fuel card. In the post-pay mode, VISA, MasterCard and Maestro have to be issued by an Austrian bank. This doesn't apply to Diners Club and American Express.

GO-Box: the full electronic toll collection

For the Austrian GO toll system you need a GO-Box. The GO-Box is an electronic device which communicates with the toll gantries via microwave technology. Inform yourself in good time before the trip about the toll in Austria and about handling and function of the GO-Box.

Composition of prices

Since 1 January 2010, the toll tariff for vehicles over 3.5 tonnes of hzG is dependent, among other things, on the EURO emission class.

On 1 January 2017 both the air pollution (EURO emissions class) and the noise pollution - the so-called "external costs" - are taken into account.

The tariff is then composed of:

- Infrastructure basic kilometers
- Surcharge for traffic-related air pollution
- Supplement for traffic-induced noise pollution

On some sections of the highways a higher fee can be imposed. These prices appear in the tables below:

Prices 2021 at a glance						
Distance-related toll including surcharges for air and noise pollution for motor vehicles with a maximum permissible weight of over 3.5 tonnes						
Tariff group	Category 2 2 axles		Category 3 3 axles		Category 4+ 4 and more axles	
	Day	Night*	Day	night	Day	night
A EURO emission class EURO VI	0.20010	0.20050	0.28077	0.28169	0.41702	0.41818
B EURO emission class EURO V and EEV	0,20980	0.21020	0.29435	0.29527	0.43399	0.43515
C EURO emission class EURO IV	0.21670	0.21710	0.30401	0.30493	0.44503	0.44619
D EURO emission class EURO 0 to III	0.23730	0.23770	0.33285	0.33377	0.47799	0.47915

Rates in EUR per km, excluding 20% VAT, valid from 1 January 2021

The night rates apply between 10pm and 5am

Remark

On the special motorways (A 9 Gleinalm- or Bosrucktunnel, A 10 Tauerntunnel, A 11 Karawankentunnel, S 16 Arlberg Straßentunnel, A 13 Brenner Autobahn), higher tariffs apply as before. For the A 12, an increased tariff (+ 25% on the basic kilometer tariff) is also applied on the Unterinntal route (national border at Kufstein to junction Innsbruck / Amras).

EURO emission classes

The EURO emission class of your vehicle over 3.5 t hzG influences the toll. The "cleaner" you are on the road, the cheaper the toll rate.

On the A13 highway, a night fare is applicable from 10 PM till 5AM. It is the double of the day price.

http://alturl.com/hhxrf

Bulgaria

Price of stamps in Bulgaria for 2020

In Bulgaria it is necessary to have a vehicle bearing the highway sign, not only in transit, highways, but also on most roads 1., 2. and (3). class. In Bulgaria, so without the highway mark probably is essential. The list of chargeable roads appears in the table below:

Type of vehicle	Time lapse	Vignette price (EUR)
All freight vehicles with more than two axles	Daily	12
	Weekly	34 - 45
	Monthly	69 - 89
	Yearly	685 - 891
All freight vehicles with two axles	Daily	12
	Weekly	21 - 27
	Monthly	41 - 54
	Yearly	413 - 537

Freight vehicles with two axles towing a trailer have to buy a second vignette for the trailer, of the same type as the one for the lorry.
The bridge on the Danube between Rousse (BG) and Giurgiu (RO) is paid. The fees range from 12 Euros for a vehicle of under 5tonnes without trailer to 37 Euros for a truck of over 16 tonnes with a trailer of over 750 kgs.

Special charges also apply to vehicles with excessive dimensions, weight or weight per axle. Moreover, heavy and/or bulky convoys, having a total mass of over 45 tonnes, a weight per axle exceeding by more than 30% the maximum axle loading for the given road, a height of over 4.3 metres, a width of over 3.30 metres or a length of over 22 metres, are subject to the requirement of a permit issued by the National Road Infrastructure Fund. The price of the permit is of 36 Euros, 72 Euros for delivery within three working days and 108 Euros for delivery within one working day.

More information is available at www.aebtri.com.

Croatia

In Croatia, all highway users are subject to highway fees. These are levied at the toll lanes. Prices depend on the number of axles of the vehicle and on its height. Two payment modes exist. First, the driver can pay directly in cash, credit cards or cheques. Second, one can buy an ETC (electronic toll collection) device for 122 HRK, then load credit and use it for rapid cashless payment in special ETC lanes. Nevertheless, the ETC payment still requires stopping at the toll collection point.

Prices
Croatian Motorways Ltd does not indicate what the price/kilometre is. Nevertheless, you will find on
http://www.hac.hr/index.php?task=ces&stask=2
For an easy to use fee calculation tool.

Czech Republic

A summary of important changes in the electronic toll system, which will come into effect on 1 January 2021 on the basis of an amendment to Regulation of the Government No. 240/2014 Coll and Decree No. 470/2012 Coll as amended

Groups vehicles	
Identification of vehicles	**Description of Vehicle**
IA	Motorcycles, motor tricycles and quadcycles
AND	Motor vehicles with two axles, height up to 1.90 m
II	a) Motor vehicles with two axles, height above 1.90 m, where the maximum permissible weight not exceeding 3,500 kg b) Motor vehicles with two axles, height below 1.90 m, with a caravan trailer, regardless of the number of axles and the height of the trailer
III	a) Motor vehicles with two or three axles, maximum permissible mass exceeding 3500 kg b) Motor vehicles with two axles, the maximum permissible mass exceeding 3500 kg, with a caravan trailer with one axle c) motor vehicles from II a) with a caravan trailer , regardless of the number of axles of the trailer
IV	a) Motor vehicles with four or more axles, with a maximum mass exceeding 3500 kg b) Motor vehicles with two axles, the maximum permissible mass exceeding 3500 kg, with a caravan trailer with two or more axles c) Motor vehicles with three axles, the maximum permissible weighing more than 3500 kg, with a caravan trailer, regardless of the number of axles of the trailer

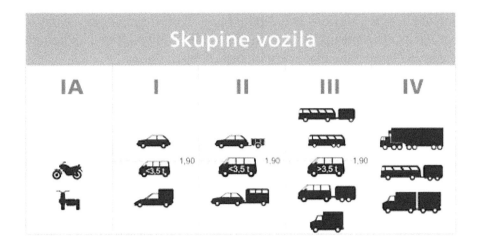

Vehicles that are subject to the toll must be equipped with a small electronic device which communicates with the tolling system. A fee for the use of a specific tolled section of a road is charged when the vehicle passes under the tolling station that corresponds to tolled section. When passing through a toll gate, an acoustic signal from the unit alerts the driver that the toll has been registered properly. The driver can use any lane without having to reduce the vehicle's speed or stop. The tolling process is fully automatic and requires no intervention on the part of the driver.

Prices:
The amount of toll for the use of a particular section of a tolled road depends on the length of the section and the category of the respective vehicle, depending on the number of axles and the emissions class. The amount to be paid for the use of a particular road section is calculated as a multiple of the applicable rate and of the length of the section.

On the highways under the jurisdiction of the Croatian Motorways Ltd. in accordance with the Regulations on the toll NN 130/13 tolls are charged for the length of the section between the two points of collection according to type of vehicle. Toll is paid at toll stations and can be paid by cash, credit cards , for which the point of sale featured visible mark that are acceptable means of payment and means of subscription. Non-residents under the regulations on foreign exchange operations tolls can pay in euros, according to the current exchange rate of the commercial banks HAC on the day of payment. On highways is governed by two toll systems: open and closed toll system. The open toll system applies to road structures (bridges, tunnels) and shorter motorway. In such a system, toll plaza is both input and output, and the cost of using the highway is determined by the type of vehicle. On motorways with multiple entry and exit apply to closed toll system.

Prosecution of toll cheats, settlement of toll discrepancies

Mobile enforcement is carried out by employees of the General Directorate of Customs of the Czech Republic. They are authorised by law to stop all vehicles identified by the tolling system to investigate discrepancies, and in the event of legal transgressions, they are also authorised to impose penalties, initiate administrative proceedings or even impound vehicles that are in violation of the law. In such cases drivers can expect to face considerable delays and complications. The access to information about transgressions is unlimited time-wise for members of the mobile enforcement units. This means that any vehicle could very well end up being detained for a long time following the discovery of such transgressions.

Newly charged toll roads

As of 1 January 2021, the network of toll roads will be extended by the newly opened sections of D48 (Rybí - Příbor Východ in the total length of 11.53 km) and D6 (Nové Strašecí - Krušovice in the total length of 9.8 km) motorways.

For more information on the electronic road toll, e-toll guide etc., go to website: https://mytocz.eu/etoll/toll-rates-2021

The website is available in many different languages.

<u>France</u>

In France, all highway users are subject to highway fees. These are levied at the toll plazas. Prices depend on the number of axles of the vehicle, its permissible total weight and its height. There are a variety of payment modes, such as cash, credit cards, fuel cards and the "Liber-t" card.

<u>French motorway tolls for HGVs:</u>

Most French motorways are toll routes. The price per kilometre varies from toll motorway to toll motorway, but generally speaking, for trucks or lorries it is between 18 centimes per kilometre and 35 cts./km

There are two **classes of tolls** for HGVs : Class 3 tolls apply to lorries with two axels; class 4 tolls apply to vehicles with more than two axels - notably articulated trucks and semitrailers.

As at 1st January 2021.

Sample   toll   charge   for   HGVs:
Paris - Strasbourg (480 km on motorways):

- Class 3 toll 86.10 € (18 centimes per kilometre)
- Class 4 toll 114.30 € (24 centimes per kilometre)
- Class 1 toll (cars) (8 centimes per km.)

More information:

https://about-france.com/hgv.htm

https://www.vinci-autoroutes.com/fr/tarifs-peage-reseaux-vinci-autoroutes

More information can be found on the web pages

Toll Tickets - http://alturl.com/mgaw2

A full price rate tool can be found at:
http://www.autoroutes.fr/en/key-rates.htm

Some tunnels and bridges are subject to extra payment.

The tunnels are:

- Fréjus, that links France and Italy (Modane - Bardoneche
- Mont Blanc, that links France and Italy (Chamonix Mont Blanc – Courmayeur / Entreves)
- Maurice Lemaire in the Vosges mountains (road N59)
- Puymorens in eastern Pyrénées mountains (road N20)
- Envalira in Andorra

The bridges are:

- Tancarville, at the Seine river delta on the A15 highway
- Normandie, at the Seine river delta, eastern part of Le Havre, near Honfleur;
- La Rochelle, linking la Rochelle with île de Ré
- Millau, in Larzac

Germany

On German highways heavy commercial vehicles and vehicle combinations with a permissible total weight of 12 tonnes or more are subject to an electronically collected toll. The system does not require vehicles to slow down or stop, nor does it restrict them to a designated lane.

Under the German toll system, two paying methods exist: the manual log-on, recommended for drivers and companies that seldom use German motorways, and the automatic log-on. Under the manual log-on, the user logs-on for the planned route at one of about 3,500 toll station terminals or over the Internet at www.maut.toll-collect.de. To log-on manually over the Internet, the company must register with Toll Collect in advance. No registration is necessary to log-on at a toll station terminal. Truck drivers can log-on manually at toll station terminals located near motorway access ramps. Terminals marked with the name "Toll Collect" can be found at service areas and filling stations in Germany and neighbouring countries. The driver enters all the relevant vehicle information, departure time, starting point and destination. The toll station terminal then calculates the shortest route within the toll road network. The user can accept this route or choose an alternative one by entering other waypoints. The user then confirms the route, selects the desired payment method, and receives a log-on receipt upon payment. This ticket should be kept in the vehicle.

Under the automatic log-on, a transport company has to register in advance with Toll Collect. It then receives On-board units (OBU), one for each truck. The OBU automatically determines how many kilometres have already been driven on the toll route, calculates the toll based on the vehicle and toll rate information that has been entered, and transmits this information to the Toll Collect computer centre for further processing. For truck drivers, automatic log-on requires the least amount of effort: He is not required to book the route himself. All key data is already stored in the On-Board Unit.

Prices:

The toll fees are based on the number of axles and emissions class of the vehicle. Based on their emissions class, the vehicles are assigned to one of the following categories (A, - F) as follows:

Toll rates per kilometre as of January 1, 2020

Category	Emission class / number of axles[1]	Toll rate
A	**S6, Euro 6**	
	2 axles	0,093€
	3 axles	0,128 €
	4 axles	0,173 €
	5 axles and more	0,187 €
B	**S5, EEV[2] Class 1, Euro 5, EEV Class 1**	
	2 axles	0,104 €
	3 axles	0,139 €
	4 axles	0,184 €
	5 axles and more	0,198 €
C	**S3 with min. PMK[3] 2, S4, Euro 3 with min. PMK**	
	2, Euro 4	0,114 €
	2 axles	0,149 €
	3 axles	0,194 €
	4 axles	0,208 €
	5 axles and more	
D	**S2 with min. PMK 1, S3, Euro 2 with min. PMK 1,**	
	Euro 3	0,140 €
	2 axles	0,181 €
	3 axles	0,226 €
	4 axles	0,240 €
	5 axles and more	
E	**S2, Euro 2**	
	2 axles	0,156 €
	3 axles	0,191 €
	4 axles	0,236 €
	5 axles and more	0,240 €

F	**S1, no emission class, Euro 1, Euro 0**	
	2 axles	0,167 €
	3 axles	0,202 €
	4 axles	0,247 €
	5 axles and more	0,261 €

More information available at:

https://www.ages.de/en/hgv-toll-germany-tariffs.html

https://www.tolltickets.com/en/country/products

www.toll-collect.de

Hungary

In Hungary, the use of toll highways is permitted only if the driver has attached a motorway sticker to their windscreen (the "vignette").

Apart from toll payment with the "Relational Ticket", toll in Hungary can also be recorded and invoiced via an on-board unit. The existing vignette will continue to be valid for vehicles up to 3.5 t with no more than 9 seats and for coaches. Except buses, all trucks over 3.5 t are subject to toll.
6,513 kilometres of road, divided into Motorways, Expressways and National Roads subject to toll.

Toll charges are based on:

- Distance
- Vehicle Type
- Emission Class
- Number of Axels

The new system is called HU-GO, and is mandatory for all vehicles over 3.5 tonnes. You can find further information regarding the parameters of Hungarian toll including rates on www.motorway.hu/Electronic-toll as well as on the www.hu-go.hu portal.

The amount of the fee to be determined (on the toll rates and the toll roads in line with European Union requirements the Government Decree No. 209/2013 (VI. 18.) entered into force on 26 November 2020. Based on the calculation method set out in the Decree, the following distance-based tolls, specified in the table below, will be applicable as of 1 January 2021.

J2 Category: Trucks over 3.5 t GVW – two axles.

J3 Category: Trucks over 3.5 t GVW – three axles.

J4 Category: Trucks over 3.5 t GVW – four or more axels.

Valid from 1 January 2021

	CATEGORY	J2 Category		J3 Category		J4 Category	
	Category Road	Speed Way	Main Road	Speed Way	Main Road	Speed Way	Main Road
Environmental Protection Department	A > EURO 111	50.63	21.53	71.03	37.29	109.95	68.58
	B = EURO 11	59.56	25.33	83.56	43.87	129.35	80.68
	C < EURO 1	68.49	29.13	96.09	50.45	155.22	96.82

The road usage fee of the value added tax which includes gross written premium (EUR / km).

For further information: http://toll-charge.hu/

Italy

In Italy, all highway users have to pay highway fees. These are levied at the toll lanes. Prices depend on the number of axles of the vehicle. Payment can be made by cash, credit cards, prepaid Viacards or by electronic means, using the Telepass. The price of a journey can be easily calculated using the calculation tool on the web page:

http://www.autostrade.it/autostrade/percorso.do.

Moreover, special fees apply to a few tunnels.
These are:

- Mont Blanc (between Italy and France)
- Fréjus (between Italy and France)
- Grand Saint-Bernard (between Italy and Switzerland) - Munt la Schera (between Italy and Switzerland)

Ireland

In Ireland, some roads are toll roads. In the table below, you will find maximum tolls applicable to goods vehicles with a design gross vehicle weight exceeding 3.5 tonnes

There are a number of different toll roads located across the Republic of Ireland with different rates, depending on your vehicle. To get special discounts on certain toll roads, you can sign up for a Toll Tag Account.

These rates are valid from 1st January 2021.

Road segment	2-3 axles	4 or more axles
M1 Motorway (Gormanston to Monasterboice)	EUR 4.80	EUR 6.20
M4 Kinnegad-Enfield-Kilnock Motorway	EUR 5.80	EUR 7.20
M8 Rathcormac/Fermoy Bypass	EUR 4.80	EUR 6.10

On M50 West-Link Toll Bridge, commercial vehicles exceeding 2 tonnes unladen weight and with not more than 2 axles pay EUR 5.30, commercial vehicles exceeding 2 tonnes unladen weight and with no more than 3 axles – EUR 5.80 and commercial vehicles exceeding 2 tonnes unladen weight and with 4 or more axles – EUR 6.40.

Macedonia

In Macedonia, the tolls are levied according travelled sections of the toll gates. Toll fees are required to pay as drivers of motorcycles and cars, as well as truck drivers, trucks and buses. Compared with other countries in Macedonia not need to pay additional fees for passage of bridges and tunnels. If you are going to pass through the Macedonian highway sections, we suggest to read map toll, or the location of toll gates. We hope you find the information contained herein help facilitate and accelerate the passage after the Macedonian highways.

For drivers of vehicles over 3.5 tons of tolling applies the same rules as drivers of motorcycles and passenger vehicles up to 3.5 tonnes. Compared with other countries, however, are not distributed according to the category of vehicle weight, but by the size, ie the length and height of the vehicle. If the vehicle is equipped with a trailer, is to determine the category of vehicle gate length and height including the trailer.

http://www.roads.org.mk/416/toll-rates

Toll payment costs in North Macedonia 2021

section/ vehicle	I	II	III	IV
Kumanovo - Miladinovci	€ 1.5	€ 2.0	€ 3.00	€ 5.00
Skopje - Petrovec	€ 1.0	€ 1.0	€ 2.00	€ 3.00

Petrovec - Veles	€ 1.50	€ 2.50	€ 4.50	€ 6.50
Veles - Gradsko	€ 1.50	€ 2.00	€ 3.50	€ 5.00
Skopje - Miladinovci	€ 1.00	€ 1.00	€ 2.00	€ 3.00
Tetovo - Gostivar	€ 0.50	€ 1.00	€ 1.50	€ 2.00
Skopje - Tetovo	€ 1.00	€ 1.50	€ 2.00	€ 3.50

Vehicle Categories.

category	I	II	III	IV
vehicle	motorcycles and vehicles with height up to 1,3m	vehicles with height up to 1,3m and more than 2 axles	vehicles with height over 1,3m and 2 or 3 axles (vans with trailers, busses)	vehicles with more than 3 axles and height over 1,3m

An extra fee is levied for the use of highways.

Norway

In Norway, the highways and some major roads are toll routes. Details on the fees applicable on different highways are available at

Automatic payment system AutoPASS : https://www.autopass.no/en/payment

If you do not reside in Norway for more than 3 months then you do not take the Onboard unit, simply use the so called AutoPASS Visitors' Payment. Toll payment is then carried through registered credit card, from the first toll gate entrained deposit 300 NOK (1000 NOK for vehicles weighting over 3,5t) and when passing each other gate subtracting a fee (your vehicle will be photographing for documentation).

If the deposit during your stay in Norway is full, it will be necessary to recharge your account.

In case the embedded deposit is exhausted, you will have up to 85 days for the recharge balance to be returned to the bank account.

The toll for stretch Svinesundforbindelsen and Atlanterhavstunnelen must be paid on the spot.

The second option is the use of additional payments (EPC). On the basis that an invoice will be sent to your address for the travelled portions.

For drivers of trucks and buses weighing over 3.5 tonnes pay for toll payment, similar rules as car drivers. The only difference is in the price of tolls individual sections and in the case of Visitors Payment contract in the amount of the deposit, that's for vehicles over 3.5 tons, is 1000 NOK

Special fees are also perceived on:

- the tunnel linking eastern and western Oslo
- entering the city centres of Oslo, Bergen and Trondheim

Poland

There are two systems for collecting tolls in Poland:

1. The open system. These tolls are collected on the motorways from a toll - booth.
2. The closed system. These tolls are collected through the viaTOLL electronic system.

The toll you pay depends on the type of vehicle and the distance travelled. This can make travelling around Poland cheaper than other neighboring countries, which have the vignette system. Only certain sections of the motorways are charged.

The rates for electronic toll roads class A and S or sections on which the charge is collected electronically

| vehicle category | The rate of electronic toll booths 1 km of the national road (in zł) | | | |
| | Class vehicles in the EURO depending on the exhaust emission limits (1) | | | |
	max. EURO 2	EURO 3	EURO 4	min. EURO 5
Motor vehicles with a permissible total weight of (2) above 3.5 tonnes and below 12 t	0.40	0.35	0.28	0.20

	max. EURO 2	EURO 3	EURO 4	min. EURO 5
Motor vehicles with a permissible total weight (2) at least 12 t	0.53	0.46	0.37	0.27
Buses regardless of the maximum permissible weight	0.40	0.35	0.28	0.20

The rates for electronic toll roads and GP class G or sections on which the charge is collected electronically

vehicle category	The rate of electronic toll booths 1 km of the national road (in zł)			
	Class vehicles in the EURO depending on the exhaust emission limits (1)			
	max. EURO 2	EURO 3	EURO 4	min. EURO 5
Motor vehicles with a permissible total weight of (2) above 3.5 tonnes and below 12 t	0.32	0.28	0.22	0.16
Motor vehicles with a permissible total weight (2) at least 12 t	0.42	0.37	0.29	0.21
Buses regardless of the maximum permissible weight	0.32	0.28	0.22	0.16

Portugal

In Portugal, as well as in the neighboring Spain, tolls are collected from drivers of motorcycles, cars and trucks and buses at the toll gates. Toll payment can be made by using prepaid coupons Toll and Toll Card Service,

Another option payment system EasyToll working in cooperation with Credit Card Master Card and Visa. For those who cross the Portuguese highway passes more often ready automatic payment system Via Verde. We hope you find the information contained herein will help facilitate orientation in the prices of tolls in Portugal.

Toll payment methods

On Portuguese motorways toll payment can be made in several ways,

If you cannot pay the exact amount in cash, there are the following systems available, Easy Toll, Toll Card, Toll Service and Via Verde Visitors.
Especially for tourists there is the Toll Card system, which are pre-paid coupons worth 5, 10, 20 and € 40.

For a few selected sections you can also use the system Toll Service, voucher worth € 20 and unlimited 3-day validity.
Another payment option Portuguese toll EasyToll, it is a system in which records the toll roads crossed automatically deducted from a linked credit cards are Visa and Mastercard.
Last of payment systems is an automatic Via Verde, a wireless electronic device allowing the passage of the charging zones without stopping the vehicle at the toll gate

There are two bridges where extra is paid:

- 25 Avril bridge in Lisbon
- Vasco da Gama north of Lisbon

Romania

Anyone driving on the Romanian roads must, according to law, (Government ordinance no. 15/2002 on the introduction of a tax for using the national road network in Romania, and ordinance no. 769/2010 on the approval of Methodological Standards for the toll levied on national road network in Romania) pay a road toll called rovinieta. Its price is set according to the vehicle category (A, B, C, D, E, F, G, H) and the period of validity (1, 7, 30 or 90 days, or 12 months).

Prices of vignettes for Romania for 2021

a) Category A – Cars

1 day   - cannot be purchased for this category;

7 days   – 3 Euros;

30 days – 7 Euros;

90 days – 13 Euros;

12 months – 28 Euros.

b) **Category B** – freight vehicles with weight less than MATW (maximum authorized total weight) less or equal to 3.5 tonnes

1 day - cannot be purchased for this category;

7 days – 6 Euros;

30 days – 16 Euros;

90 days – 36 Euros;

12 months – 96 Euros.

c) **Category C** – Freight vehicles of 3.5 t less than MATW less or equal to 7.5 t

1 day – 4 Euros;

7 days – 16 Euros;

30 days – 32 Euros;

90 days – 92 Euros;

12 months – 320 Euros

d) **Category D** – freight vehicles with 7.5 t less than MATW less than 12.0 t

1 day – 7 Euros;

7 days – 28 Euros;

30 days – 56 Euros;

90 days – 160 Euros;

12 months – 560 Euros.

e) **Category E** – freight vehicles with MATW over or equal to 12.0t, with up to (including) 3 axles

1 day – 9 Euros;

7 days – 36 Euros;

30 days – 72 Euros;

90 days – 206 Euros;

12 months – 720 Euros.

f) **Category F** – freight vehicles with MATW over or equal to 12.0t, with at least (including) 4 axles

1 day – 11 Euros;

7 days – 55 Euros;

30 days – 121 Euros;

90 days – 345 Euros;

12 months – 1.210 Euros.

g) **Category G** – vehicle for the carriage of passengers with more than 9 seats (including driver) and maximum 23 seats

1 day – 2 Euros;

7 days – 20 Euros;

30 days – 52 Euros;

90 days – 120 Euros;

12 months – 320 Euros.

h) **Category H** – vehicles for the carriage of passengers with more than 23 seats (including driver)

1 day – 7 Euros;

7 days – 35 Euros;

30 days – 91 Euros;

90 days – 210 Euros;

12 months – 560 Euros.

Note:

Drivers who do not have a valid Romanian vignette can be subject to fines of up to 4,500 lei.

www.roviniete.ro/en provides you a calculator for Romanian vignettes, in order to find out how much a vignette costs and the possibility of buying it online, payment via: bank card, payment order or payment to bank - BT24 Banca Transilvania or 24 Banking BCR.
Fees are VAT inclusive and delivery to your e-mail address is free!

Slovakia

Driving through toll, ie motorways and primary roads for vehicles over 3.5 tons are charged with the toll system. (There is a different toll system for vehicles under 3.5 tons)

In Slovakia - similar to Czechia - motor vehicles with a gross combined weight of more than 3.5 t are subject to tolls on all motorways and expressways, as well as category 1 roads.

However, sections of category 2 and 3 roads (corresponding to state and federal roads in Germany) are subject to tolls.

Tolls are charged based on kilometres driven and the number of axles, tonnage and emission class.

Tolls are collected through an open system consisting of toll portals, GPS-GNS technology and a hybrid on-board unit that communicates using microwaves and satellite technology. A toll box is mandatory for vehicles with a permitted total weight in excess of 3.5t.

Controls are performed based on DSRC technology.

In Slovakia, all vehicles over 3.5 t of permissible gross weight require the electronic SkyToll OBU for settlement of the toll.

The toll medium for vehicles up to 3,5 t is an electronic vignette. You can find information on the Toll country Slovakia here.

https://web.uta.com/en/solutions/products/toll-solutions-6x/skytoll-obu

The SkyToll OBU is available in two options:

Postpay:
Order your SkyToll OBU directly from UTA. You can then choose to have the device sent to you or you can pick it up at a contact or distribution centre. In this case, the subsequent settlement of Slovakian tolls via UTA is mandatory.

Prepay:

You can load variable credit balance amounts on your SkyToll OBU. The prepay version is available without prior order directly at a contact or distribution centre by presenting the vehicle registration document. Simply present your UTA Full Service Card to purchase as well as to load a credit.

https://www.emyto.sk/en/etoll/toll-rates-and-discounts

Slovenia

Slovenia's road user charging policy is a curious combination of manual tolls for heavy vehicles only (trucks and buses) on main highways and a vignette (time based charge) for light vehicles. The heavy vehicle toll rates are based on distance. Note the heavy vehicle toll includes buses and coaches, not just trucks. Slovenia is, of course, a major transit point between Italy/Austria and Croatia, Hungary, with transit freight (and passenger) traffic growing now Croatia is an EU Member State

Toll classes

R3 (1st toll class)		The vehicles with two or three axles whose maximum permissible weight is over 3,500 kg, and the groups of vehicles with two or three axles whose maximum permissible weight of their powered vehicle is over 3.500 kg.
R4 (2nd toll class)		The vehicles with more than three axles whose maximum permissible weight is over 3,500 kg, and the groups of vehicles with more than three axles whose maximum permissible weight of their powered vehicle is over 3.500 kg.

The toll is to be paid be electronic means by DARS d.d. (DARS Card, DARS Transporter Card or ABC electronic tag) on which EURO emission class E4 for EURO IV vehicles, E5 for EURO V or E6 for EURO EEV and EURO VI vehicles, is paid.

https://www.dars.si/DarsGo/About_DarsGo

Spain

Fee for journeys on motorways in Spain is charged when passing the toll gate.

The price paid for the journey road sections is derived according to the length of time and vehicle category; there is no need to buy a vignette.

In addition to the charges for highway and transit of certain road sections there is a charge for the use of several tunnels.

When driving in Spain, you can use a payment system Via-T which allows the use of toll gates without stopping and discounts according to the monthly spending.

Payment System Via-t

Via-T is a system that enables automatic meter travelled toll sections without having to stop when passing through the toll gate (must slow down to 30 km / h).

Records of the journeys of individual road sections sends the payments to the online system, e-billing and e-receipt. Additional information, including sales offices can be found on viat.es or customer line +34 902 200 320. http://www.tolls.eu/spain

Vehicle category for pricing Spanish motorway sections.

Category	I	II	III
Vehicle	Motorcycles, sidecars, passenger cars and vans with max. four wheels	two- and three-axle trucks and buses, two-axle vehicles with single axle trailer	More than three-axle vehicles, two and three-axle vehicles with more than single axle trailer

https://www.viat.es/descuentos   https://www.tolls.eu/spain#vehicles-over-3-5-t

Switzerland

Vignettes are compulsory in Switzerland for all motor vehicles and trailers up to and including 3.5 t.

Vignettes are compulsory in Switzerland on all national class 1 and 2 roads. There is only the 1-year vignette valid from 1 December of the preceding year until 31 January of the following year, i.e. 14 months.

From December 1st, new stickers will be available every year. They are valid for 14 months. The stickers bought in December 2020 are therefore valid until the end of January 2022. The sticker will be delivered within 5 working days after ordering (in high season within 10 working days).

The journey through the following tunnels is not included in the vignette price: Great St. Bernhard Tunnel and Munt la Schera. A special toll fee must be paid directly for this.

A valid undamaged vignette affixed on an untinted area of the windscreen interior is the only acceptable substantiation that the toll has been duly paid.

Using motorways and expressways without a valid vignette properly affixed on the vehicle is an offence against the Public Highways Act and is punishable with cash fines of at least 200 Franks.

Vehicles of a total weight above 3.5 t and used for commercial goods traffic are subject to a performance-related heavy vehicle fee (HVF).

For vehicles licensed abroad the charge is levied by using an ID card and a special HVC clearance terminal. On the first entry to Switzerland/Principality of Liechtenstein, the HVC relevant data of the vehicles are entered into the central IT system.

The driver receives a vehicle-specific ID card. At each entry, he enters the card into the clearance terminal and so calls up the saved data.

Then he enters by hand the current mileage, the details of the trailer and the method of payment (petrol card, HVC account or cash).

He receives a receipt in duplicate which he completes on exit with the current mileage and his signature. Persons paying in cash must go to the customs office and pay an additional processing fee of CHF 10.-. Customs run random checks on the data declared on entry and exit.

HVC clearance terminals may be found at almost all the border crossings. Easy instructions which are displayed on the screen and available in many languages, allow the driver to get along without help.

All foreign lorries and articulated lorries with a maximum permitted total weight of more than 3,5 tons are duly registered for taxation on the first entry to Switzerland.

Foreign drivers may fit a recording device (on-board unit) on their own accord. Besides correct use of the device, the installation is bound to the following conditions:

- Opening of an HVC account at the Directorate General of Customs
- Evidence of sufficient security
- Installation of the on-board unit at their own expense at an authorized garage (reception point) in Switzerland or the Principality of Liechtenstein.

Declaration data are read on every exit (communication via radio beacon) and the fee is billed monthly.

https://www.tolls.eu/switzerland#vehicles-over-3-5-t

Section D4 Income and Corporate Taxation

This section is concerned with income tax paid by individuals who may be employees or self-employed persons and corporate taxation levied on the profits of limited liability companies.

Income Tax

Employed individuals and self-employed sole traders and partners in a partnership business are liable to pay income tax based on their earnings, but subject to certain minimum earnings concessions and various personal allowances.

Tax Schedules

Income is assessed according to source "schedule" allocated by HRMC. Broadly, there are four schedules:

- Schedule A, which applies to income from land and property (applicable to individuals and companies)
- Schedule D, which applies to income/profits from trade or a profession, interest on savings/investments, rents and commissions (applies to both individuals and companies)
- Schedule E, which applies to wages and salaries from employment
- Schedule F, which applies to dividends and the like paid to shareholders by a UK company

Payment of Income Tax

Payment methods vary by the manner in which the tax was deducted, namely Pay As You Earn (PAYE), and payment of tax by self-employed persons on a twice-yearly basis calculated on their annual income.

PAYE

A relevant amount of income tax determined by the tax code and the National Insurance contribution is deducted from the gross earnings of employees working for a wage or salary. The employer pays these monies to HMRC monthly. Personal allowances to offset the tax due include personal allowance for all individuals which may vary according to circumstances (for example single-child-one-parent families, blind person allowance, widow's bereavement allowance, medical insurance relief, life assurance relief).

Tax for the Self-Employed

Self-employed people are taxed under a "self-assessment" system on an earnings basis. They must maintain income and expenditure records and make an annual HMRC return reflecting this information. Tax due is payable in January and July.

After the first year in business two payments on account towards the annual tax bill are due on 31 January and 31 July each year with a final payment of any balance due payable the following 31 January. In effect then, in the second year of business the self-employed individual pays one and half years' worth of tax.

Trading Accounts for the Self-Employed

The self-employed are required to compile a complete and accurate account of income received in a tax year and are responsible for the accuracy of the information even if it is assembled by an accountant.

The report must include two parts: a profit and loss or trading account showing income and expenditure, and a balance sheet showing the assets and liabilities of the business.

For very small businesses, those below £15,000 annual income before deduction of expenses, a simple three-line return will suffice (i.e. turnover, less expenses, equals net profit).

Expenses and Allowances for the Self-Employed

The only business expenses that may be used to offset income to determine gross profit are those related to business activities. Expenses not allowed include:

- personal and domestic
- entertaining and hospitality
- gifts and donations, fines and penalties
- debts other than bad debts
- life insurance and pension premiums on the business proprietor

Employee Benefits

Most benefits in kind provided to an employee in consequence of his employment are taxable. The general rule (subject to many exceptions) is that for employees who are company directors or whose annual income and benefits are more than £8,500, the benefit is assessable for an amount equal to the cost to the employer. For other employees, fringe benefits are not usually assessed. Taxable benefits include:

- provision of accommodation
- gifts of assets and gift vouchers
- loans

- provision of staff
- childcare facilities
- company car/van and fuel
- luncheon vouchers
- club memberships
- use of mobile phones
- share options
- travel

Certain benefits can be provided free of tax including:

- Canteen facilities, provided the same facilities are available to all employees.
- Car parking at or near the place of work.
- Chauffeur, provided he is only used on company business.
- Childcare facilities provided by the employer and which comply with local authority regulations.
- Clothes such as uniforms, safety clothing or bearing the company logo.
- Company car, covering use of a pool car only for company business.
- Education, full-time, but only where it meets certain criteria.
- Entertainment incidental to the employment.
- Gift, but only if unrelated to employment or not from the employer and not worth more than £150 a year.
- Housing – necessary to perform duty properly, customary for that employment, necessary for security, or free board for agricultural workers.
- Hotel bills, but only necessary food and accommodation (£5 a day personal expenses in the UK and £10 overseas).
- Laundry where the clothing qualifies for tax relief.
- Liability cover or payment, but not for a criminal offence.
- Long service awards for at least 20 years and not more than £50 per year of service.
- Luncheon vouchers, but not if worth more than 15p per working day.
- Medical treatment incurred overseas or for a routine check-up.
- Mobile telephone, but not for personal calls.
- Outplacement counselling for an employee made redundant.
- Parties and functions provided cost does not exceed £150 per person.
- Pension contributions to an approved scheme.
- Relocation up to £8,000.
- Scholarships first awarded before 1983.
- Security measures necessary to protect an employee or his family (but not a vehicle or accommodation).
- Sports facilities provided by an employer.
- Training costs related to an employee's work.
- Training expenses for courses in the UK related to work and lasting four weeks or more.
- Travel and subsistence made in the course of work.

Tax Records

Tax records including all relevant receipts must be maintain for five years from 31 January in the year following that to which the return relates. (Practically, that means six years' of data.)

Corporation Tax

UK-based companies pay corporation or corporate tax based on their annual trading profits and capital gains determined from the company's annual accounts showing sales and purchases. By deducting one from the other the gross profit is calculated. Income may include overseas trading, investment income and dividends received. Purchases/expenditure may include normal business expenses, capital allowances, charitable covenants and patent royalties.

At Summer Budget 2015, the government announced a reduction in the Corporation Tax rate from 20% to 19% for the Financial Years beginning 1 April 2017, 1 April 2018 and 1 April 2019, with a further reduction from 19% to 18% for the Financial Year beginning 1 April 2020.

This measure supports the government's objective of a more competitive corporate tax system to provide the right conditions for business investment and growth.

The measure reduces the Corporation Tax main rate to 17% for the Financial Year beginning 1 April 2020.

This is an additional 1% cut on top of the previously announced CT main rate cuts which reduced the CT main rate to 18% from 1 April 2020

http://alturl.com/pdgzq

Small Company Corporation Tax

Marginal relief eases the transition from the starting rate to the small companies' rate for companies with profits between £10,000 and £50,000. The percentage used in the calculation of this marginal relief will be 17%. Marginal relief also applies to companies with profits between £300,000 and £1,500,000, The percentage being 30%. The fraction used in the calculation of this marginal relief will be 11/400.

Double Taxation

When the same income and gains are taxable in more than one country double taxation occurs. Double taxation relief is given by:

- Means of a double tax treaty with the country concerned, whereby income is exempt from tax in one country and a credit granted for foreign taxes paid on other income.

- Allowing the foreign tax paid as a credit against the total UK tax liability.
- The foreign tax being considered as a deductible expense in calculating the business profits chargeable to tax (for example the foreign tax being treated like an ordinary business expense).

Double tax treaties take precedence over UK domestic legislation where relief is due. In most cases, the full amount of income, including income from the overseas territory, is calculated for income tax liability for the tax year. The overseas tax paid on the relevant income is then offset as a credit against the total liability to income tax. The credit is limited to the income tax liability on the income that has been subject to overseas tax. There is no relief available for any excess foreign tax paid. Any unrelieved foreign tax cannot be carried forward or back. Generally, only direct foreign taxes are taken into account for the purposes of double tax relief.

National Insurance

Most people who work pay National Insurance contributions in one of five classes: employee, self-employed person, non-employed person or employer. Depending on his status, a person may have to pay more than one class of contribution at the same time. Some contributions count towards benefits such as incapacity benefit and retirement pension.

Self-employed people are liable to pay two classes of contributions: Class 2 and Class 4, which are paid on profits and gains at, or above, a set level.

Class 2 Contributions

Class 2 contributions are a flat rate payment collected by the Contributions Agency from self-employed persons or more than16 years but who are under pension age

Payment is made in arrears either by quarterly bill every 13 weeks or by direct debit every month.

These contributions do not count for Jobseeker's Allowance but they do count for incapacity benefit, retirement pension, widow's benefit and maternity allowance.

Class 4 Contributions

Class 4 contributions are payable when an individual's profits exceed a certain amount. These contributions may have to be paid in addition to Class 2 contributions. They are based on a percentage of annual profits between a lower and upper profit level. The levels are set each year by the Chancellor in the Budget.

Class 4 contributions are normally assessed and collected by HMRC together with Schedule D tax, based on the individual's profit assessment. As with tax, if payment becomes overdue, interest may have to be paid. These contributions do not entitle the payee to any benefit, but they do help to share the cost of funding the benefits paid to all self-employed people.

Section E1 E2 E3 E4 E5 E6 E7 Payment Systems and Financial Management

Business success depends on an organised system for dealing with and tracking payments and expenses, calculating revenue and profit, and arranging credit as needed. The books are normally balanced annually for the purpose of preparing proper financial statements that reflect the year's activities for tax purposes and that allow owners, shareholders, and other interested parties to evaluate business performance and the so called "bottom line" or the current value of the business. Using this information, the business can attract potential investors and allow financial institutions to evaluate its credit worthiness for loans.

Limited liability companies are legally required to have their annual accounts independently audited. All businesses are required to submit a return of income or profit to HMRC for tax assessment purposes. In the case of a large organisation, annual accounts are made up of multiple documents but we will look at two in particular, the profit and loss (or trading) account and the balance sheet. These documents are found in the accounts of businesses of all size.

Payment Methods

Businesses use a variety of methods for payment of accounts and expenses. While it is not always convenient or safe to deal in cash, the method does have merit under certain circumstances.

Cash

While cash is the oldest and most simple means of payment, and a constraint against buying what you cannot afford, it has some disadvantages. One of these would be the need to use cash received in respect of work done or goods sold, which could lead to shortcomings in the accounting system. Cash dealings also mean repeated bank visits for withdrawals and the inherent risk of loss or theft when handling large sums. A possible advantage afforded is the ability to negotiate discounts based on immediate cash payments, although the practice of offering a lower price if cash is paid is illegal. Such instances are reflective of the fact that the recipient may not be meeting his income tax responsibilities and is also avoiding VAT registration.

Cheques

The use of cheques is contingent on having a current bank account with sufficient funds (or an agreed overdraft arrangement). Cheques eliminate the risk and inconvenience of carrying large amounts of cash. The cheque guarantee card scheme ended on the 30 June 2011 – your debit card will work as it always has.

Cheques normally clear within three working days, giving purchasers a small margin of credit between making the purchase and seeing the amount deducted from their account.

Credit/Debit Cards

Credit cards give cardholders a line of credit on which to draw to make purchases. When the amount owed is not repaid in a given billing period (normally 4 to 6 weeks), interest accrues on the outstanding balance. The interest rate will be higher compared to other forms of credit. Exceeded the account's limit and / or failing to make regular payments can lead to revocation of the card with penalties applied.

There is an advantage of using credit cards for certain purchases because the company issuing the card provides a degree of insurance or guarantee should the purchased item not perform as expected.

Debit cards are issued by banks as an alternative to cheques. The amount of the purchase is taken directly from the account with no credit attached. The withdrawal is immediate with no waiting period attached.

Charge Cards

Charge cards are a specific form of credit card issued to a customer by a supplier with the balance payable in full when the statement is presented. Charge cards are not usually valid with another supplier and they do not normally offer extended credit. Abnormally high interest rates and penalties apply when the balance is not paid. An example of a charge card would be the "store cards" issued by High Street retailers.

Promissory Notes

Promissory notes simply contain a promise to pay a person or firm a specified amount of money on a date stipulated or on demand. The notes are similar to cheques but carry more information and may, for example, refer to the transaction details.

Bills of Exchange

Bills of exchange are unconditional written orders from one person to another to pay a specified amount within a given time period, usually 60 to 90 days or on sight. They are used in international trade to pay for goods or services. Due to the bill of exchange security of payment when due, the holder may be able to raise credit on the bill.

Debit Systems

In a direct debit service the account holder authorises the bank to pay amounts directly from his account. Normally, these are made on a regular basis such as monthly, quarterly, annually or upon application by the account holder's debtors for obligations such as for mortgage payments or leasing repayments. The service saves the account holder the trouble of writing cheques and guards against a missed or late payment.

Credit Transfer

In a credit transfer arrangement, money is moved within the banking system. Many firms now pay their employees by this method, transferring their salary or wages directly into the employees' bank account. The process saves the firm from handling cash and writing cheques while making payment faster for the recipient.

Credit and Borrowing

Bank Loans

In granting loans, banks require security in the form of deposits, personal guarantees, and charges over freehold property or the lodgement of insurance policies with a guaranteed surrender value, or debentures. Such loans are usually sought to establish a new business or to finance an expansion of an existing business. Repayments are made at regular intervals for a fixed period of time. Unlike overdrafts, such loans are not subject to recall on short notice but are mid to long-term in duration.

Overdrafts

Overdrafts are provided by banks for short-term use in daily operations to overcome fluctuating cash flow problems. They are not suitable long-term capital requirements being subject to recall at short notice if, for instance, the Government or the Bank of England restricts credit. Overdraft usage is not recommended because it reduces the availability of ready cash for immediate needs such as weekly wages, fuel bills, or deliveries of supplies. Overdrafts facilities require some form of security or at least the surety of a substantial inflow of funds in a short time.

Documentary Credit

A documentary (letter of) credit is an agreement under which the importer's bank agrees to pay the exporter via his own, or a nominated bank, in his home country. Payment is tied to pre-established conditions set out in the letter of credit being met by the exporter. Letters of credit are useful where the seller does not know the buyer and cannot conclusively establish his ability to pay.

Guarantee Deposits

In guarantee deposits the buyer pays in advance for the goods by a guaranteed bank deposit, released to the seller when the goods are received.

Mortgages

A mortgage is a loan to the purchaser of a property in which the property secures the loan. If the buyer defaults, the lender takes legal charge on the property and sells it to realise the outstanding debt. In the context of small haulage businesses, an operator might raise a mortgage on his home to provide business finance and would therefore face the loss of the home in the event of a business failure.

Leases

In a lease agreement, use of a property is obtained without purchase, usually on a long-term basis. A provision is often included whereby the lease can be transferred to another lessee with a premium charged. Such an agreement is a legal document containing terms and conditions relative to the use and potentially to the maintenance of the property, as well as any exclusions on occupancy or use (called covenants). Prematurely opting out of a lease agreement may prove difficult due to penalty and forfeiture clauses, unless the remaining term of the lease can be sold (with the leaser's agreement) to another lessee.

Rents

Whereas leases apply to long-term arrangements, a rent is a short-term tenancy with payment due generally on a monthly basis in the form of rent. Such payments may be made in cash, by cheque, or be a direct debit arrangement through the bank. Termination is usually given to the landlord by a predetermined period of notice.

Factoring

The factoring of sales invoices is one means of short-term finance in instances of poor cash flow. Factoring companies pay cash against invoices deemed acceptable with a percentage of the face value deducted in fees. The prompt payment of invoices improves cash flow and speeds the receipt of payment but at a reduced amount that is often substantial. Firms on small profit margins, like haulage operations, will not find this an acceptable venue because the factors' commission eliminates the profit margin on each invoice.

Hire Purchase and Leasing

Hire purchase and leasing are long-term methods of financing for the acquisition of specific assets such as motor vehicles, workshop equipment or office machines.
In hire purchase, the finance house lends the necessary funds, the borrower buys the item and repays the loan with interest over an agreed upon period at which time the asset belongs to the borrower. (During the period of repayment he also has title to the goods.)
In leasing, the lessor provides the fund and retains ownership title to the goods. The lessee has their full use during a given period but does not become the owner. The

arrangement has the advantage of making essential equipment obtainable with a minimum of capital outlay. Heretofore, the item has not appeared on the balance sheet as an asset or as an outstanding debt. (Consequently this method was referred to as "off- balance sheet financing".) Under the new accounting rules, however, this will change so that the leased items will appear on balance sheets and trading accounts, thus providing a more accurate picture of the firm's leased assets and commitments.

Other Funds

Finance to establish and to run a business can be obtained from a number of sources each with its own advantages and disadvantages.

Proprietor's and Shareholder Funds

The founding proprietor of a new business usually puts up a portion of his own capital, which may be augmented by business loans and funds from other sources. In limited liability companies, the initial capital comes from shareholders, an amount that can also be increased by funds from other sources. Banks and other institutions regularly invest in new concerns with good ideas and sound prospects. These original funds are considered long-term investments.

Retained Profits

Retained profits normally fund operations and expansion in an established business. These are the profits held over from a previous successful year or years that have not been retained in the business or distributed to shareholders. Although an ideal method, retained profits in times of recession or during the business' formative years may be insufficient, so recourse to other sources becomes necessary.

Debentures

Debentures, also called loan stock, are long-term loans secured against the assets of the business by individuals or investment firms. Such loans are repayable with agreed upon fixed interest after a specified period. Frequently, the issue of a debenture is tied in with a charge on all or part of the firm's fixed assets. If the company collapses, debenture holders take priority over normal creditors and shareholders but not over statutory claimants (HRMC, includes VAT, the DSS) in the disposal of assets or any share of remaining funds. Invariably, however, they lose their investment.

Investment Funds

A business short of capital to meet development or expansion plans, to obtain more extensive premises, to purchase or to replace equipment may seek assistance from merchant banks, investment groups, the ICFC (Industrial and Commercial Finance Corporation) and the 3is company as well as from individual investors. The investor usually seeks a share of the equity in the business in exchange for the provision of long-term or venture capital. This means that the original owners have to surrender part of both their holdings in and control of the business.

<u>Use of Funds</u>

The merits of financial sources should be weighed against the use for the money. Raising capital from shareholders and surrendering partial equity should not be considered to meet short-term demands which can be addressed by short-term borrowing and overdrafts. Such measures do not represent loss of equity nor do they tie up valuable securities such as legal charges on freehold property. On the other hand, short-term borrowing should not be used for major capital projects or long-term development because this method reduces the availability of ready funds to meet urgent or unexpected short-term needs. Careful financial planning is an essential and vital management skill.

Balance Sheet and Assets

<u>Balance Sheet</u>

The cumulative worth of a business at a given point in time, for instance the end of the financial year, is reflected on a balance sheet showing the values of fixed and current assets, including buildings, land, equipment, bank deposits, debts, the value of stock on hand (in a haulage firm: diesel in a bulk tank, spares and tyres in the workshop stores as well as stationery in the cupboard) and liabilities including tax owed to HMRC, amounts due to creditors, outstanding loans and other debts. The balance sheet entries are in two columns, one for assets plus any trading profits and one for liabilities and any trading losses. Both sides of the balance sheet are totalled and one figure is deducted from the other to show a plus or minus balance. That figure is the so-called "bottom line", the value of the business.

A simple balance sheet may appear as follows:

Fixed Assets	Current Liabilities
Freehold premises	Mortgage
Motor vehicles	Accounts payable (creditors)
Plant and equipment	Hire purchase repayments
Fixtures and fittings	Bank loan repayable
	Bank overdraft
	Tax liability

(It should be noted that not all of these items would necessarily appear on a particular balance sheet. For example, there would not be both a trading profit and a loss figure and a firm may not have cash in the bank and an overdraft.)

Assets

Understanding the role of assets in a business is contingent upon understanding the difference between fixed and current assets.

The property and equipment owned by a business that represent a value on the balance sheet but cannot be readily converted to cash are fixed assets. They may include property owned by the business, motor vehicles, mobile and fixed plant and equipment, tools, office equipment and furniture, and building fixtures and fittings.

Cash in the business bank account, petty cash in the office, the accounts receivable, and any stocks of good that could be quickly sold for cash are current assets.

To arrive at a determination of net current assets take the value of current assets less current liabilities or debts owed. Once a firm has paid all its debts, what it has left in credit bank balances, cash in hand, and stocks that could be sold are its net current assets. When current liabilities exceed current assets a business is, in effect, insolvent and should cease trading.

Liabilities

Liabilities are debts owed by a business to suppliers, banks or any other provider of funds. As long as a business has sufficient covering assets, liabilities are not a problem for a business. When a business cannot meet its liabilities, it is said to be insolvent. To calculate the solvency of a business add the current liabilities and deduct the current assets to show a positive or negative balance. (A strong asset base and a good order book do not protect a business from cash flow problems that will leave it unable to cover its liabilities.)

Debtors and Creditors

- Debtors are people, firms or organisations that money to a company. They show on the balance sheet as current assets.

- Creditors are people, firms or organisations including banks and financial institutions to which a company owes money. They show on the balance sheet as current liabilities.

Clearly understanding the difference is extremely important for exam purposes. Ideally, the value of debtors should be greater than that of creditors.

Legal Responsibilities

Limited liability companies must have their annual accounts professionally audited and copies of the profit and loss account and balance sheet provided to shareholders. Copies are also submitted to the Registrar of Companies (at Companies House), where they are retained on file and are available for inspection by any person wishing to see them for a small statutory fee.

Non-limited, sole proprietorships and partnership businesses are not required to have annual audits, but they must prepare satisfactory annual financial records and submit a statement of income to HMRC for tax assessment purposes.

Profit and Loss Accounts

The profit and loss (or trading) account is comprised of two major sections. Payments received for work done or goods supplied is shown on one side. This is also known as sales, sales turnover, turnover or revenue and is always a single figure. The other side lists all the business expenditures for such things as purchase of materials, administrative and operating costs, and salaries. These items are normally broken down into individual headings.

Balancing both sides indicates either a trading profit (revenue exceeded costs) or a trading loss (costs exceeded revenue). These are gross not true figures since factors such as depreciation and other allowances can significantly alter the situation. Still gross profit or loss gives a good indication of business performance that should be carefully interpreted by the business manager to assess how the operation stands financially and the likelihood of future success.

Two particular points should be considered in this analysis. First, fluctuations in business expenditure items (such as local authority rates or rents on premises, fuel prices, or wages) appear and have a direct affect on this account – not elsewhere. Second, there are a number of things that cannot be established by looking at this account:

- debtors and creditors
- business asset values
- bank overdrafts
- the value of shareholder funds
- other liabilities

These items must be determined from an analysis of the balance sheet.

Profitability and Financial Ratios

While most businesses exist to turn a profit, there are others whose primary motive is to provide public services or to perform charitable functions. In such instances, the goal becomes breaking even (income matches expenses) or achieving a surplus (income exceeds expenses).

Those individuals with an interest in the viability of a business are most interested in assessing profitability, for instance the owner, the firm's bank and other lenders.

Ratios For Assessing Financial Performance

A number of basic and simple calculations are used to quickly assess business performance. The important ones include:

Working Capital Ratio

Also known as the "liquidity ratio" or "acid test", this calculation indicates how readily a business could settle its liabilities.

liquid working capital (assets)   =   liquidity/working capital ratio
current liabilities

Current Ratio

While basically the same as the working capital, this calculation shows current assets in relationship to current liabilities.

current assets   =   current ratio
current liabilities

The ideal result will be at least 2:1 - twice as many assets as liabilities. A ratio of 1:1 (equal assets and liabilities) is acceptable but not good, while less spells problems. A higher figure would indicate a surfeit of funds which should be placed on deposit to earn interest or should be used for other investment purposes.

Return on Capital

This calculation measures whether sufficient profit is being made in relationship to the capital invested in the business.

net profit   =   x 100 = x%
capital employed

Example: (add pound symbol below)

£30,000   x   100 = 10%
£300,000

Working Capital

Working capital is the money a business uses daily to pay suppliers, meet staff wages, and pay office rent and bills (for example heating, lighting, and telephone bills). Working capital enables a business to function and includes money in the bank, cash on hand and the value of debtors' invoices, less anything owed to creditors. Thus, working capital is the excess of current assets over current liabilities.

Total Capital Employed

Total capital employed is all the money employed in a business. This includes the original investment, which may have been spent on fixed assets (land and buildings, equipment and vehicles) and current assets such as cash in the bank and other reserves. Trading or financial performance is assessed against the total capital employed to determine performance in the form of return on that capital.

Cash Flow

Cash flow is one of the most vital elements of business management. When large firms are slow to pay large outstanding debts, small firms suffer severe problems from a lack of available funds to meet their immediate needs. Such problems can quickly result in closure or liquidation of a business even when it has a good client basis and generates annual profits.

Budgeting or planning finances so as to ensure regular cash flow is important. This involves assessing:

- the levels of revenue to be invoiced
- the frequency of probably payment receipt
- expenditures over the same period

If anticipated expenditures are greater than anticipated payments, plans must be made to cover the shortfall. These could include measures to:

- ensure faster payments
- obtain longer periods of credit with suppliers
- obtain bank overdraft arrangements to cover the shortfall

Net cash flow is the difference between cash received and cash paid out on a daily or weekly basis (or over longer periods).

Cash-flow forecasting ensures the availability of cash to meet future needs. When a business seeks overdraft arrangements, the bank manager may want to see a cash-flow forecast to indicate:

- the levels of overdraft needed
- when it is needed
- over what period of time it will be required

Some banks provide blank forms as worksheets on which to calculate cash-flow projections. Such assessments serve as a guide to the business owner about the sources of his revenue and the periods in which he can afford to make expenditure. By knowing the months of the year cash flow may be deficient, the businessman has the opportunity to consider ways rearranging work to overcome short falls.

Budgets

A budget of any kind is a financial plan for the future. While a budget is primarily financial, it must also include an operational plan to earn the required revenue at a calculated cost. Basically, a haulier would need to know how far and how long his vehicles must drive in a year taking into consideration the cost of fuel, maintenance and the drivers' pay (expenditure budget) against the revenue the truck would generate (revenue budget).

For projects requiring new equipment or facilities, a capital expenditure budget is required which weighs the capital expenditure or investment against the potential earnings. A cash-flow budget reflects monthly projected income from issued invoices and scheduled haulage and projected routine expenditure as well as ad hoc (one-off) purchases (for instance vehicle parts or repairs). The difference each month between cash due to be received and payments due to be made indicates whether existing cash resources are sufficient or whether an overdraft will be needed (and if so, for what amount and duration).

Purchasing and Stock Control

Expenditure control is important in any business but particularly so in transport. It is not uncommon for staff to indiscriminately purchase spare parts and to accumulate excessive stocks of incorrect and redundant components. This means that business capital is tied up and not available for immediate day-to-day commitments. Cash resources are reduced, and unless the stock can be sold quickly at a fair price, over-stocking can create liquidity problems in the event of urgent demands. To avoid such instances purchasing and stock control systems are required and should address:

- Placing limits on the value or volume of parts individuals purchase.
- Establishing expenditure budgets not to be exceeded without authority.
- Determining the best time to buy relative to cash flow and market forces (lower prices or discounts).
- Systematically recording purchases and issues.
- Taking regular inventory to make sure stock holdings agree with records.
- Analysing stock and examining requisition notes to ensure correct stock levels to demand (slow-moving and fast-moving items).
- Checking on suppliers' prices and discount structures to channel purchasing to the most economic supply sources and those maximum obtainable discounts.
- Returning obsolete and redundant stocks and surplus items for credit as soon as possible.
- Reviewing supply invoices for correct prices and applicable credits.

Assessing current stock levels from records is important (as in the case of bulk diesel fuel storage facility) and this is done by:

Opening stock or balance	+	Deliveries or purchases	-	Issues or sales	= Current Stock

Costs and Depreciation

Calculate vehicle operating costs and road haulage rates, understanding accounting paperwork, and dealing with payments are important attributes for running a haulage business.

Vehicle Costing

Determining in advance the cost of owning and operating commercial vehicles allows for the establishment of appropriate fees and gives the owner the ability to ascertain whether a particular job can be completed in such a way as to provide a margin for profit.

In own-account transport operations where profit is not the goal, costing is still necessary to determine if vehicles are operated efficiently and within budgeted financial limits.

Methods of Costing

Vehicle costing involves a number of separate elements. Various costs can be further identified as

- direct costs - directly attributable to the running of the vehicle such as fuel, maintenance, licenses and insurance
- indirect costs - those related to the operation of the haulage business such as office rent, heating and lighting costs, telephone charges, and bank charges

Understanding and differentiating between these two cost types is important.

Standing or Fixed Costs

Standing or fixed costs are incurred from the time of purchasing a vehicle regardless of how much the vehicle is used. These costs are usually calculated annually and include:

Licenses	Vehicle excise license (VED) and "O" license.
Insurance	Compulsory third party plus additional cover.
Wages	Drivers' wages plus costs of employment (for instance National Insurance and pension).
Rents and rates	A proportion of the costs attached to providing land for vehicle parking (this could be dealt with as an overhead cost item).

Interest on capital   Provision for a return on the capital invested in the vehicle on the basis that had the money been invested elsewhere it would have earned a return.

Depreciation   Provision for a reserve of capital to be built up from the vehicle earnings to pay for its eventual replacement. Usually calculated on a straight-line or on a reducing balance basis.

Depreciation

Straight-line depreciation over a fixed period of time (calculation made only once when vehicle is purchased):

$$\frac{\text{vehicle original cost - tyres - residual value}}{\text{anticipate life (years)}} = \text{£ x depreciation per annum}$$

To calculate depreciation by the reducing balance method, the amount to be depreciated is reduced by a chosen yearly percentage. If the vehicle is expected to have a life of five years, the figure can be reduced by 20 percent the first year with the balance carried forward and reduced by 20 percent each year for a progressively lower depreciation figure.

In theory, the early years of depreciation should coincide with low maintenance costs and the lower figure with the higher maintenance and downtime costs later on.

Example of calculation:
Year 1	£40,000 x 20 % = £8,000 = £32,000
Year 2	£32,000 x 20 % = £6,400 = £25,600
Year 3	£25,600 x 20 % = £5,120 = £20,480
Year 4	£20,480 x 20 % = £4,096 = £16,384
Year 5	£16,384 x 20 % = £3,276 = £13,108

So, at the end of the fifth year the vehicle has a "written down" value is £13,108.

According to the current cost accounting method, the depreciation calculation would need to be made annually during vehicle life, often more frequently. On each occasion, the current new price for the vehicle would be used instead of the original invoice amount in the straight-line calculation as shown above.

Running or Variable Costs

The direct costs incurred operating a vehicle is usually calculated on a pence per mile/km basis, including the following items:

Fuel	fuel consumed at x pence per mile/km
Tyres	cost of tyre usage; divide tyre costs by their life in miles/km to give a cost in pence per mil e/km
Maintenance	cost of maintaining the vehicle including regular servicing, safety inspections, oil changes, unscheduled repairs, breakdowns, and the annual test

Given the fact that most heavy goods vehicles are now outfitted with tachographs that indicate distance in kilometres only, and that most fuel pumps record litres only, fuel consumption figures may be increasingly referred to on a km/litre basis.

Overheads or Establishment Costs

Overhead or establishment costs are the indirect costs of operating the business calculated annually. They may include expenses relative to management and administration, workshop operation, heat and light expenses, telephone, postage, salaries, and company cars among others. Each expenditure item, with its accompanying receipt, must be recorded to produce an accurate reflection of the costs of running those aspects of the business not directly associated with the vehicles. Missed items lead to distorted cost calculations and incorrect quoting of haulage rates as well as to the production of inaccurate trading accounts.

Total Operating Costs

Total operating costs incorporate standing costs, running costs and overheads combined by calculating each item into a common denominator of time or mileage (km) to give a price per week, per day, per hour or per mile/km. These costs vary with the distances run by the vehicle. To understand the relationship of these items consider that:

- less miles/kms = higher cost per mile/km with fixed costs spread over fewer miles/kms
- more miles/kms = a reduced overall cost per mile

Marginal Costs

After the fixed and overhead costs are recovered, the remaining costs are those described as "marginal". For example, once a vehicle route has been calculated an extra included delivery would add only the marginal costs of extra time, fuel, and vehicle wear.

Profit

With a profit margin added to the total operating cost, this is the amount a haulier needs to obtain to operate his vehicles on a profitable basis. A figure of 25 percent is a useful gross margin to add.

Calculation of Haulage Rates

While many hauliers have no choice but to accept customer quoted rates, working out the cost of the operation by determining required time, mileage and other factors, plus the addition of a profit margin is an important check to make sure the rates quoted are fair for the proposed job.

To assess rates, calculate the operating cost of the type of vehicle required for the job and add a margin for profit. The resulting figure can be converted into an appropriate unit price to suit a customer's requirements. Examples might be rate per day, per hour, per load, per ton, per pallet, per cubic foot, or per litre. Rate schedules can be calculated by mileage/kilometres with progressively increasing amounts in radial distances or by tonnage starting with "up to one ton" and increasing to the price of a full load.

Financial Considerations

Exchange Rates

International transport and export of goods take on unique financial aspects due to increased direct costs and to the constantly shifting rates of currency exchange. The effect of such fluctuations can be considerable especially where foreign currencies rise in value against the pound sterling. Hauliers should beware quoting prices too far in advance as a consequence.

- "Strong" pound sterling - reduces the operator's costs. He gets more value in foreign currencies for his one-pound sterling.
- "Weak" pound sterling - results in higher direct operating costs outside Britain, especially for fuel and driver expenses. He gets less value in foreign currencies in exchange for his one-pound sterling.

European Currency Units (EUROS)

The introduction of the European Currency Unit, the euro, in connection with the Single European Market, smoothes out the wide variations in individual national currencies for inter-EU trade. Haulage rates can be quoted in Euros, the daily value of which appears in the financial press.

Costs involved in International Haulage

The international haulier confronts many additional costs including:

- The need for vehicles that meet the TIR specification or Community Transit requirements.
- The costs of employing staff experienced in international operations.
- The cost of preparing documents such as carnets and consignment notes.
- Additional insurance costs for vehicles.
- Permits.
- Other fiscal charges.
- Cross-Channel ferry fares.
- Taxes, tolls and dues in foreign countries.
- Communication.
- Driver expenses for food, accommodation, general expenses and cash for on-the-spot fines and "gratuities".
- The higher costs incurred in the event of vehicle breakdown.
- Insurance costs for CMR liability, green card, drivers' medical/accident cover and bail bonds.

- Drivers' extra costs for passport, international driving license (where necessary) and visas.

Payment and Collection of Revenue

In transport operations, drivers carry consignment and receipt notes with collection and delivery instructions and other relevant information. The consignee signs the receipt copy to acknowledge the safe delivery of the goods. The documents also assist in pricing the job according to the type of goods, their weight or volume, vehicle used, distance covered, and waiting time among others.

When the price has been calculated, an invoice can be sent to the customer identifying the job and stating the price plus VAT as appropriate. A copy of the receipt may be enclosed to prove delivery (POD) or kept for the carrier's future reference. A statement of the account can be sent subsequent to the invoice on which the customer will base payment. (Some customers pay on receipt of invoice while others wait for a statement.)

Large firms, government departments, and other authorities commonly pay their suppliers by credit transfer which places the amount owed directly into the payee's bank account, speeding clearance of the payment.

Section E8 Organisation Charts, Work Plans and KPIs

What is an organisation?

Those individuals performing roles within a group according to hierarchical rules and a division of labour, all with a common purpose are said to be part of an organisation. For commercial organisations that common purpose is a profit or return on capital invested.

Organisation Charts

An organisation chart specifies individual roles, their relative status to each other, and the lines of communication. The organisation structure tends to be stratified or layered with authority flowing downward from a "boss". More than one type of chart may be applied to various departments or chains of command with an organisation.

Work Plans - Planning and Measuring Work

Work plans set out the logical sequence of tasks to be completed and the overall deadline for the work. (These are often drawn as flow charts.) The work addressed may be simple or complex with overlapping tasks and requirements to acquire relevant materials or components or to maintain a job site to prevent impediments to progress.

Measuring work involves developing a system to determine the time required for a worker to complete a particular task. In transport operations, measurement generally relates to journeys and addresses such components as loading, delivery and running/travel time.

Typically, a delivery journey may be broken down into:

- driver/vehicle preparation time
- loading
- securing load
- travel time to destination
- driver break
- finding signatory/contact at delivery point
- preparing for unloading
- unloading
- obtaining signature for receipt of goods
- re-securing and closing vehicle
- travel time returning to base
- driver signing-off time

KPI – Key Performance Indicators

Fleet performance management is essential for the modern hauliers.

With rising fuel costs, the spread of road pricing to tackle increasing congestion, tax charges, and tighter curbs on speed having further complicated the already difficult task of those who operate the millions of vehicles in Britain's company fleets, it is important that fleets are managed properly in the haulage industry.

Efficient freight transport that delivers for business and consumers is vital to the UK economy. To effectively manage commercial vehicle fleets, managers need to have a good understanding of their operation and need to be able to identify areas for improvements.

Fleet performance management is a proven and useful tool that measures a standard set of criteria on an ongoing basis – one that is equally relevant to any organisation irrespective of the size or nature of the operation.

The most simple and effective way of measuring performance is through Key Performance Indicators; general KPIs tend to fall under the broad headings:
- costs
- operational
- service
- compliance
- maintenance
- environmental

These are applicable to the vast majority of transport operations irrespective of the nature of the business or the size of the fleet.

How to measure fleet performance management

Fleet performance management does require time and effort on the part of individuals. However, the rewards once established will save money, enhance customer satisfaction and identify potential problematic areas before they become serious. Typically under each standard headline KPI you would expect to find a range of sub headings as follows:

- Costs – per unit delivered, average running and standing costs and total maintenance costs.
- Operational – miles per gallon, total mileage, empty miles, vehicle utilisation (load fill and time)
- Service – late deliveries, damages and complaints/compliments.
- Compliance – overloads, vehicle traffic infringements, drivers' hours infringements and road traffic accidents (blameworthy and non blameworthy).
- Maintenance – percentage of inspections failed, percentage of defects rectified (in a given timeframe).
- Environmental – total fleet CO_2 and average fleet CO_2.

There are many reasons to monitor fleet performance; the majority of operators will do so for a combination of the following:

- For an early warning of possible service failure.
- For a means of troubleshooting problems.
- For the operator to compare different drivers, vehicles, contracts, depots and external providers.
- As a means of evaluating investment and performance.
- To set a published minimum standard of performance for all to see and buy into.

KPI Input will be done on either a daily or a weekly basis dependent on the size of company and the exact criteria it is measuring. The frequency at the level of detail that operators require as outputs will vary.
However the most frequent will be:

- Weekly reports – operations and costs.
- Monthly reports – operations, costs and compliance.
- Annual reports – operations, costs, performance and the entire fleet.
- KPI cumulative summary list for actual vs. target.

These can be incorporated into graphs and spreadsheets that can be used both internally and externally.

Management Tools

Many organisations have their own systems. For those that do not, the Fleet Performance Management Tool Incorporating CO2 Emissions Calculator is available free of charge from the Department for Transport's Freight Best Practice Programme. There are also many 'off the peg' and bespoke solutions that can be adopted by the Transport Manager.

Section E9 Marketing

What is Marketing?

The task of promoting a company and its services to existing and potential customers in such a way as to make the services and rates attractive is called marketing. These are the business and operational strategies that separate a road haulier from his competition. Marketing may emphasise rate structure, reliability and integrity, appropriateness of the vehicles to perform the task at hand, professionalism, or any other customer requirement that can be addressed in such a way as to enhance the customer base and the ability of the business to turn a profit. (It should be taken into account that some customers are only interested in the lowest rate and there is always a haulier prepared to work at that price.)

The Separate Functions of Marketing

Although marketing is a complex interplay of individual functions, those functions may be separated into the following component tasks:

- market research
- marketing planning
- sales (including sales promotion)
- advertising
- public relations (including customer relations)

Market Research

Market research simply means finding potential customers and what they need in the way of services. For a haulier this may be as simple as looking through the telephone directory and calling firms that might be interested in working with him. On the other end of the scale, researchers at a market research consultancy would conduct surveys directed to pre-identified potential customers to pinpoint their precise transport needs. At whatever level, the basics of market research are:

- finding firms that may be interested in your services
- determining what particular aspects of transport services they require
- evaluation what special equipment they may need
- determining the price level they are prepared to pay

Sources of Market Data

Market data can be obtained from:

- telephone and trade directories
- commercial gazetteers

- chamber of commerce directories
- trade journals
- local newspapers
- similar sources

The data collection process interviews conducted in person or via questionnaires to determine the services required and the manner in which they are prioritised, the factors influencing decisions, and the source of the final decision. The research should not neglect to identify the services that are not required. Offering services irrelevant to the potential client could lead to a negative decision about hiring the haulier.

Marketing Planning

Market planning allows the haulier to determine if he can offer the services determined by research to be required and if so, what positive methods could be used to make this fact known. Such methods might include advertising, direct selling, sales promotion, as well as indirect promotion via public relations.

Selling

Selling is nothing more than winning orders. Customers must be "sold" on the idea that by contracting for services with a given haulier they can receive better quality service at a better price than that currently being used. Care should be taken not to criticise the services presently in use, only to show that an improved opportunity is available. A haulier must convince potential clients that he offers what they want at the best price with the utmost reliability.

There are many different selling techniques with a common approach being direct mail. Personally addressed letters are sent directly to the relevant contact person at the firm or firms being "courted". Such a letter outlines the haulier's services with an explanation of why he is better than the competition. The text will carry an invitation to the potential client to try the service or simply to meet the haulier to discuss in greater detail the firm's requirements.

Another common method is "cold calling", a scenario in which a salesman telephones a potential client without prior appointment or introduction. The hope is that the relevant person will be willing to discuss the potential of doing business. With a good salesman, this method can work, but overall cold calling is difficult and carries a high risk of failure because of the turn away rate.

Sales Promotion

As an extension of the sales effort, sales promotion adds something to the selling message to sway the potential customer.
This might involve:

- providing brochures and supporting literature

- staging exhibitions and other promotional campaigns
- handing out items emblazoned with a company logo

At a much higher level, sales promotion could involve bigger, more prestigious gifts or even free travel.

Advertising

Attempts to attract customers through the media are called advertising. "Media" could include trade papers, journals, newspapers, radio or television.
Generally speaking, an advertisement does two things:

- Apprises interested parties of services offered and supplies basic contact information.
- Constitutes an invitation to try services offered, often with an offered discount or bonus or by requesting the interested party to contact the firm for more details.

Advertising that carries an invitation to contract the firm is called direct response advertising. The success and cost-effectiveness of the ad campaign can be measured by the number of responses received. For a newspaper or magazine ad, response is often 1-2 percent of the readership and 4-5 percent for a highly successful ad campaign.

The secret of advertising lies in the ability to design an eye-catching message that will hold the attention of a potential customer long enough for the name and the services offered to register. Perhaps even long enough for the interested party to take down a telephone number or fill out and mail a reply slip.

Public Relations

Simply put, practicing good public relations means that any people who come into contact with your firm gain a good impression. The goal is to present an image of quality, professionalism, and reliability (among other desirable qualities), not just in regard to services offered and performed, but also as the business functions as an aspect of the local community. Creating undue noise, polluting the environment, and leaving disreputable vehicles parked haphazardly are not examples of good PR.

Media Relations

While media relations are an adjunct function of public relations, the field forms a specialty in its own right. In our information rich world, dealing with the media requires particular knowledge and skills to make the best use of the massive opportunities for publicity presented by newspapers, magazines, radio and television. Moreover, a major function of media relations consultants is to make sure that their clients do not fall victim to adverse publicity arising from poorly handled news stories, product launches or similar events.

Market Segments in Road Haulage

The road haulage industry encompasses a wide range of road freighting activities involving considerable specialisation of methods, skills, equipment, and staff. Not surprisingly, each varies greatly in its marketing approach and areas of extensive overlap are common. One extreme might be represented by the firm running small vans and advertising they will carry anything for anybody to anywhere at any time. A good marketing message, even though it cannot be accomplished with the equipment at hand. The other extreme would be occupied by the specialist bulk road tanker operator who carries only dangerous substances. His clientele is so small and specialised, his marketing efforts would be more effectively directed to public relations, convincing the public his vehicles are save and are handled by responsible drivers operating within the law.

Other specialist sectors would include:

- express parcels carriage (same-day, next-day services)
- bulk carriage in road tankers (chemicals/foodstuffs, etc.)
- carriage of abnormal loads
- furniture removals (domestic and industrial and new furniture)
- machinery carriage (including computers)
- livestock carriage
- timber haulage
- steel haulage (including rolled steel, billets and ingots)
- boat haulage
- contract hire
- distribution and storage
- refrigerated transport (temperature-controlled)
- international haulage (specialised or general)
- groupage operations (plus export packing, labelling and shipment, etc.)
- bulk tipping (minerals, fuels, aggregates, cement, grain, animal feeds)
- ready-mixed cement (truck-mixers)
- container haulage
- vehicle/trailer hire/spot rental
- distribution of motor vehicles (car transporters)
- motor parts

Within each there are many sub-specialisations like those hauliers who provide only local or only long-distance services, those who cover only certain geographical regions within Great Britain, those who follow only particular routes, and those who serve only particular countries. Quite a number of haulage firms serve only a single customer under a long-term contract or by long-established tradition. For these firms marketing may not be all that necessary, but a good public relations image remains essential.

174

Section E10 Insurance

While overlooked in many firms, insurance is a specialised, professional service of particular importance to protect against the risks attached to conducting business. Insurance can cover buildings and property, vehicles and equipment, personal sickness and accident, and life. Ancillary cover might protect against the loss of money, goods in transit, public liability, and employers' liability among others. Insurance is provided by the insurer for a fee called a premium and while many regard this as just another unnecessary expense, insurance can reduce the risk or ruination to the business from unexpected and catastrophic events.

The insured must be aware of any policy exclusions that may prevent him from obtaining compensation. For instance, on vehicle insurance some actions can invalidate the cover, such as operating the vehicle outside the requirements of the law. The main types of insurance, both compulsory and voluntary, include the following.

Excess Clauses

In many types of insurance, including vehicle insurance, the insured is responsible for the first portion of any claim, an amount known as the "excess". This may be the first £25, £100, £250 or more, depending on the circumstances. If a vehicle is damaged in an accident requiring £500 worth of repairs, and the insured has a £100 excess on his policy, the insurance company will reimburse him only £400.

Fire (non-compulsory)

Insurance against fire provides cover in the event of loss of buildings, equipment, vehicles and other possessions. The fire brigade would generally need to be called to affect a claim. If neighbouring premises catch fire and damage the insured property, he must claim on his own insurance. His insurance company will in turn seek reimbursement from the neighbour's insurers.

Storm and flood (non-compulsory)

This is cover to provide compensation in the event of damage or loss sustained from severe weather and flooding.

Theft (non-compulsory)

This type of insurance policy covers the loss of possessions by theft, but usually requires evidence of forcible entry. Policy conditions vary, but insurers may not accept claims unless there is sound evidence of a criminal act that has been reported to the police.

Fidelity guarantee (non-compulsory)

A fidelity guarantee insurance policy is used when employees are put in responsible positions, particularly those requiring the handling of money or valuable. If the employee's background checks out, the insurers provide cover (by bond or guarantee) against the risk of the employee disappearing with the money or valuables.

Consequential loss (non-compulsory)

This type of insurance covers consequential loss resulting from an accident or fire. For example, if a warehouse burned down the buildings and contents might be covered but not the loss of trade and profits. The same applies where a haulage vehicle was out of commission for repairs for an extended period after an accident. The vehicle policy might cover the repairs, but not the resulting loss of business.

Employers' liability (compulsory)

Employers have a statutory duty to take out insurance cover (minimum £5 million) against the risk of injury to their employees while on the firm's premises or elsewhere (for instance on the road in a company-owned vehicle). Usually such policies provide unlimited cover for any eventuality. A current certificate of insurance must be displayed on the employer's premises.

Public liability (non-compulsory)

A firm should also protect itself against claims for loss or injury from the general public through public liability policies. If a member of the public is injured or suffers loss while on a firm's premises, or as a result of the action or negligence of its employees, that person has a right to claim compensation.

Life/sickness and accident/pension (non-compulsory)

A business proprietor should acquire personal insurance to cover his premature death or extended periods of incapacity due to sickness or accident. Such cover will, to an extent, protect his dependents and his business providing a cash sum (in the case of his death) or an income over a period (in the case of his incapacity). These benefits may be sufficient to keep the business going until it can be sold or until the proprietor can return to work. By the same token, proprietors should provide for eventual retirement by paying into a personal pension fund which can be provided via an insurance policy.

Motor vehicles (compulsory)

Under the terms of basic motor vehicle insurance, the insured is covered against claims by injured parties for personal injury (death or bodily injury) and medical expenses. By the terms of the Road Traffic Act, such cover is the minimum requirement and must include mandatory cover for passengers (except those in the employ of the vehicle owner/operator) and for damage to roadside property. The policy may also cover other third-party risks including damage to other property, loss of the vehicle by fire or theft, or it may be extended to become fully comprehensive cover to provide full protection against third-party claims and to provide compensation for damage to the vehicle.

Motor vehicles using the public highway must be covered against third-party claims – except those belonging to local authorities (owned, use, or directed by the police or the armed forces, and certain vehicles of the NHS). The cover may be provided by means of a security of £500,000 deposited with the Accountant General of the Supreme Court (subject to the approval of the Secretary of State for Transport) or by means of an insurance policy taken out with an authorised insurer (a member of the Motor Insurers' Bureau – MIB) – Road Traffic Act (of 1988) cover.
The insurance policy must: insure such person(s) or classes of person as may be specified in the policy in respect of any liability which may be incurred by him or them, in respect of the death or bodily injury to any person caused by, or arising out of, the use of the vehicle on a road; and must also insure him or them in respect of any liability which may be incurred by him or them relating to payment for emergency treatment.

The insured person or organisation must have in their possession a current, valid certificate of insurance (the policy is not acceptable proof) showing the cover provided and it must give particulars of any conditions subject to which the policy is issued.
It should indicate:

- The vehicles covered by registration number or by specification.
- The persons authorised to drive the vehicle.
- The dates between which the cover is effective.
- The permitted use of the vehicle.

Claims to MIB

Third parties injured in motor vehicle accidents with uninsured driver/owners can seek compensation from the Motor Insurers' Bureau.

Passenger Liability (compulsory)

Passenger liability insurance cover for motor vehicles is compulsory. This requirement includes all vehicles required by the Road Traffic Act to have third-party insurance and the cover extends to authorised passengers, other non-fare paying passengers and "unauthorised passengers" such as hitch-hikers and other people who are given lifts. It does not cover employees of the vehicle owner/operator who have cover under the employers' liability policy.

The display in a vehicle of a sign which says "No passengers" or "No liability" does not fully indemnify the owner or driver against claims by unauthorised passengers for injury or damage as a result of negligence, even if they agree to travel at their own risk. The law ensures that such liabilities are covered within the vehicle policy.

Additional Voluntary Insurance

Any insurance cover over the minimum is at the vehicle owner's discretion, but in many instances such additional coverage is advisable for the protection it affords in the event of loss of the vehicle or severe damage.

Production of Insurance Certificate

If a police officer asks to see a certificate of insurance, or if there has been an accident, the vehicle owner of a vehicle must produce a certificate of insurance. The certificate or a temporary cover note may be produced at any police station chosen by the owner or driver within seven days (five days in Northern Ireland) of the request.

The owner of a vehicle must give the police any information needed to determine whether a vehicle was being driven without valid third-party insurance.

Invalidation of Cover

Insurance cover on a vehicle can be invalidated for a number of reasons:

- Non-payment of premiums.
- Employment of unlicensed or incorrectly licensed drivers.
- Using a vehicle without an excise license or "0" license.
- The use of a vehicle in an unroadworthy condition.
- Failing to report an accident to the insurers.
- Admitting liability at the scene of an accident.
- Otherwise being in breach of policy conditions.

Cancellation of Insurance

When an insurance policy is cancelled, the certificate(s) of insurance must be surrendered to the insurer within seven days of the cancellation date.

Goods in Transit (GIT) Insurance Cover

Vehicle insurance covers risks of loss or damage to the vehicle not to the load it carries. Cover for the load is through a GIT policy which provides protection against loss or damage on a standard valuation of at least £1300 per ton (in accordance with the RHA standard conditions of carriage). If the loads carried are of greater value per ton, the cover should be extended as necessary. Usually insurers need to be advised if exceptionally valuable or vulnerable loads are carried. Failure to make this notification can result in invalidation of the cover or refusal by the insurers to pay claims.

GIT policies usually specify restrictive clauses that require vehicle owners to observe particular conditions:

- Immobiliser clause - Vehicles must be fitted with anti-theft devices that must be engaged when the vehicles are left unattended.
- Night risk clause - Loaded vehicles must be left in a closed building or yard or one which is locked or guarded.

CMR Cover for International Haulage Journeys

GIT cover is not sufficient or legally acceptable for vehicles engaged in international haulage. In most cases, the provisions of the Convention on the Contract for the International Carriage of Goods by Road, referred to in common usage as the CMR convention, governs such operations. The Convention applies automatically to international haulage trips that take place between countries where at least one is party to the Convention. UK-Eire and UK mainland – Channel Islands journeys are not defined as international journeys for this purpose.

Road hauliers who carry goods on any part of an international journey, whether they know it or whether they choose to or not, fall under the CMR Convention. The CMR compensation levels for loss or damage to goods are much higher than the standard Conditions of Carriage GIT cover applicable in national transport operations. CMR levels of cover vary according to a set standard published daily in the financial press. For this reason it is important to obtain adequate cover when involved in international transport.

Additionally, where hauliers undertake sabotage operations they should discuss the levels of cover required with their insurers or verify that extended cover is available to cover certain liabilities such as losses from unattended vehicles. Difficulties may arise where local conditions of carriage are imposed, and claims and legal wrangling arise under law other than English law.

Insurance and Carriers' Liability

Adequate insurance is also necessary as a protection against civil liability claims arising from the use of motor vehicles on international journeys. Details of the requirements are specified in EU Directive 166/72 Council Directive on the approximation of the laws of the member states relating to insurance against civil liability in respect of the use of motor vehicles, and to the enforcement of the obligation to ensure against such liability as follows:

Definitions

- Vehicle: Any mechanically propelled motor vehicle intended for travel on land and any trailer, whether coupled or not.

- Injured party: Any person entitled to compensation in respect of any loss or injury caused by vehicles.
- National Insurers' Bureau: A professional organisation which groups together insurance undertakings authorised by member states to conduct the business of motor vehicle insurance against civil liability. Such bodies are constituted in accordance with a recommendation of the Road Transport Sub-Committee of the Inland Transport Committee of the United Nations Economic Commission for Europe.
- Territory in which the vehicle is based: The state in which the vehicle is registered.
- Green card: An international certificate of insurance issued on behalf of a national insurers' bureau (see above).

Other provisions of the Directive

The Directive provides that member states need not see evidence of insurance for vehicles based in other member states. Similarly, it provides for a relaxation of checks on evidence of insurance for vehicles based in third countries when entering member states from another member state. The Directive specifies that member states must take all appropriate steps to ensure that civil liability (in the UK commonly known as third-party liability or Road Traffic Act cover) in respect of vehicles based in their territory is covered by insurance.

Member states must also make sure that the insurance provides cover for loss or injury caused in other member states according to the law in force in those states, and loss or injury suffered by nationals of member states during a direct journey between two territories in which the treaty establishing the EU is in force, if there is no national insurers' bureau responsible for the territory being crossed. In this case the loss or injury must be covered in accordance with the internal laws on compulsory insurance in force in the member state where the vehicle is normally based.

It allows for derogation (exemption) from the previous Article in certain respects. A list of exempted people must be drawn up by the member state and communicated to other member states and to the EU Commission.

Member states must ensure that compensation is paid in respect of loss or injury caused in the territory of other member states by vehicles belonging to the exempt persons. Further, derogation also applies to certain vehicles having a special plate, but member states may still request sight of valid green cards for vehicles entering their territory or they can request that suitable insurance cover is obtained at the point of entry to the territory.

The Directive also deals with action in the event of accidents. Member states are required to ensure that where an accident is caused in its territory by a vehicle normally based in another member state, the national insurers' bureau must be given details of the vehicle registration mark and the territory in which the vehicle is normally based, and details of the insurance of the vehicle from the green card or as they would appear on the green card. This information must be given to the national insurers' bureau of the state in whose territory the vehicle is normally based.

The Directive requires EU member states to ensure that vehicles normally based in third countries (non-EU members) or in the non-European territory of any member state are not used in their territory unless any loss or injury caused by those vehicles is covered in accordance with the various laws on compulsory insurance against civil liability in respect of the use of vehicles.

The Directive further requires that vehicles from third countries must have a green card or a certificate of frontier insurance before entering EU member states unless the national bureaux of all member states guarantee, in accordance with their own national laws, settlement of claims in respect of accidents caused by such vehicles.

Green Cards

An international motor insurance card (green card) issued by an insurance bureau (in the UK the MIB via insurance companies) provides evidence of insurance against compulsory insurable liabilities in those countries in which the card is valid.

While green cards are no longer essential for travel within the EU and in certain other countries, drivers should continue to carry a green card (or at least their British insurance certificate). Drivers are not subjected to routine checks, but may need to produce the card in the event of an accident or other incident.

European Accident Statement

It is usual for insurers to provide a copy of the European Accident Statement to operators who send their vehicles abroad. This document is a universally recognised form of words and layout for making a report (statement) of a motor vehicle accident. The document contains behavioural advice to drivers and instructions on completion of the form. It also instructs drivers to forward the form without delay to their own insurer (the vehicle insurer). The form should not be sent to any other official body.

Section E11 Electronic Data and Transmission

EDI — Electronic Data Interchange

Widespread computerisation in the road freight, shipping and export/import industries and by HMRC has led to the introduction of modern systems for passing shipping and export/import data via direct or indirect computer links, without the need for paper documents to pass or confirm information. This Information Technology (IT) or EDI – Electronic Data Interchange (paperless systems of trading) and its use results in automatic handling and actioning of data. To ensure uniformity in this method of trading, the United Nations has set a standard for EDI known as EDIFACT (Electronic Data Interchange for Administration, Commerce and Transport) under which there are standard procedures and messages for passing such matter as shipping instructions.

Satellite-Based Communications Systems

Technological developments in satellite-based communication systems provide facilities for long-range telephone, fax and paging links between base and vehicle, as well as positive vehicle tracking systems. Such systems are widely used in North America and are of increasing interest to UK and European transport fleet operators. A satellite navigation system with global coverage may be termed a global navigation satellite system (GNSS). As of 6 November 2020, 76 Global Positioning System navigation satellites have been launched, these include the United States NAVSTAR Global Positioning System (GPS), the Russian GLONASS and the EUs Galileo are global operational GNSSs.

The Global Positioning System

The Global Positioning System (GPS) incorporates more than 32 satellites orbiting the Earth. A GPS receiver uses the satellite signals to track location accurately and efficiently. At least three satellites are in view of the receiver at any one time. The unit decodes the received information and provides position data in longitude and latitude as well as a number of different coordinate formats. GPS can be used anywhere in the world. In-vehicle systems can now incorporate CD, radio, and GPS in a single unit. By entering the desired destination (for instance the name of a road) into the unit, the GPS provides distance, route and estimated travel. A voice gives commands for turning at the correct junctions and an on-screen map is provided for reference.

Computerisation in Transport

The current trend is towards the development of on-board systems for constant communication with drivers and their base for the transmission of data and instructions. Precise vehicle location can be determined via the GPS and other tracking systems, technology that is particularly useful for tracking high-value cargo vehicles as well as those that have been stolen.

Additionally a full range of data recording, information and analysis operations, including accounting, staff records, vehicle maintenance records and such like, can be carried out and can be accessible by all relevant staff and management via in-office and laptop or hand-held computers equipped with an Internet connection.

The use of e-mail and the Internet has led to enormous improvements in business efficiency and information, providing rapid person-to-person communication and access to unlimited data on virtually any topic.

Intelligent Transport Systems

Intelligent transport systems (ITS) using telematics (the combination of information technology and telecommunications) provide online information and control systems for all modes of transport, including vehicle-based systems. Typical of such systems used in road transport are those which operate:

- variable message signs (VMS), for example on motorways
- onboard route and traffic information, such as Trafficmaste
- traffic control and enforcement signs, like the digital speed cameras
- electronic road charging
- traffic monitoring
- vehicle-to-base communications
- electronic ticketing

The Data Protection Act 2018

This Act is designed to protect living and identifiable persons from the misuse or unauthorised disclosure of any information, including expression of any personal opinion, about them. Firms or self-employed road hauliers who hold personal employee, applicant, or customer data on file (especially in computerised format) fall under the scope of the Act. Exemptions apply when information is held:

- by persons for their own family or domestic purposes
- for historical or statistical research
- in certain instances relating to journalism, art and literature
- for the purposes of national security

In road haulage, if customer names and addresses held on file include an individual person (for instance the managing director or transport manager) then such data falls within the scope of the Act.

The Act defines data as information:

- being processed by means of automatic equipment
- recorded to be processed by such equipment
- recorded as part of a filing system, or with that intention
- relating to certain health and associated records

Processing of personal data means obtaining, recording or holding information or data or carrying out any operation on it, including its:

- organisation, adaptation or alteration
- retrieval, consultation or use
- disclosure by transmission, dissemination or otherwise making it available
- alignment, combination, blocking, erasure or destruction

Special rules apply to the processing of "sensitive" data such the racial origin of an individual.

Any firm or individual maintaining personal data is required to register with the Data Protection Commissioner and to conform to the principles of the Act.

It is a criminal offence (punishable by a fine of up to £500,000) for an unregistered person to hold or to disclose personal data about any person, and no processing of data should take place unless registration under the Act has been completed and the appropriate entry made in the Data Protection Register.

https://www.gov.uk/data-protection

Increased penalties under the GDPR

The European Data Protection Board's (EDPB) guidelines from May 2020 clarify what constitutes valid consent on websites in compliance with the GDPR.

Protection Directive (hereafter: Directive 95/46/EC) and in the e-Privacy Directive to date, has evolved. Guidelines 05/2020 on consent under Regulation 2016/679 Version 1.1 - Adopted on 4 May2020

When the General Data Protection Regulation (GDPR) is enforced breached organisations will find the fines they face increasing dramatically.
From a theoretical maximum of £500,000 that the ICO could levy (in practice, the ICO has never issued a penalty higher than £400,000), penalties will reach an upper limit of €20 million or 4% or annual global turnover – whichever is higher.

It is the responsibility of data controllers to operate within the terms of their Register entries. Such individuals can be held liable to pay compensation for any damage or associated distress suffered as a result of holding or disclosing inaccurate personal data.

When a data controller registers he must notify the Data Protection Commissioner of:

- The name and address of their principal place of business; the address of the registered office for limited companies.
- The name and address of any nominated representative for the purposes of the Act where this differs from that of the company's registered office.
- A description of the personal data that is or that will be processed and the category or categories of that data.
- A description of the purpose or purposes for which the data is or will be processed.
- A description of those to whom data will be disclosed.
- The names of countries outside the European Economic Area (EEA) to which the data controller will directly or indirectly transfer data.

It is illegal for a registered data user to:

- Hold personal data of any description other than that specified in their entry in the Data Protection Register.
- Hold any such data, or use any such data which they hold, for any purpose other than those described in their entry.
- Obtain data, or information to be contained in such data, from any source which is not described in the Register entry.
- Disclose the data which they hold to any person who is not described in the Register entry.
- Directly or indirectly transfer data they hold to any country or territory outside the EEA which does not have similar data protection laws.

The Act sets out eight "data protection principles" under which registered data users must ensure that data is:

1. Processed fairly and lawfully.
2. Used only for specified and lawful purposes.
3. Adequate, relevant and not excessive.
4. Accurate and up-to-date.
5. Not kept longer than necessary.
6. Is processed in accordance with the rights of data subjects under the Act.
7. Protected against unauthorised processing loss, destruction and damage.
8. Not be transferred outside the European Economic Area (EEA).

Individuals who know or believe that a firm or organisation holds information about them have a statutory right under the Data Protection Act and under other employment legislation to request details of that information. In the case of health records, some information must be statutorily provided on request. However, there are certain areas where information about data held will not be given, for example by the police about their records while "enquiries" are in progress.

Hardware and Software

"Hardware" refers to the computer equipment used while "software" describes the systems that enable the hardware to function.

Hardware usually comprises:

- the central processing unit (CPU) – the brains of the computer
- visual display unit (VDU)
- keyboard
- mouse or pointing device
- printers
- scanner
- modem – for Internet connection
- floppy disks (on older systems for inputting and storing data)
- CD ROM drive/writer – for installing and storing data
- zip or tape drives – for data storage
- DVD drive – for viewing video and film
- digital camera – for producing photographs

There are many other peripheral hardware devices on the market for both business and leisure use.

Software for business usually comprises:

- the operating system (Windows or the Mac OS)
- word processing (Microsoft Word)
- database
- spreadsheets
- accounts (Sage packages)
- Internet and email
- graphics
- design
- animation and video
- networking
- Web design
- other business applications (Microsoft Office)

Section E12 Terms of Business and Incoterms

Business is largely concerned with administration, a process involving the use of common terms and documentation designed to keep records, to convey information, to advise customers. Knowing and understanding this terminology and understanding which document to use for which purpose is essential to avoid confusion and costly mistakes. The following documents are commonly found in commercial practice.

Estimate

An estimate is a price approximation for a job given without access to precise job details. The operator cannot be held to the estimated price should the need to charge more become evident with full access to the details.

Quotation

A quotation is a firm officer of a price for a specific job. Normally, quotes are good for only a specified time, typically 30-60 days. The quote specifies the conditions under which the price is offered. For a haulier, such a specification would be "goods carried in accordance with our standard conditions of carriage", "ex-works", "delivered to site" or "to one delivery point only" among others. Quotes are fixed prices unless clauses are incorporated specifying otherwise or unless extreme, unforeseen circumstances arise, at which time the price can only be altered by mutual agreement with the customer.

Order

An order is made by a customer instructing the supplier to supply specified goods or service with full details of the customer's requirements included. Normally these are some combination of:

- date or period of supply
- quantity of goods
- quality
- method of supply
- labelling and packing instructions
- other special instructions, for instance "loads must be sheeted" or "notification required before delivery"

Invoice

The supplier generates an invoice to indicate job completed and/or amount owed. Invoices should identify the job clearly and contain evidence of supply or delivery. It should show:

- date of supply
- quantity of goods
- price per unit
- total price less any discount offered
- any VAT due

An invoice is in effect, a demand for payment either upon completion of a job, or in advance of a job where advance payment has been agreed upon by both parties. Usually terms for payment are shown. A note of discounts offered for prompt payment can be added, such as "2.5 per cent discount for payment in 14 days".

If the invoice bears the "E. & OE", they are a reference to "errors and omissions excepted". If the issuer of the invoice discovers that the invoice was undercharged, he can go back to the customer for increased payment. Unless the original job contract or conditions of carriage so stipulate, adding interest to unpaid or late accounts is illegal.

Incoterms

The Incoterms rules or International Commercial terms are a series of pre-defined commercial terms published by the International Chamber of Commerce (ICC) widely used in international commercial transactions. A series of three-letter trade terms related to common sales practices, the Incoterms rules are intended primarily to clearly communicate the tasks, costs and risks associated with the transportation and delivery of goods. The Incoterms rules are accepted by governments, legal authorities and practitioners worldwide for the interpretation of most commonly used terms in international trade. They are intended to reduce or remove altogether uncertainties arising from different interpretation of the rules in different countries.

 Incoterms are subdivided into two categories based only on method of delivery. The larger group of seven rules applies regardless of the method of transport, with the smaller group of four being applicable only to sales that solely involve transportation over water.

The seven rules defined by Incoterms for any mode of transportation are:

1. EXW – Ex Works (named place of delivery)

The seller makes the goods available at its premises. This term places the maximum obligation on the buyer and minimum obligations on the seller. The Ex Works term is often used when making an initial quotation for the sale of goods without any costs included. EXW means that a seller has the goods ready for collection at his premises (works, factory, warehouse, plant) on the date agreed upon. The buyer pays all transportation costs and also bears the risks for bringing the goods to their final destination. The seller doesn't load the goods on collecting vehicles and doesn't clear them for export. If the seller does load the goods, he does so at buyer's risk and cost. If parties wish seller to be responsible for the loading of the goods on departure and to bear the risk and all costs of such loading, this must be made clear by adding explicit wording to this effect in the contract of sale.

2. FCA – Free Carrier (named place of delivery)

The seller hands over the goods, cleared for export, into the disposal of the first carrier (named by the buyer) at the named place. The seller pays for carriage to the named point of delivery, and risk passes when the goods are handed over to the first carrier.

3. CPT - Carriage Paid To (named place of destination)

The seller pays for carriage. Risk transfers to buyer upon handing goods over to the first carrier.

4. CIP – Carriage and Insurance Paid to (named place of destination)

The containerised transport/multimodal equivalent of CIF. Seller pays for carriage and insurance to the named destination point, but risk passes when the goods are handed over to the first carrier.

5. DAT – Delivered at Terminal (named terminal at port or place of destination)

Seller pays for carriage to the terminal, except for costs related to import clearance, and assumes all risks up to the point that the goods are unloaded at the terminal.

6. DAP – Delivered at Place (named place of destination)

Seller pays for carriage to the named place, except for costs related to import clearance, and assumes all risks prior to the point that the goods are ready for unloading by the buyer.

7. DDP – Delivered Duty Paid (named place of destination)

Seller is responsible for delivering the goods to the named place in the country of the buyer, and pays all costs in bringing the goods to the destination including import duties and taxes. This term places the maximum obligations on the seller and minimum obligations on the buyer.

Rules for Sea and Inland Waterway Transport

The four rules defined by Incoterms 2010 (Revised INCOTERMS® took effect on January 1, 2011) for international trade where transportation is entirely conducted by water are:

1. FAS – Free Alongside Ship (named port of shipment)

The seller must place the goods alongside the ship at the named port. The seller must clear the goods for export. Suitable only for maritime transport, but NOT for multimodal sea transport in containers (see Incoterms 2010, ICC publication 715). This term is typically used for heavy-lift or bulk cargo.

2. FOB – Free on Board (named port of shipment)

The seller must load the goods on board the vessel nominated by the buyer. Cost and risk are divided when the goods are actually on board of the vessel (this rule is new!). The seller must clear the goods for export. The term is applicable for maritime and inland waterway transport only, but NOT for multimodal sea transport in containers.

3. CFR – Cost and Freight (named port of destination)

Seller must pay the costs and freight to bring the goods to the port of destination. However, risk is transferred to the buyer once the goods are loaded on the vessel (this rule is new!). Maritime transport only and insurance for the goods is NOT included. This term is formerly known as CNF (C&F).

4. CIF – Cost, Insurance and Freight (named port of destination)

Exactly the same as CFR, except that the seller must in addition procure and pay for the insurance (Maritime transport only).

Section E13 Third Part Transportation Systems

Working in road haulage operations means contact with other modes of transport and other organisations such as:

- Freight forwarders
- Haulage subcontractors
- Transport clearing houses
- Groupage operators

It is important to understand the different roles fulfilled by these organisations.

Freight Forwarders

Many firms with goods to despatch, particularly to overseas destinations, use the services of freight forwarders who provide a complete transport service in connection with the export or import of goods (as well as for inland movements) covering some or all of the following aspects:

- Advice on the best method of movement (i.e. road, sea, air).
- Advice on legal/commercial requirements.
- Advice on the best services.
- Making necessary bookings with appropriate transport services.
- Completing all documentation.
- Advising on and arranging packing and labelling.
- Arranging insurance cover as necessary.
- Arranging for collection and following through until delivery is effected.
- Arranging Customs clearance for export/import consignments.
- Ensuring that all charges are reasonable and presenting a comprehensive final account.

Subcontract Hauliers

Subcontract hauliers (often owner-drivers) have no direct contact with customers but pick up work from other hauliers and clearing houses. They undertake work that others have contracted to carry, which saves them the costs and efforts of marketing. It also means, however, that they exist on haulage rates reduced by the main contractor's commission, and they usually have to wait a considerable time for payment.

Clearing Houses

A clearing house is an organisation which arranges with shippers (consignors) of goods to move those goods by subcontracting the work to road haulage operators. The clearing house agrees on one price with the customer and another, lower, price with the haulier and keeps the difference.

Alternatively, the clearing house advises the haulier of the price to be paid by the customer then deducts a commission for handling and administrative charges from what is due to the subcontract haulier. Usually, the commission is around 10 percent of the original rate.

Hauliers seeking return loads for vehicles frequently accept loads from clearing houses to save searching around. Problems, however, can arise on both sides. Unscrupulous clearing houses deduct excessive commission and take a long time to pay the haulier. Hauliers sometimes pick up loads and deliver to the wrong place, or do not obtain proof of delivery, or take a long time to effect delivery. Additionally, subcontract hauliers are sometimes not adequately covered by Goods in Transit insurance, and if loads are lost or damaged and substantial claims arise, financial problems can result.

Groupage

This is the practice of bringing small consignments together (in industry terminology less than container loads – LCLs) and consolidating them into bulk loads in a large vehicle or container. Break-bulk is a term used to describe the unloading of consolidated loads ready for delivery of individual consignments to their respective destinations. In the case of import/export groupage, much of this work is carried out at inland clearance depots where HMRC have a presence for clearing the necessary documentation.

Section F1 F2 F3 F4 F5 Operator Licensing and Documentation

The operators' ("O") licensing system seeks to regulate the quality of goods vehicle operators entering the industry in the interest of public safety. A Traffic Commissioner administers the system for each of the traffic areas covering England, Wales and Scotland. In Northern Ireland the Department of the Environment administers the Road Freight Operators' licensing system.

Quality and Quantity Licensing

For purposes of licensing "quality" equates with an ability to operate a vehicle safely, legally and professionally. Quantity licensing restricts the number of license holders or the total volume of freight license holders can move. The present UK system and that of Northern Ireland are quality based.

Trade or business users of most goods vehicles of more than 3.5 tons maximum permissible weight are required to hold an "0" license. This license is necessary whether the vehicles are used for carrying goods in connection with the operator's main business or are used for hire road haulage operations. Certain goods vehicles, including those used exclusively for private purposes are exempt from the licensing requirements.

The Regulatory System

The Transport Act 1968 established the original system of operators' licensing. Its relevant provisions are now consolidated into the Goods Vehicle (Licensing of Operators) Act 1995. It forbids any person using a goods vehicle on a road for hire or in connection with any trade or business carried on by him to do so without an operator's license.

Substantial changes were made to the "O" licensing system by the Goods Vehicle (Operators' licenses) Regulations 1977 which took effect on 1 January 1978. These regulations introduced a three-tier system of "O" licensing. The Goods Vehicles (Operators' licenses, Qualifications and Fees) Regulations 1984 (as amended 1986, 1987, 1988, 1990, 1993 and 1994) further changed the system and gave Traffic Commissioners the power to consider "O" license applications in relation to the environmental nuisance or discomfort local residents might suffer by the presence of goods vehicles operating from particular locations.

On 1 January 1996 the system of continuous "O" licensing was introduced. Once granted, the license remains valid indefinitely so long as the license holder meets all relevant conditions and pays his fees on time. Failure to pay the fees can result in loss of the license. A license may become invalid and a new license issued if a major variation is required such as an increase in the authorised number of vehicles or a change to or addition of a new operating Centre. The requirement for five-yearly license renewals has been lifted where details remain unchanged, although operating Centres are subject to periodic reviews.

The 1995 Act also provided new definitions for vehicle operating Centres, which must be large enough to accommodate all the vehicles used under the license. The legislation addresses the placement of newspaper advertisements (in one or more local newspapers circulating in the locality) and the period of time in which objectors and environmental representatives may make their case (five years for environmental representatives). Finally the TCs have greater powers in relation to road safety matters, particularly in regard to situations where vehicles may cause danger to the public.

After 1 October 1999 new UK regulations implemented EC Council Directive 98/76/EC (1 October 1998), which amends Directive 96/26/EC. These provisions provide for stricter good repute requirements, increased financial commitments for new (and later for existing) operators, a more extensive professional competence examination syllabus, and a more stringent examination process. These measures are intended to ensure higher levels of professionalism, greater law abidance in road haulage, and a harmonised approach throughout all the member states of the EU.

Vehicle operators: updated guidance from Traffic Commissioners
Revised statutory documents introduced from 1 January 2017 (updated 28th October 2020)
From 28 October 2020, revised versions of the statutory documents covering:

Most of the amendments relate to updated legal references (following Upper Tribunal appeal cases), which have allowed some minor grammatical corrections.
Operators and licence applicants are advised to pay particular attention to the changes.

The Statutory Documents are clearly defined. They are published as an available resource for all applicants, operators, transport managers, vocational drivers, and other interested parties. From 28 October 2020, revised versions of the statutory documents covering:

1. Finance
2. Transport Managers
3. Operating Centres, Stable Establishments and Addresses for Service
4. Legal Entities (including Insolvency and Regulation 31 & Section 57 Applications)
5. Vocational Driver Conduct
6. Impounding
7. Delegation of Authority (in terms of Staff and Multiple Licence Holders)
8. Case Management
9. Principles of Decision Making & the Concept of Proportionality
10. Format of Decisions (including Publication, Written Reasons and Decisions)
11. Appeals
12. PSV Operations
13. Local Bus Services in England (outside London) and Wales will take effect.

All statutory documents can be accessed here: http://alturl.com/xh8bj

Administration of Licensing System

The central licensing office is responsible for processing applications for heavy goods vehicle (HGV) and public service vehicle (PSV) operator licences and providing administrative support to traffic commissioners. ALL licence applications are processed in Leeds, along with bus registrations for England and Wales. Bus registrations in Scotland are dealt with by staff at the Office of the Traffic Commissioner (Scotland).

Central Licensing Office

Hillcrest House
386 Harehills Lane
Leeds
LS9 6NF

Email: enquiries@otc.gsi.gov.uk

Phone 0300 123 9000

Fax 0113 249 8142

Opening hours

Office hours: 9.30am to 4.00pm, Monday to Friday
Telephone hours: 8.30am to 5.00pm, Monday to Friday

The Traffic Area Network (TAN) is now merged with the Vehicle Inspectorate (VI) to form DVSA, the Drivers and Vehicle Standards Agency.

Office information and opening times for the Central Licensing Office and the offices of the traffic commissioners.   http://alturl.com/x6f5w

The Vehicle User

An "O" license is required by the "user" of an appropriate vehicle, the person who operates and drives the vehicle (owner-driver), or who employs a person to drive the vehicle for him in connection with any trade or business. Ownership of the vehicle is not a relevant factor in determining who the user is. In Northern Ireland own-account users of vehicles are exempt from road freight operators' licensing.

Definition of a Goods Vehicle

For the purposes of "O" licensing, a goods vehicle is one used in connection with the trade or business of the license holder and has a permissible maximum weight (pmw) of more than 3.5 tons unless it is otherwise exempt.

Exemptions from "O" Licensing

The following small vehicles are exempt from "O" licensing:

- Rigid vehicles plated of not more than 3.5 tons maximum permissible weight or unplated with an unladen weight of not more than 1,525kg.
- Drawbar combinations with plated weights totalling not more than 3.5 tons gross or unplated with a total combined unladen weight of not more than 1,525kg (trailers of not more than 1,020kg unladen weight need not be included in the calculation).
- Articulated vehicles with a combined plated weight of not more than 3.5 tons gross or, if either is not plated, if the total of the unladen weights is not more than 1,525kg.

A number of further exemptions apply to specialised vehicles or vehicles used for specialised purposes.

Restricted "O" Licenses

Own-account operators who only carry their own goods or goods in connection with any trade or business in which they are engaged (other than professional haulage) may hold a restricted "O" license to operate within the UK and internationally. The license does not permit the holder to carry any goods for hire or reward, or in connection with a trade or business other than their own.

Standard "O" Licenses — National / International Operations

Professional haulage operators and own-account operators who wish to carry goods for hire or reward solely within the UK are required to hold a standard "O" license. They may also carry their own goods nationally and internationally.

Standard "O" Licenses - International Operations

Professional haulage operators and own-account operators who wish to carry goods for others in addition to their own goods both nationally and internationally need to hold a standard "O" license covering both national and international operations.

Definition of International Operations

For the purposes of the "O" license regulations international operations are those in which the:

- Driver or vehicle undertakes a journey where all or part of the vehicle leaves the UK loaded.
- Vehicle or part of the vehicle has entered the UK from another country loaded.

Only a standard "O" license cover national operations is required if the driver:

- Takes a loaded trailer or semi-trailer to a British port for unaccompanied onward movement.
- Collects an unaccompanied loaded trailer or semi-trailer from a port and does not leave the country himself.

Conditions for the Granting of Restricted/standard "O" Licenses

The conditions which must be met to receive a restricted or standard "O" license are:

- Restricted "O" licenses - The applicant must be a fit and proper person of appropriate financial standing.
- Standard national "O" licenses - The applicant must be of good repute, of appropriate financial standing, and professionally competent in national transport operations.
- Standard international "O" licenses - The applicant must be of good repute, of appropriate financial standing, and professionally competent in both national and international transport operations.

In each case, the license applicant must illustrate his willingness and ability to comply with the conditions of the declaration of intent on the "O" license application form GV 79. The operating Centre at which vehicles on the license are based must be suitable for the purpose and environmentally acceptable.

Number of "O" Licenses

Only one "O" license may be held by a person/firm in any one traffic area. A separate "O" license is required in each traffic area in which goods vehicle operations are based.

Observance of Legal Requirements

It is a condition of "O" licensing that operators must observe the laws regarding:

- Drivers' hours and the keeping of drivers' records (including tachographs).
- The overloading of vehicles.
- The maintenance, roadworthiness and use of vehicles.
- Vehicle plating and testing.
- Speed limits and traffic rules.
- Drivers' licensing.
- International road haulage permits.
- Use of rebated fuel oil.
- Parking restrictions.
- Prohibitions on loading/unloading.
- The reporting of vehicle defects by drivers.

- Regular safety inspection of vehicles.
- The keeping of maintenance records (driver defect reports, safety inspection reports and defect repair records).

Declaration of Intent

An applicant for an "O" license or a variation of an "O" license must make a legally binding declaration of intent that all the requirements will be strictly observed. This promise must be kept throughout the duration of the license and if broken the TC can curtail, suspend or revoke the license.

Maintenance

Operators must make arrangement acceptable to the TC for vehicle maintenance and repair by either maintaining his own workshop or engaging the services of an outside repairer. In the latter cast, the TC would require evidence of a written agreement between the operator and the repairer detailing the arrangement and the manner and frequency of the inspection and repairs. Even if repairs are carried out by the third party the license holder is completely responsible for the mechanical condition of the vehicles and cannot blame the repairer for faulty work so far as the "O" license is concerned.

Maintenance Records

Whether the maintenance records are prepared in an operator's own workshop or supplied by a repairer, they must be up to date and available for inspection for at least 15 months.

Fit Persons/Good repute

The TC must be satisfied that "O" license applicants are fit and proper persons of "good repute". To determine this the TC requires details of any convictions in connection with the operation of goods vehicles against the applicant, any partners, or any other directors of a limited company. Good repute is automatically lost if a person is convicted of more than one serious offence or of road transport offences.
A serious offence is one that incurs:

- More than three months' imprisonment.
- A community service order of more than 60 hours.
- A fine exceeding level 4 on the standard scale (currently £2,500).

Rehabilitation of Offenders

The TC is concerned with convictions that occurred prior to the granting of the license for a period of:

- Five years prior if a fine or community service order was imposed.
- Seven years if a prison sentence of not more than six months was imposed.
- Ten years if a prison sentence of more than six months was imposed.

If the person concerned was under age 17 the applicable periods of interest are 2.5, 3.5, and 5 years prior to the granting of the license

Convictions prior to these periods do not count against the applicant under the terms of the Rehabilitation of Offenders Act 1974. The rehabilitation periods are:

- Six months for an absolute discharge.
- Three years for a detention Centre order.
- Seven years for a borstal order.

Financial Status

The TC must be satisfied as to the financial status of "O" license applicants to determine whether the applicant has sufficient money to operate and maintain the licensed vehicles according to statutory requirements. Detailed questionnaires (form GV 79F) are frequently sent out by TCs for completion to obtain details about the resources and projected operating expenditures of an applicant.

Operating Centres and Parking

"O" license applicants must supply the address of the place where the vehicles will be parked when they are not in use, a location known as the "operating Centre". The TC will consider the location and suitability of the premises for the parking of goods vehicles under provisions contained in the Transport Act 1982 (section 52 and schedule 4) amending the Transport Act 1968.

By the provisions of the Act an operating Centre includes any place where vehicles are regularly parked. Therefore, when drivers regularly take vehicles home, the place where they park the vehicle may become an operating Centre subject to TC approval and to representation by any local resident environmentally affected by such parking.

Powers of Traffic Commissioners

"O" license applications are made to the TC for the area in which the vehicles to be operated are based. The TC has the sole power (apart from appeal decisions of the Transport Tribunal) of:

- Considering applications.
- Granting or refusing licenses.
- Placing environmental restrictions on the use of vehicles at operating Centres.

The TC requires completion of the appropriate forms and must be satisfied of the following:

- That the applicant is of good repute and is a fit person to hold a license.
- That he has suitable facilities or has made satisfactory arrangements for vehicle maintenance.
- That he has made satisfactory arrangements for ensuring that the law concerning drivers' hours and records and the overloading of vehicles will be complied with.
- That, where appropriate, he is professionally competent or employs somebody who is professionally competent.
- That he is of adequate financial standing.
- That the applicant has suitable parking facilities (with appropriate planning permission) for his vehicles.
- That the operating Centre is environmentally suitable.

The TC has the power to call an operator to public inquiry so he can:

- Publicly consider the application for an operator's license.
- Question an operator about offences which have been committed in contravention of the "O" license requirements. (A Section 69 Inquiry granted as a power of the TCs under Section 69 of the Transport Act 1968.)
- Listen to environmental representations by local residents about the suitability of the vehicle operating Centre and the use of vehicles at the Centre.
- Listen to statutory objections to the granting of a license by specified objectors.

TCs have powers to impose conditions on operating Centres under provisions contained in the Transport Act 1982. These include:

- Number of vehicles parked.
- Manner in which they are parked.
- Size of the vehicles.
- Times when vehicles arrive and depart.
- The route followed going in and out.
- Maintenance.
- Vehicle loading and unloading.

License Penalties

Under Section 69 of the Transport Act 1968 the TC can impose the following penalties on holders of an "O" license:

- Revocation - the complete license can be revoked for a stipulated period or in extreme cases the person can be forbidden from ever holding a license again.
- Suspension - the TC can suspend the complete "O" license or a number of vehicles from the license temporarily.
- Curtailment - the TC reduces the number of vehicles that may be operated under the license.

In the case of curtailment or suspension the TC can rule that the vehicles concerned must not be used under any other "O" license for a period of up to six months.

Objections to an "O" License Application

The bodies listed below may object to the granting of an "O" license within 21 days of the publication of the application in the booklet Applications and Decisions (commonly referred to as "As and Ds") on the grounds that the applicant does not meet the necessary qualifications, because:

- The applicant is not of good repute.
- He is not of appropriate financial standing.
- He does not meet the requirements of professional competence.
- He is not likely to comply with the law regarding drivers' hours and records and vehicle overloading.
- There are not satisfactory arrangements or facilities for vehicle maintenance.
- The applicant does not have suitable parking facilities.

The bodies are:

- A chief officer of police.
- A local authority.
- A planning authority.
- The Freight Transport Association (FTA).
- The Road Haulage Association (RHA).
- The British Association of Removers (BAR).
- The General and Municipal Workers' Union (GMWU).
- The National Union of Railwaymen (NUR).
- The Transport and General Workers' Union (TGWU).
- The Union of Shop, Distributive and Allied Workers (USDAW).
- The United Road Transport Union (URTU).

When an objection is raised by any of the listed bodies the objector must provide the applicant with a copy of the objection.

Appeals to the Transport Tribunal

An "O" license applicant who has been refused, or an existing operator whose license is revoked, suspended or curtailed, may appeal to the Transport Tribunal. An operator may also appeal the decision of a TC following representations on environmental grounds or against conditions placed on a license. People making environmental representations have no such appeal rights. Appeals must be made within one month of the TC's decision being published in Applications and Decisions.

Admission to the Occupation — Professional Competence

There are a number of changes taking place to the regulation of the CPC examination. The student should check with DVSA and OCR to check for current regulations.

Examination

The official examination for those who do not qualify for professional competence by other means is conducted four or more times a year at various Centres throughout the country on behalf of OCR, the current official examining body. (Copies of the examination syllabus can be obtained from OCR.)
The examining body may change in the future, so be advised to check for any updates regarding any of these changes.

Fees and Validity

Certificates of Professional Competence were granted on a once-only basis with no renewal, and were free. Obtaining the professional competence qualification costs nothing beyond the price of studying for and sitting for the examination or payment of Institute annual subscriptions. Once acquired, the professional competence qualification does not require renewal and is valid so long as the current system remains in place.

Issue of Certificates of Professional Competence

Certificates of Professional Competence were issued only to those who qualified under Grandfather Rights. A valid membership in qualifying professional institute is sufficient proof of competence, although the institutes will issue a confirmatory certificate if needed.
(Please be advised to check any changes regarding these rights.)

A pass certificate from the examination board will be issued for those qualifying through the official examinations.

Setting Up a Road Transport Undertaking

The goods vehicle operator licensing scheme is administered by the Driver and Vehicle Standards Agency (DVSA) on behalf of the traffic commissioners.

Applications for "O" licenses

Before making an application

You are advised to consider the following questions:

- Why do you require an operator's licence?
- What type of operator licence do you need?

- How many vehicles and trailers will you need?
- Have you someplace suitable to park your vehicles and trailers?
- Have you someone competent to conduct regular vehicle maintenance and inspections?
- Can you provide evidence of 'financial standing' to the Traffic Commissioner?
- Do you have sufficient knowledge of drivers' hours to ensure operator compliance?

There are other criteria that you may need to satisfy, depending on the type of licence you require

You can apply on-line here:
https://www.gov.uk/apply-vehicle-operator-licence

Nine weeks (or more) before commencing operations, "O" license applicants should complete and submit form GV 79 to the Traffic Area Office where the specified vehicles will be based. This submission should be accompanied by form GV 79A listing the vehicles to be specified. The TC may also require further evidence of financial standing through submission of accounts, accountant's letter, bank statements or other proof of resources. An applicant may be asked to complete form GV 79F detailing projected expenditure and earnings. If, after publication of the application, environmental representations arise, form GV 79E must be completed.

Form GV 79

Form GV 79 is the basic application for an "O" license requiring name, trading name, address, telephone and fax numbers for the applicant and the following information:

- Details of any subsidiary companies whose vehicles are to be included on the license.
- Details of the previous experience of the applicant, his partners or fellow directors in operating or driving goods vehicles.
- Details of any other operator's license held or previously held.
- Details of the operating Centres for the vehicles to be included on the license and the number of vehicles and trailers in possession or to be acquired.
- Details of any previous convictions which the applicant, his partners or fellow directors may have had during the past five years relating to the roadworthiness of vehicles, overloading offences or drivers' hours and records offences which have resulted in a fine or imprisonment.
- Details about the financial status of the business proprietor, his partners or the directors of the business, and whether any of them have been made bankrupt in the past three years.
- Details about the professionally competent person in the case of applications for standard operator's licenses.

In addition to these basic questions form GV 79 requires a declaration of intent regarding ability and willingness to comply with the law. The points included in the declaration are as follows:

I declare that the statements made in this application are true. I understand that the license may be revoked if the licensed operator does not comply with the undertakings made below and that it is an offence to make a false declaration.

I, or the licensed operator, undertake to make proper arrangements so that the rules on drivers' hours are observed and proper records are kept:
Motor vehicles and trailers are not overloaded.
Vehicles operate within speed limits.
Motor vehicles and trailers, including those hired, are kept fit and serviceable.
Drivers report promptly any defects or symptoms of defects that could prevent safe operation and that any defects are promptly recorded in writing.
Records are kept (for 15 months) of all driver defect reports, all safety inspections, routine maintenance and repairs to vehicles and trailers, and these are made available on request; and that in respect of each operating Centre specified, the number of authorised motor vehicles and the number of authorised trailers kept there will not exceed the maximum numbers recorded against the operating Centre (named in section 14 of Form GV 79).
If the license is granted these undertakings may be recorded in the license.

I, or the licensed operator, understand that failure to comply with the conditions or undertakings recorded on a license can result in disciplinary action being taken against the license holder and that failure to comply with the conditions is a criminal offence.

Form GV 79E (environmental information)

If the Licensing Authority receives representations from local residents after application details are published, Form GV 79E is sent to the applicant. The form requires details concerning:

- The applicant and his proposed operating Centre.
- The vehicles normally to be kept there.
- The number and types of trailer to be kept there.
- Any other parking place in the vicinity of the Centre.
- Proof of permission to use the premises where the applicant does not own same.
- Operating times of authorised vehicles (when they will leave and arrive).
- Vehicle use on Saturdays and Sundays including arrival and departure times
- Hours of maintenance work and if such work will be done on Saturdays and Sundays.
- Covered buildings in which maintenance work will be conducted.
- The parking positions for authorised vehicles.
- Entry and exit points.
- Main buildings.
- Names of surrounding roads.
- Any applications for or planning permission granted to use the site as a vehicle operating Centre.

Form GV 79F (financial information)

When the TC requires additional financial information for consideration of ability to meet necessary financial requirements, the applicant will receive Form GV 79F. An application will be refused unless the TC is satisfied that the applicant has sufficient resources to set up and run the business. Information required on the form includes details concerning:

- The vehicles to be included on the license.
- Their average annual mileage.
- Estimated running cost for each individual vehicle type.
- Available funds to start the business.
- Where said funds are held.
- Start-up costs of the business including purchase price and vehicle down payments.
- The sum to be held in reserve as working capital.
- Forecast of annual expenditure and income.

The TC expects this information to give a clear indication of the business finances for the year ahead.

Form GV 79A

Form GV 79A, a supplement to GV 79, requires the details of every vehicle currently in possession including:

- Registration number.
- The official (Vehicle Inspectorate) plated maximum permissible weight or gross train weight.
- Body type (van, tipper, tanker, platform) and whether articulated.

Form GV 79A will eventually become incorporated into the operator's license form, if granted. The Traffic Area Office will place its stamp in the right-hand column alongside authorised vehicles. This stamp will be cancelled when the vehicles are removed from the license. In some instances a new computerised form is being used.

Form GV 80

Form GV 80 is used to change the total number of vehicles authorised on an existing "O" license. The form requires details of both the applicant and the vehicles to be added or removed. A period of one month is allowed to notify the Traffic Area Office as to the details of vehicles added to a license within the margin (the total number authorised).

Form GV 81

Form GV 81 addresses requests to increase the total number of vehicles authorised on a license. It is also used for:

- Changes to operating Centres, including additions and deletions.
- Changes to the maintenance arrangement.
- Changes to the type of license (from restricted to standard or vice versa).
- To request a change or removal of conditions from the license.

This form requires details of the applicant and any convictions against him, his partners or co-directors; reiteration of the declaration of intent made on the original application; and placement of an advertisement in a local newspaper as previously described.

Advertising of Applications

Applicants for new, varied or renewed "O" licenses must run a local newspaper advertisement for up to 21 days before and not more than 21 days after the TC receives their application. The advertisement must give the address of the proposed operating Centre or Centres for vehicles covered by the license. This provides residents with the chance to make valid representations to the TC (not those that are vexatious, frivolous, or irrelevant) against the granting of the license on environmental grounds only, in that it would prejudicially affect their enjoyment of land owned or occupied. Such representatives have 21 days from the appearance of the advertisement to write to the TC setting out their complaint. For the representation to be valid a copy must be sent to the license applicant.

Publication of Applications

The TC publishes applications for new "O" licenses or for variations of existing licenses in the booklet Applications and Decisions for the benefit of potential objectors who have 21 days to raise their concern. Decisions to grant licenses or variations of licenses or refusals for same may also be published in this document which is available at Traffic Area Offices.

Subsidiary/Associate Companies

A holding/parent company may include vehicles from a subsidiary, a company in which more than a 50 percent shareholding is held, on the "O" license application. Those of an associate company in which less than 50 percent shareholding is held may not be included.

Transfer of Vehicles

If vehicles will be operating in another traffic area for more than three months, they must be specified on an existing "O" license in that area or application for a new license must be submitted at least nine weeks before operations begin. Operating goods vehicles of more than 3.5 tons maximum permissible weight from a base in a Traffic Area in which no "O" license is held is illegal.

License Margin

In making an "O" license application it is permissible to receive permission to operate more vehicles than those actually required to serve as a surplus or "margin" in the event of vehicles being off the road for any reason or to cater to peak trade periods.

Adding Vehicles

The number of authorised vehicles may be increased at any time so long as the TC is informed of their details within one month by submission of form GV 80.

Notification of Changes

If any changes to the legal entity of a business occur such as alteration of name, partners or if a limited company is formed, the existing license is no longer valid and application for a new license is required. The TC must be apprised of changes to business addresses within three weeks. Other changes requiring notification include those affecting a nominated professionally competent person:

- Where such a person dies.
- Becomes physically disabled.
- Becomes mentally disordered.
- Where the license holder or a partner or director is declared bankrupt.
- Where company goes into insolvent liquidation.

Failure to notify can result in a fine, revocation, suspension, or curtailment.

Fees and Validity

The fee for an "O" license is calculated on a per vehicle per quarter basis plus a license fee. Licenses run continuously but must be reviewed every five years when payment of the appropriate fees is due. Failure to pay the fee will result in automatic termination.

Interim licenses

A TC may grant an interim "O" license pending consideration of an application for a full license. Receiving an interim license does not guarantee issuance of a full license.

Temporary Derogation

Holders of a standard "O" license may operate without a professionally competent person if the person dies or becomes physically or mentally incapacitated (the TC must be notified in writing) for no more than 12 months, after which time the license will be revoked unless the TC accepts that there are exceptional circumstances and permits an extension of this period (the maximum is 18 months).

Community Documentation

Documentation to be carried on the vehicle for international journeys is described below. You should note that international haulage operations depend on correct documentation at points of entry and exit. Incorrect documentation can results in both delays and extra expense. The following documents should be carried:

For the driver:

- his national (EU-type) driving license
- an international driving license where appropriate
- a translation of the driving license where appropriate
- his current and valid passport
- an entry visa where appropriate
- a letter of authority to have charge of the vehicle on company letter-heading
- a bail bond (for Spain only, usually issued with the insurance green card)
- tachograph charts where applicable
- ADR training certificate if applicable

For the vehicle:

- the registration document (original form V5 log book for NI vehicles)
- the current "O" license disc displayed in the windscreen
- the certificate of insurance
- insurance green card (not compulsory but advisable)
- copies of the vehicle annual test and plating certificate
- road haulage/cabotage authorisation permit (as appropriate)

Carnet de passage en Duane for certain countries:

- France (no longer required for plated trailers and semi-trailers)
- Gibraltar
- Greece (if staying more than 10 days)
- Italy (for vehicles remaining more than three months)
- Portugal (triptype for spare parts)
- nationality plate (in the UK, a GB plate)
- Eco-points card and stamps (for Austria)

For the load:

- road haulage/cabotage permit/Community Authorisation (where applicable)
- CMR consignment note (for haulage operations or own-account certificate)
- carnet (as appropriate)
- TIR
- ATA (for temporary importation of goods)
- copies of invoices for the goods
- certificate of origin/health/consular certificates (where appropriate)
- certificates issued under the following conventions (as appropriate)
- ADR (for dangerous goods)
- ATP (for perishable foodstuffs)

Full details of the requirements for documents in respect of individual countries may be obtained from the International Road Freight Office. When on an international journey, certain documents may be required only in particular circumstances; others are required at all times.

A national identification plate should always be fixed to the vehicle when it is travelling in a country other than that of its registration.

The driver should carry his passport (and visa, which is usually stamped in the passport) with him at all times. The passport provides a means of identification and carrying it everywhere helps to prevent it being stolen.

The driver should have with him in the vehicle, the original of the vehicle registration document and a letter of authorisation from the vehicle owners, confirming that he is authorised to be in possession of the vehicle.

In some countries a British/Euro driving license is not sufficient to meet national requirements. In these circumstances the driver should have an international driving permit (IDP) which is obtainable from the AA, RAC or RSAC and the National Breakdown Recovery Club. An applicant for an IDP must be a UK resident and aged 18 years or over.

A visa is required by the driver for visiting certain countries (not EU member states). Employers should obtain the visas from the relevant country's embassy in Britain or from the British embassy in countries to be visited.

Planning and Requirements for International Journeys

International Movements

Several countries have introduced COVID-19 testing requirements for hauliers. The rules are different in each country. Check the rules before you travel and take the necessary action.

What UK goods vehicle operators need to do to carry out international road haulage as of 31st December2020.

From 1 January 2021, HGV drivers must have a KAP to travel through Kent to the Port of Dover or the Eurotunnel and on to the EU. The permit helps manage traffic by confirming drivers have the right documents for EU import controls.

You must have tested negative for coronavirus (COVID-19) up to 72 hours before you cross the border into France. Check the latest advice for HGV drivers using the Port of Dover or Eurotunnel at: http://alturl.com/n9yja

You do not need a Kent Access Permit (KAP) if the HGV is under 7.5 tonnes or leaving from a different port. Further details here: http://alturl.com/wyx6a

Border Controls

Your driver will need to carry the right vehicle documents with them during international journeys. These include:

- vehicle registration documents
- vehicle and trailer insurance documents
- GB stickers
- vehicle operator licences and permits

Your driver will need to carry the right documents about themselves with them during international journeys. These include:

- a valid UK driving licence
- a valid Driver Certificate of Professional Competence (CPC) card
- a valid passport
- an international driving permit (IDP) if they need one for the countries they're travelling in
- healthcare documents

Community Road Haulage Authorisations

A road consignment (CMR) note is a standard contract used by companies who want to use a provider to transport goods internationally by road.

The CMR note confirms that the haulage company has received the goods and has a contract from the supplier to carry them.

You must have a CMR note on all international journeys if you're carrying goods on a commercial basis.

The CMR note can be filled in by either:

- you (the haulier)

- the company sending the goods abroad
- a freight forwarder

You will need 3 copies of a CMR note, including one:

- for the supplier of the goods
- for the eventual customer
- to accompany the goods while they are being transported

Full Details here: http://alturl.com/szdyr

International Carriage

For the purposes of this regulation, "international carriage" means:

- where a goods vehicle departs from one and arrives in another country (whether transiting other countries en route)
- where a vehicle departs from a country and arrives in a another country or vice versa (with or without transit through one or more countries en route)
- where a vehicle departs from and arrives in a country but travels via a another country en route

UK Licence for the Community for International Road Haulage.

From January 2021 the UK Licence for the Community has replaced the EU Community Licence.

You will have to get a UK Licence for the Community to transport goods by road to or through the EU, Liechtenstein, Norway and Switzerland, and the rules you have to follow.
It's a single permit that covers trips between these countries. It also allows transit traffic through these countries to and from non-EU countries - but you need extra permits for the non-EU countries.
Check which international road haulage permits you need: http://alturl.com/wa5xs

UK Issue of Community Authorisations

You should have received your replacement UK Licence for the Community by 31st December 2020 if you had an EU Community Licence.
You should destroy your old EU Community Licence.

You must have a standard international vehicle operator licence for Great Britain or standard international vehicle operator licence for Northern Ireland to apply for a UK Licence for the Community.
You can call DVSA to get a licence. You need your vehicle operator licence number.

Rules for using the licences

You can only use licences that have been issued to you. You cannot transfer them to another operator or company.

The licence includes:

- an office copy - you must keep this at your main office so that it can be inspected by enforcement agencies
- certified copies - you can get a certified copy for each of the vehicles authorised by your standard international vehicle operator licence

Certified copies of the licences are not specific to any one vehicle.

You must carry a certified copy of your UK Licence for the Community in your vehicle when transporting goods in or through EU countries.
You must also carry a certified copy if you're transporting goods using another type of permit. The driver must show it to any enforcement officer when asked to.

You can use UK Licences for the Community in the 27 EU countries and 4 other countries:

Austria, Belgium, Bulgaria, Croatia, Republic of Cyprus, Czech Republic, Denmark, Estonia, Finland, France, Germany, Greece, Hungary, Ireland, Italy, Latvia, Liechtenstein, Lithuania, Luxembourg, Malta, Netherlands, Norway, Poland, Portugal, Romania, Slovakia, Slovenia, Spain, Sweden, Switzerland and the UK.

International Road Haulage Permits For Some Non-EU Countries

Bilateral Road Haulage Permits

You can apply for permits for 8 non-EU countries that the UK has agreements with to transport goods to or through those countries. These countries are:

Belarus, Georgia, Kazakhstan, Morocco, Russia, Tunisia, Turkey and Ukraine.

Each country has single-journey permits. Whether or not you need a permit depends on:

- the size of the vehicle
- the nature of the goods being carried

You need a permit in some of the 8 countries if your vehicle is carrying goods in connection with your own business, and not for hire or reward
(sometimes called 'own account traffic').

There are also 2 extra types of permits for Morocco to:

- enter Morocco with an empty vehicle
- take in filming equipment and material for film or TV products, or equipment for exhibitions (including racing)

Countries where you need permits for 'own account' journeys

You must have a permit for 'own account' journeys to:

- Belarus
- Morocco
- Russia
- Tunisia
- Turkey

Single-journey permits are valid for one complete journey. The outward and return trips count as one complete journey.

Multiple-journey permits are available for Morocco which authorises 15 return trips during the validity of the permit.

You can use the permits to travel to or through:

- Belarus
- Georgia
- Kazakhstan
- Morocco
- Russia
- Tunisia
- Turkey (you only need a permit when you're continuing on to another third-country)
- Ukraine (you only need a permit if you have a Euro III or Euro IV vehicle)

.

Rules for Using the Permits

You can only use the permit in one vehicle at a time.
You must return all special entry permits for Morocco within 15 days of them expiring - whether you've used them or not.

What to do when you make journeys
You must carry the permit in your vehicle for the whole of the outward and return journey.

You need to show the permit at the border, and you'll be allowed to pass into or through that country.

You must show the permit to any enforcement officer when asked to.
Depending on the terms of the bilateral agreement, you may still have to pay certain local taxes.
Check what other vehicle documents and driver documents the driver needs to carry on international journeys.

<u>Lost or Stolen Permits</u>

Road haulage permits are valuable transit documents. They are not transferable to another operator. Such misuse is illegal, with harsh penalties attached. Replacement of lost or stolen permits is not normally automatic, and requires a full written explanation together with a copy of the police report.
Contact DVSA straight away if you lose or damage a permit, or if one is stolen.

Single-journey permits for all 9 countries, and multiple-journey permits for Morocco

Fees

Country	Permit Type	Cost
Belarus	Single-journey permit	£8
Georgia	Single-journey permit	£8
Kazakhstan	Single-journey permit	Free
Morocco	Single-journey permit	£8
Morocco	Multiple-journey permit (15 return journeys)	£50
Morocco	Empty entry	£8
Morocco	Hors contingent (film and TV equipment, or exhibition equipment)	£8
Russia	Single-journey permit	£8
Tunisia	Single-journey permit	£8
Turkey	Single-journey permit	£8
Ukraine	Single-journey permit	£8

Apply For Permits

Apply to DVSA at least 5 working days before you start your journey from the UK.

Include a cheque or postal order to pay the fee. If you want to pay by debit or credit card, DVSA will contact you to take the payment when your application arrives.

International Road Haulage Permits Office
DVSA
Hillcrest House
386 Harehills Lane
Leeds
LS9 6NF

DVSA International Road Haulage Permits Office
irhp@dvsa.gov.uk
Telephone: 0330 678 1117
Monday to Thursday, 9am to 5pm
Friday, 9am to 4:30pm

Journeys To or Through Non-agreement Countries

If vehicles are to travel to or through a country with which there is no agreement, permission to operate in that country has to be sought directly from that country's transport authority. Application should be made well in advance with full details of the vehicle, the load and the route supplied.

ECMT Permits for Non-EU Journeys

Each year a number of permits are allocated to the UK for haulage journeys between ECMT European countries. These include all European countries plus:

Albania
Armenia
Azerbaijan
Belarus
Bosnia Herzegovina
Croatia
Georgia
Iceland
Macedonia
Moldova
Norway
Switzerland
Turkey

The validity of some permits is limited in certain countries, particularly Austria.

ECMT permits allow laden or empty journeys between countries as well as third country journeys to other ECMT countries prohibited by certain bilateral agreements. The permits cannot be used for transit of ECMT countries on journeys to non-ECMT states or for cabotage. The permits are for hire or reward journeys only and may not be used by unaccompanied trailers or semi-trailers. They allow unlimited journeys for one calendar year but may be used with only one vehicle at a time. The quota for issue of the permits is limited, so they are allocated before the beginning of the year of issue. Usually, no further permits are available during the course of the year, but should the quota be increased an announcement is made in the trade press.

ECMT Removals Permits

Specialist removals companies can apply for an international removal permit for European Conference of Ministers of Transport (ECMT) member countries.

You can apply for a permit for laden or empty journeys if you're a specialist removal company and you move household goods and business possessions between or across European Conference of Ministers of Transport (ECMT) countries.

There are no limits on the number of available permits.

These permits are quota-free and can be used for international removals between, or across, ECMT countries. They are available only to firms employing the specialised equipment and staff needed to undertake such operations and are valid for one year.

Permit Checks

You need an ECMT permit to transport most types of goods (or drive an empty vehicle) through the EU (except Cyprus), Liechtenstein, Norway and Switzerland to these 13 countries:

Albania, Armenia, Azerbaijan, Belarus, Bosnia and Herzegovina, Georgia, North Macedonia, Moldova, Montenegro, Russia, Serbia, Turkey, and Ukraine.

Cyprus is not part of the ECMT scheme. You cannot use an ECMT permit to transport goods through Cyprus to ECMT countries.

After a number of cases of permit fraud, stringent regulations now prevent vehicles on international journeys from travelling without valid permits. Checks are made on vehicles to ensure compliance, and vehicles with no valid permits will not be allowed to continue on their journey. In the UK, the International Road Haulage Permits Act 1975 makes forging or altering a permit an offence as is making a false statement to obtain one or allowing use of a permit by another person.

Eco-points System for Transit Journeys through Austria

Journeys through Austria now involve the issue of Eco-point stamps, a system intended to reduce the effects of air pollution and by design to benefit operators with "less polluting" vehicles. The number of Eco-points available will decrease annually thus reducing the total number of permitted transit journeys unless more ecologically-friendly vehicles are used. The system works so that the greater the potential exhaust emission, the greater the number of Eco-point stamps required to fulfil a journey. The lower the emissions, the fewer the stamps required. Vehicle emissions will be verified by a Conformity of Production (CoP) document issued to operators that must be produced at the Austrian border. For journeys terminating in Austria, existing permit requirements apply but Eco-point stamps are not required, nor are they needed for operations carried out under an ECMT permit.

Eco-point Exemptions

Certain transport operations are exempt from the Eco-points system:

- Occasional freight movements by road to and from airports in the event of diversion of air services.
- Transport of baggage in the trailers of vehicles intended for the carriage of passengers and baggage transport using vehicles of any kind to and from airports.
- Transport of post.
- Transport of damaged vehicles or vehicles requiring repair.
- Transport of refuse and faecal matter.
- Transport of animal carcasses intended for disposal.
- Transport of bees and fish fry.
- Funeral transport.
- Transport of objects d'art and works of art for exhibitions and for professional purposes.
- Occasional freight transport for reasons exclusively relating to publicity and education.
- Removals transport (i.e. household removals) carried out by companies employing qualified workers and having the necessary equipment.
- Transport of instruments, accessories and animals to and from theatrical, musical, cinema, sport and circus performances, exhibitions or fairs, and to or from radio recordings, filming sessions or television recordings.
- Transport of spare parts intended for ships and airplanes.
- An unladen journey by a freight transport vehicle intended to replace a vehicle which has broken down en route and the subsequent transport operation carried out by this replacement vehicle under cover of the authorisation allocated to the defective vehicle.
- Transport of emergency medical aid (in particular during natural disasters).
- Transport of securities (for example precious metals) in specialised vehicles, accompanied by the police or other security services.

The Eco-points System

The Eco-points system comprises Eco-point stamps, Eco cards, and the issue of the CoP document for relevant vehicles. To undertake international road haulage journeys which involve a transit crossing of Austria, operators need a supply of Eco-point stamps and an Eco card on which to affix the stamps or each leg of the journey.

The Council and the European Parliament in the Conciliation Committee reached an agreement on a proposal for a Regulation establishing a transitional transit system applicable to heavy good vehicles travelling through Austria from 2004. This agreement is now endorsed by the Parliament (majority of votes cast) and the Council (qualified majority voting procedure) for the Regulation to be adopted.

In the context of a global compromise package, the Conciliation Committee settled all the questions arising from the amendments adopted by the European Parliament in second reading. The agreement includes notably:

- *On the territorial aspect:* The Regulation will be applied to the entire Austrian territory, thus maintaining the global protection of the environment as well as facilitating both the administrative and technical management of the system.
- *On the system of ecopoints:* As from 1st January 2004 and until 31 December 2006 at the latest,

  - No transit will be allowed for heavy goods vehicles using more than 8 points. An exemption to this rule has been agreed for Greece and for highly specialised vehicles.

Quota system for heavy goods vehicles will be applied to vehicles using 8,7 and 6 points.
Unrestricted transit is granted to vehicles using 5 points or less.
(Update: 24-01-2017)

Eco Cards

Eco cards are readily available on application to national transport authorities (in the UK, the International Road Freight Office IRFO). Cards are normally given free with the issue of Eco-points stamps or they may be purchased at the Austrian border. Haulage operators must fill out the three-page Eco card prior to entering Austria:

- Page one has space for affixing the Eco-points stamps, which must be cancelled by the driver's signature across their face before crossing into the country this page will be detached and retained by the Austrian authorities.
- Page two (with carbon copies) requires details to be completed of the vehicle, load and journey (including, where possible, the postcode of both loading and unloading locations, however an offence is not committed if this information is omitted). This page will be stamped by the authorities at the border, confirming the number of Eco-points stamps used, and a copy will be given to

the driver to be carried for the rest of the journey as proof that Eco-points stamps have been paid.*

- Page three lists the appropriate codes for the Austrian border controls and international distinguishing signs to be used when completing page two of the document.

* Note that page two of the Eco card must be returned to the issuing authority, complete with operator's name, address and reference number within seven days of use. Future issues of Eco-points stamps will depend on it.

Eco-points Stamps

Eco-points stamps are each worth one Eco-point. They are issued solely by national transport authorities in connection with international road haulage journeys involving transit through Austria. Vehicles are "charged" with Eco-points according to the following rules:

- For vehicles first registered prior to 1st October 1990 and those not carrying a CoP document, 16 Eco-points.
- For vehicles carrying a CoP document the number of Eco-points equal to the rounded (up or down) CoP value shown.

Conformity of Production (CoP) Documents

CoP documents are issued upon application by the relevant transport authority for vehicles first registered from 1st October 1990 whose engines have a lower NOx emission than older vehicles.

Operators are required to supply the following information in respect of each vehicle:

- vehicle registration number
- the date of first registration
- the type approval number
- the chassis number

The non-transferable CoP document for each vehicle shows the NOx emission value and the CoP value (the NOx emission value plus 10 per cent). The document also indicates the number of Eco-points stamps needed for each single-leg journey. The document must be carried on the vehicle.

Own-Account Transport Operations

Permits to carry goods for your own business. Not for hire and reward.

'Own account' is where either:

- your vehicle is only carrying goods in connection with your own business
- your delivery contents are not for hire or reward

Own account journeys in Europe

The UK Licence for the Community has replaced the EU Community Licence.

You need an UK Licence for the Community if you make journeys for hire or reward within the EU, Liechtenstein, Norway and Switzerland.

You do not need a UK Licence for the Community for own account journeys between the UK and EU if the following conditions apply:

- The goods carried must be the property of the business or must have been sold, bought, let out or hired, produced, extracted, processed or repaired by the business.
- The purpose of the journey must be to carry the goods to or from the business or to move them, either within the business or outside, for its own needs.
- Motor vehicles used for the carriage must be driven by employees of the business.
- The vehicles carrying the goods must be owned by the business or have been bought by it on deferred terms or hire (this does not apply where a replacement vehicle is used during a short breakdown of the vehicle normally used).
- Road haulage must not be the major activity of the business.

Own-account operations between the UK, Austria, Cyprus and Hungary are free from permit requirements, but drivers should have on hand the following information to confirm that the operation is solely for own-account purposes:

- The name and address of the vehicle operator.
- The nature of the operator's trade or business.
- The nature of the goods being carried.
- The location of the loading and unloading points.
- The registration number of the vehicle on which the goods are carried.
- Details of the route to be followed.

In all cases, own-account vehicle operators (and their drivers) should be aware that they may be asked to provide satisfactory evidence to help the authorities to determine the ownership of the goods, and also to prove that the goods are being carried solely for own-account purposes.

Road Haulage Cabotage

Cabotage, provided for under the Treaty of Rome, is internal haulage by foreign transport operators - the collection and delivery of goods by road within a country by a road haulier with an established business in another country.

If you're a UK goods vehicle operator (haulier) working in the EU, you need both of the following:

- a standard international licence
- a UK Licence for the Community

UK Licences for the Community have replaced EU Community Licences. If you have an EU Community Licence, you'll automatically be sent a UK Licence for the Community.

Distortion of Domestic Haulage Markets

Where cabotage operations cause serious disturbance of the national transport market in a given geographical area, Regulations provide for safeguard measures to be implemented on the authority of the UK Licence for the Community.

The Permanent Cabotage Regime

Cabotage and cross-trade

Cabotage is the loading and unloading of goods for hire or reward in one country by a vehicle registered in a different country.

Cross-trade is the haulage of goods between 2 countries by a vehicle registered in another country.

When and where UK hauliers can carry out cabotage and cross-trade jobs

You can usually carry out up to 2 haulage jobs within the EU after dropping off goods from the UK. Only one of the jobs can be cabotage.

The cabotage job must be completed within 7 days of dropping off the goods you brought into the EU.

If you are carrying out jobs in Ireland

You can carry out up to 2 cabotage jobs in Ireland if both of the following apply:

- you are registered as a goods vehicle operator in Northern Ireland
- you have travelled from Northern Ireland

Both cabotage jobs must be completed within 7 days of dropping off the goods you brought into Ireland.

If you have a European Conference of Ministers of Transport (ECMT) permit for 2021

You can carry out one additional cross-trade job (3 haulage jobs in total) before returning to the UK.

Your right to carry out cabotage or cross-trade jobs may be removed temporarily or permanently if you breach safety rules.

When you're carrying out cabotage jobs in the EU you must have documents with you to show the following:

- the name, address and signature of the sender and haulier
- the place and the date you picked up the goods
- the place you are delivering to
- the name, address and signature of the international consignee with the date of delivery
- a description of the goods, the method of packing, the number of packages and their special marks or numbers
- the gross mass of the goods or their quantity
- the number plates of the vehicle and trailer

The so-called permanent cabotage regime replaced the former quota system on July 1st 1998. All international road hauliers holding Authorisations are entitled to operate temporary road haulage services in countries other than their own without any restriction as to quantitative limits or any need to maintain a registered office in that country. Operators must comply with the laws, regulations and administrative provisions of the "host" country concerning:

- Rates and conditions incorporated in haulage contracts.
- Weights and dimensions of road vehicles which may exceed those of the home country, but not those of the vehicle's design standards.
- Dangerous goods, perishable foodstuffs and live animals.
- Drivers' hours and rest periods.
- VAT on transport services.

Cabotage permit holders may temporarily enter another country and carry out internal road haulage journeys as required. It does not mean that they have the right to establish a permanent haulage operation in that country. If a haulier is established on a permanent basis within another country, or wishes to be so, he must conform to the relevant national legislation.

VAT on Cabotage Operations

You may have to register for and pay VAT in the country where the journey took place.
Internal transport operations under cabotage authorisation must comply with national VAT regulations. Operators may need to register in the member states in which they are operating or appoint a suitable VAT agent or fiscal representative.

Prohibited Operations, Offences and Penalties

Cabotage by hauliers and own-account operators in non-EU states is prohibited. Non-resident hauliers who infringe either the cabotage rules when operating in a state other than that in which their business is established, or who otherwise offend against Community or national transport legislation while in such states, may be penalised by the host nation, on a non-discriminatory basis. Penalties may comprise an official warning or, in the case of more serious or repeated infringements, a temporary ban on cabotage. Where falsified cabotage documents are found, these will be confiscated immediately and returned to the appropriate authority in the haulier's own country. You are required to co-operate in applying the cabotage rules and may ask another country to impose penalties on its own hauliers who are found to have breached these rules even to the point of withdrawing an offending haulier's right to operate (in the case of a UK haulier this could mean loss of his "O" license). Additionally, the haulier may be prosecuted for relevant offences and brought before a court in his home country for offences committed in another EU country.

TIR

Under the Customs Convention on the International Transport of Goods by Road (TIR Carnets) 1959, goods in Customs-sealed vehicles or containers may travel through intermediate countries with the minimum of Customs formalities provided a TIR carnet has been issued in respect of the journey.

The carnet is a recognised international Customs document intended purely to simplify Customs procedures not to substitute for other documents. Its use is not mandatory nor does it give any operator the right to run vehicles in any European country. Use of a carnet frees the operator from the need to place a deposit of duty in respect of the load he is carrying in each country through which the vehicle is to pass.

The issuing authorities for the carnets,(in this country the FTA and the RHA), act as guarantors on behalf of the IRU (International Road Transport Union the international guarantor). Consequently, carnets are only issued to members of these two associations.

Goods may only be carried under a TIR carnet provided the vehicle in which they are carried complies with special requirements and has been approved for this purpose by the Vehicle Inspectorate (an agency of the Department of the Environment, Transport and the Regions).

Approved vehicles must have a load-carrying space that can be sealed by Customs, after which it must not be possible for any goods to be removed from or added to the load without the seals being broken. There must be no concealed spaces where goods may be hidden.

Detailed requirements are laid down concerning the structure of the body, particularly regarding the manner in which it is assembled, so that there is no possibility of panels being removed by release mechanisms. The manner in which doors and roller shutters are secured must also meet stringent specifications. Sheeted vehicles or containers may be used, provided conditions relating to the construction of the sheet are observed that once the closing device is secured attempts at entry leave obvious traces.

The VI ensures vehicles meet the technical requirements for operation under the TIR Convention and issues a certificate of approval which must be carried in the vehicle operating under a TIR carnet and must be renewed every two years. Customs authorities make random checks on vehicles leaving the UK to ensure that the required certificate is present.

Application for the examination of vehicles or containers must be made to the VI, (DVSA), in the Traffic Area in which they are available for inspection. The GVTS will provide the application form GV 62, and the required technical conditions. If a TIR-approved vehicle is sold to another operator, the TIR certificate (form GV 60) is not transferable. The new owner must have the vehicle re-certified if he wishes to use it for TIR operations.

TIR Plates

Approved vehicles must display front and rear plates showing the letters "TIR" in white on a blue background. Such plates are obtainable from the FTA and RHA. They should be removed or covered when the vehicle is no longer operating under TIR.

TIR Carnets

TIR carnets are internationally recognised Customs' documents. They are in four parts and contain 6, 14 or 20 pages (volets in French). A 6-page carnet is valid only for a journey between the UK and one other country. Journeys to more than one other country require 14 or 20 page carnets which are valid for two and three months respectively. A carnet covers only one load. If a return load is to be collected, a separate carnet is needed and the driver should take this with him on the outward journey.

Carnets are in pairs and have counterfoils in a bound cover. At each Customs point en route, a voucher is detached and the counterfoil is stamped. Therefore a 14-page carnet may be used to cross six frontiers, the other pair of vouchers being required at the Customs Office of Departure.

The four parts of the carnet include:

- Part 1 - Details of the issuing authority, the carnet holder, the country of departure, the country of destination, the vehicle, the weight and the value of the goods as shown in the manifest.
- Part 2 - A declaration that the goods specified have been loaded for the country stated, that they will be carried to their destination with the Customs seals intact and that the Customs regulations of the countries through which the goods are to be carried will be observed.
- Part 3 - A goods manifest giving precise details of the goods, the way in which they are packed (the number of parcels or cartons) and their value.
- Part 4 - Vouchers which Customs officials at frontier posts will remove, stamping the counterfoil section which remains in the carnet.

Before obtaining a carnet, the member must sign a form of contract with the issuing authority, agreeing to abide by all the legal and administrative requirements. A financial guarantee is required to ensure that the member meets any claims that may be made against him.

Carnets are valid for limited periods only and if not used, they must be returned to the issuing authority for cancellation. Those which are used and which bear all the official stampings acquired en route must also be returned within ten days of the vehicle's return.

Strict instructions regarding the use of carnets are supplied by the issuing authorities, both for the operator and the driver. For example, the driver should never leave the carnet with any Customs authority without first obtaining a signed, stamped and dated declaration quoting the carnet number and certifying that the goods on the vehicle conform to the details contained in the carnet. Drivers should also ensure that the Customs officials at each departure office, transit office and arrival office take out a voucher from the carnet and stamp and sign the counterfoil accordingly.

If a Customs seal on a TIR vehicle is broken during transit for any reason, Customs officials or the police must be contacted immediately to endorse the carnet to this effect.

Carnets

Carnets de passage

Most European countries permit the temporary importation of foreign vehicles and containers (not to be confused with the loads they carry) free of duty or deposit and without guaranteed Customs documents. However, a carnet de passage en Duane pour l'admission temporaire is required for vehicles and trailers entering Gibraltar, Iran, Iraq, Jordan, Kuwait, Lebanon, Saudi Arabia, Syria, Turkey and other Middle East countries. It is also required for vehicles remaining in Greece for more than ten days, in Italy for more than three months, and those remaining in Portugal for more than one month.

A deposit of duty in lieu of a carnet de passage is required for unaccompanied trailers entering Norway and Denmark. Vehicles entering the Benelux countries (The Netherlands, Belgium and Luxembourg) do not require carnets provided they show signs of use (they are not new imports).

Carnets de passage are issued by the Automobile Association, the Royal Automobile Club and the Royal Scottish Automobile Club.

ATA carnets

Goods that are only being imported temporarily can be moved under an ATA carnet, an international Customs clearance document valid for 12 months. Normally these documents are used in connection with the movement of samples for demonstration, display material for exhibitions and trade fairs and equipment for use by service or maintenance personnel fulfilling overseas contracts. They are issued by Chambers of Commerce or by the RHA to members without the need for duty payments or deposits. Operators are still required to observe the Customs regulations in each individual country.

Other Customs/Transit Documentation

Bills of Lading

A Bill of Lading is a legal document of title that acts as a receipt for goods and as evidence of a contract of carriage for such goods. A bill comes in both the traditional "long" form and the new shortened form. The General Council for British Shipping and SITPRO (Simplification of International Trade Procedures) devised the shortened bill to reduce the costs of export documentation and to simplify completion procedures.

House Bill

This is an alternative to a bill of lading used by shipping and forwarding agents and groupage operators when making up consolidated loads or arranging through-transit of goods by land and sea. This document is also referred to as a "combined transport document."

Invoice

An invoice is a document giving details of a sale of goods showing the supplier, the purchaser and any other parties involved. It identifies the goods, the quantity, the price and any other charges to be paid to the supplier, the terms or arrangements for payment, and details of the origin of the goods. Some countries insist on details of invoices being certified by suitable authorities such as Chambers of Commerce.

Consular Invoice

This is an invoice document prepared on a special form and given legal status by the Consul of the importing country. Consular invoices are required by some countries to confirm the specific details of the goods and the transaction, as well as the origin of the goods - this conforms to the Customs requirements of the country concerned. Forms can usually be obtained from the Consul of the appropriate country and when completed, normally have to be lodged with the country for visa purposes.

Certificates of Insurance

Certificates of insurance are issued as confirmation and evidence that a policy exists to cover risks involved in the movement of goods for export. The certificate indicates the type of risks covered.

ECGD Certificates

The Export Credits Guarantee Department provides insurance to British exporters against the risks of export movement. Guarantees are given in respect of goods manufactured in this country for sale abroad and the risks covered include loss or damage in transit plus the risk of non-payment by the overseas customer. The ECGD certificate provides evidence of the cover against specified risks.

Guarantee Vouchers

To avoid having to make individual guarantees or deposits of duty in respect of individual consignments when moving goods under the full Community Transit documentation system, operators can obtain guarantee vouchers against possible Customs claims for duty. Vouchers are obtainable from the FTA, RHA on payment of the appropriate fee. Guarantee vouchers are valid in all EU member states plus Switzerland.

Bail Bonds

Spain requires additional insurance cover for vehicles crossing their borders to protect the driver in the event of his being involved in an accident or infringing local regulations.

It is the practice of the Spanish police, in the event of an accident or incident, to hold all the parties involved until the blame has been clearly established. The purpose of the bond is to secure the release of the driver and the vehicle, pending the outcome of any investigation into the event.

The bonds are supplied by insurance companies.

SITPRO

In 1968 the National Economic Development Council set up The UK Committee for the Simplification of International Trade Procedures to "study documentation in international trade and the commercial and governmental procedures associated with it and to make recommendations to assist the more efficient flow of trade".

The purpose was to establish simplified procedures and forms of documentation to ease trade between countries, thus reducing costs and improving efficiency in the administration of export and import trade. The documentation is referred to as "aligned documentation".

With the "aligned" method, the size of essential documents is standardised and their layout designed so as to be produced in a unified set from a single master document. By typing the details on the master, the aligned forms can be prepared by the "one-run" system.

Items of information that are not required can be omitted by the use of plastic masks or other techniques. This system reduces time and costs.

Section G1 Weights and Dimensions of Vehicles and Loads

Definition of Vehicle Weights

Weight specifications are determined by different means and used for various purposes. The following definitions generally apply.

Unladen Weight (ULW)

The weight of the vehicle including the heaviest of any alternative body and the normal parts. The ULW does not include the weight of water, fuel, loose tools, equipment and batteries where these are used for propelling the vehicle.

Kerb Weight

The weight of a vehicle in road-going condition inclusive of oil, water and fuel but without its load, the driver, or any passengers.

Tare Weight

The weight of a vehicle in road-going condition including the weight of the driver and any passenger prior to loading. This is the weight deducted from the gross weight to determine the actual or potential "payload".

Maximum Laden Weight (MLW)

The actual total weight of a vehicle and its load including the weight of fuel, driver and any passenger. This weight should not exceed the legal limits.

Gross Vehicle Weight (GVW)

The maximum weight at which a rigid vehicle is designed and permitted to operate as indicated on the vehicle plate or the "Ministry" (DVSA) plate and plating certificate (showing the permitted maximum weight to be transmitted to the road by all the wheels of the vehicle in Great Britain). This is sometimes called gross plated weight (gpw) – or gross mass – but more correctly, is the permissible maximum weight (pmw).

Gross Train Weight (GTW)

The total weight of a drawbar combination including its load, fuel and driver and as defined for gross vehicle weight.

Gross Combination Weight (GCW)

The total weight of an articulated vehicle with its load, fuel and driver and as defined for gross vehicle weight.

Permissible Maximum Weight (pmw)

Permissible maximum weights for goods vehicles and trailers depend on:

- wheelbase
- number of axles
- outer axle spread (distance between the centre of the wheels on the front and rear axles)
- relevant axle spacing in the case of articulated vehicles

All goods vehicles of more than 3,500kg gross weight (and trailers of more than 1,020kg ulw) should be fitted with a "Ministry" plate showing the permissible maximum axle and gross weight (or for articulated vehicles, the gross train weight). These weights must not be exceeded.

The current permissible maximum weights for different types of vehicle are specified in both Construction and Use regulations and the Authorised Weight regulations.

Combined Transport Vehicles

The Government introduced rules in March 1994 to boost rail freight prior to rail privatisation that permit swap-body and container-carrying lorries running to and from rail terminals to operate at up to 44 tons gross weight. This increased weight limit applies only to articulated vehicles and drawbar combinations equipped with at least six axles and road-friendly suspensions (or those that have no axle exceeding 8.5 tons), and to articulated vehicles comprising specially built bi-modal semi-trailers (capable of running on road or rail), used in combined road-rail transport operations.

When operating at this weight the driver must carry documentary evidence to show that the swap-body or container load is -

      (a) on its way to a rail terminal, identified by name with the date of the contract and the names of those party to it.

      or

      (b) is on its way back from a rail terminal identified by name with the date and time the unit load was collected. There is no restriction on the distance that may be travelled to or from a rail terminal.

Gross Weight Calculation

The gross weight of a goods vehicle is the unladen weight of that vehicle plus the weight of its driver, any passengers, fuel, the load, and the load-securing devices. The VI plate and plating certificate show the permissible maximum weight. Vehicles may only be operated up to the maximum legal limit as shown on this plate, which is not necessarily the same as that shown on the manufacturer's plate.

Axle Weight Calculation

The major problem is axle plated weight. Whereas gross vehicle weights can be easily checked and controlled, axle weights are more difficult. Although gross vehicle plated weight may not be exceeded, a load incorrectly distributed on the vehicle, often results in axle plated weight being exceeded.
If a vehicle is uniformly loaded the weight imposed on axles can be ascertained by the use of a simple formula.

The only information required, is the total weight of the payload, the distance of the centre of the load to the rear axle, and the wheelbase of the vehicle.

The Formula is:

$$\frac{\text{Payload x distance of centre of load to rear axle}}{\text{Wheelbase}}$$

= Front Axel Load

It must be remembered that weights and dimensions must be in kilograms and millimetres or pounds and inches, to mix the two would necessitate a further conversion.

Example:
Payload = 6 ton
Centre of load from rear axle = 4m
Wheelbase = 10m

$$\frac{6 \text{ ton x 4 metres}}{10 \text{ metres}}$$

24 ÷ 10 = 2.4 ton on front axle
Payload = 6 ton
Weight on front axle = 2.4 ton
Weight on rear axle = 3.6 ton

The amount of payload imposed on any axle must be added to the axle kerbside weight to ascertain if the axle plated weight has been exceeded.

The permissible axle load, i.e. the amount of the payload that can be legally imposed on any axle, should be known. It is obtained by deducting the axle kerbside weight from the axle plated weight.

An area of concern is the diminishing load problem of a payload comprising of multi-drop deliveries. The same formula is used to ascertain axle loading, but it must be remembered that any load put on a vehicle and having the centre of the load behind the rear axle, will act as a counter weight to the front axle.

Two or three sections of a load could be places on a vehicle in such a manner as to cause the front axle to be overloaded. A forth section could be placed on the vehicle with the centre of the load behind the rear axle. (Use of the formula would give the weight being lifted of the front axle acting like a pivot point.) This could result in the front axle now being within the axle plated weight, but when the section was off-loaded it would revert to being overloaded.

Calculations for articulated vehicles are the same, except that there must now be two calculations, one for the trailer and one for the tractive unit.

For the trailer, the kingpin replaces the front axle and the trailer wheelbase is the distance from the kingpin to the rear axle. The formula will give the amount of payload being imposed through the kingpin onto the drawing unit. Add to this the trailer kerbside weight and the weight of the coupling to obtain the total weight being imposed.

For the tractive unit, the centre of the payload to the rear axle is replaced by the distance of the centre of the coupling to the rear axle.

All relevant plated weights must be known and it is the operator's and the driver's responsibility to ensure that at no time are they exceeded.

Overloading and GV 160 Procedure

Overloading a goods vehicle is an offence and subject to examination at a weighbridge upon the order of a police constable, VI examiner or trading standards officer. If the vehicle is found to be overloaded, both the driver and the driver's employer are liable for prosecution and penalty.

After being weighed, a certificate is issued which exempts the vehicle from further weighing on that journey with that load – whether the vehicle is overloaded or not. If the vehicle is overloaded and appears unsafe or to be a danger, a prohibition notice (Form GV 160) will be issued requiring the excess weight to be off-loaded (potentially at a designated location) and reduced to the legal limit before the vehicle proceeds.

A vehicle may be sent up to five miles to a weighbridge without the owner being able to claim compensation for costs incurred should the weight prove to be legal. If sent beyond this distance, and the vehicle is found to be legal, a claim for any losses incurred can be made to the Highway Authority.

Dynamic Weighing

The Weighing of Motor Vehicles (Use of Dynamic Axle Weighing Machines) Regulations 1978 provides for roadside weight check with dynamic weighing machines. As the vehicle is driven slowly across the machine, each separate axle weight is printed out or manually recorded by an authorised examiner. The weights shown are presumed to be accurate to within plus or minus 150kg, unless proved otherwise.

Overall Vehicle Length and Width

The overall length and width of a motor vehicle is the total distance between two vertical planes passing through its extreme projecting points but exclusive of the following items:

- driving mirror
- starting handle
- hood
- fire escape or turntable
- snow plough
- container for Customs seal

Maximum overall lengths and widths for vehicles/trailers are as follows:

Lengths (in metres):

- Locomotives, 2.75
- Motor tractors, 2.55
- Heavy motor cars, 2.55
- Motor cars, 2.55
- Trailers, 2.55
- Trailers when drawn by a vehicle not exceeding 3500kg gross weight, 2.3
- Specially designed refrigerated vehicles with insulated side walls at least 45mm thick, 2.6
- Rigid goods vehicles, 12
- Articulated vehicles (except those constructed to carry indivisible loads of exceptional length, low loaders and those with semi-trailers complying with the items below), 15.5
- Composite trailers (comprising towing dolly plus semi-trailer), 14.04
- Articulated vehicles with semi-trailers complying with item below and satisfying conditions as to turning circles*, 16.5

- Lorry and drawbar trailer combinations, 18.75
- Articulated low-loader type vehicles, 18 ~

Widths (in metres):

- Drawbar trailers (with four wheels and over 3500kg gross weight), 12
- Other trailers not exceeding 3500kg gross weight, 7
- Semi-trailers built since 1 May 1983 (not of a type in item below and not a low-loader) (internal load space dimension), 12.2 ^
- Semi-trailers used in combinations up to 16.5m (see item 3 above):
  - kingpin to rear, 12
  - kingpin to rear (car transporters), 12.5
  - kingpin to front*, 2.04
  - kingpin to front's (car transporters), 4.19   12   12.5   2.04   4.19

* Articulated vehicles exceeding 15.5 metres overall length must be capable of turning within minimum and maximum swept circles with radii of 5.3 metres and 12.5 metres respectively (no part of the vehicle must pass outside concentric circles of these radii). This does not apply to articulated vehicles which are car transporters, low loaders or step-frame low-loaders and those constructed and used for the carriage of indivisible loads of exceptional length.

~ This dimension must comprise a minimum driving-cab length of 2.35m and a minimum coupling distance of 0.75m. This leaves a potential load space of 15.65m within a 16.4m "envelope" measured from the back of the cab to the rear of the trailer.

^ This dimension does not apply when such semi-trailers are used in international operations.

"Front" in this context means the dimension is measured to the furthest point of the semi-trailer forward of the kingpin (i.e. the front corners).

Overhang

The overhang of a vehicle is the distance measured between the centreline of the rear axle and the extreme rear projection of the body or chassis. The overhang distance must not exceed 60 percent of the vehicle wheelbase.

In the case of vehicles with twin rear axles, the overhang distance to the extreme rear projection is measured from a point 110mm to the rear of the centre of the two rear axles.

There is no overhang limit for trailers and the overhang limit does not apply to tipping vehicles if the distance from the centre of the rear axle to the rearmost point of the vehicle does not exceed 1.15 metres.

Dimensions of Vehicles and Loads

Apart from the actual maximum length and width limitations on vehicles and trailers, additional regulations specify the maximum dimensions for vehicles and their loads. These apply to:

- Vehicles operating under the Construction & Use (C&U) Regulations.
- Vehicles which comply with the Regulations but which are constructed and normally used for carrying indivisible loads of exceptional length.
- Vehicles operating under the provision of the Special Types General Order (STGO) carrying abnormal loads.

Vehicle type	Two days' police notification	Attendant to be carried
LENGTH		
Rigid vehicle and load over 18.3m	Yes	yes
Articulated vehicle and load mover 18.3m	Yes	yes
Articulated vehicle for carrying long loads over 18.3m excluding length of tractive unit	Yes	yes
Combination of vehicles and load (excluding the length of the drawing vehicle) over 25.9m	Yes	Yes
over 24.7m (exclusive of drawing unit)	Only by special order from the Secretary of State for Transport.	Only by special order from the Secretary of State for Transport.
WIDTH		
Vehicles and trailers over 2.9m	Yes	Yes
over 3.5m	Yes	Yes
over 4.3m (on C&U vehicle but operating under STGO*)	Yes	Yes
over 5.1m up to 6.1m (under STGO*)	Only by special order from the Secretary of State for Transport.	Only by special order from the Secretary of State for Transport.

Where notification of the police is required, said notification must be made for every district through which the vehicle and load is to pass. The notification must be given at least two clear working days (excluding weekends and bank holidays) in advance of the movement. In the interests of road safety, the police may delay the movement or direct that particular routes should or should not be used. Where three or more vehicles and loads requiring statutory attendants travel in convoy, attendants are only required on the first and last vehicles.

Projecting Loads

A projecting load extends beyond the foremost and/or rearmost points of a vehicle. Depending on the length of the projection, certain requirements (such as police notification, carrying attendants and displaying side and/or end marker boards) have to be met.

Forward Projections

If a vehicle carries a load which projects to the front:

- more than 2m — side and end markers and attendant required
- more than 3.05m — side and end markers, attendant and two days' notice to the police
- more than 4.5m — side and end markers, attendant and two days' notice plus additional side markers within 2.5m of first and subsequent sets

Rearward Projections

If a vehicle carries a load which projects to the rear:

- more than 1m — it must be made clearly visible
- more than 2m — end marker boards required
- more than 3m – side and end markers, attendant and two days' notice to the police
- more than 5m – as in 3 above plus additional side markers within 3.5m of the first and subsequent sets

Side Projections

If a vehicle carries a load which projects to the side:

- more than 400mm beyond the existing front or rear position lamps –extra position lamps must be carried within 400mm of the outer edges of the load (this is a requirement of The Road Vehicles Lighting Regulations 1989 as amended)
- more than 305mm on either side or more than 2.9m overall – two days' notice to the police
- more than 3.5m – two days' notice to the police and an attendant is needed
- more than 5m – see note above about need for approval from Secretary of State for Transport

For these purposes, unless the load comprises loose agricultural produce or is indivisible, it must not be carried if the side projection exceeds the dimensions given in item 2 above.

Vehicle Weights and Dimensions in Europe

Height

There is a height limit of 4 metres on goods vehicles entering Austria, Belgium, Denmark, Germany, Greece, Italy, Luxembourg, Netherlands, Portugal, Spain and Switzerland. Where vehicles registered in EU member states enter other states this limit is not usually enforced.

Carriage of Abnormal Indivisible Loads

The provisions of the C&U Regulations regarding length, width and weight do not apply to vehicles specially designed, constructed and used solely for the carriage of abnormal indivisible loads. Such vehicles come within the scope of The Motor Vehicles (Authorisation of Special Types) General Order.

An abnormal load is defined as one which cannot, without undue expense or risk of damage, be divided into two or more loads for a journey by road and which cannot be legally carried by a vehicle complying with the C&U Regulations (one having a permissible maximum weight not exceeding 38,000kg and complying with dimensional limitations and all other requirements for such vehicles).

Certain conditions apply to these vehicles when abnormal indivisible loads are carried. To ensure the safe carriage of large loads, such vehicles (locomotives and trailers) may be up to a maximum of 6.1m wide (including the width of the load). The overall length of a special types vehicle and its load or a combination of vehicles/ trailers and the load must not exceed 27.4m.

Special Types Vehicles

Special types vehicles used for carrying abnormal indivisible loads are divided into three categories according to total laden weight. Such vehicles must observe varying speed limits.

Cat.	Laden Weight		Speed Limits Not Exceeding	
		Motorways	Dual Carriageways	Other Roads
1	50,000kg	60	50	40
2	80,000kg	40	35	30
3	150,000kg	40	35	30

Vehicles operating under this order must display an identification sign at the front with white letters on a black background reading as follows:

- STGO - Letters 105mm high
- CAT - Letters and figures 70mm high

A figure 1, 2 or 3 must follow the word "CAT" as appropriate.

Under the provisions of the Road Vehicles (Marking of Special Weights) Regulations 1983 such vehicles falling in categories 2 and 3 must display "special types plates" showing the maximum operational weights recommended by the manufacturer when travelling on a road at varying speeds as follows: 12, 20, 25, 30, 35, 40mph. The weights to be shown are the maximum gross and train weights and weights for each axle. Plates on trailers (including semi-trailers) will show maximum gross weight and the maximum weights for each axle.

Attendants

An attendant must travel on special types vehicles where:

- the vehicle or its load is more that 3.5m wide
- it is more than 18.3m long (excluding the drawing vehicle), or in combination with other vehicles is more than 25.9m long
- the load projects more than 1.83m to the front or more than 3.05m to the rear

If three or more vehicles carrying abnormal loads or other loads of dimensions requiring statutory attendants travel in convoy, attendants are only necessary on the first and last vehicles in the convoy.

Police Notification

The police of every district through which a special types vehicle combination passes must be given two clear working days' notice (i.e. excluding Saturdays, Sundays and bank holidays):

- if the vehicle or its load is more than 2.9m wide
- if it is more than 18.3m long (excluding the drawing vehicle), or in combination with other vehicles is more than 25.9m long
- if the load projects more than 3.05m to the front or rear
- if the weight of the vehicle combination and the load is more than 80,000kg

When notice has been given to the police of the movement of an abnormal load, they have the power to delay the vehicle if it is obstructing traffic or in the interests of road safety.

Extra-Wide Loads

When the width of a vehicle and its load exceeds 5 metres, Form VR1 must be used to apply for approval from the Secretary of State for Transport and the form must be carried on the vehicle at all times during the authorised movement.

Notification to Highway and Bridge Authorities

The highways and bridge authorities in an area must be given five clear days' notice of the passage of a vehicle and load that weighs more than 80,000kg or that does not in some other way comply with C&U Regulations. The vehicle's operator must also indemnify the authorities against damage to any road or bridge over which the load passes. Schedule 2 to the Special Types General Order sets out an appropriate form for this purpose. Two days' notice must be given to these authorities in any case where a vehicle exceeds the overall C&U weight limit (38,000kg) or a maximum axle weight.

A special types vehicle must not knowingly be driven on to a bridge at the same time as any other such vehicle or parked on a bridge unless the circumstances are beyond the driver's control. If such a vehicle, weighing more than 38,000kg, has to stop on a bridge for any reason it must be moved as soon as possible. The highway department should be consulted before a broken down vehicle is jacked up on the bridge.

Movement of Abnormal Loads Abroad

The national transport authority must be consulted and must grant authorisation when an abnormal load is to be moved either through EU member states or other European countries. There are no standard rules as to vehicle/load weights and dimensions or the manner of conducting such loads in transit. Each country has its own legal requirements.

Each country has their own regulations governing weights and dimensions of commercial vehicles allowed on their roads. The following is a comprehensive list.

COUNTRY	HEIGHT	WIDTH	LENGTH		
	Lorry or Trailer			Road Train	Articulated Vehicle
Albania	4m	2.50 m	12 m	18.35 m	16.50 m
Austria	4 m	2.55 m (3)	12 m	18.75 m	16.50 m
Azerbaijan	4 m	2.50m	12 m	20 m	
Belarus	4 m	2.55 m	12 m	20 m	20 m
Belgium	4 m	2.55 m (3)	12 m	18.75 m	16.50 m
Bosnia-Herzegovina	4 m	2.50 m	12 m	18 m	17 m
Bulgaria	4 m	2.55 m	12 m	18.75 m	16.50 m
Croatia	4 m	2.55 m (3)	12 m	18.35 m	16.50 m
Czech Republic	4 m	2.55 m (3)	12 m	18.75 m	16.50 m
Denmark	4 m	2.55 m (3)	12 m	18.75 m	16.50 m
Estonia	4 m	2.55 m	12 m	18.75 m	16.50 m
Finland	4.20 m	2.60 m	12 m	25.25 m	16.50 m
France	not defined	2.55 m (3)	12 m	18.75 m	16.50 m
FYR Macedonia	4 m	2.50 m	12 m	18 m	16.50 m
Georgia	4 m	2.50 m	20 m	20 m	
Germany	4 m	2.55 m (3)	12 m	18.75 m	16.50 m
Greece	4 m	2.55 m (3)	12 m	18.75 m	16.50 m
Hungary	4 m	2.55 m (3)	12 m	18, 75 m	16.50 m
Iceland	4.20 m	2.55 m	12 m	22 m	18 m
Ireland	4.25 m	2.50 m (3)	12 m	18.35 m	16.50 m
Italy	4 m	2.55 m (3)	12 m	18.75 m	16.50 m
Latvia	4 m	2.55 m (3)	12 m	18.75 m	16.50 m
Liechtenstein	4 m	2.55 m	12 m	18.75 m	16.50 m
Lithuania	4 m	2.55 m (3)	12 m	18.75 m	16.50 m
Luxembourg	4 m	2.55 m (3)	12 m	18.75 m	16.50 m
Malta	4 m	2.55 m (3)	12 m	18.75 m	16.50 m
Moldova	4 m	2.50 m	12 m	20 m	16.50 m
Netherlands	4 m	2.55 m (3)	12-m	18.75 m	16.50 m
Norway	not defined	2.55 m (3)	12 m	19.50 m	200 m
Poland	4 m	2.55 m (3)	12 m	18.75 m	16.50 m
Portugal (2)	4 m	2.55 m (3)	12 m	18.75 m	16.50 m
Romania	4 m	2.55 m (3)	12 m	18.75 m	16.50 m
Russia	4 m	2.55 m (3)	12 m	20 m	20 m
Serbia	4m	2.50 m	12m	18 m	16.50 m
Slovakia	4 m	2.55 m (3)	12 m	18.75 m	16.50 m
Slovenia	4 m	2.55 m (3)	12 m	18.75 m	16.50 m
Spain	4 m	2.55 m (3)	12 m	18.75 m	16.50 m
Sweden	N/D	2.60 m	24 m	24 m	25.25 m
Switzerland	4 m	2.55 m (3)	12 m	18.75 m	16.50 m
Turkey	4 m	2.55 m (3)	12 m	18.75 m	16.50 m
Ukraine	4 m	2.65 m	12 m	22 m	22 m
United Kingdom	N/D	2.55 m (3)	12 m	18.75 m	16.5 m

DVSA's roadworthiness and traffic enforcement work involves carrying out roadside spot checks on commercial and other vehicles for compliance with regulations relating to:

- safety and environmental standards
- overloading
- drivers' hours
- operator licensing
- vehicle licensing and vocational drivers' licences

DVSA's specialist enforcement staff are either, Vehicle Examiners, (VEs) responsible for checking the mechanical condition of a vehicle, or Traffic Examiners, (TEs) responsible for checking tachographs, drivers' hours regulations, vehicle weight, licensing and other documentation.

Checks are held all over the country, either at the roadside or at permanent sites such as weighbridges. Vehicles selected for examination are directed into the check site either by specialist DVSA staff or by a police officer. The vehicle will then be examined.

Roadworthiness Enforcement Action

For non-compliant vehicles, enforcement action is taken by using a Prohibition Notice (PG9) prohibiting vehicles from use, or by prosecuting drivers and vehicle operators and reporting to the Traffic Commissioner for Operator Licensing action.

Vehicle Examiners use the "Categorisation of Defects on Road Vehicles" at the roadside checks. This provides guidance on the action to take when roadworthiness defects are found during vehicle inspections. Copies of this document can be purchased from DVSA.

If significant defects are found, an immediate prohibition will be issued which prevents further use of the vehicle. In cases in which a defect is not considered to be an immediate risk, a delayed prohibition will be issued. This allows the continued use of the vehicle until the prohibition comes into force, usually up to 10 days from the date that the prohibition was issued.

Details about how to clear a prohibition are given on the reverse of the prohibition notice. Clearance will usually be by a full or partial test at a DVSA test station.

Prohibitions can be issued by Traffic Examiner's for matters relating to weight, drivers' hours and records, hazardous goods and visual construction and use (such as length, insecure loads etc.). If during the check an offence is found for which the driver and/or operator may be prosecuted, the driver will be advised at the roadside that he will be reported for the offence. This may subsequently lead to prosecution. Details of prohibitions issued are copied to the Licensing Authority/ Traffic Commissioner.

DVSA and the Traffic Commissions

The central licensing office is responsible for processing applications for heavy goods vehicle (HGV) and public service vehicle (PSV) operator licences and providing administrative support to traffic commissioners. ALL licence applications are processed in Leeds, along with bus registrations for England and Wales. Bus registrations in Scotland are dealt with by staff at the Office of the Traffic Commissioner (Scotland).

Central Licensing Office

Hillcrest House
386 Harehills Lane
Leeds
LS9 6NF

Email: enquiries@otc.gsi.gov.uk

Phone 0300 123 9000

Fax 0113 249 8142

Opening hours

Office hours: 9.30am to 4.00pm, Monday to Friday
Telephone hours: 8.30am to 5.00pm, Monday to Friday

Section G2 Vehicle Selection

Choice of Vehicle

The weight and volume of loads to be carried and their nature are initial considerations in selecting a vehicle. The choice will also be significantly affected by the need for the vehicle to be specified on an operator's license and to employ LGV-licensed drivers.

Selection for Operational Needs

A badly chosen vehicle unsuited to its work will prove costly in terms of:

- inefficient use
- under use
- repeated breakdowns
- excessive downtime
- driver discontent
- disruption of delivery schedules
- customer discontent
- reduced vehicle life

Savings in initial capital cost are frequently offset by higher operating costs and shorter life. The best approach is to buy on the basis of likely "total life cost" (purchase price plus operating costs throughout the vehicle life, less its residual value).

Selection to Achieve Environmental Objectives

With increasing attention to the adverse environmental impact of large vehicles relative to fuel consumption, noise, and air pollution, technology to reduce these factors has give the transport operator a number of choices for more environmentally friendly vehicles such as:

- Road-friendly suspensions (usually air) allowing for greater permissible axle and vehicle gross weights and reduced drive-by noise levels.
- The Reduced Pollution Certificate (RPC) scheme to reduce your vehicle tax ended on 31 December 2016.

Your vehicle can be tested for a Low Emissions Certificate if it:

- was registered in the UK before 1 October 2006
- is fitted with a full filter to Low Emission Zone emissions standards
- You don't need a Low Emission Certificate for a vehicle with a Euro 4, 5 or 6 engine.

Book a Low Emissions Certificate test

Contact an authorised testing facility or Driver and Vehicle Standards Agency (DVSA) test station to book the test.

You need:

- your vehicle registration number
- your vehicle identification or chassis number
- the make, model and date of manufacture
- details of any modifications made to meet the emissions standard
- to pay the fee

Definition of Vehicle Types

The Road Traffic Act 1991 defines vehicles as follows:

Goods vehicle
A vehicle (or trailer) constructed or adapted for use in the carriage of goods.

Motor Car

A vehicle constructed to carry goods or passengers with an unladen weight not exceeding 3,050kg. Otherwise any other vehicle with an unladen weight not exceeding 2,540kg.

Heavy Motor Car

A vehicle constructed to carry goods or passengers with an unladen weight exceeding 2,540kg.

Motor Tractor

A vehicle which is not constructed to carry a load and which has an unladen weight not exceeding 7,370kg.

Light Locomotive

A vehicle which is not constructed to carry a load and which has an unladen weight of more than 7,370kg but not exceeding 11,690kg.

Heavy Locomotive

A vehicle which is not constructed to carry a load and which has an unladen weight exceeding 11,690kg.

Articulated Vehicle

As defined in the C&U Regulations a motorcar or heavy motorcar with a trailer so attached that when the semi-trailer is uniformly loaded at least 20 percent of the weight of the load is imposed on the drawing vehicle.

Definition of relevant vehicles as found in other legislation:

Small Vehicles (for "O" licensing purposes)

- Rigid vehicles which have plated weight of not more than 3.5 tons.
- Vehicle and trailer outfits which have a total combined plated weight of not more than 3.5 tons. (For "O" licensing only trailers with an unladen weight of less than 1,020kg should not be included.)
- Articulated vehicles which do not exceed 3.5 tons. (The weight is calculated as the plated weight of the semi-trailer plus the unladen weight of the tractive unit.)

Medium-sized Goods Vehicle

A vehicle constructed or adapted for the carriage of goods, which has a maximum gross weight between 3.5 and 7.5 tons.

Heavy Goods Vehicle

A vehicle constructed or adapted for the carriage or haulage of goods, which is an articulated vehicle or has a maximum gross plated weight exceeding 7.5 tons. (Used to determine if an LGV driving entitlement is required).

Rigid Vehicle

Under C&U Regulations – a vehicle not constructed or adapted to form part of an articulated vehicle. (A vehicle where the driving cab and the load-carrying space are mounted on a rigid chassis.)

Tractive Unit

 A motor vehicle which forms the towing unit of an articulated vehicle with a semi-trailer so that when uniformly loaded, at least 20 percent of the weight of the load is borne by the tractive unit.
It is not designed to carry a load other than when a semi-trailer is attached and should not be confused with a "tractor".

Tractor

A towing unit which does not have part of the weight of the trailer superimposed upon it (as described above for articulated tractive units). Usually tractors are employed in heavy haulage operations and carry ballast to give them sufficient traction for pulling very heavy loads at low speeds.

Semi-trailer

A trailer drawn by a tractive unit where at least a proportion of its weight is superimposed on the tractive unit (at least 20 percent of the weight of the load when uniformly loaded) and connected by means of a kingpin and fifth wheel mounting plate or by an automatic-type coupling.

Drawbar Trailer

One which has axles on both the front and the rear and the steerable front axle is connected to the rear of the rigid towing vehicle by means of a solid drawbar with flexible brake and electrical connections. No part of the weight of the trailer is imposed on the towing vehicle.

Composite Trailer

A semi-trailer connected to a towing dolly to comprise a drawbar trailer.

Section G3 G4 Mechanical Conditions, Plating and Testing

Goods Vehicle Type Approval

The Motor Vehicles (Type Approval) Regulations 1980 (as amended)
These Regulations may be cited as the Motor Vehicles (Approval) Regulations 2001 and shall come into force on 1st February 2001.
This provides for vehicles and their components to be "type approved," meaning that manufacturers can submit product examples which conform to an established specification for "Ministry" and receive a Type Approval Certificate (Certificate of Conformity). All subsequent identical products are legally approved for sale and use. Purchasers receive a certificate confirming that the product conforms to that approved type, a document required when first registering a type-approved vehicle. After the initial registration all the requirements of the C&U Regulations in respect of the vehicle and all its component parts must be observed.

New-style vehicle test certificate

There is no longer a requirement to display a vehicle test certificate on the windscreen of your vehicle.
A new-style A4 size, plain paper, vehicle test certificate will be issued following the inspection of your vehicle.
This change took effect on 6 April 2015 and applies to all vehicle categories, including cars, motorcycles, goods vehicles or buses.
Motorists are encouraged to remove all expired discs from the vehicle windscreen.

Goods Vehicle Plating and Testing

The Road Traffic Act 1988 and the Goods Vehicles (Plating and Testing) Regulations 1988 (as amended 2001) requires goods to conspicuously display plates showing the permissible maximum weight and the respective maximum weights for any axle.

The same regulation requires annual tests at a Vehicle Inspectorate (VI) goods vehicle test station, with the first test due no later than 12 months from the date of original registration. Trailers must be tested no later than 12 months from the date they were first supplied or sold retail. Trailers have no identification by registration and are given a serial number indicating the testing due date. The number is usually welded to the trailer on to the chassis side frame on the nearside.

Vehicles Covered – Plating

The following vehicles are required to be plated:

By the manufacturer (showing the vehicle design weights or legal weights, whichever are the lower):
- all goods vehicles
- trailers over 1,020kg unladen

By the VI (Ministry plating showing permissible maximum weights):
- articulated vehicles
- rigid goods vehicles over 3,500kg gross weight
- trailers over 1,020kg unladen

Vehicles Covered – Annual Testing

The following vehicles are required to be tested:

At MoT-approved garages (by the third anniversary of the date of their original registration and annually thereafter):
- private cars and dual-purpose vehicles
- goods vehicles up to 3,500kg gross weight

At VI goods vehicle test stations (annually after the first year):
- articulated vehicles
- rigid goods vehicles over 3,500kg gross weight
- trailers over 1,020kg unladen

Manufacturers' Plates

As a statutory requirement, all manufacturers of goods vehicles, and trailers over 1,020kg unladen, must affix a plate showing the maximum weights at which the product is designed to operate. Where such weights exceed current legal limits in Great Britain, the legal maxima will normally be shown.

The information to be shown on the plate includes:

- Manufacturer's name.
- Date of manufacture.
- Vehicle type.
- Engine type and power rating.
- Chassis or serial number.
- Number of axles.
- Maximum weight allowed on each axle.
- Maximum gross weight for the vehicle (including the weight imposed on the tractive unit by a semi-trailer in the case of articulated vehicles).
- Maximum train weight.

In the case of a trailer:

- Manufacturer's name.
- Date of manufacture.
- Chassis or serial number.
- Number of axles.
- Maximum weight allowed on each axle.

- Maximum weight imposed on the drawing vehicle if it is a semi-trailer.
- Maximum gross weight for the trailer.

"Ministry" Plates

Upon initial registration of a goods vehicle or trailer, a plate and plating certificate are issued showing the maximum operating weights. The gross weight and axle weight figures shown on the "Ministry" plate and certificate may coincide with those on the manufacturer's plate or may be lower if the maximum legal limit for the class in which that vehicle falls is lower.

The plate will include:
- Registration/identification mark.
- Chassis/serial number.
- Year of original registration.
- Make.
- Model.
- Maximum Axle weights.
- Maximum gross weight.
- Maximum train weight.
- Design weights (where these are greater than the above).

Using a vehicle loaded in excess of the gross, train and axle weights shown on the plate or for the class of vehicle is an offence.

Standard Lists

VI testing stations use "standard lists" to determine relevant plated weights. The lists identify every vehicle and trailer by type, code and serial number and give the appropriate gross and axle weights. The Stationery Office supplies copies of standard lists.

Notifiable Alterations

The Goods Vehicle centre, Swansea, must be advised (on form VTG 10) of any structural alterations to a vehicle before it is used on the road. The following constitute alterations:

- Alterations to the chassis frame or structure or the attaching of equipment to alter carrying capacity.
- Changes to the steering, suspension, wheels and axles (including stub axles and wheel hubs).
- Fitting an alternative body of a different design, construction or type.
- Alterations to the braking system.
- Other alterations to the structure or fixed equipment.

Annual Testing

The following forms are used to apply to the Goods Vehicle centre, Swansea, for vehicles:

- VTG 1L: first test of vehicle.
- VTG 2L: first test of trailer.
- VTG 40L: subsequent annual tests of vehicles and trailers.

Application should be made not less than one month or more than three months before the expiration of the previous test certificate. Subject to availability, an appointment for the test will generally be made at the testing station of the operator's choice.

The Test

Goods vehicle annual tests are categorised as follows:

- First test (first annual test of a goods vehicle or trailer).
- Part 2 re-test (examination of a vehicle/trailer which fails its first test).
- Periodical test (annual test applicable to all vehicles/trailers after the first test).
- Part 3 re-test (examination of a vehicle/trailer which fails its periodical annual test).
- Part 4 test (examination of a vehicle/trailer following a notifiable alteration).
- Re-test following appeal (examination of vehicle/trailer after an appeal to the VI).

(Additionally, the goods vehicle test stations conduct the "Group V" test, the light vehicle MoT test for large passenger vehicles that cannot get into normal MoT test garages.)

The vehicle will be subjected to an inspection covering the points listed in the HGV Inspection Manual (copies available from The Stationery Office). The inspections are carried out in four main areas:

- Outside - external aspects of the vehicle cab and bodywork, lights, equipment and fittings are examined and the engine is tested for smoke emission.
- Inside the station - over the pit, where the underside is inspected including the vehicle's steering, suspension, transmission, wheels and tyres, wiring and pipework.
- In the next area - where headlamp beam settings are checked.
- The roller brake tester - where braking efficiency is checked.

Test Certificate

There is a new version of the test certificates now in use for trucks, trailers, buses and coaches – the VTG5, VTG5A and VTP20. These test certificates have been updated to comply with EC Roadworthiness Directive 2010/48.

The directive means that test documents must capture three new elements of information not previously recorded by these certificates:

- Country of registration
- Vehicle Identification Number, or VIN –verified by the vehicle manufacturer's plate
- Odometer reading – recorded at the time of test where an odometer is fitted in the cab. Hub odometer readings are not recorded.

Vehicles in satisfactory mechanical condition receive a form VTG 5 test certificate valid for one year. Test certificates must be produced to a police constable on request. Vehicles may not be driven without a valid certificate unless they are being taken to a testing point for a prior appointment. The certificate is also required in order to re-tax the vehicle when its excise license expires.

Refusal to Test

The test station may issue a form VTG 12 (Refusal to Test) on the following grounds:

- Arrival after the appointed time.
- If the appointment card or vehicle registration document is not produced.
- If the vehicle brought to the test station does not conform to the details given on the application form.
- If the vehicle was booked for the test with a trailer but the trailer is not taken to the test station.
- If the chassis number cannot be found by the examiners, or if the serial number given for the vehicle by the VI is not stamped on it.
- If the vehicle is in a dirty or dangerous condition.
- If the vehicle lacks sufficient fuel or oil to enable the test to be carried out.
- If the test appointment card specifies that the vehicle should be loaded for the test and it is taken to the test station without a load. (This decision to test loaded or empty is normally up to the operator but the Goods Vehicle centre may ask the vehicle to be submitted loaded in order to accurately check the brakes.)
- With a trailer, if the vehicle submitted with it is not suitable to draw it.
- If a vehicle breaks down during the test.
- If the vehicle is submitted for its annual test (not the first test) or a re-test and the previous test and plating certificates are not produced.

Test Failure and Re-test

A vehicle found to have defects will not pass and necessary repairs must be made before the vehicle can be re-tested. If the vehicle is re-submitted at the same station within 14 days the fee is reduced.

Temporary Exemption

In the event of special circumstances (bad weather, fire, industrial dispute, epidemic, and such) a test can be suspended for three months and a Temporary Exemption Certificate (form VTG 33) issued. The Secretary of State for Transport may extend the exemption for up to 12 months.

Appeals Against Test Decisions

Appeals must be made to the Goods Vehicle centre at Swansea within 14 days of the test. If no satisfaction is achieved, a further appeal to the Secretary of State for Transport may be made.

Northern Ireland Certification of Vehicles

Commercial Vehicle Testing in Ireland is conducted by approved Vehicle Test Centres (formerly known as DOE Test Centres). All centres licensed to provide HGV (Heavy Goods Vehicles) and LGV (Light Goods Vehicles) tests are listed on their website. www.vehicletesting.ie/

Under The Goods Vehicles (Licensing of Operators) Regulations (Northern Ireland) 2012 These Regulations may be cited as the Goods Vehicles (Licensing of Operators) Regulations (Northern Ireland) 2012 and shall come into operation on 1st July 2012.

Application for a certificate must be made to the Department of the Environment, Vehicle and Driving Test centre in Belfast at least one month before the date on which the certificate is to take effect.

Re-test fees apply where application is made within 21 days from the date of service of the notice and the vehicle is presented for re-examination within 28 days.

Applications by Non-NI Based Bodies

Where an application is made by a corporate body with its principal or registered office outside Northern Ireland or by a person residing outside Northern Ireland the following conditions must be observed:

- During the period in which the certificate is valid, a place of business must be retained in NI.
- They must be prepared to accept any summons or other document relating to any matter or offence arising in NI in connection with the vehicle in question.

- They must undertake to appear at any court as required.
- They must admit and submit to the jurisdiction of the court relative to the subject matter of such summons.
- Failure to comply with any of the above requirements will involve immediate certificate revocation.

Examination of Vehicle

The applicant must present the vehicle for examination when notified and the vehicle must be reasonably clean and accompanied by the registration book and previous certificate (if any). The time and the centre will be specified in the notice.

Issue of Certificate

A certificate will be issued if the Department finds that the vehicle complies with regulations concerning construction, use, lighting and rear marking.

Refusal of Certificate

If the vehicle does not meet the requirements, a certificate will be refused and the reasons for the refusal supplied.

Re-examination of Vehicles

When defects specified in a refusal are corrected, the vehicle may be submitted for re-examination. If this occurs within 21 days, the applicable fees will be reduced.

Refund of Fees

Prepaid test fees may be refunded if:

- The Department cancels an appointment for an examination.
- The applicant cancels the appointment with three clear working days' notice.
- The vehicle is presented on time but the examination does not occur.
- The applicant proves the vehicle could not be presented due to exceptional circumstances occurring no more than seven days prior and notice is given within three days of the occurrence.

Duplicate Certificates

For a fee, certificates lost, defaced, or destroyed may be replaced. Duplicates are subject to return if the original is located.

Display of Certificates

Certificates must be attached to the vehicle in a secure, weather-proof holder and displayed on the nearside windscreen or on the nearside of the vehicle not less than 610mm and not more than 1830mm above the road surface so as to be visible at eye level of a person standing at the nearside of the vehicle.

Conditions of Certificate

By condition of the certificate the vehicle owner:

- Must not permit the vehicle to be used for any illegal purpose.
- Must prevent defacement or mutilation of the certificate.
- Must, at all reasonable times, for the purpose of inspection, examination or testing of the vehicle to which the certificate relates:
    - produce the vehicle at a time and place specified by any Inspector of Vehicles
    - afford to any Inspector of Vehicles full facilities for such inspection, examination or testing including access to his premises
- Must ensure that the vehicle and all its fittings are maintained in good order and must take all practical steps to ensure that all parts of the mechanism, including the brakes, are free from defects and in working order.
- Must immediately notify the nearest examination centre of any alteration in design or construction since a certificate was issued.

Transfer of Certificates

If a vehicle owner sells or changes the ownership of a vehicle, he must return the certificate to the nearest examination centre and notify the Department of the name and address of the transferee. The Department may then transfer the certificate on request by the new owner.

If a vehicle owner dies or becomes infirm of mind or body, the Department may transfer the certificate to another person, on application.

Change of Address

The nearest examination centre must be informed of a certificate holder's change of address during the period of time in which a certificate is valid.

Markings on Vehicles

When certificates have been issued for vehicles, those vehicles must be legibly and conspicuously marked with the name and address of the owner on the nearside of the vehicle; and where the unladen weight of the vehicle exceeds 1,020kg, the unladen weight should be conspicuously and clearly painted or marked on the offside of the vehicle. In the case of articulated vehicles the unladen weight of the tractive unit and the trailer must be marked on the respective unit and trailer.

Offences

Offences include:

- operating a vehicle with an expired certificate
- defacing or mutilating a certificate
- failing to display a certificate
- to assign or to transfer a certificate to another person

Any of the above may result in invalidation of the certificate. Fines or six months' imprisonment may be imposed for such offences or up to two years' imprisonment upon any further conviction or indictment.

Renewal of Certificates

One month before the expiration of a certificate the holder should apply for a new one using an application form obtainable from any examination centre or Local Vehicle Licensing Office of the Department.

Exemptions from Certification

The following vehicles are exempt from the requirements of NI certification:

- Vehicles constructed or adapted for the sole purpose of spreading material on roads or used to deal with frost, ice or snow.
- A land tractor, land locomotive or land implement.
- An agricultural trailer drawn on a road only by a land tractor.
- A vehicle exempted from duty under section 7(i) of the Vehicles (Excise) Act (Northern Ireland) 1972 and any trailer drawn by such a vehicle.
- A motor vehicle for the time being licensed under the Vehicles (Excise) Act 1971, paragraph (a).

- A trailer brought into NI from a base outside the province if a period of 12 months has elapsed since it was last brought in.
- A pedestrian-controlled vehicle.
- A track-laying vehicle.
- A steam-propelled vehicle.
- A vehicle used within a period of 12 months prior to the date of it being registered for the first time in NI or the UK.

Where a vehicle has been used on roads in NI or elsewhere before being registered, the exemption applies for the period of 12 months from the date of manufacture, rather than from the date of registration. For this purpose, any use before the vehicle is sold or supplied retail is disregarded.

Selection to Achieve Environmental Objectives

With increasing attention to the adverse environmental impact of large vehicles relative to fuel consumption, noise, and air pollution, technology to reduce these factors has give the transport operator a number of choices for more environmentally friendly vehicles such as:

- Road-friendly suspensions (usually air) allowing for greater permissible axle and vehicle gross weights and reduced drive-by noise levels.
- The Reduced Pollution Certificate (RPC) scheme to reduce your vehicle tax ended on 31 December 2016.

Your vehicle can be tested for a Low Emissions Certificate if it:

- was registered in the UK before 1 October 2006
- is fitted with a full filter to Low Emission Zone emissions standards
- You don't need a Low Emission Certificate for a vehicle with a Euro 4, 5 or 6 engine.

Book a Low Emissions Certificate test

Contact an authorised testing facility or Driver and Vehicle Standards Agency (DVSA) test station to book the test.

You need:

- your vehicle registration number
- your vehicle identification or chassis number
- the make, model and date of manufacture
- details of any modifications made to meet the emissions standard
- to pay the fee

Section G5 Periodic Vehicle Maintenance

Comprehensive preventive maintenance ensures vehicles are kept fully serviceable and do not suffer mechanical problems between regular safety inspections or manufacturer's recommended service. Such a programme also ensures compliance with C&U Regulations relative to the mechanical condition of vehicles. Being found on the road with a legally defective vehicle, can result in a prohibition notice, possibly followed by prosecution. The vehicle could then be off the road until satisfactory repairs are effected and cleared with enforcement authorities (DVSA). Such a circumstance risks penalty to the firm's "O" license. Finally, in a simple business sense, breakdowns are costly both in terms of money and time and are not good for customer relations.

Systems of Preventive Maintenance

Reading a copy of the DVSA booklet on preventive maintenance systems, Guide To Maintaining Roadworthiness (available from The Stationery Office) is useful for examination candidates. Owners may carry out vehicle maintenance operations in their own workshop or contracted out to a garage or repair specialist.

Responsibility for Contracting Out

When repair work is contracted out, the TC will expect the vehicle owner, as the "0" license holder, to make proper arrangements for regular inspection and repair on an established schedule according to time or mileage. Even if the work is completed on a contract basis, the owner or operator is responsible for proper completion of the work and that the vehicles comply fully with the law. Copies of all documents relating to regular inspection and repair, including drivers' defect reports and responses to them, must be obtained from the repairer.

Safety Inspections

As a condition of "O" license issue, vehicles and trailers are inspected at regular intervals of time or mileage. These inspections are intended to ensure that the vehicles meet all legal requirements and are safe to operate. A written report of the inspection (usually in the form of a pre-printed checklist) and any defects found should be made and a written record kept of the corrective action taken.

Driver Defect Reporting

As a further condition of "O" license issue, goods vehicle operators must provide drivers with a means to report defects. The best method is to issue pads of defect reports, so any problem can be noted during the day. Ideally, if there is nothing wrong with the vehicle, the driver should write "nil" to so signify to the operator.

When action is taken to correct a reported defect, the date and repairer should be noted on the defect report or on another record filed with the defect report.

Regular Servicing

Oil changes, lubrication, and regular replacement of parts such as diesel fuel injectors should be carried out according to manufacturer recommendation. These services may coincide with safety inspections to reduce vehicle downtime.

Maintenance Records

As a condition of "O" license issue records of inspections, defects, repairs and other maintenance work on vehicles should be kept for at least 15 months. To comply with this requirement record systems should ideally consist of the following:

- Wall charts: To indicate "at a glance" when vehicles/trailers are due for safety inspections, service or annual testing and subsequently, when the work was done.
- Vehicle history files: To contain all relevant details of the vehicle – date of purchase, price, specification, engine/chassis numbers, supplier, and body manufacturer. All other records such as those relating to regular inspections, driver defect reports, servicing and repair should be kept in this file.
- Safety inspection reports: Should be completed at regular intervals of time or mileage in accordance with promises made to obtain the "O" license. Ideally, the checklist used should cover all the items shown in the HGV Inspection Manual (available from The Stationery Office).
- Driver defect reports: These are important records which TCs expect operators to keep as promised when obtaining their "O" licenses. They should be made by drivers in writing, ideally with a "nil" report in the absence of defects, and should be acted upon immediately.
- Repair sheets: A record of the work carried out to repair defects identified on safety inspection reports and as reported by drivers as well as other necessary repairs.
- Service records: A record of manufacturers' recommended services – lubrication, adjustments, and replacements.
- Tyre records: A separate record of tyres on the vehicle, tyre repairs and changes.
- Repair invoices: When work is carried out by outside repair garages a copy of the repair invoice should be kept in the vehicle history file as evidence of maintenance work done, together with a record of the replacement components fitted and the cost. The garage should also provide copies of their safety inspection, servicing and defect repair reports to accompany the invoice – the invoice alone does not satisfy the legal requirement relating to maintenance record keeping.

GUIDE TO MAINTAINING ROADWORTHINESS – HGV DRIVERS' WALKAROUND CHECK PULL-OUT

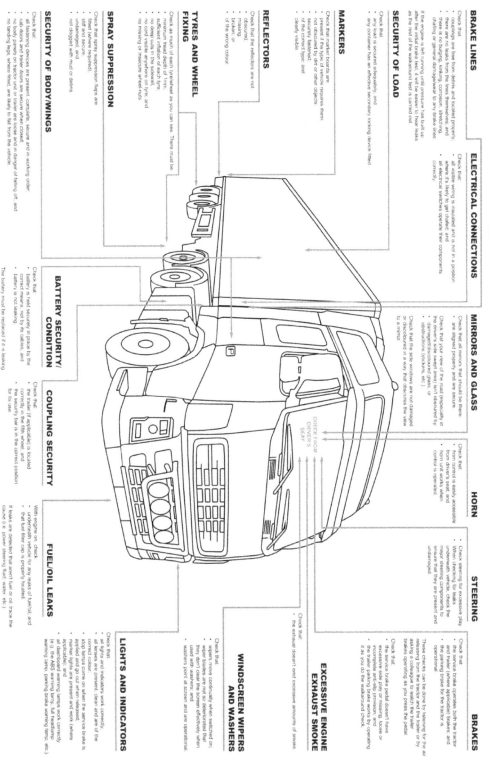

BRAKE LINES

Check that:
- couplings are free from debris and located properly;
- there are no leaks from the lines themselves, and
- there is no bulging, kinking, corrosion, stretching, chafing or general damage/wear to any brake lines.

If the engine is left running until pressure has built up after the initial brake test, it will be easier to hear leaks as the rest of the walkaround test is carried out.

SECURITY OF LOAD

Check that:
- any load is secured adequately, and
- any container has an effective secondary locking device fitted.

MARKERS

Check that marker boards are:
- present if the type of vehicle requires them;
- not obscured by dirt or other objects;
- securely fastened;
- of the correct type; and
- clearly visible.

REFLECTORS

Check that the reflectors are not:
- obscured;
- missing;
- broken; or
- of the wrong colour.

TYRES AND WHEEL FIXING

Check as much of each tyre/wheel as you can see. There must be:
- minimum tread depth of 1mm;
- sufficient inflation of each tyre;
- no deep cuts in the sidewall;
- no cord visible anywhere on tyre, and
- no missing or insecure wheel-nuts.

SPRAY SUPPRESSION

Check that spray suppression flaps are:
- fitted (where required);
- stiff and secure;
- undamaged; and
- not clogged with mud or debris.

SECURITY OF BODY/WINGS

Check that:
- all fastening devices are present, complete, secure and in working order
- cab doors and trailer doors are secure when closed;
- no body panels on tractor unit or trailer are loose and in danger of falling off and
- no landing legs, where fitted, are likely to fall from the vehicle.

ELECTRICAL CONNECTIONS

Check that:
- all visible wiring is insulated and is not in a position where it's likely to get chafed; and
- all electrical switches operate their components correctly.

MIRRORS AND GLASS

Check that all mirrors that should be there:
- are aligned properly and are secure.

Check that your view of the road (especially in the driver's side swept area) isn't obscured by:
- damage/discoloured glass; or
- obstructions (stickers, etc.)

Check that the side windows are not damaged or discoloured in a way that obscures the view to a mirror.

HORN

Check that:
- horn control is easily accessible from driver's seat, and
- horn unit works when control is operated.

STEERING

Check steering for excessive play.
When checking for leaks underneath vehicle check the major steering components to ensure that they are present and undamaged.

CHECK FROM DRIVER'S SEAT

BATTERY SECURITY/ CONDITION

Check that:
- battery is held securely in place by the correct means, not by its cables, and
- battery is not leaking.

The battery must be replaced if it is leaking.

COUPLING SECURITY

Check that:
- the trailer (if applicable) is located correctly in the fifth wheel; and
- the security bar is in the correct position for its use.

FUEL/OIL LEAKS

With engine on, check:
- underneath vehicle for any leaks of fuel/oil; and
- that fuel filler cap is properly located.

If leaks are detected that aren't fuel or oil, trace the cause (i.e. power steering fluid, water etc.)

BRAKES

Check that:
- the service brake operates (both the tractor and trailer where applicable) brakes; and
- the parking brake for the trailer is operational.

Check that:
- the service brake pedal doesn't have excessive side play or missing, loose or incomplete anti-slip provision; and
- the trailer parking brake works by operating it as you do the walkaround check.

These checks can be done by listening for the air releasing from the tractor and the trailer or by asking a colleague to watch the trailer brakes operating as you press the pedal.

EXCESSIVE ENGINE EXHAUST SMOKE

Check that:
- the exhaust doesn't emit excessive amounts of smoke.

WINDSCREEN WIPERS AND WASHERS

Check that:
- wipers move continually when switched on;
- wiper blades are not so deteriorated that they don't clear the screen effectively when used with washers; and
- washers point at screen and are operational.

LIGHTS AND INDICATORS

Check that:
- all lights and indicators work correctly;
- all lenses are present, clean and are of the correct colour;
- stop lamps come on when the service brake is applied and go out when released;
- marker lights are present and work (where applicable); and
- all dashboard warning lamps work correctly (e.g. the ABS warning lamp, full headlamp warning lamp, parking brake warning lamp, etc.)

Source: VOSA Guide to maintaining roadworthiness (Revised 2007)

Example Safety Inspection Record

Vehicle registration	Odometer reading

Make and type

Date of inspection	Operator

Notes
IM ref. (col 2) – for more details on each item listed, look under this reference number in the VOSA Inspection Manual
Serviceable (col 4) – enter the appropriate code:
✔ = Satisfactory   R = Repair required   ✗ = Safety item defect   **N/A** = Not applicable

Part 1 – Inspection

A: Inside cab (motor vehicles)

Check no.	IM ref.	Item inspected	Serviceable	Defect found	Rectified by
1	18	Driver's seat			
2	3	Seat belts			
3	22	Mirrors			
4	23	Glass and view of the road			
5	25	Windscreen wipers and washers			
6	26	Speedometer/tachograph			
7	27	Horn			
8	28	Driving controls			
9	30	Steering control			
10	37	Service brake pedal			
11	38	Service brake operation			
12	34	Pressure/vacuum warning and build-up			
13	36	Hand levers operating mechanical brakes			
14	39	Hand-operated brake control valves			
15	17	Cab floors and steps			

B: Ground level and under vehicle (motor vehicles and trailers, see items marked * for trailers)

16	16	Cab doors			
17	15	Cab security			
18*	19	Security of body			
19*	20	Condition of body			
20	5	Exhaust emissions			
21*	6	Road wheels and hubs			

Check no.	IM ref.	Item inspected	Serviceable	Defect found	Rectified by
22*	7	Size and type of tyres			
23*	8	Condition of tyres			
24*	9	Sideguards, rear under-run devices and bumper bars			
25*	10	Spare wheel and carrier			
26*	41	Condition of chassis			
27	11	Vehicle to trailer coupling			
28*	12	Trailer parking, emergency brake and air line connections			
29*	13	Trailer landing legs			
30*	14	Spray suppression, wings and wheel arches			
31	33	Speed limiter			
32	42	Electrical wiring and equipment			
33*	43	Engine and transmission mountings			
34	44	Oil leaks			
35*	45	Fuel tanks and system			
36	46	Exhaust systems			
37	54	Steering mechanism			
38*	48	Suspension			
39*	53	Axles, stub axles and wheel bearings			
40	57	Transmission			
41*	59	Brake systems and components			
42*	62	Rear markings and reflectors			
43*	63	Lamps			
44*	66	Direction indicators and hazard warning lamps			
45	67	Aim of headlamps			
46*		Ancillary equipment			
47*	74	Other dangerous defects			

C: Brake performance (roller brake/decelerometer test)

Check no.	IM ref.	Item inspected	
48*	71	Service brake performance	%
49*	72	Secondary brake performance	%
50*	73	Parking brake performance	%

Check no.	Fault details

Signature of inspector

Name of inspector

Part 3 – Action taken on faults found

Action taken on fault	Rectified by

Part 4 – Declaration

I consider that the above defects have been rectified satisfactorily

Signature of supervisor ....

Sample Maintenance Planner

Vehicle registration number	Vehicle make and type	Week	JANUARY					FEBRUARY				MARCH					APRIL			
			1	2	3	4	5	6	7	8	9	10	11	12	13	14	15	16	17	18

Vehicle registration number	Vehicle make and type	Week	MAY				JUNE					JULY					AUGUST			
			19	20	21	22	23	24	25	26	27	28	29	30	31	32	33	34	35	36

Vehicle registration number	Vehicle make and type	Week	SEPTEMBER				OCTOBER				NOVEMBER				DECEMBER			
			37	38	39	40	41	42	43	44	45	46	47	48	49	50	51	52

S = SAFETY INSPECTION

I = INTERMEDIATE INSPECTION

M = MAJOR SERVICE AND INSPECTION

A = ANNUAL TEST PREPARATION
(including major service and inspection)

O = VEHICLE EXCISE DUTY RENEWAL

X = WORK COMPLETED

Section G7 Transport Systems

The following information is a brief outline of the principal forms of transport modes and systems that may be used by exporters solely or in combination.

Freight Forwarders

Freight forwarders negotiate carriage, complete documentation, clear Customs, and attend to other arrangements for exporters who do not want to deal directly with the process. Freight forwarders may arrange for all or part of the export operation. Information on freight forwarders and their services may be obtained from BIFA (the British International Freight Association).

Roll-on/Roll-off

Roll-on/roll-off (ro/ro) short sea-ferry ships allow goods vehicles and trailers to travel abroad without being lifted on to a ship or unloaded. The process is fast and efficient, reducing the risks of loss or damage through transhipment. A wide variety of services and cross-Channel routes are now available to international transport operators.

The Channel Tunnel

The Channel Tunnel opened in 1994 providing another alternative for international transport. Freight may travel through the Tunnel on a driver-accompanied basis, with complete road vehicles using Eurotunnel's Freight Shuttle rolling motorway system. Via this method the vehicles are driven on at Folkestone and off at Calais (or vice versa) with only an 80-minute transit time between. Other freight is carried on an intermodal basis by container or swap body on through train services from inland terminals in the UK to destinations in Europe. Conventional rail freight is also carried through the Tunnel.

Containerisation and Swap Bodies

Containers carry the benefits of providing exporters with a means of transport conforming to rigid dimensions which can be tightly sealed, handled with the correct equipment, and is strong enough to protect goods under all the circumstances typically encountered on overland journeys and sea crossings.

Similar functions are performed by swap bodies, but they cannot be stacked. This form of transport is used extensively in Europe, and with the opening of the Channel Tunnel the potential exists for a significant increase of such use in the UK.

The terms "combined" or "road-rail" transport have become common. Legislative provision has been made in the UK and Europe for vehicles used in this traffic to be permitted to run at 44 tons gross weight. Information on the use of containers and swap bodies may be obtained from many sources, including the Inter-Governmental Maritime Consultative Organisation (IMCO).

Other Methods of Unitisation

Other methods of unitisation used in international include:

- Sealed TIR vehicles and trailers.
- On pallets with goods secured by:
    - netting
    - banding
    - shrink wrapping
- In airfreight-type igloos (small, specially shaped containers).
- For liquids, in tanks.

Unitisation of loads ensures more efficient handling and reduces the risks of the consignment being dispersed, lost, or damaged.

Groupage

When consignments are too small to fully occupy TIR vehicles or trailers or containers, the services of groupage companies are useful. These firms combine consignments to fill vehicles and containers as an economical means of sending "less-than-container-load" (LCL) shipments.

Road/Rail

In rail transport, the practice of carrying trailers, semi-trailers or containers in a train atop a railway flatcar. In intermodal freight transport this is referred to as "piggybacking".

Some European national rail networks provide a system for road vehicles to be carried by rail. The rail rate may be less than the vehicle operating cost over the route and heavy lorry usage is reduced on congested road networks helping both traffic conditions and lowering pollution. In the UK, there are limited piggyback services but major expansion is inhibited by restricted rail gauge clearances through bridges and tunnels on key routes.

Intermodalism

The UK White Paper, A New Deal for Transport: Better for Everyone, the Transport Ten Year Plan 2000: Delivering Better Transport – progress report (December 2002) and the EU's own 10-year transport plan, European Transport Policy for 2010: Time to Decide (September 2001) all promoted intermodalism as an effective means of reducing road congestion, exhaust pollution, road traffic accidents, noise and vibration by encouraging a switch of long-haul freight traffic to rail and water way freight systems.

Transport 2010: The Ten Year Plan' (DETR, 2000a) sets out the Government's strategy to tackle congestion and pollution and deliver better integrated, high quality, transport systems over the next decade. A background paper 'Transport 2010: The Background Analysis' (DETR, 2000b) ('Background Paper') has also been published which provides an overview of the modeling and analytical work that has informed the Plan. The Background Paper includes forecasts of emissions of oxides of nitrogen and particles from road and rail transport in England in 2000 and in 2010 under a number of different scenarios. It also includes an assessment of the impact of the measures in the Plan on ambient NO_2 and PM_{10} concentrations based on the methods described in the Air Quality Strategy for England, Scotland, Wales and Northern Ireland (DETR et al, 2000) (AQS) and supporting technical reports (Stedman et al, 1998a, Stedman et al, 1998b). These methods have been updated to incorporate more recent ambient air monitoring results, understanding of atmospheric chemistry and emissions estimates and projections. This report describes these methods and presents the results of the site specific analyses of NO_2 and PM_{10} concentrations.

The emissions projections derived for the scenarios described in the Background Paper are set out in section 2. Sections 3 and 4 describe the methods that have been used to derive estimates of NO2 and PM10 concentration in 2010 from a combination of ambient monitoring data and emissions information. Site specific projections have been calculated for both pollutants. This method has the advantage of not incorporating the additional uncertainty that would be introduced by the use of a dispersion model or mapping method. The site specific projection method involves separating the measured concentration into a number of component parts, projecting each of these parts forwards and recombining to derive an estimate of the concentration in 2010. The results of the analysis for the Plan are listed in sections 5 and 6 and discussed in section 7.

Section G8 Carriage of Dangerous Goods

The Carriage of Dangerous Goods and Use of Transportable Pressure Equipment Regulations 2009 ("CDG 2009"), SI 2009 No 1348, came into force on 1 July 2009. They replace the 2007 regulations.
The Regulations implement ADR 2015 (with a number of exceptions). The main duties are now covered by a single regulation, namely Regulation 5.
Variations in GB which arise from derogations are now in a DfT Approved Document (HSE NI),
Information on the operation of the regulations may be found in the Carriage of Dangerous Goods Manual, available here:
http://www.hse.gov.uk/cdg/manual/index.htm

The Carriage of Dangerous Goods and use of Transportable Pressure Equipment (EU Exit Regulations 2020)

This further amends the Carriage of Dangerous Goods and Use of Transportable Pressure Equipment Regulations 2009 (S.I. 2009/1348) ("the 2009 Regulations"), to ensure that Great Britain ("GB") has a functioning statute book at the end of the transition period ("IP completion day").   Full details from this link:
http://alturl.com/fm9y7

ADR 2021

The GB regulations were substantially restructured for 2009 with direct referencing to ADR for the main duties. Amending regulations were made in 2011, mainly to reflect changes to the EU Transportable Pressure Equipment Directive

ADR is highly structured and prescriptive. It follows that if care and time are taken, the answer to most problems can be found, and for that reason there is little or no need for extensive explanatory literature or guidance.

The European Agreement Concerning the International Carriage of Dangerous Goods by Road (ADR) 2021

This revised version is based on changes applicable from 1 January 2021.

It contains new or revised provisions concerning in particular the transport of electrical storage systems (including lithium batteries installed in goods transport units and defective batteries), medical waste and radioactive materials.

The COVID-19 pandemic has led to an increase in demand for medical gases (particularly medical oxygen), which, along with infectious, hazardous or radioactive substances are being transported with special care and are covered in this edition.

The Agreement concerning the International Carriage of Dangerous Goods by Road (ADR) is an important trade facilitation tool and thus helps reduce the risk of protectionism.

Except for dangerous goods which are totally prohibited for transport, and except when transport is regulated or prohibited for reasons other than safety, the international transport of dangerous goods by road is authorized by ADR in the territories of the Contracting Parties, provided that the provisions of the agreement are respected.

http://alturl.com/cwwb3

Exemptions

Subject to conditions and qualifications ADR does not apply to:

- Carriage of dangerous goods by private individuals where the goods are packed for retail sail and intended for their personal or domestic use or for leisure or sporting activities.
- Carriage of machinery or equipment not specifically appearing on the Dangerous Goods List and which contains dangerous goods in internal or operational parts.
- Carriage undertaken by enterprises which is ancillary to their main activity.
- Carriage undertaken by or supervised by the emergency services, particularly by breakdown vehicles carrying vehicles that has been involved in accidents, or have broken down and contain dangerous goods.
- Emergency transport to save human lives or to protect the environment.

Exemptions Related to Dangerous Goods in Limited Quantities

If a vehicle is carrying under the small load threshold, many of the requirements of ADR are not applicable. The table below summarises the position. Some care needs to be taken, as "what is not exempted is still required". In most cases the remaining obligations are:

- General training for driver (ADR 1.3.2). A record should be kept (ADR 1.3.3)

- Carry one 2 kg dry powder fire extinguisher or equivalent (ADR 8.1.4.2)

- Stow the dangerous goods properly (ADR 7.5.7)

 This is in transport category 2. The "small load threshold" is 333 kg and there is no LQ provision.. The result is that all cylinders count towards the load limit, but if that is less than 333 kg, the "minimum" ADR requirements apply.

All vehicle marks (orange plates) must be removed when no dangerous goods are being carried.

<u>Exemptions Related to Quantities per Transport Unit</u>

Dangerous goods are assigned to a transport category under ADR 1.1.3.6 appearing in column 15 of the Dangerous Goods List. The exemption applies where the goods carried are all in one transport category and the quantity does not exceed the value of column 3 or where the goods are in more than one transport category and the total quantity does not exceed the value in column 3.

For small loads (ADR 1.1.3.6) there is no need in GB to carry the documentation except for explosives and radioactive materials.
The need for the consignor to provide documentation to the carrier remains (ADR 1.4.2.1.1(b) and Regulation 5.

<u>Other Exemptions</u>

ADR also includes exemptions for:

- Carriage of gases.
- Carriage of liquid fuels.
- Empty uncleaned packagings.
- Carriage in a transport chain including maritime or air carriage.
- Use of portable tanks approved for maritime transport.
- Carriage other than by road.

Classification of Dangerous Goods

Dangerous goods should not be consigned for road carriage unless they have been classified according to:

- The relevant ADR 2.1 requirements
- The requirement to assign UN number, name and description, and packing group to these goods as indicated in columns 1, 2, and 4 of the Dangerous Goods List.
- Any relevant class-specific requirements of ADR 2.2 as indicated in columns 3a and 3b of the Dangerous Goods List.
- The relevant test methods as set out in ADR 2.2 and 2.3.

<u>Principles of Classification</u>

Dangerous goods covered by each UN Class are defined based on their properties according to ADR 2.2.x.1, where x indicated the UN Class:

- Class 1 - Explosive substances and articles
- Class 2 - Gases
- Class 3 - Flammable liquids

- Class 4.1 - Flammable solids, self-reactive substances and solid desensitized explosives
- Class 4.2 - Substances liable to spontaneous combustion
- Class 4.3 - Substances which emit flammable gases upon contact with water
- Class 5.1 - Oxidizing substances
- Class 5.2 - Organic peroxides
- Class 6.1 - Toxic substances
- Class 6.2 - Infectious substances
- Class 7 - Radioactive material
- Class 8 - Corrosive substances
- Class 9 - Miscellaneous dangerous substances and articles

Articles or substances not listed on the Dangerous Goods List or defined elsewhere in the ADR have to be assigned to a Class according to the dangers they present in terms of their physical or chemical properties.

Dangerous Goods List

ADR Table A, Chapter 3.2 is the Dangerous Goods List. It identifies all such goods in UN number order with relevant information including name, class, packing groups, labels to be affixed, among others. Entries for each substance refer to "specific provisions" or detailed carriage requirements.

The following types of entries appear:

- Single entries relative to well-defined substances or articles including entries for substances covering several isomers.
- Collective entries made up of:
- Generic entries for well-defined substance groups or articles "not otherwise specified".
- Specific NOS entries covered a substance group with a particular chemical or technical nature.
- General NOS entries covering substance groups having one or more dangerous properties.

Cautions in using the Dangerous Goods List

There are more than 2,000 entries in the UN Dangerous Goods List. Each entry consists of 11 columns and each column includes very useful info.
Be advised that the Dangerous Goods List occasionally contains multiple entries with matching UN number and name. These entries will vary in columns 3a-20. Some multiple entries result from a given substance having more than one form (liquid and solid). Additionally, there may be more than one UN number for the same article or substance. When in doubt, consult the alphabetic index or an electronic version of the Dangerous Goods list from here: http://alturl.com/hs8iu

General Training

Any operator involved in the carriage of dangerous goods by road must ensure that both they and their employees are appropriately trained in the handling of said goods. This training must include:

- Awareness training covering the general ADR requirements.
- Function-specific training covering the detailed ADR requirements.
- Safety training addressing hazards presented, safe handling, emergency response.

Both the operator and the employee must keep records of said training, which must be verified upon starting at a new place of employment.

Driver Training

By law, drivers carrying dangerous goods in a vehicle with a permissible maximum mass exceeding 3.5 tons, tank vehicles, and vehicles carrying Class 1 dangerous goods or Class 7 (radioactive) material must hold a vocational training certificate (VTC) from the Department for Transport secured by attending training courses and passing an examination. The certificate must be presented on request by the police or any goods vehicle examiner. (Drivers not required to hold a VTC are still covered by the general training requirement.)

The main objectives of the training are to:

- Make drivers aware of the associated hazards of dangerous goods.
- Provide them with basic information to minimize potential incidents.
- Enable them to take measures to ensure their safety, the public and of the environment.
- To limit the effect of an incident that does occur.

Moving dangerous goods by road is governed by international regulations and is strictly policed. Most European countries are signed up to the European Agreement concerning the International Carriage of Dangerous Goods by Road (ADR). Each country that complies with ADR implements specific safety measures through its own national legislation.

The purpose of ADR is to ensure that dangerous goods (including clinical and other dangerous waste) being carried by road can cross international borders freely, as long as goods, vehicles and drivers comply with its provisions. ADR has been in force since 1968 and is administered by the United Nations Economic Commission for Europe (UNECE). It's updated every 2 years to take account of technological advances.

Safety Obligations

By law, anyone involved in the carriage of dangerous goods by road must:

- Act to avoid damage or injury.
- Minimise the effects of potential damage or injury.
- Act to avoid foreseeable dangers.
- Notify emergency services of any immediate risk to public safety and supply all necessary information.

When dangerous goods are being consigned for a third party, that party must inform the consignor in writing that the goods are dangerous and make all necessary information and documentation available to them.

Safety Advisers

Every operator involved in the carriage of dangerous goods by road and related loading or filling must appoint one or more safety advisers (DGSAs). It is the duty of the advisers to make sure all activities related to the carriage comply with requirements and are conducted as safely as possible. In particular, the DGSAs advise on and ensure compliance with regulations regarding:

- Identification of dangerous goods.
- Equipment used in carriage and loading.
- Training of employees.
- Maintenance of training records.
- Emergency procedures in the event of an accident or incident.

DGSAs prepare an annual report for management and must ensure that in the event of an incident an accident report is drawn up. DGSAs must undergo training, sit an examination, and hold a VTC valid for five years.

The following organisations do not have to appoint DGSAs:

- Those whose activities involve the carriage of dangerous goods in quantities per transport unit below those referred to in ADR 1.1.5.
- Those whose main or secondary activity is not the carriage or loading of dangerous goods, but which occasionally engage same posing little danger or risk of pollution.

Following discussions within the Working Group on Tanks at the September 2020 session of the Joint Meeting the United Kingdom reflected on the requirements in RID/ADR/ADN 1.1.5.

At the meeting, it was noted that other contracting states / parties appeared to have a slightly different interpretation of these requirements compared to the United Kingdom, which we believe to be due to slightly different interpretations of the various language versions.

The difference in interpretation we believe concerns the use of the word 'conflict' which is used in the English language version of RID/ADR/ADN 1.1.5.

In our opinion, RID/ADR 1.1.5 would better reflect the intention if the word "conflict" were to be replaced by the word "contradict". This would, in our view, make it clear that referenced standards can apply additional requirements over and above those in RID/ADR/ADN.

A discussion on replacing the word "conflict" with "contradict" took place at the second inter-seasonal meeting of members of the "London" group on 18 December 2020.

Many delegates were content with the term "conflict" as this translated well, but a consensus emerged that it would be helpful to add a note indicating that a standard could include requirements that enhance or supplement those set out in RID/ADR/ADN.

We therefore propose inserting the following note in RID/ADR/ADN 1.1.5:

Note: A standard provides details on how to meet the provisions of RID/ADR/ADN and may include requirements in addition to those set out in RID/ADR/ADN.

European agreements concerning the International Carriage of Dangerous Goods by road, applicable as from the 1st January 2021 are available from this link:

https://unece.org/transportdangerous-goods/adr-2021-files

Accident Reports Involving Dangerous Goods

Certain accidents must be reported to the Department for Transport including those where:

- Dangerous goods were released.
- There was an imminent risk of loss of product and personal injury.
- There was material or environmental damage estimated to exceed €50,000.

The Department of Transport has a guidance note available for such reports entitled Notification of Occurrences Involving Dangerous Goods.

(Under the Reporting of Injuries, Diseases and Dangerous Occurrences Regulations 1995 reports must also be made to the HSE.)

You must keep a record of any reportable injury, disease or dangerous occurrence for three years. This must include:

- the date and method of reporting;
- the date, time and place of the event;
- personal details of those involved;

- the injury;
- A brief description of the nature of the event or disease.

You must still keep a record of all over-three-day injuries. If you are required to keep an accident book, under the Social Security (Claims and Payments) Regulations 1979, that record can be treated as a record for the purposes of RIDDOR.

Under the Safety Representatives and Safety Committees Regulations 1977 and the Health and Safety (Consultation with Employees) Regulations 1996, employers must make relevant health and safety documents available to safety representatives.

RIDDOR 2013 Changes

From 1 October 2013, RIDDOR 2013 came into force, which introduced significant changes to the existing reporting requirements. The main changes are to simplify the reporting requirements in the following areas:

■ The classification of 'major injuries' to workers is being replaced with a shorter list of 'specified injuries';

■ The previous list of 47 types of industrial disease is being replaced with eight categories of reportable work-related illness;

■ Fewer types of dangerous occurrence require reporting.

There are no significant changes to the reporting requirements for:

■ Fatal accidents;

■ Accidents to non-workers (members of the public);

■ Accidents which result in the incapacitation of a worker for more than seven days.

Recording requirements remain broadly unchanged, including the requirement to record accidents resulting in the incapacitation of a worker for more than three days.

The full document is available at: https://www.hse.gov.uk/pubns/hsis1.htm

Packaging Dangerous Goods

Dangerous goods must be packed in good quality packagings including intermediate bulk containers (IBCs), large packagings, and pressure receptacles that have sufficient strength to withstand shocks normally encountered during carriage. These provisions apply to new, reused, repaired or remanufactured packagings and IBCs. Columns 8 and 9a of the Dangerous Goods List give specific and special packing provisions for each article or substance. Certain dangerous goods may be packed together or with other goods in combination packing provided they will not dangerously react to one another and that compliance of all mixed packing provisions is maintained. (Mixed packing provisions are given in column 9b of the Dangerous Goods List.)

Package Marking and Labelling

Packages must be clearly, durably marked with the letter "UN" followed by the UN number and the labels indicated in column 5 of the Dangerous Goods List must be placed on each package: In addition:

- Special provisions indicated in column 6 may vary or add to the basic required labelling.
- If two or more dangerous goods are packed together, the outer packaging must be labelled for each.
- A further label ("model number 11" orientation arrows) has to be applied in certain circumstances and there are additional marking provisions for Classes 1, 2, and 7 and special labelling provisions for Classes 4.1, 5.2, 6.2, and 7.

Vehicles - Marking and Placarding

Every operator whose activities include loading, consigning, carriage by road or filling of dangerous goods into specified equipment for carriage by road, of dangerous goods must ensure all vehicles and containers display appropriate placards and marks, orange-coloured plates, and hazard identification numbers (HINs) or emergency action codes (EACs).

Placards must correspond with the labels specified in columns 5 and 6 of the Dangerous Goods List. They are affixed to the outside surface of the vehicle and/or containers. Placards not relating to the dangerous goods or their residue must be removed or covered.

Domestic Journeys and EACs

EACs not HINs must be displayed by the loader, filler, consignor and carrier when dangerous goods are being carried:

- By road.
- In tanks or in bulk.
- With the transport unit registered in GB and the whole of the journey taking place in GB.

Orange-coloured plates must be displayed when:

- A transport unit or tank-vehicle is carrying one dangerous good in a tank or in bulk in either the transport unit or in a single container.

- Where a transport unit or tank vehicle is carrying more than one dangerous good in a tank, or in bulk in either the transport unit or a tank vehicle with more than one tank or container.

Tanks carrying dangerous goods must display a telephone number where information on the load can be obtained at any time.

Carrying and Retaining Documentation

Those who carry or consign dangerous goods by road must ensure the transport document accompanies each consignment and a carrier must retain a written record of all the information contained therein for three months.

Transport Unit

Transport units for dangerous goods to be carried by road must comply with the following:

- A transport unit loaded with dangerous goods must not include more than one trailer or semi-trailer.
- Transport units carrying dangerous goods have to be placarded and marked.
- Transport units carrying dangerous goods must carry appropriate fire-fighting equipment.
- Transport units carrying dangerous goods must be equipped with one portable fire extinguisher for the inflammability classes A, B, and C, with a minimum capacity of 2 kg dry powder or an equivalent capacity of any suitable extinguishing agent.
- Transport units other than those carrying dangerous goods have to be equipped with at least the above mentioned equipment and one or more additional fire extinguishers of greater capacity depending on the vehicle's permissible net mass.

A transport unit carrying dangerous goods should also have:

- For each vehicle a minimum of one chock suitable to the weight of the vehicle and its wheel diameter.
- Two self-standing warning signs.
- Suitable warning vest or warning clothes for each member of the crew.
- A pocket lamp for each member of the crew.
- A respiratory protective device conforming to the necessary requirements.
- Personal protection equipment necessary to take addition and/or special actions referred to in the required written instructions.

Documentation

The following documents must be carried on the transport unit:

- Copies of any applicable special agreements.
- Permit authorising transport operation (when carriage is on the basis of such agreements).
- Transport documents.
- Container packing certificate.
- Instructions in writing.
- Driver's training certificate as required.
- Certificate of approval for each transport unit as required.

Any written instructions regarding the load must be carried in the cab at all times and be readily identifiable. The carrier must make sure the driver in question understands and is capable of carrying out said instructions, especially in the event of an accident or emergency.

Carriage

The driver and each crew member must make sure the ADR requirements in relation to the following are met:

- Attendance.
- Carrying passengers.
- Ability to use fire-fighting equipment.
- Opening of packages containing dangerous goods.
- Use of lighting apparatus that contains a flame or produces sparks.
- Prohibition of smoking inside or near vehicles during loading and unloading.
- Shutting off the vehicles engine during loading and unloading.
- Applying parking brakes.

Carriage by Private Individuals

The Carriage Regulations do not apply to the carriage of dangerous goods by private individuals under circumstances set out in ADR 1.1.3.1(a) and where the net mass of explosive substance does not exceed 50kg for fireworks and 30kg for other explosives or a combination of fireworks and other explosives.

As of the 1st Oct 2020 ... ADR exempts completely private, non-work related carriage subject to some conditions (ADR 1.1.3.1(a)). Work related carriage may be exempt or the individual must make sure the explosives are loaded, stowed, carried, and unloaded safely.

The following ADR requirements do apply to private citizens:

- Mixed loading requirements.
- Prohibition of smoking.
- Prohibition of fire or naked flame near Class 1 substances.

https://www.hse.gov.uk/cdg/commonproblems/petrol.htm

Attendance for Carriage of Class 1

For a transport unit carrying Class 1 goods, when the vehicle is not parked the driver must be accompanied by an attendant competent to ensure the security of the goods, with appropriate training, who has been given detailed instructions. An attendant is not required where the quantity of Class 1 goods does not exceed the maximum total quantities allowed per transport unit.

Completion of Class 1 Carriage in a Reasonable Time

The carrier and driver of a vehicle carrying Class I goods must make sure:

- Carriage is completed in a reasonable length of time.

- Any trailer containing Class 1 goods is not detached except in a safe, secure location or in an emergency.
- The goods are delivered to the consignee, consignee's agent, or an authorised person who can take custody of and ensure the security of the explosives.
- If there are compelling reasons not to accept the goods, the consignee makes arrangements for them to be delivered to an alternate secure location.

Security Precautions with Class 1 Carriage

Anyone involved with Class 1 carriage must take reasonable steps to prevent unauthorised access to the goods. In addition:

- The consignor and carrier must ensure the transport unit is suitable secure for Class 1 goods.
- The driver and vehicle crew must take all proper precautions to secure the goods in the event of an accident or emergency.
- In the event of an accident or emergency the driver and any attendant must inform the carrier as quickly as possible who in turn must inform HSE.
- The carrier and driver of a transport unit carrying more than 5 tons of Class 1 Division 1 goods must ensure the route has been approved by the chief officer of police for the relevant areas.

Any vehicle travelling on the European road network could be carrying dangerous goods. A vehicle must be marked up only if it is carrying a quantity greater than a threshold determined in the ADR legislation.
The threshold quantity will vary depending on the dangerous goods and their associated risks. For example, you can carry 1000 litres of diesel (UN1202) without being obliged to mark up the vehicle but only 20kg of chlorine (UN1017). Equally, you can carry as many matches (UN1331) or firelighters (UN2623) as you like without any warning marks at all. Just because the vehicle has no markings does not mean it is not carrying potentially dangerous goods.

Tankers are the vehicles people commonly associate with carrying dangerous goods. However, the goods could be in liquid, gas or powder form. The construction of the tanker will give an indication of the type of product it may contain.

Gas tankers are quite distinctive, often with a box at the rear with the valve gear within it. They also have a tank access plate at one end which is bolted in place with numerous large bolts in a ring and typically no access platform on the top of the tank.

Powder tankers are distinctive in terms of the shape of the tank. Flour or cement tankers are fairly common examples of powder tankers, albeit these loads are not classified as dangerous goods.

Liquid tanker construction can even give clues to the product that they may contain.

Corrosives tankers tend to have smaller diameter barrels due to the dense product. Fuel tankers often have oval tanks to aid drivability when transporting comparatively less dense fuels.

Shipping containers come in various shapes and sizes. Goods can be transported in containers in one of three ways.

In a tank container which is just the same as a normal tanker except the tank is mounted in a standard container frame.

The more frequently seen 'box' containers carry goods either in packages (boxes, bottles, drums etc.) or can carry dry goods in bulk. If carrying goods in 'bulk' a large plastic bag lines the container and is filled in situ via filling ports on the container.

Powder or granular dangerous goods can be transported in tipper trucks although the load area must be sealed to prevent any loss of product as the vehicle makes its journey. Fertilizer is often moved in this way.

Packaged dangerous goods in boxes, bottles, drums etc. are transported in all vehicle types from small vans to full 44t articulated vehicles. In fact they could be in what appears to be a domestic vehicle.

If the vehicle is not marked up at all, it is very difficult to spot what may be dangerous but from the above section it is important that dangerous goods are considered at an early stage in any incident. Vehicles come in all shapes and sizes, but a big clue is the company logo on the trailer. There are certain hauliers that regularly carry dangerous goods whilst others do so less frequently. For example, fuel companies regularly transport large quantities of petrol whereas a furniture delivery van is unlikely to contain dangerous goods.

The common markings requirement for all vehicles carrying dangerous goods is an orange board with black border mounted on the vehicle front and rear. The exact marking requirements will vary in relation to the way the goods are being transported and if the load is on a domestic or international journey.

Certain load types and/or vehicles will supply more information on the goods being carried. The UN number, emergency action codes and specialist advice phone number are displayed on road tankers for example, but this is not required for packaged goods. The only way of knowing exactly what a vehicle carrying packaged goods is actually carrying is the paperwork held by driver and the haulier. The load should have the UN number on its packaging, but would you want to enter the load area without knowing the risks?

The Carriage of Dangerous Goods and Use of Transportable Pressure Equipment Regulations 2009 ("CDG 2009"), SI 2009 No 1348, came into force on 1 July 2009. They replace the 2007 regulations.

This is a draft item of legislation. This draft has since been made as a UK Statutory Instrument: The Carriage of Dangerous Goods and Use of Transportable Pressure Equipment (Amendment) (EU Exit) **Regulations 2020, No. 1111**

Variations in GB which arise from derogations are now in a DfT Approved Document (HSE NI), available here.http://alturl.com/uokow

Information on the operation of the regulations may be found in the Carriage of Dangerous Goods Manual, available here:
http://www.hse.gov.uk/cdg/manual/index.htm

European agreements concerning the International Carriage of Dangerous Goods by road, applicable as from the 1st January 2019 are available from this link: https://unece.org/adr-2019-files

Detailed guidance on the requirements of ADR and the Carriage Regulations can be found in the HSE publication "Working with ADR: An Introduction to the Carriage of Dangerous Goods by Road ". It is available as a free download at:-

https://www.hse.gov.uk/cdg/introduction.htm

The following material is only a summary of the major topics contained in that document.

The IMDG code

The IMDG Code, 2018 Edition (inc. Amendment 39-18) came into force on 1 January 2020 for two years and may be applied voluntarily as from 1 January 2019.

The IMDG Code Supplement, 2018 Edition renders obsolete the previous 2014 edition

The IMDG code contains internationally agreed guidance on the safe transport of dangerous goods by sea, and most commonly relates to the carriage of dangerous goods in freight containers and tank containers. Primarily it is used by shipping operators but it is also relevant to those transporting dangerous goods on journeys involving a sea crossing. In the UK many operators do not undertake complete international journeys but only visit a port to deliver or collect trailers, freight containers or tank containers which have been placarded with IMDG labels for sea journeys. Where there is full compliance with the IMDG Code, vehicles are exempted from the placarding requirements of CDG 2007. However, all other relevant matters including training, information in writing, provision of fire-fighting equipment etc., apply as under the regulations. For the exemptions on placarding to apply, the journey must involve dangerous goods being carried to a port for carriage by sea, or from a port having been carried by sea.

The Code has undergone many changes over the years, in both format and content, in order to keep up with the rapid expansion of the shipping industry.
Amendment 39-18 includes revisions to various sections of the Code and to transport requirements for specific substances.
It was adopted by IMO's Maritime Safety Committee (MSC) at its ninety-ninth session in May 2018.
Amendment 39-18 of the Code is mandatory as from 1 January 2020 but may be applied by Administrations in whole or in part on a voluntary basis from 1 January 2019.

Many maritime countries have taken steps to regulate the carriage of dangerous goods by sea, based on the safety considerations set out by the 1974 SOLAS Convention. More recently, as marine pollution has become a serious concern, countries have taken further steps to regulate the carriage of marine pollutants, as described in Annex III of MARPOL.

The International Maritime Dangerous Goods (IMDG) Code, which was first published in 1965, amplifies the requirements of both Conventions and has become the standard guide to all aspects of handling dangerous goods and marine pollutants in sea transport

http://alturl.com/9anf5

Hazardous Goods Warning Labels

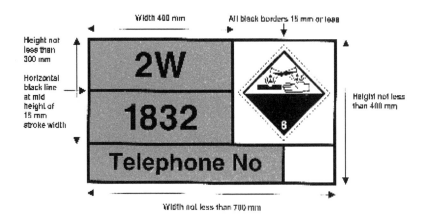

Hazard Warning Panel

RID/ADR (Hazard Identification Number) orange coloured plate and placard

Danger Labels

The following are danger labels that will be shown during the transport of dangerous goods: CLASS 1 – Explosive substances or articles

CLASS 2 – Gases

Flammable gases   Non-flammable,
Non-toxic gases

Toxic gases
CLASS 3 – Flammable liquids

CLASS 4.1 – Flammable solids, self-reactive substances and desensitized explosives

CLASS 4.2 – Substances liable to spontaneous combustion

CLASS 4.3 substances which, in contact with water, emit flammable gases

CLASS 5.1 – Oxidising substances

CLASS 5.2 – Organic peroxides

CLASS 6.1 – Toxic substances

CLASS 6.2 – Infectious substances

CLASS 7 – Radioactive material

CLASS 8 – Corrosive substance

CLASS 8 – Corrosive Goods (Limited Quantity)

CLASS 8 – Corrosive Goods (Limited Quantity) air mode journey

CLASS 9 – Miscellaneous dangerous substances and articles

Section G9 Carriage of Perishable Foodstuffs

The Regulations give effect to the detailed requirements of two international agreements to which Ireland is a signatory, namely the ATP, or more correctly, the 'Agreement on the International Carriage of Perishable Foodstuffs and on the Special Equipment to be Used for such Carriage'. This Agreement dates from Geneva in 1970. The other is the Agreement on the Rules governing the Carriage of Frozen and Deep Frozen Foodstuffs by equipment with thin sidewalls, to and from Italy. It was signed in 1986.

The Regulations apply to insulated, refrigerated, mechanically refrigerated and heated transport equipment used or intended to be used, for the international carriage of perishable foodstuffs. Foodstuffs and classes of foodstuffs known as perishable foodstuffs are prescribed, as designated in the ATP. Temperature limits, standards for insulation and other requirements for transport equipment of these foods are specified. The Regulations also make provision for testing and examination of transport equipment and certification of compliance and issue of certification plates. The National Standards Authority of Ireland is the Competent Authority for certification of equipment.

The ATP Agreement

ATP (formally, the Agreement on the International Carriage of Perishable Foodstuffs and on the Special Equipment to be used for such Carriage **(ATP))** **as amended on 6 July 2020.**
Britain acceded to L'Accord relatif aux Transports internationaux de den rees Perissables et aux engins speciaux a utilizer pour ces transports from October 1st 1979 by implementation of the International Carriage of Perishable Foodstuffs Act 1976 and The International Carriage of Perishable Foodstuffs Regulations 1985. The purpose is to improve the preservation of perishable foodstuffs during carriage, particularly in international trade. It applies to road or rail journeys or a combination of both and to related sea crossings that do not exceed 150 kilometres. It does not apply to national transport of such goods within the UK.

http://alturl.com/bhrsd

Additional practical information

Any query concerning the application of ATP should be directed to the relevant competent authority. Additional information may also be found on the UNECE Transport Division web site at the following link:
http://www.unece.org/trans/main/wp11/atp.html

This information, updated on a continuous basis, concerns:
- The status of ATP;
- Depositary notifications (e.g. new Contracting Parties, amendments or corrections to legal texts);
- Publication details (corrections, publication of new amendments);
- List and details of competent authorities and ATP Test Stations.

This comprises the Agreement itself and its annexes with the latest amendments which enter into force on 6 July 2020.

Principal terms of the Agreement

The use of the following terms is prohibited unless the equipment complies with the standards set out in the Agreement:

1. Insulated
2. Refrigerated
3. Mechanically Refrigerated
4. Heated

The equipment referred to above must be inspected and tested for compliance at six-year intervals. Certificates of compliance must be carried on the vehicle and produced for inspection on request by an authorised inspecting officer. When a certificate has been issued, vehicles/containers must be fitted with a "designated mark" showing the month and year of the expiration (blue figures on white background).

The Agreement applies to carriage, if the carriage is between two different states, on own-account or for hire and reward by rail or road of:

- Quick (deep) frozen and frozen foodstuffs.
- Other foodstuffs (including meats, offal, game, milk, fish, poultry and rabbits and dairy products) which are not quick frozen or frozen - this condition applies if the original vehicle containing the goods having travelled by road or rail is subsequently carried on a sea crossing of less than 150km between one or more land journeys.

The equipment referred to in the first point must be used in movements covered by the Agreement unless the temperatures to be anticipated during the carriage make this unnecessary; otherwise the equipment must be used to maintain temperatures laid down in the Agreement. The Agreement does not apply to carriage in containers by land preceded by or followed by a sea crossing other than as described in point 3 above.

Parties to the Agreement must ensure observance of its conditions. Countries which are party to the ATP Agreement include all EU member states plus Bosnia-Herzegovina, Croatia, Georgia, Kazakhstan, Macedonia, Morocco, Norway, Russia, Serbia and Montenegro plus Switzerland (signed but not ratified).

Vehicles, trailers and containers used on ATP operations must be examined at one of five approved establishments in Great Britain. A certificate or a metal certification plate for affixing to the vehicle/trailer/container is issued and valid for six years. The certificate is transferable to a new owner on request.

Transport of Perishables to Italy

The International Carriage of Perishable Foodstuffs (Vehicles with Thin Side Walls) Regulations 1987 requires that vehicles used for the transport of frozen and deep frozen foodstuffs to Italy from April 1st to October 31st must be tested for compliance with specific regulations relating to carriage in vehicles with thin sidewalls.

Section G10 Carriage of Live Animals

Legislation

The welfare of animals during transport is protected by retained EU legislation. You must transport animals in a way that is not likely to cause injury or undue suffering to them.

When you transport animals you must:

- plan the journey properly and keep it as short as possible
- check the animals during the journey to make sure you meet their needs for water, feed and rest
- make sure the animals are fit to travel
- design, construct and maintain the vehicle and loading and unloading facilities to avoid injury and suffering
- make sure anyone handling the animals are trained or competent in the task and do not use violence or any methods likely to cause unnecessary fear, injury or suffering
- give the animals sufficient floor space and height

Legislation on the protection of animals during transport applies to the transport of live vertebrate animals in connection with an economic activity (a business or trade). This includes:

- livestock and equine hauliers
- farmers
- commercial pet breeders
- pet couriers
-

The requirements apply to those working at:

- markets
- assembly centres
- slaughterhouses

The requirements do not apply to the transport of animals where this is not in connection with economy activity. For example, journeys which are:

- not in the course of business or trade
- not for hire or reward

The transport of animals to and from markets, to slaughter, and particularly on export journeys, is a matter of some public concern. Government recognises this and ensures that the welfare of animals is protected during transport in line with compulsory EU legislation, as implemented by domestic legislation in England and the Devolved Administrations.

The Government is often urged to ban the exports of live animals for slaughter or further fattening. We would prefer to see meat (or germ plasm) exported rather than live animals, since animals would not be subjected to long periods in transit. But the clear legal position, confirmed by two past judgements of the European Court, is that this is a legitimate trade within the European Community and that restricting it or banning it could not be defended in law. Our policy is therefore to ensure full application of the EU rules on our territory, and, importantly, to encourage other member states to do the same.

As expected, the report is purely factual and does not contain any proposals for legislative change. It concludes that the Regulation has had a beneficial impact on the welfare of animals during transport, however, it also acknowledges that 'severe animal welfare problems during transport persist'. The Commission's proposed solution to these problems involves adopting new implementing rules concerning satellite tracking systems; an increase in the number of inspections (where needed) to improve existing controls; better reporting on compliance by Member States; a study into the welfare of fish during transport; increased co-operation and communication between the competent authorities and NGOs, and, most crucially, the dissemination of Commission guidance on the interpretation of the Regulation and development of guides to good practice, which would help implement the latest scientific findings identified by the European Food Safety Agency (EFSA) in its own report issued in December 2010.

The Regulation includes a provision for a review of its impact to be carried out within four years of it coming into force i.e. January 2011. The European Commission's report on its review of the Regulation was published on 10 November 2011. The report and accompanying documentation can be found on the Commission's website.

General Rules

It is illegal to transport any animal in a way likely to cause injury or unnecessary suffering. The person in charge of animals in transit must ensure compliance to these provisions while animals are waiting to be loaded or after being unloaded. On journeys over 50 kilometres, animals must be given sufficient space relative to their weight, size and physical condition, to weather conditions and to the realistic journey time. They must be fed and watered before and during a journey at specified intervals and must be transported to their destination without delay.

Fitness of Animals to Travel

It is illegal to transport any animal unless it is fit for the journey and suitable provision has been made for its care while travelling and upon arrival. Animals are not considered fit if they are ill, injured, infirm or fatigued, unless the intended journey is not likely to cause them unnecessary suffering.

Animals may be transported to the nearest available place for veterinary treatment or diagnosis, or to the nearest available place of slaughter, provided they are not likely to suffer unnecessarily. When transported under this provision, they must not be dragged or pushed by any means, or lifted by a mechanical device, except under the supervision of a veterinary surgeon. Animals which fall ill or are injured, must be given first aid or veterinary treatment as soon as possible, or be slaughtered without unnecessary suffering.

https://www.gov.uk/guidance/animal-welfare

Journey Times, Feeding and Watering

In most cases travel times for cattle, sheep, pigs, goats and horses must not exceed eight hours. However, where the transporting vehicle meets the following additional requirements, journey times may be extended:

- Sufficient bedding on the floor of the vehicle.
- Appropriate feed for the length of the journey.
- Where there is direct access to the animals.
- Where adequate adjustable ventilation is provided.
- Where movable panels can create separate compartments.
- If equipped for connection to a water supply during stops.
- If, when transporting pigs, sufficient liquid is carried for drinking during travel.

Provided the above requirements are met, watering and feeding intervals, journey times and rest periods may be extended as follows:

- Unweaned calves, lambs, kids and foals and unweaned piglets must be rested for at least one hour after nine hours of travel. After this, they may be transported for a further nine hours.
- Pigs may be transported for a maximum of 24 hours, but they must have continuous access to liquid during the journey.
- Horses may be transported for a maximum of 24 hours, but they must be given liquid during the journey and, if necessary, be fed every eight hours.
- All other cattle, sheep and goats must be rested for at least one hour after 14 hours of travel. After this, they may be transported for a further 14 hours.

When the maximum journey times specified have been reached, animals must be unloaded, fed and watered and be rested for at least 24 hours. Where it is solely in the interests of the animals, the maximum journey times mentioned above may be extended by two hours, depending on the proximity to the final destination.

Unweaned calves, lambs, kids and foals and unweaned piglets may be transported for nine hours from a market if the journey to the market took not more than four hours (or nine hours if it was in a vehicle as described above). Pigs or horses may be transported for nine hours from a market if the journey to market took not more than four hours (or eight hours if it was in a vehicle complying with items one to four listed above). All other cattle, sheep and goats may be transported for 14 hours from a market if the journey to market took not more than four hours (or 14 hours if it was in a vehicle as described above).

Accompaniment by Competent Persons

Hauliers carrying animals on journeys of over 50 km in length, or a person accompanying the animals must have had specific or equivalent practical training to handle the animals properly and administer care.

Competence must be established in the handling of and care for animals in transport. Those with practical experience (as opposed to specific training) must be assessed as to their ability, competence and knowledge. A record to this effect must be kept by the transporter while the person is engaged on livestock journeys and for six months afterwards. The record must be produced on request by an inspector.

The Order specifies the "framework of competences" – the necessary knowledge people responsible for the welfare of animals during transport must have, including an understanding of:

- When to seek veterinary help and knowledge.
- Which body or organisation to contact with general questions.
- Matters of law or documentation.
- Knowledge of enforcement authorities' power to inspect animals, documentation and vehicles before, during and after a journey.
- Basic knowledge of authorisation requirements for transporters and when such authorisation is necessary.
- Knowledge of how to plan a journey (taking account of such factors as maximum travelling times, required rest periods, and the time taken to load and unload).
- The ability to anticipate changing conditions and make contingencies for unforeseen circumstances.
- Understanding of when route plans or documentation are required and how to complete these documents.
- Knowledge of vehicle construction and use requirements in current welfare legislation.
- The ability to load, operate and control a vehicle safely, efficiently and effectively so as to ensure the welfare of the animals.
- Knowledge of the appropriate methods for handling animals (and those prohibited) during loading and unloading, including the use of visual fields and flight zones, lighting and the appropriate use of sticks, boards, blindfolds and electric goads.
- Knowledge of the specific requirements of the Order relating to different animal species for the provision of rest, feed and liquid.
- Knowledge of stocking densities and headroom and segregation requirements, taking account of the species being transported, methods of transport, sex, condition, age, length of journey and ambient conditions.

- An understanding of the importance, for animal welfare, of temperatures both inside and outside the vehicle, including the effect on different species and the need for the adjustment of ventilation.
- An ability to clean and disinfect vehicles and knowledge of when it is necessary to do so before and after the journey.
- Elementary knowledge of the causes of stress in animals, ability to recognise the signs of stress and ill health, and basic knowledge of how to reduce such symptoms.
- An ability to care for animals which become unfit or injured during transport, including an understanding of when to seek veterinary advice.
- Knowledge of the limited circumstances when it is permissible to transport unfit animals for veterinary treatment or for slaughter.

From 1 July 1998 persons in charge of animals during transportation must have demonstrated that they are qualified to handle, transport, care for and safeguard the welfare of the animals. The Ministry of Agriculture, Fisheries and Food (MAFF) has produced a guidance booklet on the subject for employers, Assessment of Practical Experience in the Handling, Transport and Care of Animals.

Authorisations and Registration

You must have a transporter authorisation if you transport animals as part of an economic activity (a business or trade), for a distance over 65km.
You will need a:
- type 1 transporter authorisation for journeys over 65km and up to 8 hours
- type 2 transporter authorisation for journeys over 8 hours

You need to contact APHA's Welfare in Transport team for a transporter authorisation application pack. This will include the forms you need to submit, and guidance on what to include in your application.

http://alturl.com/8j8sf

In your application you will need to declare any:

- Home Office simple cautions or convictions under legislation on the protection of animals
- current court orders restricting ownership, keeping or being in control of animals

This declaration includes you and anyone transporting animals under the authority of your Authorisation. Anyone who has been convicted or given a Home Office simple caution under such legislation, in the 3 years before their application, will normally be refused an authorisation.

Applicants for authorisations must be persons fit to transport animals. Authorisations may be suspended or revoked for breach of the Order or of **European Commission Directive 95/29** whether this results in conviction or not.

The Minister issues specific authorisations to a named transporter only to cover activities described in the authorisation. General authorisations do not name individual transporters but cover individual transporters resident in Great Britain or transporter companies incorporated in Great Britain undertaking activities described in the authorisation. Since 1 October 1997, a specific authorisation has been required for transporting cattle, sheep, pigs, goats and horses in a road vehicle on journeys exceeding eight hours' duration. For journeys of less than eight hours only a general authorisation is needed

Although a transporter may be covered by a general authorisation for certain activities, this does not prevent him from also holding a specific authorisation for the same activities. However, where a specific authorisation has been issued the general authorisation no longer applies to animals covered by the specific authorisation. The transporter must not carry out any transport of those particular animals except under the terms of the specific authorisation. Furthermore, if the specific authorisation is revoked or limited in any way then the transporter may not transport the animals concerned under the general authorisation.

The Minister may amend or revoke both specific and general authorisations. Specific authorisations require written notice; general authorisations by a publication in a manner determined by the Minister. In the case of general authorisations the Minister may exclude a transporter from transport operations or impose additional conditions on him different from those in the general authorisation.

Revocation or suspension of a specific authorisation, or removal of a transporter from a general authorisation, either temporarily or permanently, would occur if the transporter or any associate, employee or agent of the transporter:

- Repeatedly infringes this Order in Great Britain (or any other Order implementing **European Commission Directive 95/29**).
- Commits a single act resulting in serious suffering to animals (whether or not such an act leads to a criminal conviction).
- In the case of a journey taking place partly within and partly outside Great Britain, breaches the rules relating to route plans or repeatedly infringes **European Commission Directive 95/29**, or a single such infringement involving serious suffering to animals (whether or not this leads to a criminal conviction).

The Minister must notify an offending transporter in writing of a planned revocation of the authorisation, or suspend it until a specified date or indefinitely.

Route Plans

Where horses, cattle, sheep, pigs and goats are traded between member states or exported to third countries on journeys exceeding eight hours, the transporter must draw up and sign a route plan. This route plan must be submitted, along with an application for an export health certificate, for approval by the Ministry. It will be returned with authorisation stamping and appropriate health certificates. Where more than one transporter is involved, the route plan requirements must be met by the person consigning the animals for the whole of the journey.

It is an offence to transport animals on such journeys without an approved route plan. The original of the route plan and the attached health certificates must accompany the consignment throughout the journey. All reasonable steps must be taken to comply with the route plan.

Feeding and watering times during the journey must be endorsed on the route plan as they occur by the person in charge of the animals.

When a route plan journey is completed, the person who signed the plan when it was originally submitted must certify compliance to the plan in writing or must describe the actual journey together with the reasons for deviation from the planned route.

Within 15 days of completion of the journey, the route plan must be returned to the issuing office. The sender must keep proof to this effect for six months. The transporter must also keep a second copy of the route plan for six months from completion of the journey, and produce it on demand at the request of an inspector and allow copies to be taken.

The information to be provided on the route plan is as follows.

Section 1– information to be completed before the journey:

- Name, full address, business name, telephone number and fax number of the transporter.
- Number and species of animals to be transported.
- Health certificate number(s).
- Number of the transporter's authorisation (if any).
- Registration number of the vehicles to be used, and the trailers if different.
- Name of the person(s) in charge of the transport during the journey.
- Place where the animals are to be first loaded, and full address.
- Planned date and time of departure.
- Full itemised itinerary of the journey.
- Full address of the final destination.
- Estimated date and time of arrival at the final destination (local time).

Section 2 – information to be completed during the journey:

- Actual date and time of loading the first animal.
- Actual time of departure from the place of loading.
- Full itemised itinerary of the journey.
- Actual date and time of arrival at the final destination (local time).

Animal Transport Certificates

Where animals are transported other than under a route plan they must be accompanied by documentation showing:

- The name and address of the transporter.
- The name and address of the owner of the animals.
- Where the animals were loaded and their final destination.
- The date and time the first animal was loaded.
- The date and time of departure.
- The time and place where rest period requirements were met.

This requirement does not apply where poultry and domestic birds are transported for distances of not more than 50 kilometres and where the number is less than 50, or the entire journey is on land occupied by the owner of the poultry and domestic birds.

In the case of animals which are not cattle, sheep, pigs, goats, horses or poultry and domestic birds, the documentary requirement mentioned above does not apply to journeys of 50 kilometres or less.

Transporters are required to retain a copy of the documentation for six months from the completion of the journey, and must produce it to an inspector on demand and allow a copy to be taken. Where such copy is kept in electronic or magnetic form, the inspector may request its production in written form and for copies to be taken in writing.

Powers of Livestock Inspectors

Inspectors appointed for the purposes of the Animal Health Act 1981 by the Minister or by a local authority* may serve notice on the person in charge of animals that are being or are about to be transported in a manner likely to cause injury or unnecessary suffering requiring action to ensure compliance and giving reasons for the requirements. In practice, these inspectors will be veterinary inspectors from the State Veterinary Service, a local veterinary inspector of MAFF, or an officer from the trading standards department of a local authority.

In particular the inspector may:

- Prohibit that movement of the animals, either indefinitely or for a specified period.
- Specify conditions under which the animals may be transported.
- Require the journey to be completed or the animals to be returned to their place of departure by the most direct route, provided this would not cause unnecessary suffering to the animals.
- Require the animals to be held in suitable accommodation with appropriate care until the problem is solved.
- Require the humane slaughter of the animals.

Inspectors may, where necessary for identification, mark an animal. It is an offence for any person to remove, deface, obliterate or alter such marks.

Construction of Vehicles

The Order specifies general requirements for the construction and maintenance of vehicles and receptacles. In particular they must:

- Be safe and not cause injury or suffering during transport, or while loading or unloading.
- Be weather-proof.
- Allow space for animals to lie down.
- Have strong, non-slip floors which are free of protrusions.
- Protect animals from the weather and from excessive humidity, heat and cold.
- Be free of sharp edges.
- Allow appropriate cleaning and disinfection.
- Be escape-proof.
- Prevent animals from undue exposure to noise or vibration.
- Provide sufficient natural or artificial light to enable proper care.
- Have partitions if necessary which provide adequate support and prevent animals being thrown about during transport, are of rigid construction and strong enough to bear the weight of any animal, and do not obstruct ventilation.

When transporting animals (all mammals and birds) they must:

- Not be subject to severe jolting or shaking.
- Not be injured during loading or unloading.
- Be driven without excessive use of prods and such like.
- Be carried in a vehicle with means for emergency unloading.
- Be segregated from goods carried on the same vehicle.
- Not be carried on the same vehicle with carcasses except those of animals that die on the journey.
- Be carried on a vehicle or receptacle that has been thoroughly cleaned and, where appropriate, disinfected.
- Remove dead animals, soiled litter and droppings as soon as possible.
- Cover the vehicle/receptacle floors with sufficient litter, unless alternative arrangements are made or urine and droppings are regularly removed.
- Mark or label the receptacles to indicate they contain live animals of a named species.
- Be carried in an upright position.
- Be carried in receptacles secured during transport.
- Be accompanied by at least one attendant unless -
- Receptacles are secure.
- Adequately ventilated.
- Contain sufficient food and liquid, in dispensers which cannot tip over, for a journey of twice the anticipated time.

- The transporter (driver) acts as the attendant
- The consignor has appointed an agent to care for the animals at stopping or transfer points.

http://alturl.com/naygg

Additional provisions relating to the construction and maintenance of vehicles and receptacles and for the transport of animals are as follows:

- There must be sufficient space for animals to stand normally.
- They must allow adequate ventilation and provide space above the animals to enable air to circulate properly.
- They must allow for the inspection of animals and their feeding and watering.
- Road vehicles must have a roof to protect against the weather.
- Have barriers (for horse-carrying vehicles, straps) to prevent animals falling out when doors are opened.
- Ramps on vehicles must:
- Prevent slipping.
- Not be too steep for the animals being carried.
- Not have a top or bottom step which is too high.
- Not have gaps at the top or bottom which are too wide.
- Road vehicles must enable inspection of the animals from the outside (and must have suitable footholds).

For animals which are normally tied, tying facilities must be provided and ties must be:
- Strong enough not to break during normal transport conditions.
- Designed to eliminate any danger of strangulation or injury.
- Long enough to allow animals to lie down and to eat and drink.
- Animals must not be tied by their horns or by a nose ring.
- On multi-deck vehicles, suitable ramps or lifting gear of sufficient strength must be provided.

Certain animals must be segregated during transport as follows:

- A cow with a suckling calf.
- A sow with un-weaned piglets.
- At mare with a foal at foot.
- A bull more than 10 months old.
- A breeding boar more than 6 months old.
- A stallion.

Bulls, boars and stallions may be carried with others of the same species/sex if they have been raised in compatible groups or are accustomed to one another. Other animals of mixed species may be carried together if separation from their companions would cause them distress.

Animals must not be carried together if, due to differences age and size, injury or unnecessary suffering may be caused. Also, animals hostile to each other or fractious must not be carried together.

Other animals which must not be carried together are:

- Uncastrated male adults with female animals (unless accustomed to each other).
- Horned cattle with unhorned cattle.
- Broken horses with unbroken horses (unless they are all secured).

Animals must not be suspended by mechanical means, lifted or dragged by the head, horns, legs, tail or fleece.

Excessive force must not be used to control animals including no use of:

- Electric shock instruments.
- Stick, goad or other instrument (to hit cattle under 6 months old).
- Stick, non-electric goad or other instrument (to hit or prod pigs). Use of such items is allowed on the hindquarters of cattle more than 6 months old and on adult pigs that refuse to move forward when there is space to do so – but such action must be avoided as far as possible.

Attendants must look after animals including, if necessary, feeding and watering them.

As required animals must be milked at appropriate intervals – in the case of cows about 12 hours but not exceeding 15 hours.

Horses being transported in groups must wear halters unless they are unbroken and have their hind feet unshod.
Horses must not be transported in vehicles with more than one deck in operation.

When poultry and domestic birds and domestic rabbits are carried, further requirements are specified for vehicle and receptacle construction and maintenance:

- Adequate ventilation and air space must be provided.
- Receptacles must allow inspection of and care for the animals.
- Receptacles must be of such size as to protect the animals from injury or unnecessary suffering during transport.
- Receptacles for carrying birds must prevent the protrusion of heads, legs or wings.
- Birds must not be carried in a sack or bag.
- Birds must not be lifted or carried by the head, neck, wing or tail except:
- Ducks which may be lifted or carried by the neck.
- Geese which may be lifted or carried by the base of both wings.
- Birds must not be tied by the neck, leg or wing.

- Rabbits must not be carried in the same undivided pen, receptacle or road vehicle as an animal of any other species.
- Birds must be segregated according to sex and species except that:
- Female birds may be transported with their broods
- Male and female chicks may be transported together
- Male and female birds which are familiar with one another may be transported together
- Chicks must be segregated from all other poultry except their mother or other chicks
- Birds must not be transported next to any animal which is hostile to them or in the presence of any animal likely to cause them unnecessary suffering.

Additional standards for road vehicles

Formerly, we had advised that vehicles built before and in use before 5 January 2007 could be exempt from the ramp angle requirements up to a deadline of 4 January 2012.
This decision has now been legally challenged by the EU Commission.
Therefore, as of 1 January 2011, any vehicle found on inspection for enforcement purposes to be non-compliant with the Regulation's ramp angle specifications could be subject to enforcement action.

Means of transport (road vehicles), and containers, used for transporting animals on 'long journeys' (those in excess of eight hours) must be inspected and approved by the competent authority of a EU Member State or a body designated by a EU Member State (Articles 7 and 18).
Approval criteria for containers differs from that for road vehicles (paragraph 5.15 refers). 5.10 Compulsory inspection and approval in relation to animal welfare is a departure from previous requirements.

Vehicles making journeys over 8 hours transporting cattle, sheep, pigs, goats or unregistered domestic equidae need to be equipped with a satellite navigation (tracking) system. There is an exception to this rule for journeys of up to 12 hours within GB.

Approvals are dependent on those vehicles (and containers) meeting specific requirements of the Regulation (Annex I, Chapters II & VI) covering:
- basic construction requirements (for all species);
- equipment for loading and unloading;
- additional requirements for long journeys involving domestic cattle, sheep, pigs, goats or domestic Equidae-roof, partitions, water/feed equipment, ventilation and satellite navigation (tracking) systems (excluding registered equidae)

Container approval is required for all journeys over eight hours where domestic cattle, sheep, goats, pigs or domestic Equidae are being carried (Article 7.3). The derogations permitted under Article 18.4 of the Regulation do not extend to these journeys.
https://www.gov.uk/guidance/animal-welfare

Section H1 Drivers, Driving Tests and Driver CPC

Safety and competence, knowledge of the rules of the road, the significance of traffic signs and signals, and an appreciation of the attendant dangers are the main goals of driver testing. The purpose of LGV/PCV entitlements is to ensure that such drivers are competent to safely drive large vehicles carrying heavy loads or passengers. Vocational testing also provides a measure of professionalism. It is more comprehensive and complex than the ordinary driving test and, consequently, demands greater skill and knowledge.

Proof of Identity

Candidates for both ordinary and vocational driving tests must produce satisfactory photographic evidence of identity. Acceptable documents for this purpose include existing driving licenses, a passport or an employer-issued identity card bearing the holder's name, signature and photograph. If a test candidate cannot produce such proof, the test will not be conducted and the fee will be forfeited.

Ordinary Driving Test

Applicants for a driver's license must pass both a written theory and a practical driving test on the applicable class of vehicle. An entitlement will not be gained until both parts are passed. The theory test must be passed before the practical driving test can be taken.

The Theory Test

Driving test candidates must take and pass a written theory test carried out by DriveSafe Ltd (a private company) on behalf of the Driving Standards Agency (DSA – an Executive Agency of the DETR) at a nationwide network of dedicated theory test centres.

The LGV test has 100 multi–choice questions, and you need to get 85 correct to pass. You'll have 115 minutes to complete the test.
 The questions concern such matters as driver attitude, traffic signs and regulations, the effects of alcohol and drugs, driver fatigue, and safety and environmental aspects of vehicles. All these topics are covered in the Highway Code and the DSA's Driving Manual. The DSA has also published The Complete Theory Test for Cars and Motorcycles. These publications are available from The Stationery Office or main booksellers.
https://theorytest.org.uk/lgv-theory-test/

Practical Driving Tests

Examiners from the DSA carry out the 30-minute practical driving test. Candidates must present a theory test pass certificate for the driving test to occur.

Test candidates must meet the following requirements:

- They must show that they are fully conversant with the contents of the Highway Code.
- They must prove that they are able to read in good daylight (with the aid of spectacles, if worn) a motor vehicle's registration number in accordance with the vision requirements.

They must show that they are competent to drive without danger to and with due consideration of other users of the road, including being able to:

- Start the engine of the vehicle.
- Move away straight ahead or at an angle.
- Overtake, meet or cross the path of other vehicles and take an appropriate course.
- Turn right-hand and left-hand corners correctly.
- Stop the vehicle in an emergency and in a normal situation, and in the latter case bring it to rest at an appropriate part of the road.
- Drive the vehicle backwards and while doing so enter a limited opening either to the left or to the right.
- Cause the vehicle to face the opposite direction by the use of forward and reverse gears.
- Carry out a reverse parking manoeuvre which involves stopping the vehicle next to and parallel with a parked vehicle, then reversing to position and park the vehicle in front of or behind the other vehicle, level with and reasonably close to the kerb.
- Indicate their intended actions at appropriate times by giving appropriate signals in a clear and unmistakable manner (in the case of a left-hand drive vehicle, or a disabled driver for whom it is impracticable or undesirable to give hand signals, there is no requirement to provide any signals other than mechanical ones).
- Act correctly and promptly on all signals given by traffic signs and traffic controllers and take appropriate action on signs given by other road users.

New Test Requirements

Besides extending the duration of the test by some five to seven minutes and including, where possible, de-restricted dual carriageway driving, a more stringent marking system is now applied under which candidates are allowed a maximum of 15 minor (nonhazardous) faults after which the test is terminated (as well as termination in the event of a serious driving error). Cars used for the ordinary (category B) driving test must be fitted with a seatbelt and a head restraint for the front seat passenger and an additional rear view mirror for use by the examiner. An oral explanation is given to candidates who fail.

Highway Code Proposed Changes

The government plans to include a 'hierarchy of road users' in a revised Highway Code that could make truck drivers responsible for the actions of vulnerable road users around their vehicle.

The proposed changes could lead to a situation where drivers of larger vehicles will be responsibility in the event of a collision.

This will be giving cyclists the right of way when undertaking or overtaking a turning vehicle at junctions.

The proposals are said that it could encourage dangerous and irresponsible behaviour.

Details at: http://alturl.com/26svh

Driving Instruction

Only approved instructors (ADIs – approved by the DSA) are permitted to give driving instruction for payment on private cars and goods vehicles not exceeding 3050kg unladen weight. More stringent standards have been introduced for driving instructors; in particular, extended training periods are necessary before they can become qualified.

Tuition given for payment on heavy goods vehicles does not come within the scope of this legislation. To ensure that the level of driving instruction available to learner LGV drivers is of a consistently high standard, a new scheme for the voluntary registration of LGV driving instructors has been established. Entry to the register is currently via a two-part examination of both driving and instructional abilities.

LGV Driver Testing

In order to drive a large vehicle it is necessary to pass both the theory and a practical driving test on a large goods or passenger vehicle of the appropriate category.

Theory Testing

The LGV test has 100 multi–choice questions, and you need to get 85 correct to pass. You'll have 115 minutes to complete the test.

The test including a wide range of topics such as fuel economy, environmentally sensitive driving and safety issues.

The LGV Driving Test

Since 1 January 1997 in order to undertake an LGV/PCV driving test, candidates must produce a large vehicle theory test pass certificate. The LGV practical driving test is conducted by DSA examiners and booking has to be made through the local offices of the DSA. The staged system of testing means that:

- Applicants for LGV tests must already hold a full category B (car and light vehicle) driving entitlement before taking a test to obtain a category C entitlement.

- Category B entitlement holders have to pass a test on a rigid goods vehicle in category C before being able to take a test to qualify for driving articulated vehicles and drawbar combinations in category C +E.
- Category C1 entitlement holders wishing to drive vehicles in category C1+E must take a further test for this type of vehicle combination.

In each case the driver must hold a provisional entitlement for the category of vehicle on which he wants to be tested.

Identification

Test candidates must produce satisfactory identification or the examiner may refuse to conduct the test and the fee will be forfeited.

Vehicles for the LGV Driving Test

The candidate has to provide the vehicle (or arrange for the loan of a suit able vehicle) on which he wishes to be tested and it must comply with the following requirements:

- It must be unladen and of the category for which an LGV driving entitlement is required.
- It must display ordinary T plates front and rear (learner drivers in Wales may display a "D" plate instead).
- It must be in a thoroughly roadworthy condition.
- Seating accommodation in the cab must be provided for the examiner.
- It must have sufficient fuel for a test lasting up to two hours.

Minimum Test Vehicles (MTVs)

LGV driving test candidates must supply vehicles which meet the following requirements as regards their minimum weight and speed capability:

- Vehicles for category B tests must have at least four wheels and be capable of a speed of at least 100kph.
- For category B+E tests the vehicle itself must comply with category B requirements (see above) and must be drawing a trailer of at least 1 tonne gross weight (1 ton maximum authorised mass – mam).
- For category C1 tests the vehicle must be of at least 4 tons mam and capable of a speed of at least 80kph.
- For category C 1 +E tests the vehicle must comply with the requirements for category C tests (see above) and must be drawing a trailer of at least 2 tons mam – the combined length of the combination must be at least 8 metres.
- For category C tests (rigid goods vehicles exceeding 3.5 tons pmw) the vehicle must be of at least 10 tons pmw (or mam), at least 7 metres long and capable of at least 80kph.

- For a category C+E test (articulated vehicles) the vehicle must be articulated and have a permissible maximum weight (mam) of at least 18 tons, be at least 12 metres long and capable of at least 80kph.
- For a category C+E test (restricted to drawbar vehicle combinations only) the rigid towing vehicle should meet the requirements for a category C test and the trailer should be at least 4 metres long. The combination must have a minimum total weight of at least 18 tons, a minimum overall length of 12 metres, and the 80kph minimum speed capability also applies.

The LGV Driving Test Syllabus

The recommended syllabus to prepare for the LGV driving test is to be found in the DSA publication, The Goods Vehicle Driving Manual (available from The Stationery Office). The syllabus comprises 10 main sections containing advice and detailing specific requirements as well as an introductory section outlining the prior "thorough" knowledge that a candidate should acquire.

LGV Test Passes and Failures

A driver who passes the LGV/PCV driving test is issued with a certificate valid for a period of two years, and the holder can apply for an LGV driving entitlement of the appropriate category to be added to his unified driving license. A driver who fails the LGV/PCV driving test is given a written statement of failure and an oral explanation. He may apply for an immediate re-test.

What is Driver CPC?

The Driver CPC is for LGV and PCV drivers who drive professionally throughout the UK. It has been developed as a requirement of the EU Directive 2003/59, which is designed to improve the knowledge and skills of professional LGV and PCV drivers throughout their working life. This was implemented for LGV drivers on 10th September 2009.

There are two parts to the legislation:

The Initial Qualification that must be achieved by new LGV and PCV drivers along with their vocational licence to enable them to use their licence professionally. It involves periodic training, which involves all professional drivers undertaking 35 hours of training every 5 years.

The qualification which is obtained following the successful completion of driver training and an examination which is designed for all UK professional drivers. It is being developed as a requirement of the EU Directive 2003/59, which is designed to improve the knowledge and skills of LGV and PCV drivers throughout their working lives.

The Training Directive stipulates that all persons wishing to drive Goods Vehicles in excess of 3.5 tonnes (C1 licence) in a professional capacity will have to undergo training for, and obtain, a vocational Certificate of Professional Competence (CPC), further to the LGV/PCV licence.
Vocational training leading to the CPC will be kept, but the number of exemptions will be reduced and incentives will be introduced to reward drivers who undergo the training to have earlier access to larger vehicles.

Basic vocational training is divided into three areas:

- Advanced training in rational driving based upon safety rules.
- Compliance with regulations.
- Health, safety, service and logistics.

The Driver CPC will unify for the first time further training for existing drivers and new guidelines on training for new drivers entering the profession as a career.

What is Involved?

Training will affect all professional LGV and PCV drivers. For new drivers it introduces a new initial qualification, the Driver Certificate of Professional Competence (CPC), which increases the amount of knowledge that drivers need before they can drive. The theory test questions were increased from the proposed 60 in April 2007, to 100 by July 2008. There will also be 19 hazard perception clips in the theory test and along with the appropriate practical test, will have to be taken by both PCV and LGV drivers.

Since the 10th September 2009 LGV drivers also have to do 3 case studies and a half hour extra practical test module that constitute the initial Driver CPC.

All new and existing professional drivers will have to undertake 35 hours of training every five years to ensure that their driver CPC is current, this is known as Periodic Training. It is designed to confirm and expand on the existing knowledge and skills of each driver to ensure that they continue to be confident, safe and fuel-efficient drivers.

Only courses that have been approved and are being delivered by a training centre that has been approved by the Joint Approvals Unit for Periodic Training (JAUPT) on behalf of the Competent Authority will count towards the Periodic Training requirement.

Training will be delivered in three modules, which will enable drivers to keep up to date with the ever-changing regulations and to benefit from state of the art training throughout their whole career. The Directive became effective for PCV in September 2008 and LGV in September 2009.

Training courses must be at least seven hours in duration. Where courses are seven hours in duration, they can be divided into two equal parts, but the full course must be delivered within 24 hours. Please note, the total course length must be a full or half hour e.g. 7 hours or 7.5 hours not 7.25 hours. Where courses are over seven hours, but can be delivered in blocks of seven hours (i.e. course of 14, 21, 28, or 35 hours), the full course must be delivered within the year of approval.

NB: drivers must complete the full course for any of the hours to count towards Periodic Training e.g. if a driver completes only 28 hours of a 35 hour course, except in exceptional circumstances, none of the hours will count as the full course has not been completed. The review of these exceptional circumstances will be at JAUPT's discretion.

Who is affected by the requirements for periodic training?

In essence, every driver of a PCV or LGV. However, there will be exemptions in the shape of those drivers not driving for hire or reward, and those running the community bus permit scheme i.e. the majority of Community Transport.

All professional LGV drivers who hold a full, valid category C, C1, C+E or C1+E licence will from 10th September 2009 need to complete the 35 hours of periodic training by 10 September 2014. For all new Drivers who gained their initial Driver CPC after 10th September 2008 (PCV) or 10 September 2009 (LGV), they will immediately begin their period of periodic training and will need to complete 35 hours of training within five years of attaining their initial Driver CPC.

For holders of both a PCV and an LGV licence

They will have to complete only one course of 35 hours of Periodic Training every five years. They will not have to undertake 35 hours of training for each licence category.

For drivers with LGV/PCV licences in other EU states

Their periodic training must be completed in the country of employment or residence.

Exemptions

Drivers are not required to hold a Driver CPC if the vehicle they drive is:

- Not authorised to exceed 45 kph.
- Being used by or under the instructions of the armed forces, the police or a fire and rescue authority.
- Undergoing road tests for technical development repair or for maintenance purposes.
- Being used in a state of emergency or as part of a rescue mission.
- Being used for driving lessons for either driving licence or Driver CPC purposes.
- Not being used to carry passengers or goods for commercial purposes.

- Carrying materials or equipment for the driver's work, where driving is not the driver's principal activity.

This list is not necessarily exhaustive and is intended only as a guide. It is recommended that in all cases, where it is felt an exemption applies, drivers and operators seek independent legal advice.

Commercial vehicle training objectives will be to load the vehicle with due regard for safety rules and proper vehicle use, including:

- forces affecting vehicles in motion
- use of gearbox ratios according to vehicle load and road profile
- calculation of payload of vehicle or assembly
- calculation of total volume
- load distribution
- consequences of overloading the axle
- vehicle stability and centre of gravity
- types of packaging and pallets
- main categories of goods needing securing
- clamping and securing techniques
- use of securing straps
- checking of securing devices
- use of handling equipment
- placing and removal of tarpaulins

Section H2 Traffic Rules for Europe

Many traffic rules in the EU are universal across the whole continent. We shall examine the main rules and road signs that apply to driving across the EU area.

Speed Limits

Speed limits in Great Britain are applied to various types of vehicle on various types of road. Where speed limits for different classes of vehicle and road vary, the lower limit always applies.

A "restricted" road is one which has street lights placed not more than 200 yards apart and with the 30mph (or other indicated speed) limit shown on a circular sign at the beginning of the restricted section of road. On other roads where lower limits are indicated these must be observed (30mph, 40mph and 50mph areas).

Type of road	Maximum speed, any vehicle
Motorways	70mph
Dual carriageway roads	70mph
Single carriageway roads	60mph
Restricted roads	30mph

Advisory/Mandatory Speed Limits on Motorways

Advisory speed limits on motorways are shown by illuminated signs and indicate hazardous situations and roadworks ahead. The amber flashing warning lights located on the nearside of motorways indicate danger ahead – you should slow down until the road is clear. Failure to observe these signs can lead to prosecution for offences such as "driving without due care".

Mandatory limits may also be found on motorways at roadworks sites (indicated by a white sign with black letters and red border). Failure to comply with these particular signs can result in speeding prosecutions.

Exemptions from Speed Limits

Fire, police or ambulance service vehicles, when necessary in the performance of their duty, may exceed speed limits if they can do so in safety.

Speed Limits for Goods Vehicles

	Motorways	Dual carriageways	Other roads
Car derived vans			
Solo	70	70	60
Towing caravan or trailer	60	60	50
Goods vehicles not exceeding 7.5t mlw			
Solo	70	60	50
Articulated	60	60*	50
Drawbar	60	60*	50
Goods vehicles exceeding 7.5t mlw			
Solo	60	60	50
Articulated	60	50	40
Drawbar	60	50	40

MLW: maximum laden weight (i.e. maximum permissible weight for a vehicle as specified in Construction and Use regulations)
*In Northern Ireland these two limits are 50mph only. Also in NI, learner drivers and those who have only recently passed their driving test (when displaying "T" and "R" plates respectively) are restricted to a maximum speed of 45mph on all roads where higher limits are otherwise permitted.

Locally set speed limits

Local councils can set their own speed limits in certain areas, and these must be clearly signed.

For example:

- 20 mph zone in a built-up area near a school
- 50 mph (rather than 60 mph) limit on a stretch of road with sharp bends

Speed limiters

A speed limiter must be fitted on:

- vehicles with more than 8 passenger seats, eg buses, minibuses, coaches, stretch limousines
- goods vehicles with a maximum laden weight of more than 3.5 tonnes

Speed limiters are designed to reduce accidents. They limit the maximum speed of a vehicle by restricting the fuel supply to the engine. Having a speed limiter may mean that your vehicle can't reach the speed limit.

Speed Limits in Europe

Some European states and other neighbouring countries do not allow goods vehicles to use the roads at weekends or on public holidays. Operators should make inquiries about this with the transport association before planning journeys since public holidays vary from country to country.

Country	Built-up areas	Motorways	Other roads
Austria	50kph	80kph	70kph
		70kph (road trains)	60kph (road trains)
Belgium	50kph	90kph (over 7.5t)	60kph (over 7.5t)
		70kph min speed	
Denmark	50kph	80kph	70kph
Republic 0f Ireland	48kph		64kph
France	50kph	90kph (0ver12t)	80kph
		80kph (DG)	60kph (DG)
Germany	50kph	80kph	80kph (up t0 7.5t)
			60kph (over 7.5t)
Great Britain	30mph (48kph)	60mph (96kph)	40mph (64kph)
Greece	50kph	85kph (main r0ads)	80kph
	40kph (DG)	70kph (DG)	
Italy	50kph	100kph	80kph
	30kph (DG)	80kph (DG)	
Luxembourg	60kph	90kph	75kph (0ver 5t)
	40kph (DG)	60kph (DG)	60kph (DG)
Netherlands	50kph	80kph	80kph (A roads)
			60kph (B roads)
Portugal	50kph	90kph	80kph
Spain	50kph	80kph	70kph
Switzerland	50kph	80kph	80kph

As at July 2020

DG = Vehicles carrying dangerous goods
Where member states have no motorways or where common speed limits apply to motorways and other roads (usually classified as being outside built-up areas) these are shown above midway between the two headings.

EU Member States and Neighbouring Countries Where Vehicle Bans Apply

Austria - over 3.5 tonnes and when drawing trailer (except for carriage of milk); after 15.00 hours Saturday; all day Sunday; on public holidays until 22.00 hours.

Republic of Ireland - no traffic/vehicle bans in operation but it is not possible to pass through Customs posts (from Northern Ireland) except between 09.00 and 17.00 hours daily (weekdays only) except by special request and fee payment.

France - vehicles over 6 tonnes laden weight (except those carrying perishables, live animals, newspapers, hydrocarbons and vehicles returning to their home country); 22.00 hours Saturday (or the day before a public holiday) to 22.00 hours Sundays and public holidays; vehicles carrying dangerous goods; 12.00 hours Saturday (or the day before a public holiday) to 24.00 hours Sunday and public holidays.

Germany - vehicles over 7.5 tonnes laden weight (except en route to Berlin and those carrying fresh milk, meat and produce); Sundays and public holidays.

Greece - goods vehicles (except those carrying perishables); 17.00 hours Saturday to 24.00 hours Sundays and public holidays.

Italy - goods vehicles with pmw over 5 tonnes, lorries with trailers (even if unladen) and those carrying dangerous goods; 08.00 to 22.00 hours Sundays (Jan, Feb, Mar, Oct, Nov, Dec) - 07.00 to 24.00 hours Sundays (May, June, July, Aug, Sept).

Portugal - goods vehicles using certain main national routes: - 14.00 hours to 22.00 hours Saturdays; 06.00 hours to 24.00 hours Sundays and public holidays vehicles carrying dangerous goods; 12.00 hours to 24.00 hours Saturdays; 06.00 to 24.00 hours Sundays and public holidays.

Spain - goods vehicles except those carrying perishables; Sundays and public holidays 17.00 - 24.00 hours goods vehicles carrying dangerous goods; Saturday 13.00 hours to Sunday 24.00 hours.

Switzerland - vehicles above 3.5 tonnes; all day Sundays and public holidays; 22.00 to 05.00 hours daily.

Road Signs

Speed limit/End speed limit.
(In this case, 60kph). In most parts of Europe, this is considered more of a suggestion than a guideline.

Minimum speed/End minimum speed zone.

Do not enter.

Highway begins/Highway ends.
Note that major highways (autobahn / autoroute / autostrada) are usually tagged with green signs, while smaller highways are in blue. That means if you see two signs, one blue pointing right and one green pointing left, both reading "ROMA" you would turn left to take the autostrada to Rome, or right to follow a lesser highway to the Eternal City.

Keep to the right.
(Also available in "Keep to the left".) This often appears in divided roadway situations or at roundabouts.

No parking
(On whichever side of the street the sign is hanging/posted.)

No stopping.

No passing.

Parking.
Usually, this means paid parking, so look for a common meter, pay the required amount and leave the receipt on your dashboard.

You have
The right of way over oncoming traffic
A necessary sign where roads often narrow to significantly less than two full lanes.

You must yield to oncoming traffic.

Yield.
This is a good direction to follow at all times, regardless of signage, since the local drivers have a much better idea of what they're doing and where they're going than you do.

One Way.

Centre of Town
It may be called Zentrum, centre, or centro.

Britain's road sign system follows that of most European countries with the use of internationally recognised signs. (See a current copy of the Highway Code.) Certain road signs in Belgium and parts of northern Spain (Basque and Catalonian regions) are shown in dual language.

Driving on Right/Priority at Junctions

The whole of Europe (except the UK and Republic of Ireland) drives on the right and vehicles must overtake to the left. Priority at road junctions is mainly to traffic approaching from or turning right: Triorite a droite.

Sources of Information

It is essential for operators, when sending vehicles on international journeys, to be aware of the requirements in foreign countries for the following:

- Driver licensing.
- Vehicle licensing.
- Traffic regulations.
- Restrictions on vehicle movement.
- Accident procedures.
- Movement of abnormal loads.

Information on these matters may be obtained from a number of sources:

- The motor organisations: AA, RAC, and RSAC.
- Your Lorry Abroad, International Road Freight Office.
- International Services Manual, Freight Transport Association.
- Road Haulage Association.
- Transport authorities for individual countries (e.g. the DETR in the UK).
- Insurance companies, in the case of accident procedures.

Driving in Fog and Limited Visibility

When driving in fog and limited visibility you should:

- Slow down, keep a safe distance, and ensure that you can pull up within your range of vision.
- Do not keep close to the taillights of the vehicle in front; this gives a false sense of security.
- Check your speed; you may be travelling faster than you think.
- Remember that if you are driving a heavy vehicle, you need a greater distance in which to stop.
- Warning signals are there to help and to protect, so observe them.
- See and be seen — use headlights or fog lamps.

- Check and clean your windscreen, lights, reflectors and windows whenever you can.
- If you must drive in fog, allow more time for your journey.

Use of Lights in Poor Visibility

Front and rear position lamps and headlamps must be used during the daytime in poor visibility caused by heavy rain, mist, spray, fog or snow. Rear fog lights, where fitted, should also be used. It is an offence to drive in poor visibility without using lights.

Segregation

Drivers of cars, light goods vehicles and coaches should move out of the left-hand lane when it is safe to do so, unless they will soon be turning off the motorway. When desiring to leave the motorway, they should start their move to the left well before the exit. They should be prepared to miss the exit if they cannot reach it safely.

Drivers of heavy lorries should keep to the left-hand lane but should be ready to let other drivers into the lane at entry points and well before exit points.
(UK and Rep. of Ireland, rest of Europe right hand side)

Section H3 Drivers Walkaround Checks, Safety checks and Defect Reporting

<u>Daily walkaround checks and first-use inspections</u>

This section looks at the first of two essential roadworthiness inspections - the daily walkaround check and first-use inspection. It offers best practice advice on setting up a system for reporting faults and looks at defect reports, while clearly stating your legal position.

A responsible person must undertake a daily walkaround check before a vehicle is used. As a driver, you may carry out the check before you first drive the vehicle on the road each day.

The person made responsible by the operator must carry out a minimum of one check in 24 hours. The check should consist of a walkaround look over the whole vehicle or combination. On multi-trailer operations a defect check should be made on each trailer being used.

The check should cover the external condition, ensuring in particular that the lights, tyres, wheel fixings, bodywork, trailer coupling, load and ancillary equipment are serviceable.

Assistance may be required at some time during the inspection, for example to see that lights are working. Alternatively, a brake pedal application tool may be used as an effective way of making sure stop lamps are working and that the braking system is free of leaks. In addition, a torch, panel lock key or other equipment may be needed.

There must be a system of reporting and recording faults that may affect the roadworthiness of the vehicle and having them put right before the vehicle is used. Daily defect checks are vital, and the results of such checks should be recorded.

It is important that enough time is allowed for the completion of these checks and that staff are encouraged and trained to carry them out thoroughly. Drivers should be made aware that daily defect reporting is one of the critical elements of any effective vehicle roadworthiness system.

If you are the user of the vehicle, it is your responsibility to ensure that any hired, leased or borrowed vehicle is in a roadworthy condition and has all the necessary certification when used on the road. Therefore it is essential that you do a daily walkaround check before any such vehicle is used. It is your responsibility to be able to provide maintenance records covering the period of use.

Furthermore, if a vehicle has been off the road for a period longer than between planned maintenance inspections, it should be given a full safety inspection prior to being brought back into use.

The details recorded should include:

- Vehicle registration or identification mark.
- Date.

- Details of the defects or symptoms.
- The reporter's name.

It is common practice to use a composite form that also includes a list of the items checked each day. It is advisable that where practicable the system should incorporate 'Nil' reporting when each driver makes out a report sheet - or confirms by another means that a daily check has been carried out and no defects found. Electronic records of reported defects are acceptable and must be available for 15 months along with any record of repair.

Drivers' defect reports

The driver is responsible for the condition of their vehicle when in use on the road.

Drivers must be able to report any defects or symptoms of defects that could prevent the safe operation of the vehicles. In addition to daily checks you must monitor the roadworthiness of your vehicle when being driven and be alert to any indication that the vehicle is developing a fault (e.g. warning lights, exhaust emitting too much smoke, vibrations) or other symptoms.
When a vehicle is on site work, you should walk around the vehicle to identify any serious defects. If any defects are found, you must not use the vehicle on the road until it is repaired.

Any defects found during the daily check, while the vehicle is in use or on its return to base must be the subject of a written report by you or some other person responsible for recording defects.

All drivers' defect reports must be given to a responsible person with sufficient authority to ensure that any appropriate action is taken. This might include taking the vehicle out of service. Any report listing defects is part of the vehicle's maintenance record and must be kept, together with details of the remedial action taken, for at least 15 months.

'Nil' defect reports, if they are produced, should be kept for as long as they are useful. Normally this is until the next one is received or until the next scheduled safety inspection is undertaken. 'Nil' defect reports are not required under the conditions of operator licensing. However, they are a useful means of checking that drivers are carrying out their duties in this respect.

If you are an owner-driver, you will probably not have anyone to report defects to, except to your transport manager (if you have one). In these cases, defects can simply be recorded and held for at least 15 months.

Drivers must be made aware of their legal responsibilities regarding vehicle condition and the procedures for reporting defects. This can be achieved by writing a letter to each driver, describing defect reporting systems as well as any other duties they are expected to perform.
The driver should sign this letter to show in writing that they have received the letter and understand what is required. Drivers share the responsibility for the vehicle's

roadworthiness with the operator. Drivers may be prosecuted for the existence of defects found on the vehicles they drive if they are considered partly or wholly responsible for the existence of them. Failure to take these responsibilities seriously could result in the loss of the driver's licence to drive.

If you are an operator, you should bear in mind that drivers who are expected to repair minor defects in service, e.g. light bulb replacement, might need basic training.

Regular safety inspections

Regular safety inspections are essential to an effective roadworthiness maintenance system. Although a part of the overall vehicle maintenance plan, the inspections should ideally be undertaken as a separate, albeit often sequential, operation to routine servicing and repair. This provides the maintenance programme with the flexibility to intensify or otherwise change the frequency of inspections. It also allows the introduction of ad hoc inspections, should they be required, without affecting frequency of servicing and other routine work (e.g. when the operating conditions call for more regular checks or when first-use inspections are required).
In addition, freestanding inspection reports can be produced which provide the operator with the means of determining not only the roadworthiness of individual vehicles in service but also the overall effectiveness of their vehicle maintenance system, thus enabling the instigation of any changes that might be necessary.

Although primarily undertaken in the interest of safe vehicle operations, roadworthiness inspections, together with prompt remedial action, are also cost effective. The early indication of wear, damage or maladjustment may prevent the sudden failure of a component - resulting in unscheduled downtime - or prevent wear becoming so advanced that premature replacement becomes necessary.

A roadworthiness inspection can be a freestanding inspection of just those items affecting road safety and certain environmental issues. Or it can be part of a more comprehensive inspection that, in addition, takes into account items relating to the vehicle's work performance and economic operation.

A roadworthiness safety inspection must include all the items covered by the statutory annual test. Reference should be made to manufacturers' recommended tolerances to ensure that each item covered by the safety inspection is inspected properly and limits of wear and tolerance adhered to. In addition, DVSA produces annual test inspection manuals for use at annual tests. These give details of inspection methods and pass/fail criteria. These manuals are useful as a guide when safety inspections are carried out. However, higher standards may be needed during safety inspections to allow for deterioration in service before the next inspection.

Adapting your systems

If you are an operator, you are free to tailor these inspections to suit the nature of your operations and vehicle characteristics. You may even deploy more than one system across a fleet, where vehicles and the nature of the work vary. Systems will be judged primarily on their effectiveness in maintaining roadworthiness.

Safety inspection intervals

In order to maintain an inspection regime that is sufficiently flexible to accommodate these changing criteria it might be more appropriate to adopt an inspection frequency determined by, for instance, the vehicle's mileage.

Operational needs must not over-ride safety considerations. Safety inspections should, where it is practicable, be programmed to follow a time-based pattern. The frequency at which inspections are undertaken should be determined by assessing the level of mechanical degradation likely to be incurred over a period as a result of the vehicle's usage.

This will depend on such factors as:

- The type of vehicle, the nature of its load and the equipment and fittings it carries or supports.
- The type and range of operations on which it is likely to be engaged.
- The type of terrain and the nature of the environment in which it operates or is likely to operate.

Once established, operators wishing to change safety inspection frequencies, or the basis on which the frequencies are determined, must notify the DVSA Traffic Area Office.

If you are a new operator, you will need to know where to start. However, you will not have the benefit of past experience or vehicle maintenance records to call upon.

Mileage-based inspection programmes may be more suitable for some operators but will need to be linked to time.

Assessing the above factors for each vehicle will, in the majority of cases, enable a time- based programme of inspections to be formulated. Some operations, however, are subject to continuous change, or vehicles can frequently be re-assigned alternative tasks or routes, making the adoption of a strictly time- based inspection programme impracticable.

The frequencies shown are in weekly increments and take account of the type of work undertaken, the operating conditions and mileages covered. Whatever the safety inspection interval is, its effectiveness in ensuring that the vehicle is safe for use on the road must be regularly monitored. Monitoring is especially important in the early stages.

A written report must be completed for each safety inspection separately for both vehicles and trailers. If the record of the safety inspection is to be stored electronically, the checklist used for the inspection need not be retained. This does not rule out the use of an electronic device (e.g. PDA) in place of a checklist.

Each report must show at least the following:

- Name of owner/operator.
- Date of inspection.
- Vehicle identity.
- Odometer (mileage recorder) reading (if appropriate).
- A list of all items to be inspected.
- An indication of the condition of each item inspected.
- Details of any defects found.
- Name of inspector.
- Details of any remedial/rectification or repair work and by whom it was done.
- A statement that any defects have been repaired satisfactorily.

The report may contain details of any work to be carried forward. In particular, further checks may be needed on certain items deemed likely to deteriorate during service and make the vehicle unroadworthy before the next scheduled inspection or routine service.

With some types of vehicle and operation it may be necessary to check some components more often than at full safety inspections. For example, a vehicle used in urban areas, such as a public service vehicle or a local delivery vehicle, or vehicles used in hilly areas may require a weekly brake component and adjustment check together with a steering and suspension inspection. It is sometimes necessary to check components following repair work.

Safety inspections may be needed at times outside the scheduled programme. Examples include when the vehicle is used for harder work or covers greater distances than usual (e.g. vehicles used on site).

Safety inspection and repair work records, whether undertaken by operators or contracted out, must be kept for at least 15 months as part of a vehicle's maintenance history.
Operators must, however, ensure that the records are complete and available, or can be made available on request for inspection at the operating centre. If you hire, lease or borrow a vehicle you are responsible for its roadworthiness and to have available, if required, copies of any inspections that have been carried out while the vehicle is in your possession.
Electronic capture and/or storage on computer of details of defects found or work done (e.g. bar coding or scanning), is acceptable provided that a means of interpreting each code is readily available.

Safety inspection records can be stored electronically, using a computer. The system must be tamper-proof and capable of producing hardcopy information for use at public inquiries held by Traffic Commissioners. Computer records must contain the same information with the exception of:

- A full list of the items inspected. (these can be indicated on the paper report used for the inspection)
- An indication of the condition of each item inspected. (it is sufficient to provide details of defective items only)

Internet-based systems are becoming more common. These provide significant opportunities for improving the ease with which operators can plan and monitor the maintenance of their vehicles, thus leading to higher standards and improved compliance.

Safety inspectors

A person undertaking safety inspections must be technically competent and operationally aware of the safety standards that apply to the vehicles they examine. They should have been trained in the techniques of vehicle examination, diagnosis and reporting, and possess a sound working knowledge of the relevant inspection manuals produced by DVSA.
A safety inspector should not be expected to carry out repair or servicing work during the course of the examination.
There may be times during the course of an inspection when the inspector will require the assistance of someone to operate certain vehicle controls. The operator must ensure that this assistance is available when required. The vehicle's driver can often provide such assistance.

If you are the operator, you must ensure that someone within your organisation, at all times, has the authority to decide whether a vehicle is fit for service and to take it off the road if it is not.
That person must be available to decide whether a vehicle can be allowed back into service after repairs. This responsibility may be delegated, in writing (i.e. in the form of a standard agreement), provided that it is made clear what their responsibilities are.

Vehicles should be cleaned regularly on top, inside and underneath. This will make it easier to spot defects at scheduled safety inspections and during the daily walkaround checks.

It is important that all staff with an involvement either directly (e.g. drivers and workshop staff) or indirectly (e.g. transport management) are made fully aware of the company's legal and moral responsibilities as an operator of road vehicles. They should also be made aware of the subsequent importance of ensuring the effective operation of the vehicle maintenance programme.

Drivers, workshop staff and those otherwise responsible for the condition of vehicles should be individually informed in writing of their specific duties and responsibilities - particularly regarding safe vehicle operation.

Emphasis should be placed on the importance of maintaining an effective safety inspection programme and the role they play in promoting and sustaining its integrity.

One method might be to write to each relevant employee in duplicate, thus permitting a returned signed copy to be retained by the company.

HGV DRIVERS' WALKAROUND CHECK

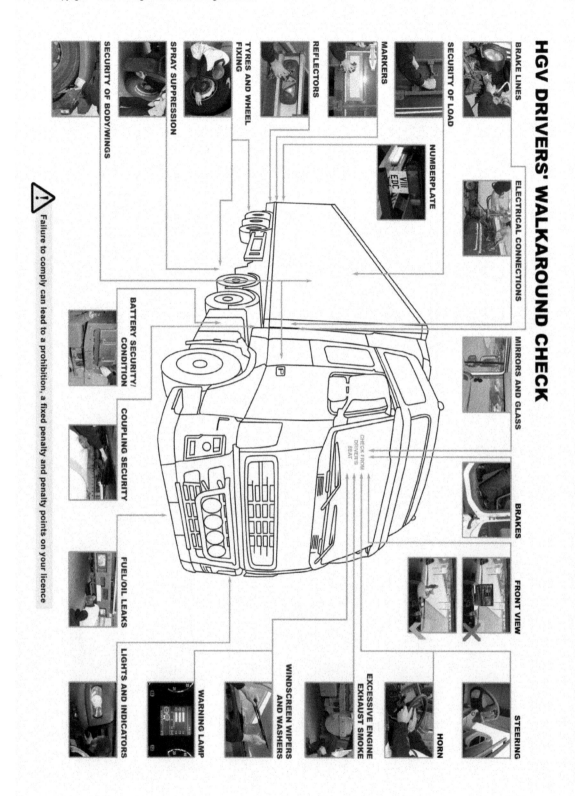

BRAKE LINES

SECURITY OF LOAD

MARKERS

NUMBERPLATE

REFLECTORS

TYRES AND WHEEL FIXING

SPRAY SUPPRESSION

SECURITY OF BODY/WINGS

ELECTRICAL CONNECTIONS

MIRRORS AND GLASS

BATTERY SECURITY/ CONDITION

COUPLING SECURITY

FUEL/OIL LEAKS

BRAKES

FRONT VIEW

STEERING

HORN

EXCESSIVE ENGINE EXHAUST SMOKE

WINDSCREEN WIPERS AND WASHERS

WARNING LAMP

LIGHTS AND INDICATORS

CHECK FROM DRIVER'S SEAT

⚠ Failure to comply can lead to a prohibition, a fixed penalty and penalty points on your licence

328

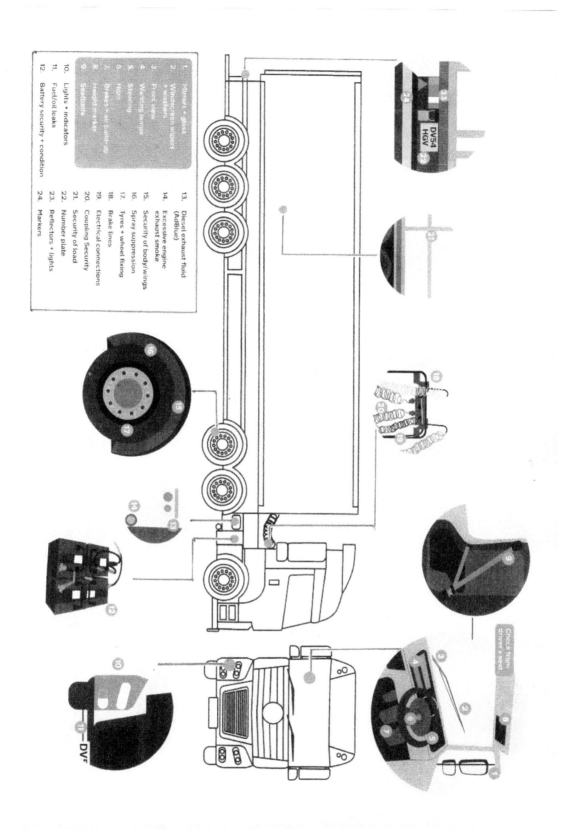

1. Mirrors + glass
2. Windscreen wipers + washers
3. Front view
4. Warning lamps
5. Steering
6. Horn
7. Brakes + air build-up
8. Headlamp aim
9. Seatbelts
10. Lights + indicators
11. Fuel/oil leaks
12. Battery security + condition
13. Diesel exhaust fluid (AdBlue)
14. Excessive engine exhaust smoke
15. Security of body/wings
16. Spray suppression
17. Tyres + wheel fixing
18. Brake lines
19. Electrical connections
20. Security of load
21. Coupling Security
22. Number plate
23. Reflectors + lights
24. Markers

Direct Vision Standard

The introduction in 2020, of the Direct Vision Standard (DVS) assesses and rates HGVs in terms of direct driver.

Transport for London is developing a Direct Vision Standard (DVS) for larger HGVs (category N3 vehicles over 12 tonnes) operating in London will be introduced by the end of the current Mayoral term in 2020.

The Direct Vision Standard is a measure of how much HGV drivers can see from their cab directly (without the use of mirrors or video cameras).
From October 2020, Transport for London will require all HGVs over 12 tonnes entering London to have at least a one-star rating and from 2024 they will need at least a three-star rating.

To meet the one-star standard, a driver will need to be able to see someone's head and shoulders from within an acceptable distance. For the one-star rating, that corresponds to 4.5m at the side and 2m in front.
The scheme will be enforced 24/7 and permits will be issued free of charge.

Fines of £550 will be issued to any vehicle entering London without a permit, with drivers fined £130.

Some haulage companies complained that the new standard placed a burden on their companies because they would have to contact the manufacturer to find out their safety rating. However, TfL's head of delivery planning said "The disproportionately high number of HGVs involved in fatal collisions with pedestrians and cyclists is a tragedy.

This is why we've worked closely with the freight and logistics industry and vulnerable road user groups to develop the Direct Vision Standard and HGV Safety Standard Permit Scheme. Together we hope that these new safety measures will help to save many lives in the future.

In 2016, shortly after taking office, the Mayor of London, Sadiq Khan announced plans to introduce a Direct Vision Standard (DVS) for larger HGVs operating in London by the end of the current Mayoral term in 2020. N3 (goods vehicles over 12 tonnes) are being assessed on the amount of direct vision and given a star rating. Zero-star rated vehicles would be banned from the Capital's roads from 2020 and those not meeting at least three stars will be affected from 2024.

How many vehicles will be affected?

Initial estimates from Transport for London (TfL) suggest that 50-60 per cent of N3 vehicles would not meet the one-star DVS rating. For HGVs used in the construction sector and in particular N3G off-road tippers, approximately three-quarters of vehicles are zero-star rated.

What do I do if my vehicle doesn't meet the one-star rating?

TfL is proposing that all HGVs over 12 tonnes would require a safety permit to enter or operate in London. HGVs with a DVS rating of one-star and above would automatically be granted a permit. HGVs with zero-star ratings would be granted a permit if they meet specific measures in a 'safe system.' The 'safe system' will build on best practice from existing, industry-recognised schemes. Measures could include:

- Sensors and other indirect vision devices
- Audible or visual warning around the vehicle
- Physical protection to deflect vulnerable road users away from the vehicle
- Driver safety training

What will happen in the next phase of the scheme?

Phase two of the scheme in 2024 would require HGVs rated two-star and below, to meet the requirements of a 'progressive safe system'. It is anticipated that these requirements will be more stringent than those from phase one to account for future developments in technology and safety measures, and to give the industry additional time to prepare for these changes. The progressive system will be subject to further consultation at an appropriate point before 2024.

The FTA's view

FTA's position is that standards for HGVs should be set at a national or international level as manufacturers design vehicles for a European market, not by individual cities.

This could lead to London becoming a niche market for the manufacturers, increasing the costs of new vehicles. There must be a clear evidence base for new standards, otherwise we cannot be sure that the additional investment required will actually lead to improved safety. Whilst increasing direct vision has a role to play, it not the most effective way of addressing safety issues and technical developments will mitigate the requirement for improved direct vision. Often cameras and mirrors will give drivers a view that no amount of direct vision will be able to replace. As technology advances, these systems will be become even more sophisticated and the benefits greater.

Whilst the safe system proposal is a welcome move away from the narrow focus on direct vision, it has the potential to make the regulatory environment in London even more complex. If driver safety training is included as a mandatory element of the scheme, there are practical issues about how and where the training will be delivered, in particular for drivers who rarely visit London or for non-UK based fleets. It is also undecided how the standard will be assessed and a permit granted. FTA is pressing for self-certification (the same system used for Operator Licensing) to minimise bureaucracy and cost.

Section H4 Traffic Accident Procedure

Duty to Stop and Give Information

If involved in a road traffic accident, where injury to people (other than the driver himself) or to specify animals (other than those carried in the vehicle) or damage occurs to another vehicle or to roadside property, the driver must stop. He should remain at the scene at least long enough to provide the requisite information, namely his name and address, the name and address of the vehicle owner, and the registration number of the vehicle, to anybody who has reasonable grounds to request such information.

If he does not give this information to a person requesting it at the scene of the accident, he must report the details to the police as soon as is reasonably practicable afterwards, but in any case not later than 24 hours later.

A police constable can ask the driver to give his name and address and his age, and the name and address of the vehicle owner. The driver may be required to produce his driving license at the scene of the accident by a police constable, or at the police station when reporting the event or within seven days at a police station of his own choice. The police may ask to see proof of insurance for the vehicle (a certificate of insurance or a temporary cover note) and the vehicle test certificate, if appropriate.

In the case of injury to third persons, an insurance certificate must be shown to a police constable or any other person at the scene of the accident who has reasonable grounds to ask to see it. If the driver is not able to produce the insurance certificate at the time of the accident or within 24 hours at a police station, he will be requested to produce it within seven days at a police station of his own choice. The accident must also be reported to the vehicle owner and the insurers.

For the purposes of these requirements "roadside property" means items "constructed on, fixed to, growing on, or otherwise forming part of the land in which the road is situated or land adjacent thereto". This includes damage to trees, hedges, gardens, gate-posts, street furniture, and other vehicles.

Animals for these purposes are specifically any horse, cattle, ass, mule (in Northern Ireland also a hinnie), sheep, pig, goat or dog. Injuries to "people" do not include those to the driver. Other people injured in an accident are the "third party" who may ultimately make a claim direct to the vehicle driver or the insurers for compensation for their injuries.

The Highway Code

https://www.gov.uk/guidance/the-highway-code

The Highway Code gives additional advice for situations where an accident involves a vehicle carrying dangerous goods. It states that the police and fire brigade should he given as much additional information as possible about the labels and other markings on the vehicle; other people should be kept away and, if it is necessary to act to save life, it should be done with the utmost caution because of the possible presence of dangerous liquids leaking on to the road and dangerous dust or vapours blowing in the wind.

The government plans to include a 'hierarchy of road users' in a revised Highway Code that could make truck drivers responsible for the actions of vulnerable road users around their vehicle.

The proposed changes could lead to a situation where drivers of larger vehicles will be responsibility in the event of a collision.

This will be giving cyclists the right of way when undertaking or overtaking a turning vehicle at junctions.

The proposals are said that it could encourage dangerous and irresponsible behaviour.

Details at: http://alturl.com/26svh

Accident Report to the Insurers

Drivers are required to report accidents to the vehicle insurers (or via their employer) and the main points to be included are:

- The date, time and place of the accident.
- A description of the weather and road conditions at the time.
- The speed of the vehicle.
- The direction of its travel and its position on the road in relationship to other vehicles.
- The position on the road and direction of travel of any other vehicles involved.
- A description of the damage caused to the insured vehicle and any other vehicle.
- A description of the damage or injury caused to any other property (including any other vehicle) or person.
- The names, addresses and the name of the insurers of any other person involved.
- The names and addresses of any witnesses to the accident.
- A note of any comments made by people at the scene of the accident.
- The name or number of any police constable in attendance at the accident.
- Details of any instructions given regarding the removal of the vehicle from the scene of the accident.

It is also advisable to provide a sketch of the accident showing the relative position of the vehicles involved prior to and immediately after the accident.

Accident Claims Procedure

In the event of an accident where damage or injury is sustained, the driver should report the event to the vehicle owner and to his insurer or the vehicle owner's insurer, usually within seven days. An accident report/claim form should be completed.

At the scene it is unwise to admit liability, to apologise to the other party, or to enter into an argument about responsibility with the third party or with any other person. Such remarks could prejudice the outcome of any claims. It should be left for the insurers to establish blame and liability.

Where damage or injury is confined to the vehicle and driver and comprehensive insurance cover is operative, a claim can be made for loss or damage, apart from any excess. A vehicle owner can volunteer to pay the first part of an amount of a claim, usually £25 to £250 or even more depending on circumstances, so that for minor damage repairs any "no claims bonus" on the policy is not jeopardised. Volunteering to pay an excess can result in premium discounts. In special cases, the insurers will impose a compulsory excess, often in the case of young or inexperienced drivers. The insurers will assess the claims and will require estimates for repair work to vehicles, property or loss through injury. If claims are met, the "no claims bonus" will be affected and this will result in a higher premium on renewal of the policy.

Where the damage or injury is confined to the insured vehicle and driver and no comprehensive insurance cover is operative, no claim can be made against the insurers for loss, damage or injury.

If no damage or injury is caused to the driver or the vehicle but is caused to roadside property, other vehicles, animals or people, the insurers will deal with any claims from third parties.

Claims which are received from third parties who have suffered loss or damage should be passed immediately to the insurers. The driver should not enter into correspondence directly with third parties. The insurers will assess the claims and will require estimates for repair work to vehicles, property or loss through injury. If claims are met, the "no claims bonus" (if applicable) may be affected and this could result in a higher premium on renewal of the policy.

European Accident Statement

The purpose of the European Accident Statement is to provide road accident victims, principally vehicle drivers, with a standardised and widely recognised means of recording accident details, especially relevant driver and vehicle details, nature of the road and weather conditions, position of vehicles prior to and at the moment of impact, witness information, and any other important details. This form of accident recording makes it easier for insurance companies to resolve matters relating to claims and where necessary, in apportioning blame.

Legislation

Road Traffic Acts

Road traffic in the UK is controlled by many separate pieces of legislation – Acts of Parliament, regulations and statutory orders. Mainly, the legal provisions are to be found in successive Road Traffic Acts, in particular those of 1972, 1974, 1988 and 1991. These, together with the Road Traffic Offenders Act 1988, the Road Traffic Regulation Act of 1984, the Transport Act 1981 and the Highways Act 1980 (plus others), deal with traffic offences and penalties, vehicle construction and use, plating and testing, licensing of drivers, vehicle insurance requirements, seatbelt fitment and use, speed limits, parking and waiting, motorway driving, powers of police and other enforcement staff among other.

ROAD TRAFFIC ACT 2010 – REVISED (Updated to 17 April 2016)

New legislation with 'EU Exit' in the title that references (and therefore may change) this legislation item:

Due to a high volume of changes being made to legislation for EU exit, we have not been able to research and record them all. More information is available about EU Legislation and UK Law. The following results are legislation items with 'EU Exit' in their title that directly reference and therefore may change this item of legislation. To understand whether or not the text of this legislation is up to date, please check those references in the following pieces of legislation.

There are currently no additional references that you need to check.

Changes to legislation:

Road Traffic Act 2016 is up to date with all changes known to be in force on or before 24 February 2021. There are changes that may be brought into force at a future date.

There are currently no known outstanding effects for the Road Traffic (Amendment) Act (Northern Ireland) 2016.

Acts which affect or previously affected this revision

• Vehicle Clamping Act 2015 (13/2015)
• Road Traffic (No. 2) Act 2014 (39/2014)
• Road Traffic Act 2014 (3/2014)

• Local Government Reform Act 2014 (1/2014)
• Taxi Regulation Act 2013 (37/2013)
• Road Safety Authority (Commercial Vehicle Roadworthiness) Act 2012 (16/2012)
• Road Traffic (No. 2) Act 2011 (28/2011)
• Road Traffic Act 2011 (7/2011)
• Road Traffic Act 1961 (24/1961)
All Acts up to and including Criminal Justice (Spent Convictions and Certain Disclosures)
Act 2016 (4/2016), enacted 11 February 2016, were considered in the preparation of this revision.

Statutory instruments which affect or previously affected this revision

• Road Traffic Act 2010 (Section 54(d)) (Defective or Worn Tyres) (Commencement) Order 2016   (S.I. No. 168 of 2016)

• Road Traffic Act 2010 (Section 13) (Prescribed Form and Manner of Statements) Regulations 2015   (S.I. No. 398 of 2015)

• Road Traffic Act 2010 (Impairment Testing) (Commencement) Order 2014
 (S.I. No.536 of 2014)

• Road Traffic Act 2010 (Impairment Testing) Regulations 2014
(S.I. No. 534 of 2014)

• Road Traffic Act 2010 (Section 53(3)(c))(Commencement) Order 2012
 (S.I. No. 560 of 2012)

• Road Traffic Act 2010 (Section 21)(Costs and Expenses) Regulations 2012
(S.I. No.477 of 2012)

• Road Traffic Act 2010 (Section 48)(Commencement) Order 2012
(S.I. No. 293 of 2012)

• European Union (Occupation of Road Transport Operator) Regulations 2011 (S.I. No. 697 of 2011)

• Road Traffic Act 2010 (Fixed Penalty Notice - Drink Driving) Regulations 2011
(S.I. No. 595 of 2011)

• Road Traffic Act 2010 (Section 33) (Commencement) Order 2011
 (S.I. No. 544 of 2011) ii

• Road Traffic Act 2010 (Certain Provisions) (Commencement) (No. 2) Order 2011
(S.I. No. 543 of 2011)

• Road Traffic Act 2010 (Section 13) (Prescribed Form and Manner of Statements) Regulations 2011   (S.I. No. 541 of 2011)

• Road Traffic Act 2010 (Sections 15 and 17) (Prescribed Forms) Regulations 2011
 (S.I. No. 540 of 2011)

• Finance (Transfer of Departmental Administration and Ministerial Functions) Order 2011   (S.I. No. 418 of 2011)

• Road Traffic Act 2010 (Certain Provisions) (Commencement) Order 2011
(S.I. No. 255 of 2011)

• Road Traffic Act 2010 (Certain Provisions) (Commencement) Order 2010
(S.I. No. 394 of 2010)

All statutory instruments up to and including Road Traffic Act 2010 (Section 54(d)) (Defective or Worn Tyres) (Commencement) Order 2016 (S.I. No. 168 of 2016), made 17 April 2016, were considered in the preparation of this revision.

Full updated Statutory Instrument can be found here: http://alturl.com/io6aa

Accident Prevention

Road traffic accidents involving goods vehicles are mainly caused by:

- Driving too fast.
- Driving while tired, unwell or under the influence of drink or drugs.
- Driving too close to the vehicle in front, especially on motorways "tailgating".
- Turning across the path of other vehicles.
- Not signalling intentions. (or signalling too late)
- Careless overtaking.
- Driving a defective vehicle. (inadequate brakes, steering, tyres, lights/signals)
- Overloading.

Assessing the Risks

It is the statutory duty of road haulage employers under health and safety legislation to assess the risks faced by their employees in loading, unloading and particularly driving goods vehicles. These risks would include:

- People being struck or run over by vehicles manoeuvring in premises.
- People falling from vehicles while loading/unloading/roping and sheeting.
- Drivers slipping while entering or alighting from vehicle cabs/load areas.
- Maintenance staff being injured while working on/beneath vehicle/ trailers.
- Injuries caused by loads falling from vehicles/fork-lift trucks during loading/unloading.
- Drivers speeding/taking insufficient care on the road.
- Drivers reversing without assistance to guide them.

Risk Prevention

Steps must be taken to reduce the identified risks by establishing suitable procedures covering the following:

- Policies on drinking and drug taking.
- Safety controls and monitoring.
- Accident/incident reporting.
- Accident/risk awareness.
- Safety information.
- Training and retraining.

Drink Driving

The legal maximum limit of alcohol is 80mg per 100ml of blood.
Laws are in discussion for the limit to be reduced from 80mg to 50mg. This will bring England and Wales in line with Scotland and Northern Ireland for the 50mg to be adopted.There will be a 20mg limit for Lorry Drivers and Taxi Drivers.

Drink-driving penalties

You could be imprisoned, banned from driving and face a fine if you're found guilty of drink-driving.

The actual penalty you get is up to the magistrates who hear your case, and depends on your offence.

You may be able to reduce your ban by taking a drink-drive rehabilitation scheme (DDRS) course if you're banned from driving for 12 months or more.

It's up to the court to offer this.

Being in charge of a vehicle while above the legal limit or unfit through drink you may get:

- 3 months' imprisonment
- up to £2,500 fine
- a possible driving ban

Driving or attempting to drive while above the legal limit or unfit through drink you may get:

- 6 months' imprisonment
- an unlimited fine
- a driving ban for at least 1 year (3 years if convicted twice in 10 years

https://www.gov.uk/drink-driving-penalties

The Use of Mobile Phones

Using a hand-held mobile phone while driving is illegal. It is also illegal if you are a passenger supervising a learner driver.

From 1 March 2017, the penalty being caught using a mobile phone while driving now carries a penalty of six points and a £200 fine.

You can use a hand-held phone if either of these apply:
- you're safely parked
- you need to call 999 or 112 in an emergency and it's unsafe or impractical to stop

<u>Penalties</u>

You can get 6 penalty points and a £200 fine if you use a hand-held phone when driving. You'll also lose your licence if you passed your driving test in the last 2 years.

You can get 3 penalty points if you don't have a full view of the road and traffic ahead or proper control of the vehicle.

You can also be taken to court where you can:
- be banned from driving or riding
- get a maximum fine of £1,000 (£2,500 if you're driving a lorry or bus)

https://www.gov.uk/driving-disqualifications

Reporting of Accidents

Employers, self-employed operators and, where relevant, employees are required by law to report certain accidents as follows:

- Road traffic accidents causing personal injury.
- Damage to vehicles, animals or property under the Road Traffic Act 1988.
- Industrial/works accidents causing death or more than three days' incapacity for work under RIDDOR. (The Reporting of Injuries, Diseases and Dangerous Occurrences Regulations 1995)

<u>International Accident Procedures</u>

Call the police. It is the law in most countries that the police must attend any accident involving a foreign vehicle. However, if you have insufficient command of the local language to do so, you will normally find that the other party will call them, if only to overcome the language problem.

Do not admit liability and do not sign any documents, other than the European Accident Statement or "Constat Amiable".

You may be asked for and should be prepared to produce:

- Your driving license.
- The registration document for the vehicle, to prove ownership. Other evidence may be acceptable.
- Your insurance certificate or Green Card. In many countries, even those within the European Union, where your UK insurance certificate is acceptable in law, you may be expected to produce a Green Card as this has for many years been the only acceptable/ understandable evidence of insurance for foreign registered vehicles.

It is perfectly safe for you to complete and sign the European Accident Statement. It is simply a method of ensuring that the parties to an accident exchange the relevant information and if possible agree how the accident happened. Make sure that you are given a copy and that you understand the information written by the other party.

If you do not understand the police, you should try and explain that you need an interpreter. However, most police are very helpful in dealing with visitors and may be able to make themselves understood. However, in countries outside the European Union, you should be aware that the police can be responsible for deciding fault at the scene of the accident. In some countries, drivers may be arrested and their vehicles impounded, when the accident is serious, to allow time for fault to be determined.

If you are arrested, you should ask to contact the British Consul or equivalent as soon as possible.

Section H6 EU Road Layouts

There is a European policy on main arterial routes that is beginning to come into force. This is the AGR Convention. It is an international convention concerned with route marking - especially the European/Trans Europe E Road system.

The international E-road network is a network of roads in Europe, numbered E1 and up. They cross national borders and are the responsibility of the United Nations Economic Commission for Europe (UNECE). The network also reaches central Asian countries like Kazakhstan, since they are members of the UNECE.

In most countries, roads carry the European route designation beside national road numbers. Other countries like Belgium and Sweden have roads with exclusive European route signage. E-roads in the United Kingdom are not signposted at all, and are not recognised by the UK authorities.

In general, north-south reference roads have two-digit numbers terminating in the figure 5 and increasing from west to east. East-west reference roads have two-digit numbers terminating in the figure 0 and increasing from north to south.

Intermediate roads have two-digit odd (north-south) and two-digit even (west-east) numbers between the numbers of the reference roads between which they are located. Class-B roads have three-digit numbers, the first digit being that of the nearest reference road to the north, the second digit being that of the nearest reference road to the west, and the third digit being a serial number.

North-south Class-A roads located eastwards of road E99 have three-digit odd numbers from 101 to 129.

The European routes are signposted with the green number sign at right.
There are different strategies for determining how frequently to signpost the roads. Sweden, Norway and Denmark have integrated the E-road numbers into their networks, meaning that the roads usually have no other national number.
In most of the countries the E-roads form a network on top of the national network. The green signs are frequent enough to show how to follow the roads, but do not usually show how to reach them. In Belgium, E-numbers are associated with motorways: for those, only the E-number is signposted, while for non-motorways only the national number (if any) is shown.

European Cities

Below is a list of some of the major European cities, together with their time zones.

Western European Time
London, England
Edinburgh, Scotland
Dublin, Ireland
Lisbon, Portugal

Central European Time
Amsterdam, Holland
Berlin, Germany
Paris, France
Madrid, Spain

Eastern European Time
Helsinki, Finland
Athens, Greece
Ankara, Turkey
Bucharest, Romania

Russia Zone 2
Moscow, Russia

Maps of Europe and European Traffic Arteries

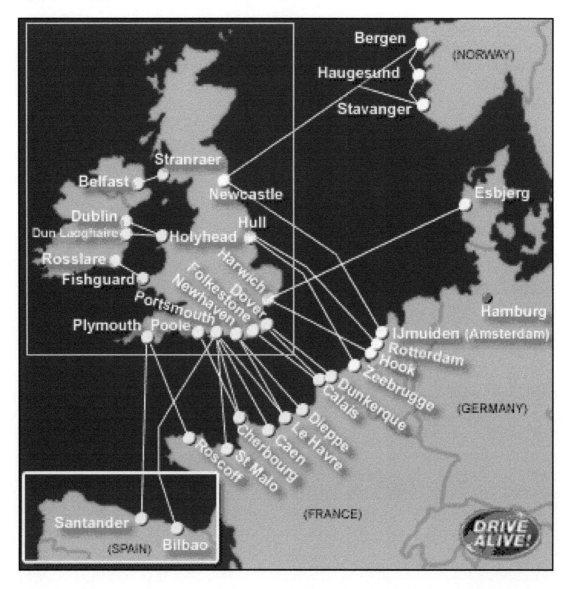

Stranraer •
• Edinburgh

Belfast •

Dublin • Hollyhead • Liverpool

Dun Laoghaire •

Rosslare •
• Amsterdam

• Fishguard   Harwich
• Hoek van Holland

Pembroke •
Dover
Portsmouth • Newhaven •Ostende
•Dunkerque
Plymouth •   Pool   Calais
• Dieppe

Guernsey •Cherbourg

Jersey •   Caen Le Havre
Roscoff •

•St. Malo

Santander
•
• Bibao

345

European E Road System

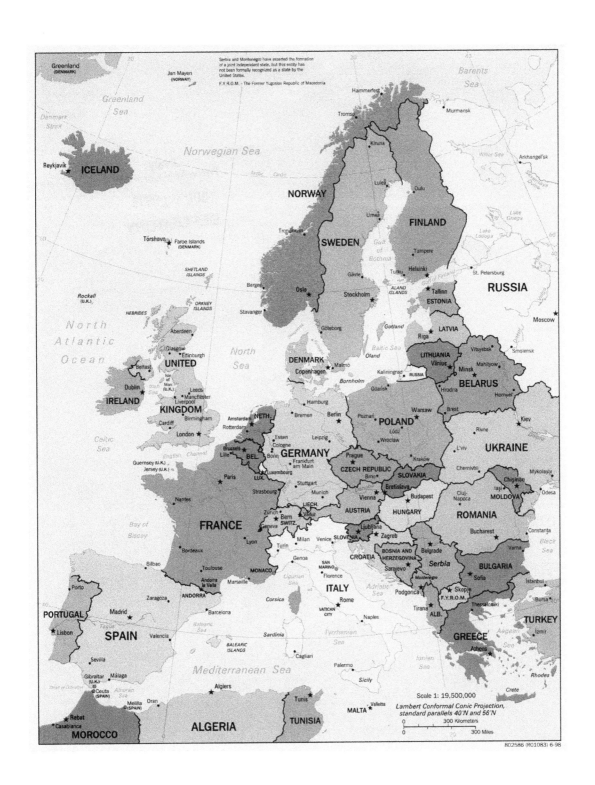

347

Sample Questions

Business Operation - Sample questions

1. An organisation which, on behalf of the sender of goods, makes the necessary transport arrangements prepares the documentation required and obtains any necessary customs clearance is:

a. Shipping broker
b. Freight forwarder
c. Importer
d. Clearing house

2. A company which accepts parcels or goods from customers, combines them and then conveys them on, is known as a:

a. Sub-contractor
b. Clearing house
c. Groupage operator
d. Warehouse

3. Karman Transport has arranged to move some goods for OCP Ltd. On the day in question Karman Transport has no vehicles available to do the work and therefore arranges with Balands Transport to do the job for them. Karman Transport would therefore be:

a. A common carrier
b. An authorised agent
c. An alternate contractor
d. A sub-contractor

[Answers: 1. (b)   2. (c)   3. (d)   ]

Safe Loading and Hazardous Operations - Sample questions

1. Statutory records relating to the movement of animals must be kept by the transport operator for a minimum period of:

a.   3 months
b.   6 months
c. 12 months
d. 15 months

2. Operators involved in the carriage of dangerous goods must keep records of the information they provide to their drivers for a specified minimum length of time. This minimum specified period is:

a.   2 weeks
b.   1 month
c.   3 months
d.   1 year

3. Under dangerous goods legislation, a road tanker carrying more than one dangerous substance must display:

a.   A list of the different substances carried.
b.   A plate containing the word 'multi-load' on the rear of the vehicle.
c.   Three orange reflective plates.
d.   A substance identification number on each compartment.

4. A carrier registers for the carriage of controlled waste. The registration will be valid for a maximum of:

a.   1 year
b.   2 years
c.   3 years
d.   4 years

5. The Department of Transport Code of Practice 'Safety of Loads on Vehicles' states that a load restraint system should be able to withstand a forward force of:

a. The total weight of the load.
b. Twice the total weight of the load.
c. Half the total weight of the load.
d. A quarter of the total weight of the load.

6. Where must the animal transport certificate relating to a commercial movement of livestock be kept during the journey?

a. in the vehicle
b. in the vehicle operator's office
c. in the consignor's office
d. in the Divisional Veterinary Manager's office

[Answers: 1. (b) 2. (c) 3. (d) 4. (c) 5. (b) 6. (a)]

Extended Question

Your haulage business has been offered a contract to carry all of the products produced by a large chemical manufacturing company. Your instructions are that most of the products are Class 3 Flammables, will be transported in 210 litre metal drums and have been allocated to UN Packing Group II. These shipments are likely to vary from 6,000 to 18,000 kg and should be transported on curtain sided vehicles.

Your haulage business has never operated the transport of dangerous goods. You have been asked to advise your company's chief executive on the legal requirements which would apply to your haulage business, including the drivers, should you take on this work.

Sample Answer

These movements are governed by the provisions of the Carriage of Dangerous Goods by Road Regulations 1996.   The following sections will form part of the operator's responsibilities under the Regulations:

- Documentation for the drivers.
- Marking of vehicles.
- Plain reflective orange plates displayed on the front and rear of the vehicles.

The company is also required to equip the vehicles with fire extinguishers, including 2 kg dry powder or equivalent for cab fires and 6 kg dry powder or equivalent for load fires.

The drivers would also be subject to the provisions of the Carriage of Dangerous Goods by Road (Driver Training) Regulations 1996; requiring drivers to undergo approved training and pass the relevant examinations to obtain a relevant vocational training certificate.

The company must appoint a Dangerous Goods Safety Adviser.

Traffic Accident Procedure - Sample questions

1. A driver is involved in an accident in which a pedestrian is injured. A police officer asks the driver for their certificate of insurance but they do not have it on them. They must produce the certificate at a police station within:

a. 5 days
b. 7 days
c. 10 days
d. 14 days

2. A driver injures his head in an accident. No one else is injured and there is no damage to any other vehicle or property. The driver:

a. Is not required to report the accident to the police.
b. Must report the accident to the police as soon as possible.
c. Must report the accident to the police within 5 days.
d. Must report the accident to the police within 7 days.

3. Under the Road Traffic Act 1988, which of the following circumstances would require the driver of a goods vehicle to stop at the scene of an accident on a public road?

a. The driver runs over and injures a cat belonging to a person living alongside the road.
b. The driver brakes hard and some of the sheep being carried on the vehicle are injured.
c. The vehicle hits a kerb, the driver's arm is injured but no other damage or injury is caused.
d. The driver's vehicle collides with a parked car, causing damage but no injuries.

4. A driver is driving their employer's rigid goods vehicle and is involved in an accident. Which of the following statements describes the employers' legal liabilities?

a. The employer has no legal liability to identify the driver to the police.
b. The employer only has a legal liability to identify the driver to the police if the police are intending to prosecute the driver for a road traffic offence.
c. The employer only has a legal liability to identify the driver to the police if the accident involved personal injury to a third party.
d. The employer has a legal liability to identify the driver to the police if requested.

5. A major accident occurs on a motorway involving a number of vehicles and personal injury to a number of people. In such circumstances, which of the following pieces of information must the driver of a 38 tonne articulated goods vehicle who was involved in the accident produce (if requested)?

1. His name and address.
2. His employer's name and address.
3. His driving licence details.
4. His load details.
5. The certificate of insurance for his vehicle.

a. 1, 2 and 3 only
b. 2, 3 and 4 only
c. 1, 3 and 5 only
d. 1, 2 and 5 only

6. Following an accident between two vehicles, which of the following items of information must a driver provide to the driver of the other vehicle (if so requested)?

1. His name and address.
2. The name and address of the vehicle owner.
3. His driving licence details.
4. His date of birth.
5. The vehicle registration number.

a. 1,2 and 5 only
b. 2,3 and 4 only
c. 3,4 and 5 only
d. 1,2 and 4 only
e. all of the above

7. Following a minor traffic accident, what must you give (if asked) to the driver?

a. The name of your insurance company.
b. Your insurance certificate.
c. Your name and address.
d. Your driving licence.

[Answers: 1. (b) 2. (a) 3. (d) 4. (d) 5. (d) 6. (a) 7. (c)]

Costings - Sample Questions

1. A local haulage company operates 20 HGVs. Each of these vehicles covers 10,000 kms a month, fuel consumption averages 4 kms per litre. The current price of fuel is £1.00 per litre,
Calculate the monthly budget for fuel.

………………………………………………………………………………………

The calculation will be required to multiply the number of vehicles, 20, by the number of kilometres, 10,000 which equals 200,000 km. Fuel consumption is 4 kms per litre, therefore divided 200,000 by four to give the number of litres of fuel used, in this case 50,000. The price of fuel is £1 per litre, therefore the monthly budget is £50,000.

Answer

20 x 10,000   = 200,000 kms

200,000 / 4   = 50,000

Monthly Budget = £50,000

2. You plan to buy a new vehicle for £81,000. The tyres included in the price are valued at £10,000. At the end of the vehicle's five-year life you expect a resale value of £16,000. Using the straight-line method, the annual amount you would allow for depreciation is:

a. £11,000
b. £ 8,760
c. £12,320
d. £10,800

3. Which of the following is an example of an indirect cost?

a. oil
b. admin staff wages
c. drivers' wages
d. vehicle insurance

4. You operate a number of 8 wheeler vehicles. Each tyre for this vehicle costs £220 and has a planned life of 32,000 miles. How much are tyres costing you on this vehicle, in pence per mile?

a. 0.6 pence
b. 5.5 pence
c. 30 pence
d. 16 pence

5. To calculate a company's net return on capital employed, you need to use:

a. gross profit
b. net profit after tax
c. net profit before tax

6. Which of the following would you refer to as a fixed cost when calculating your vehicle costings?

a. vehicle fuel used
b. repairs and maintenance
c. vehicle insurance
d. tyres

7. The total standing costs of a vehicle are £24,000 per annum. The vehicle covers 40,000 miles per year on hire. The running costs of the vehicle are 60 pence per mile. If the company wishes to make a 20% gross profit, its total charge out rate per mile will be:

a. 120 pence
b. 144 pence
c. 172.66 pence
d. 26.66 pence

8. An operator examines the following cost items associated with his business:

1. vehicle excise duty
2. depreciation
3. drivers' guaranteed wages
4. Office staff wages
5. Business rates on the premises.

Which items could be categorised as indirect costs?
a. Item 5 only
b. Items 4 and 5
c. Items 1 and 2
d. Items 2 and 3.

9. A transport operator has a single 17 tonne rigid vehicle. The vehicle is estimated to run 50,000 miles this year, and the costs involved in operating are as follows:

Standing costs   £20,000 pa
Overheads   £10,000 pa
Running cost   30 pence per mile

If a profit margin of 20% on costs is to be added, the charge out rate to customers will be:

a. 66 pence per mile
b. 72 pence per mile
c. 84 pence per mile
d. 108 pence per mile

10. A vehicle covers 50,000 miles a year. If the standing costs are £20,000, running costs are 30 pence per mile, the charge to the customer is 84 pence per mile, what percentage profit on costs is the operator making?

a. 25%
b. 20%
c. 15%
d. 10%

11. Which of the following are fixed costs?

1. vehicle excise duty
2. depreciation
3. tyres
4. lubricants

a. all items
b. 2, 3 and 4 only
c 1 and 2 only
d. 3 and 4 only

12. Writing off the value of an asset over its estimated life is called:

a. depreciation
b. erosion
c. apportionment
d. diminution

[Answers: 1. (50k) 2. (a) 3. (b) 4. (b) 5. (c) 6. (c) 7. (b) 8. (b) 9. (d) 10. (b) 11. (c) 12. (a)]

Operator Licensing - Sample questions

1. Which of the following vehicles require an 'O' licence?

a. Electrically propelled vehicle with an unladen weight of 1,750 kg.
b. Local authority road roller with an unladen weight of 5,500 kg.
c. Vehicle used for the carriage of horses with a gross plated weight of 5,000 kg.
d. Vehicle used for the carriage of milk with a gross plated weight of 3,500 kg.

2. An operator has an 'O' licence specifying 5 vehicles with no margin. They are now operating 5 vehicles and wish to acquire 2 more. Should they:

a. Surrender his 'O' licence and apply for a new one.
b. Apply for a variation to his licence.
c. Do nothing and operate the two extra vehicles until the existing 'O' licence expires.
d. Appeal to the Transport Tribunal.

3. Your company operates a fleet of 20 vehicles specified on an 'O' licence, and changes its business address. You must inform the Traffic Commissioner of the change within:

a. 42 days
b. 28 days
c. 21 days
d. 14 days

4. Which of the following may object to the granting of an 'O' licence?

a. National Union of Mineworkers.
b. Confederation of British Industry.
c. Chamber of Commerce.
d. Rail, Maritime and Transport Union.

5. In determining the 'good repute' of an applicant for a standard 'O' Licence, the Traffic Commissioner will take into account convictions for specified offences occurring during the preceding:

a. 2 years
b. 3 years

c. 4 years

d. 5 years.

6. When a statutory objector makes an objection to an application for an 'O' licence, a copy of the objection must be sent to:

a. The applicant.

b. The local authority.

c. The planning authority.

d. The Chief Officer of Police.

7. An operator has the following vehicles and trailers in their fleet:

1. A rigid goods vehicle of 2.5 tonnes gross plated weight.
2. A rigid goods vehicle of 3.5 tonnes gross plated weight.
3. A rigid goods vehicle of 7.5 tonnes gross plated weight.
4. A tractor unit of an articulated vehicle with a gross plated weight of 24 tonnes.
5. A semi-trailer with a gross plated weight of 20 tonnes.

Which of the above must display an 'O' licence disc?

a. 4 and 5 only

b. 1, 2 and 3 only

c. 2, 3 and 4 only

d. 3 and 4 only.

8. Representations, on environmental grounds, against the granting of an 'O' licence can be made by:

a. A county council.

b. A parish council.

c. A planning authority.

d. A person living near the operator's premises.

9. A representation, on environmental grounds, against the granting of an 'O' licence must reach the Traffic Commissioner by:

a. 21 days of the application being published in 'Applications and Decisions'.
b. 21 days of the application being advertised in a local newspaper.
c. 42 days of the application being published in 'Applications and Decisions'.
d. 42 days of the application being advertised in a local newspaper.

[Answers: 1. (c) 2. (b) 3. (b) 4. (d) 5. (d) 6. (a) 7. (d) 8. (d) 9. (b)]

Extended Sample Question

East River Haulage Ltd have been in business for about three years and are currently operating 6 x 3500 kg GVW vans on work delivering "panic" consignments. The management of East River Haulage Ltd are close to finalising a contract with a major supplier of replacement parts to the transport industry, to provide a dedicated delivery service for the company's customers. This will necessitate the acquisition of an additional ten 7.5 tonne curtain sided rigid vehicles. You have been asked by Acme's directors to explain briefly the criteria they will have to meet in order to obtain an operator's licence for the additional vehicles.

Specify the key criteria which East River Haulage Ltd must meet and, for each of these criteria, give a brief explanation of what is required.

Sample Answer

The key criteria which East River Haulage Ltd must meet in order to gain an operator's licence are:

- Fitness.
- Maintenance.
- Operating centre.
- Undertakings.
- Finance.
- They must reveal convictions for transport offences during last 5 years.
- They must provide suitable facilities of their own, with suitable staff and systems, or contract with external maintenance provider.
- They must provide suitable premises for parking the authorised number of vehicles.
- They should control drivers' hours and records.
- They must undertake to keep vehicles in a fit and serviceable condition.
- They must undertake to provide an effective defect reporting and rectification system.
- They must undertake to keep maintenance records for a minimum of 15 months.
- They must undertake to ensure that the maximum number of vehicles authorised for each operating centre is not exceeded.
- They must demonstrate sufficient resources to keep vehicles in a fit and serviceable condition.

As East River Haulage Ltd will be applying for a Standard 'O' licence, they will need to meet the following additional criteria:

- Good repute: They must reveal all convictions during the past 5 years.
- Finance: Must be sufficient working capital to start up and run the business.
- Professional competence: East River Haulage Ltd must employ one or more professionally competent people to manage the operation.

HGV/LGV Driving Licenses - Sample Questions

1. Simon Fowler passed his HGV test in an articulated vehicle. He now holds a licence showing full entitlement to drive category C+E vehicles. Which vehicles, from the list below, is he entitled to drive?

1. Articulated vehicles
2. Rigid vehicles
3. Rigid vehicles with drawbar trailers

a. 1 only
b. 1 and 2 only
c. 1 and 3 only
d. 1,2 and 3

2. A transport company operates a fleet of articulated goods vehicles. All of the vehicles have a maximum authorised mass exceeding 7500 kg. What category of entitlement would the company's drivers require in order to drive the vehicles legally?

a. C + E
b. C1 + E
c. C1
d. C

3. LGV entitlement must be renewed annually from the age of:

a. 45
b. 55
c. 65
d. 70

4. Category C entitlement will permit the holder to tow a trailer with a maximum authorised mass not exceeding a limit of:

a. 500 kg
b. 750 kg
c. 1020 kg
d. 3500 kg

5. David Mathews has had his LGV entitlement revoked on the grounds of misconduct. Should he wish to challenge this decision, he should make his appeal to:

a. The Transport Tribunal
b. County Court
c. The Court of Appeal
d. A Magistrate's Court

6. What minimum entitlement is required to drive a 4 axled rigid vehicle with a gross weight of 32,000 kg?

a. Category B
b. Category C
c. Category C1
d. Category C + E

7. Ivor Morris obtains a Category C licence entitlement at the age of 23. When will he next have to renew this entitlement?

a. After 5 years.
b. After 10 years.
c. When he is 45.
d. When he is 55.

8. What minimum category of licence entitlement must the driver of a rigid goods vehicle of 3.6 tonnes MAM have?

a. C
b. C1
c. C + E
d. D

9. A "vocational" entitlement to drive is required once a vehicle has a maximum authorised mass (MAM) exceeding which of the following thresholds?

a. 1020 kg
b. 1525 kg
c. 3500 kg
d. 7500 kg

[Answers: 1. (d) 2. (a) 3. (c) 4. (b) 5. (d) 6. (b) 7. (c) 8. (b) 9. (c)]

Conduct and disciplinary matters - Sample question

Robert Jones has had his LGV entitlement revoked on the grounds of misconduct. Should he wish to appeal challenge this decision, how would he make an appeal?

<u>Sample answer</u>

Under the regulations, it would be necessary to make an appeal to the Magistrate's Court. All persons who have had their license revoked are entitled to make an appeal to the Magistrates courts in England and Wales, and the Sheriff in Scotland. However, the revocation remains in effect until the result of the appeal is known.

Insurance - Sample questions

1. One of the vehicles belonging to a road transport operator is involved in a road traffic accident which results in a pedestrian being taken to hospital for emergency medical treatment. In these circumstances, the legal obligation of the transport operator in respect of emergency hospital treatment is covered by:

a. employer's liability insurance
b. consequential loss insurance
c. third party motor insurance
d. public liability insurance

2. Your company wishes to take out insurance against loss of money caused by dishonesty of employees. The type of insurance required is:

a. goods in transit
b. fidelity guarantee
c. loss of use
d. consequential loss

3. Which of the following types of insurance are compulsory for a road haulage company which operates 20 of its own vehicles and employs 30 drivers and 8 administrative and sales staff?

1. public liability insurance
2. third party motor insurance
3. goods in transit insurance
4. employer's liability insurance
5. consequential loss insurance

a. 2 and 4 only
b. 1 and 5 only
c. 3, 4 and 5 only
d. 2 and 3 only

4. On your company's goods in transit insurance, your insurance company has added an immobiliser clause. This means that:

a. Your vehicles must be attended at all times.
b. No liability will be accepted for costs incurred by late delivery.
c. The vehicles are only insured whilst on your own premises.
d. The vehicles must be fitted with an approved anti-theft device.

5. Which of the following documents may be produced to the police to prove that a current, valid vehicle insurance is in existence?

1. Certificate of Insurance
2. Insurance policy
3. Cover note
4. Renewal notice
5. Schedule to the insurance policy

a. 2 and 5 only
b. 1 and 3 only
c. 2, 4 and 5 only
d. 1, 2 and 4 only

6. An operator wishes to insure themselves against loss of profit resulting from a major incident, such as a fire, which would keep their vehicles off the road. Which of the following types of insurance should they take out?

a. Third party
b. Fidelity guarantee
c. Fire and theft
d. Consequential loss

[Answers: 1. (c) 2. (b) 3. (a) 4. (d) 5. (b) 6. (d)]

Further Sample Question

You are the manager of a medium sized road haulage company operating a dedicated shop delivery service within the Midlands for a major confectionery manufacturer. The company has taken out the necessary, legally required insurances - namely, comprehensive motor insurance to cover the vehicles and employer's liability insurance to cover the employees. In addition, the company has goods in transit insurance covering liabilities in line with the RHA conditions of carriage, under which it operates. The only amendment to the basic goods in transit cover is that the company has elected to pay a higher premium to get cover in excess of the normal £1300 per tonne. This is because of the higher value of the confectionery being carried.

Name other voluntary insurances that the business might wish to consider to guard against possible future liabilities. For each of the insurances, explain briefly the liabilities the insurance would cover.

Sample answer

- Loss of Use - covers the cost of hiring a replacement vehicle if one of the fleet is off the road following an accident.

- Public Liability - this general insurance provides businesses with insurance cover in the event of being sued. Typical situations covered by public liability insurance include - defective loading of the vehicle, unlicensed vehicles covered, occupier's liability, covering claims for death or injury to visitors, incorrect first aid treatment applied by an employee, third party fire risk, covering damage to other people's property on the operator's premises.

- Fire Insurance - to cover for the cost of replacing or rebuilding following a fire at the operator's premises.

- Storm and Flood Damage - covers for damage to property caused by storm or flood.

- Theft and Money - to cover situations such as theft of money or property, or damage caused by thieves on entry.

- Fidelity Guarantee - this covers the operator against loss of money or other property caused by the dishonesty of employees.

- Consequential Loss - covers against loss of revenue or profit following a major event such as a fire or flood at the operator's premises.

Business Law - Sample question

The two official bodies an operator may deal with in regard to disputes with employees are ACAS and Employment Tribunals. What is the difference between these two bodies and what are their prime functions?

Sample answer

ACAS

ACAS is the advisory, conciliation and arbitration service that deals with employment disputes. It is staffed by civil servants and has a council comprising a chairman and nine members appointed by employers' organisations, trade unions and other independents.

ACAS offers:

- Advice to employers and employees on industrial relations.
- Provides a conciliation service to settle disputes.
- Looks into employment relations generally or for particular industries or employment sectors.
- Publishes codes of practice and advisory literature for employers, employees and trade unions.

Employment Tribunals

Employment tribunals function as a kind of court, convened for specific disputes. The tribunal or court is adjudicated by a chairman, who is legally qualified, and two lay members. This is in order to provide a less formal way to address disputes.

Employment Tribunals deal with:

- discrimination
- equal pay
- employment protection and employee rights
- minimum wage
- violation of working time regulations
- transfer of business
- wrongful dismissal
- health and safety matters

Drivers hours and tachographs - Sample question

It is the responsibility of the driver to operate the tachograph correctly. In the case of vehicles fitted with analogue tachographs, list 10 specific responsibilities of the driver.

Sample answer

1. To verify that the instrument is correctly calibrated, by inspecting the attached plaques, and ensure that the time displayed on the device is set correctly.

2. To carry sufficient charts for the whole journey, including spare charts in case they are needed.

3. To use a second chart if the first chart is damaged in use, and to attach the second chart to the first chart where the journey is completed.

4. To ensure that the chart is being used for the specific model of tachograph.

5. To use a chart for no longer than 24 hours.

6. To enter centre-field details when the chart is first used, when changing vehicles and when completing the use of the chart.

7. To correctly operate the mode switch in order to record their activities accurately.

8. To make manual entries on the chart for activities undertaken away from the vehicle.

9. To make manual entries should be tachograph become faulty.

10. To permit an authorised examiner or police officer to inspect the tachograph.

Note that the question asked for you to list 10 specific responsibilities of the driver.

There are more responsibilities that you could have listed, but you will not gain further marks for doing this. Instead, you will only waste time that would be better spent moving onto the next question.

Social Legislation - Sample question

A haulage company has expanded its operation and as part of running local deliveries has employed a number of part time drivers. The hourly rate of pay for full-time drivers is £8 per hour. The part-time drivers are employed at a rate of £7 per hour. In addition the part-time drivers are not allowed access to the employer's pension scheme and may not be entitled to sick pay.

In what manner has the employer breached the social legislation in regard to the new part-time drivers?

Sample Answer

The Part-time Workers Regulations 2000 require that part-time workers are entitled to equality with full-time workers in respect of:

- hourly rates of pay
- access to pension schemes
- contractual sick pay
- denial of these equalities is a breach of the act

Vehicle Specification - Sample question

Your company is considering replacing four 36 tonne articulated lorry tractor units with new vehicles. List four of the main factors you would take into account when choosing the replacements.

Sample answer

1. Fuel Economy
   In order to make the best possible use of fossil fuels, both in terms of environmental impact and vehicle running costs, the best fuel economy figures would be a major consideration.

2. Exhaust Emissions
   Again, in order to lessen the environmental impact of running this kind of vehicle, it would be vital to consider those vehicles with the lowest emission figures.

3. The Vehicle
   It should be of the correct size and capacity for the kind of work anticipated for that vehicle. Considerations would include the plated gross vehicle weight, power output of the engine for the kinds of journeys considered, provision of 5th wheel and axles. The overall vehicle size should have sufficient capacity for the type of work anticipated.

4. Compatibility
   Existing maintenance arrangements for the company fleet would be an important consideration. This could include training and certification of those responsible for maintenance and repairs, availability of spares and even familiarity of drivers with particular or unusual vehicle types.

Part Two – R2

Part Two of the CPC Examination consists of scenario-based questions. In this manual we have included the key points only of the subjects covered in R2. However, they are more fully covered in the first manual for examination R1. Students should make sure they are fully conversant with these subjects to prepare for the scenario-based examination.

The CPC is the Certificate of Professional Competence in Road Haulage and Passenger Transport. These qualifications are for individuals who want to enter the profession of Transport Manager, or demonstrate their professional competence to meet Operator Licensing requirements - holding a CPC is one of the elements an applicant must satisfy for the Transport Commissioner to grant an O license. After 4th December 2011 the examinations changed to the new requirements for 2012.

The new exam consists of a single multiple-choice assessment and a single case study assessment. Both elements test national and international knowledge/application. So, to achieve a new International CPC, candidates will need to take two units.

The multiple-choice assessment R1 is available as a paper-based test from March 2012. From June, it is also be available on screen and on demand, allowing candidates to sit or re-sit an assessment at a time convenient for them and to enable them to receive their results quickly.

This second manual, R2, covers the second part of the exam, the case study; a scenario will be issued with the papers at the start of the two hour fifteen minute assessment. This shorter case study will contain no distractions and will only contain information that will enable the candidate to demonstrate application of the knowledge they have acquired. It now only assesses the core areas. Candidates will need to achieve 50% over the whole paper to pass. The case study will focus on the application of knowledge. Candidates will be able to take any notes or books of their choice into the case study assessment and questions will test application of knowledge only.
For example, candidates will no longer be asked to identify and explain but just to explain, allowing them to demonstrate they can apply their knowledge and use relevant sources of information.

The multiple-choice element will be assessed by one OCR set and marked timetabled assessment consisting of 60 multiple-choice questions (and thus 60 marks). In order to pass this unit, candidates must achieve a score of at least 70% across the paper. This paper will test knowledge of both national and international elements of the syllabus. The minimum and maximum number of questions will be asked from each broad area (A, B, C, etc.) of the syllabus.

CASE STUDY ASSESSMENT

This paper is assessed by means of a marked timetabled assessment of a case study with extended answer questions. This paper tests applications of knowledge of both national and international elements of the syllabus. There will be between five and eight questions. Each question is worth between seven and twelve marks; there are 60 marks available in the case study paper. There will be no part A and part B. In order to pass this unit, candidates must achieve a score of at least 50% of the marks available across the paper.

All questions are based upon a single scenario that will be given to candidates as a separate booklet made available at the start of the assessment. The assessment is two hours fifteen minutes in length. This paper will be open book. Candidates will be allowed to take any notes or texts of their choice into the assessment.

The following syllabus areas will be tested in every case study paper. These subjects are also more fully covered in the first manual, R1.

C4 Drivers' hours, working time and records
E7 Operational costings
F1, F2, F3 Operating licensing
At least one of F1, F2 or F3 will be tested in each paper.

The following syllabus areas may be tested in a case study paper:

A5 Compensation claims (see syllabus)
E6 Budgets
E8 Organisational charts
G2 Vehicle selection
G5 Vehicle maintenance and roadworthiness
G6 Safe loading of vehicles (see syllabus)
G8 Dangerous goods and waste
H1 Driver licensing
H3 Vehicle checks

The CPC examination is designed to ensure that candidates for the position of transport manager are properly qualified and knowledgeable to carry out the efficient and safe operation of the business.

Compulsory Examination Subjects

Drivers' Hours. Working Time and Records

Operational Costings

Operator Licensing

Optional Syllabus Subjects

(These may or may not form part of the R2 examination)

Compensation Claims

Business Contracts

Budgets

Organisational Charts

Vehicle Selection

Vehicle Maintenance and Roadworthiness

Safe Loading of Vehicles

Dangerous Goods and Waste

Driver Licensing

Vehicle Checks

Sample Case Study/Scenario

Condoco International Haulage Limited

This is a fictitious transport company such as may be described in the scenario given to the candidate at the exam. Candidates will be asked to give an extended answer to the case study scenario question. Sometimes candidates will be asked to calculate figures, add information to part completed tables, draw up lists or write instructions to staff to answer the specific question.

Note that in this fictitious example, we have split the questions and sample answers into separate sections for clarity.

The Company

Condoco International Haulage Limited is a transport company. It operates from two small operating centres, but is looking to consolidate operations at one new purpose built centre.
The current standard Operator licence gives approval for 33 vehicles and 33 trailers.

The current fleet is as follows:

- 2 x 3,500 kg pmw vans
- 2 x 6,000 kg pmw vans (one is used to tow a 4,000kg PMW drawbar trailer)
- 2 x 17,000 kg pmw 2 axle rigid vehicles with flat bodies
- 3 x 32,000 kg pmw 4 axle rigid vehicles with tipper bodies
- 14 x 41,000 kg pmw 3 axle artic tractor units with 20 x 13.6 m flat semi-trailers
- 2 x 75,000 kg pmw 3 axle artic tractor units with 3 low loader semi-trailers used for Special Types work
- 2 x 40,000 kg pmw rigid vehicle/drawbar trailer combinations (3 axle rigid vehicles, each with a 2 axle trailer)

The largest customer is a company that produces heavy steel fabrications for the engineering and construction industries. A second customer is a French international road haulage operator who utilises Condoco to collect unaccompanied semi-trailers that have been sent from France to one of the Channel ports. From there, the Condoco vehicles deliver to locations in the UK. The Condoco vehicles then reload in the UK with traffic for the continent. These are finally taken back to France.

A third customer provides regular work for the two Special Types vehicles, carrying large items of earthmoving equipment. The weight of a single item of this equipment can be as much as 50 tonnes.

The company has taken out insurance policies to cover a range of potential liabilities. The insurances held cover:

- motor vehicles - Road Traffic Act third party cover, plus fire and theft
- employers' liability
- fidelity guarantee
- loss of use
- consequential loss
- goods in transit - with cover in line with the RHA Conditions of Carriage,
- fire
- public liability - with specific cover for the following risks:
- defective loading
- unlicensed vehicles on site occupier's liability
- incorrect first aid treatment
- third party fire risk at the company's premises

For the last financial year the company generated total revenue of:

- gross revenue from haulage work   £1,790,000
- other income   £10,000

During the same period the following costs were incurred:

- vehicle maintenance	£122,000
- office salaries	£114,000
- telephone/fax/postage	£ 12,000
- fuel/lubricants	£407,000
- VED/'O' licences	£ 51,000
- rent and rates	£ 14,000
- heat and light	£ 12,000
- depreciation of vehicles	£225,000
- directors' remuneration	£ 66,000
- vehicle insurance	£105,000
- bank charges and interest	£ 18,000
- audit and accountancy fees	£ 8,000
- drivers' wages	£352,000
- tyres	£ 62,000
- sundry expenses	£ 12,000

Vehicle Costing

The cost of fuel bought by the company is currently £5.80 per gallon

Question 1

Given the nature of the company's operations as described in the scenario, suggest TWO specific additional insurances which the company ought to consider to cover potential liabilities. Give the reasons why you have selected these particular insurances and brief descriptions of the cover provided.

Sample Answer

Insurance 1: Damage to Public Highways

The vehicles operating under Special Types must notify the Highways and Bridges Authorities in advance of all movements. The Authorities can make claims against the operator for any damage done to roads/bridges etc discovered in the 12 months following. Given the potential for large claims, this insurance must be considered

Insurance 2:

The company's vehicles and trailers undertake international road haulage journeys. They are therefore subject to the international CMR conditions, so any claim for loss or damage to the goods could not be limited to the £1300 per tonne of the RHA conditions, but the 8.33 SDRs per kg of CMR - a much higher liability.

Question 2

From the financial information provided, complete the trading account and profit and loss account for Condoco International Haulage Limited for the last financial year and calculate the gross and net profit percentages on sales.

Sample Answer

TRADING ACCOUNT

Gross revenue from haulage work	£1,790,000
Other income	£ 10,000
Total income	£1,800,000

Less cost of sales:	
Vehicle maintenance	£ 22,000
Fuel/lubricants	£ 407,000
VED/ O licences	£ 51,000
Depreciation of vehicles	£ 225,000
Vehicle insurance	£ 105,000
Drivers' Guaranteed Wages	£ 352,000
Tyres	£ 62,000
Total costs	£1,324,000

Gross Profit	£ 476,000
	(26.44%)

PROFIT AND LOSS ACCOUNT

Gross Profit	£ 476,000
(brought forward from Trading Account)	
Less other expenses:	
Office salaries	£ 114,000
Telephone	£ 12,000
Rent & Rates	£ 14,000
Heat & Lighting	£ 12,000
Directors' Remuneration	£ 66,000
Bank Charges & Interest	£ 18,000
Audit & Accountancy Fees	£ 8,000
Sundry Expenses	£ 12,000
Total	£ 256,000

Net Profit Before Tax	£ 220,000
	(12.22%)

Question 3

All of the 41 tonne articulated vehicles together have incurred the following costs during the past year.

fuel   £290,500
lubricants   £   4,340
tyres   £ 43,750
maintenance   £ 85,700

The total mileage covered by all of the 41 tonne vehicles during the year was 700,000. Calculate the pence per mile figures for each of the running cost elements for a single vehicle. (calculate all answers to 2 decimal places)

Sample Answer

Fuel	41.50 ppm
Lubricants	0.62 ppm
Tyres	6.25 ppm
Maintenance	12.25 ppm
Total	60.62 ppm

If the cost of fuel increases from £5.80 to £6.22 per gallon, and all other running costs increase by 7.5 %, recalculate the individual running cost elements and total running cost per mile for a 41 tonne vehicle.

Sample Answer

The increase in the fuel price is 42p per gallon, which is 7.25%. The increases in all other running costs are 7.5%. Using these figures the revised running costs are:

fuel	44.50 ppm
lubricants	0.67 ppm
tyres	6.72 ppm
maintenance	13.17 ppm
Total	68.29 ppm

Question 4

The company is planning changes to its fleet operating centre and operations during the coming months. For each proposed change briefly describe:

a. What contact needs to be made with the Traffic Area Office?

Sample Answer

The proposed change of operating centres constitutes a major change to the Operator licence. An application for a major change (using form GV81) must be submitted to the Traffic Area Office at least 9 weeks in advance.

b. What documents need to be completed?

Sample Answer

An advertisement, in statutory form, must be placed in local newspapers and the entire page sent to the Traffic Area Office 21 days before or after the submission of the application.

c. What timescales need to be observed?

Sample Answer

The Traffic Commissioner must be informed within one month of the identity of the additional vehicles, using form GV80.

Question 5

The company has recently had its quotation accepted for the movement of the following items of steel fabrication from its customer in Hereford to a delivery point in Birmingham:

5 x steel fabrications. Each is 17.1m long, 2.5m wide and 3m in height. The weight of each is approximately 7 tonnes.

All of the 5 loads are to be transported at the same time, using existing company vehicles and equipment.

a. State which vehicle type(s) would be most suitable for this work.

Sample Answer

The 41 tonne articulated vehicles with 13.6m semi-trailers.

b. Calculate the amount by which the loads are likely to project beyond the rear of the vehicle(s) specified above.

Sample Answer

Length of rearward projection - approx 3.5m.

c. With regard to these movements, what are the essential arrangements that the operator must put in place in the period before the movements take place?

Sample Answer

Before the movement: Contact the police at least 2 clear days before the proposed movement.

On the Day of the movement: The loads will project to the rear by approximately 3.5 metres. The loads will therefore require marker boards to be fitted:

- 1 x end marker board
- 2 x side marker boards (one fitted on each side of the projection)

The vehicles must carry a statutory attendant. If the vehicles travel in convoy, the statutory attendants need only be located in the frontmost and rearmost vehicles

Question 6

A rolling plan has been drawn up specifying the timing of the acquisition of new vehicles for the fleet. The new vehicles will be used as replacements of existing vehicles as they reach the end of their planned life. The split of vehicles has already been decided between rigid, articulated and rigid vehicle/drawbar trailer combinations. The company has also decided on the types of body required for each vehicle and the load handling equipment necessary.

In helping to decide between the advantages and disadvantages of vehicles offered by a variety of manufacturers, list some of the additional factors which should be considered before the final selection is made. Give THREE environmental considerations, SIX economic considerations and ONE crew comfort consideration which might be included in the evaluation process.

Sample Answer

Environmental Considerations:

- fuel economy
- emissions - Euro1 and Euro2
- whole vehicle recycling
- noise
- road wear

Economic Considerations:

- maintenance cost
- fuel economy
- tyre life
- downtime
- depreciation
- insurance

Crew Comfort:

- air conditioning
- higher powered engine for easier driving

Question 7

Draw up a set of brief instructions for the company's lgv drivers, explaining SIX of their key responsibilities with regard to tachographs and the keeping of tachograph records.

Sample Answer

The key responsibilities of drivers subject to EU Regulation 3821/85 dealing with tachograph records are:

- Keep tachograph records on each day when driving a vehicle subject to Regulation 3820/85 - any goods vehicle with a pmw exceeding 3500 kg.
- Complete the centre field details at the beginning and end of the working day.
- Note any changes of vehicle or other occurrences on the chart.
- Operate the activity switches on the tachograph to record accurately your work activities.
- Retain completed charts for the current week and the last day of the previous week in which you drove vehicles subject to the regulations.
- Produce tachograph records at the request of an authorised inspecting officer or police officer.
- Ensure that the tachograph clock is accurate and agrees with official British time.
- Return all completed charts to your employer within 28 days.
- Keep manual records if the tachograph breaks down.

<u>Question 8</u>

List FOUR of the key responsibilities of Condoco as operators under EU tachograph regulation 3821/85.

The key responsibilities of the operator under EU Regulation 3821/85 are:

- Issue sufficient blank charts to the driver.
- Keep all completed charts in good condition for at least 12 months.
- Produce records at the request of an authorised inspecting officer.
- Provide copies of charts to drivers who request them.
- Ensure that drivers return completed charts within 28 days.

Question 9

Describe the minimum category of driving licence entitlement and minimum age at which employees may drive certain vehicles legally.

Sample Answer

The following table describes the current legal minimums:

Vehicle Type	Category	Minimum Age
Vans not exceeding 3,500 kg pmw	B	17
Vans - 6,000 kg pmw	C1	18
Vans - 6,000kg pmw with 4,000kg pmw drawbar trailer	C1+E	18
3 axle rigids - 26,000 kg pmw	C	21
6 axle artics - 75,000 kg pmw	C+E	21
5 axle rigid/drawbar combinations	C+E	21

Question 10

Your contract involves a number of journeys to France and further European countries, as business requires. Which rules in particular would you ensure that your drivers follow in respect of their drivers' hours?

Sample Answer

When driving in Europe outside of the UK, they are subject to European regulations which limit their driving hours and impose minimum periods of rest. They must take a break of no less than 45 minutes after no more than 4.5 hours of driving, although this break can be divided into two periods - the first at least 15 minutes long and the second at least 30 minutes - taken over the 4.5 hours.

During any single day they may only drive for a maximum of 9 hours, although this can be extended to ten hours on two occasions each week. During any single week, they may drive a maximum of 56 hours. Over a two-weekly period, a maximum of 90 hours. When the vehicle is on a ferry, the daily rest period may be interrupted (no more than twice) by other activities of not more than 1 hour's duration in total, provided that the driver is accompanying the vehicle that is travelling by ferry or train and has access to a bunk or couchette.

These are the minimum requirements; further rules apply in certain circumstances, such as double manning of vehicles.

Glossary of Acronyms

A
AA - Automobile Association
ACAS - Advisory, Conciliation and Arbitration Service
ADR - Accord européen relatif au transport international des marchandises dangereuses par route
AETR - European Agreement Concerning the Work of Crews of Vehicles Engaged in International Road Transport
AIL - Abnormal Indivisible Load
AILV - Abnormal Indivisible Load Vehicle
AIRSO - Association of Industrial Road Safety Officers
ANPR - Automatic Number Plate Recognition
ATM - Automated Traffic Management
AU - Authorised Weight (Regulations)

B
BERR - Dept for Business, Enterprise and Regulatory Reform
BIFA - British International Freight Association

C
C&U - Construction and Use (Regulations)
CDG - Carriage of Dangerous Goods
CMR - Convention on the Contract for the International Carriage of Goods by Road
CSS - Cascading Style Sheets
CFIT - Commission for Integrated Transport
CILT - Chartered Institute of Logistics and Transport
CMPS - Centre for Management and Policy Studies
CO - Company
COSHH - Control of Substances Hazardous to Health
CPC - Certificate of Professional Competence
CRF - Customer Record Form

D
DFT - Department for Transport
DGSA - Dangerous Goods Safety Advisor
DSA - Driving Standards Agency
DTI - Department of Trade and Industry
DTLR - Department of Transport, Local Government and the Regions
DVLA - Driver and Vehicle Licensing Agency
DVLC - Driver and Vehicle Licensing Centre
DVO - Driver Vehicle and Operator
DVSA – Driver and Vehicle Standards Agency

E
ESDAL - Electronic Service Delivery for Abnormal Loads
EC - European Community
ECHR - European Court of Human Rights
ECJ - European Court of Justice

EEA - European Economic Area
EEC - European Economic Community
EFTA - European Free Trade Association
EU - European Union

F
FAQ - Frequently Asked Question
FCO - Foreign and Commonwealth Office
FTA - Freight Transport Association

G
GDP - Gross Domestic Product
GFPN - Graduated Fixed Penalty Notice
GLA - Greater London Authority
GO - Government Office
GPS - Global Positioning System
GTW - Gross Train Weight
GV - Goods Vehicle
GVW - Gross Vehicle Weight

H
HA - Highways Agency
HACCP - Hazard Analysis Critical Control Point
HAD - Horizontal Amending Directive
HAZCHEM - Hazardous Chemicals
H&S - Health and Safety
HGV - Heavy Goods Vehicle
HMRC - Her Majesty's Revenue & Customs
HMSO - Her Majesty's Stationery Office
HR - Human Resources
HTML - Hyper Text Markup Language
HSC - Health and Safety Commission
HSE - Health and Safety Executive

I
IAM - Institute of Advanced Motorists
IE - Internet Explorer
INT - International
IP - Internet Protocol
ISP - Internet Service Provider
IT - Information Technology
ITEA - Integrated Transport Economics and Appraisal
ITS - Intelligent Transport Systems
ITSO - Integrated Transport Smartcard Organisation
ITU - Intermodal Transport Unit

J
JIT - Just In Time

K

KG - Kilogram
KM - Kilometre
KPH - Kilometre per Hour
KPL - Kilometres per litre
KPI - Key Performance Indicator
KSI - Killed or Seriously Injured

L

LA - Local Authority
LHA - Local Highway Authority
LGV - Large Goods Vehicle
LTD - Limited

M

MAPP - Major Accident Prevention Policy
MID - Motor Insurance Database
MIDAS - Motorway Incident and Detection Signalling System
MOT - Ministry Of Transport road-worthiness test
MOVA - Microprocessor Optimised Vehicle Actuation - a traffic signal control system
MPG - Miles per Gallon

N

NAO - National Audit Office
NAT - National
NATS - National Air Traffic Services
NB - nota bene, a Latin expression meaning "note well"
NDC - National Distribution Centre
NDPB - Non-Departmental Public Body
NGO - Non-Governmental Organisation
NIP - Notice of Intended Prosecution
NTM - National Transport Model

O

OCRS - Operator Compliance Risk Score
OECD - Organisation for Economic Co-operation and Development
OTS - On-The-Spot (accident database)

P

PCV - Passenger Carrying Vehicle
PDF - Portable Document Format
PI - Public Inquiry
PPL - Pence Per Litre
PSA - Public Service Agreement
PSR - Passenger Services Requirement
PSV - Passenger Service Vehicle
PTA - Passenger Transport Authority
PTE - Passenger Transport Executive
PMMW - Passive Millimetric Wave Facility

Q
QA - Quality Assurance

R
RDC - Regional Distribution Centre
RHA - Road Haulage Association
RIDDOR - Reporting of Injuries, Diseases & Dangerous Occurrences
RoSPA - Royal Society for Prevention of Accidents
RP - Roads Performance Division
RPC - Reduced Pollution Certificate
RPI - Retail Price Index
RPS - Roads: Performance and Strategy Directorate
RS - Roads Strategy Division
RTA - Road Traffic Accident
RTDF - Rural Transport Development Fund
RTP - Rural Transport Partnership Directorship
RTWTD - Road Transport Working Time Directive
RUS - Road User Safety Division
RVSS - Road and Vehicle Safety and Standards

S
SACTRA - Standing Advisory Committee on Trunk Road Assessment
SLA - Service Level Agreement
SR - Statistics Roads Division
STGO - Special Types General Orders

T
TAN - Traffic Area Network
TC - Transport Category
TEMPO - Trans-European Intelligent Transport Systems Project
TFL - Transport for London
TGWU - Transport and General Workers Union
TIR - Transit International Routier
TM - Transport Manager
TMA - Traffic Management Act
TPI - Targeted Programme of Improvements
TPT - Transport
TQM - Total Quality Management
TRL - Transport Research Laboratory
TSG - Transport Supplementary Grant
TTS - Transport Technology and Standards Division
TUPE - Transfer of Undertakings Protection of Employment

U
UCC - Urban Freight Consolidation Centre
UN - United Nations
UTC - Urban Traffic Control
UMTC - Urban Traffic Management and Control
URTU - United Road Transport Union

V
VCA - Vehicle Certification Agency
VED - Vehicle Excise Duty
VI - Vehicle Inspectorate
VOSA - Vehicle and Operator Services Agency (Now the DVSA)
VU - Vehicle Unit

W
WAI - Web Accessibility Initiative
W3C - World Wide Web Consortium
WIMS - Weigh in Motion System
WTD - Working Time Directive
WWW - World Wide Web

X
XHTML - Extensible Hyper Text Markup Language
XI - Irritant
XRD - X-ray diffraction